Protection of Property Rights in Discovered Petroleum Reservoirs

Energy and Environmental Law & Policy Series Supranational and Comparative Aspects

VOLUME 27

The aim of the Editor and the Editorial Board of this series is to publish works of excellent quality that focus on the study of energy and environmental law and policy.

Through this series the Editor and Editorial Board hope:

- to contribute to the improvement of the quality of energy/environmental law and policy in general and environmental quality and energy efficiency in particular;
- to increase the access to environmental and energy information for students, academics, non-governmental organizations, government institutions, and business;
- to facilitate cooperation between academic and non-academic communities in the field of energy and environmental law and policy throughout the world.

Protection of Property Rights in Discovered Petroleum Reservoirs

Joseph A. Tolorunse

Wolters Kluwer
Law & Business

Published by:
Kluwer Law International
PO Box 316
2400 AH Alphen aan den Rijn
The Netherlands
Website: www.kluwerlaw.com

Sold and distributed in North, Central and South America by:
Aspen Publishers, Inc.
7201 McKinney Circle
Frederick, MD 21704
United States of America
Email: customer.service@aspenpublishers.com

Sold and distributed in all other countries by:
Turpin Distribution Services Ltd
Stratton Business Park
Pegasus Drive, Biggleswade
Bedfordshire SG18 8TQ
United Kingdom
Email: kluwerlaw@turpin-distribution.com

Printed on acid-free paper.

ISBN 978-90-411-5604-4

Printed and Bound by CPI Group (UK) Ltd, Croydon, CR0 4YY.

Table of Contents

Preface

This book examines the problem of unilateral capture of petroleum from straddling reservoirs. Unilateral capture of petroleum from straddling petroleum reservoirs, which traditionally emanated from the United States' oil and gas industry in 1850s has occurred in the Domanial petroleum ownership regime in spite of the compulsory unitisation provisions in the petroleum laws and regulations either because the Regulators permitted it or because of their laxities. This shows that the problem of unilateral capture is not only confined to regime where private ownership of petroleum resources is emplaced.

Where unilateral capture occurs, it raises a number of issues both at the domestic and international levels given the current Administrative and Judicial policies on its applicability to oil and gas extraction from straddling fields. The Judicial and Administrative policies on unilateral capture appeared to have conflicted with the provisions of the licensing granting and unitisation clauses in the petroleum laws and regulations. At the domestic level, there are problems of competitive drilling resulting into wastes – both physical and economic – as well as non-recognition of property rights in discovered petroleum reservoir. At the international level, it raises concerns for investment treaties and human rights violations by the Host State especially where foreign investors are involved. From energy conservative perspective, it defied unified development and exploitation of petroleum from straddling reservoirs, thereby defeating energy conservative policies of both energy producing and consuming nations.

There are number of ways in which the problems of unilateral capture had been addressed. These include enactment of Conservation laws (Pro-rationing, well spacing, Pooling and Unitisation) and the common law doctrine of Correlative rights. These measures are not enduring as they have neither prevented unilateral capture nor eliminate its negative effects. Moreover, in spite of the fact that there is no statutory codification of the rule of capture in the selected countries examined in this book, the potential for parties failing to unitise or Regulators failing to enforce unitisation provisions has not been completely removed.

The objective of this book is to investigate how unilateral capture of petroleum from straddling reservoirs can be prevented considering its engendered externalities that far more outweigh its positive effects. This book argues that the solution lies in

Judicial and Administrative recognition of protectable 'Property Rights in Discovered Petroleum Reservoir' and that where this is not done; it has a wider implication on the States' obligations under Investment treaties and International human rights instruments. This is because Host State's measures - failure to order unitisation at the appropriate time or to order it retroactively where unilateral extraction has occurred - may amount to breach of its international obligations under relevant investment treaty and Human rights law (ECHR) in certain circumstances. A re-examination of the rule of capture or Unilateral capture in light of the above development is therefore crucial to the relationship or interaction between the Host States and the Investors, licensees or lessees. A theoretical framework is necessary in order to determine whether an Investor or licensee has property rights to discovered petroleum reservoir and thus, entitled to protection of this right under Investments treaties and International human rights instruments. It is also the aim of this book to provide such a theoretical framework.

List of Abbreviations

A1P1	Article 1, Protocol 1
BITs/MITs	Bilateral Investment Treaties/Multilateral Investment Treaties
CDR	Coordinated Reservoir Development
CS	Continental Shelf
CNSOPB	Canada-Nova Scotia Offshore Petroleum Board
CP Act	Consequential Provisions Act
DCF	Discounted Cash Flow
DECC	Department of Energy and Climate Change
DTI	Department of Trade and Industry
DPR	Department of Petroleum Resources
ECHR	European Convention on Human Rights
ECtHR	European Court of Human Rights
EEZ	Exclusive Economic Zone
FDP	Field Development Plan
FET	Fair and Equitable Treatment
FRN	Federal Republic of Nigeria
HRA	Human Rights Act, 1998
ITQ	Individual Transferable Quotas
ICCHR	Inter-American Commission and Court of Human Rights
ICSID	International Centre for Settlement of Investment Disputes
ICJ	International Court of Justice
IOC	International Oil and Gas Company (Majors and Independents Private sector included)

JOA	Joint Operating Agreement
IPA	International Petroleum Agreement
LCIA	London Court of International Arbitration
MER	Maximum Efficient Rate
NAOC	Nigeria Agip Oil Company
NAFTA	North Atlantic Free Trade Agreement
OPGGSA.	Offshore Petroleum and Greenhouse Gas Storage Act
OEL	Oil Exploration Licence
OPL	Oil Prospecting Licence
OML	Oil Mining Lease
OPCOM	Operating Committee
PEP	Petroleum Exploration Permits
PSA	Production Sharing Agreement
PSC	Production Sharing Contract
PCIJ	Permanent Court of International Justice
PRL	Petroleum Retention Lease
PPL	Petroleum Production Licence
PSLA	Petroleum (Submerged Lands) Act
ROC	Rule of Capture
SPDC	Shell Petroleum Development Company
SSLA	Seas and Submerged Lands Act
UKCS	United Kingdom Continental Shelf
UNCLOS	United Nation Convention on Law of the Sea
UNCITRAL	United Nations Commission on International Trade Law
UC	Unilateral Capture
VAT	Value Added Tax
WMC	Western Mining Corporation Ltd
ZOC Act	Petroleum (Australia-Indonesia Zone of Cooperation) Act

Acknowledgements

This book is derived from the updates and modifications of my PhD thesis submitted to the Centre for Energy, Petroleum and Mineral Law and Policy, University of Dundee in 2013. The thesis was supervised by Dr Abba Kolo and Dr Sergei Vinogradov, CEPMLP, University of Dundee. They have been extremely helpful in the writing of this book. Their critical and insightful comments during the course of writing the PhD thesis have brought my thoughts into a sharper focus. I cannot but acknowledge the PhD group; both Academic Staff and PhD students at the bi-weekly PhD seminar. Their insightful criticisms, suggestions and comments are highly inspirational in the writing of the thesis. I also thank the past PhD students of CEPMLP, Dr Obindah Gershon, Dr Adebayo Adaralagbe, Dr Adedayo Ayoade, Dr Chioke Nwaozuzu and Dr Malumfashi for their suggestions and keen interests in my successful outcome. I am equally grateful to all the Administrative Staff of CEPMLP, especially Linn McFarlane, Angela Dunsire, Rebecca Cree, Katheleen Shortt and Audery McLaughlin. They were very helpful, patient and also demonstrated excellent disposition to all my enquiries.

The rigorous VIVA conducted by my Examiners, Professor John Paterson, University of Aberdeen, Dr Ian Robson, Mr Stephen Dow and Professor Peter Cameron, (Director of CEPMLP, though absent from the VIVA due to exegesis of work) of CEPMLP, University of Dundee is a constant reminder for me to turn the thesis into a book as the whole thesis was thoroughly examined and areas for improvement was also highlighted. Mr Stephen Dow encouraged me and gave me the boldness to approach Kluwer Law International for publication of the thesis into a book. I am eternally grateful to him and the rest of the Examiners. My Supervisors, Examiners and all that offered me suggestions in the course of writing the thesis and this book are however exonerated from any error or omission either of facts or law that may be found in this book.

A number of individuals and institutions too many to mention have contributed immensely to the success of the thesis. Chief amongst them are – Professor Pieter Bekker (Chair in International Law, CEPMLP) and Mr Gerrit Vriezen (Legal Manager NAM, Netherlands but now Associate General Counsel, Shell International BV) for providing me contacts and inroad for my investigations at Netherlands, Mr Ad van der Zanden, (Managing Director, ConocoPhilips, Netherlands) for sending me materials and granting an interview electronically, A. Olufemi (SPDC, Nigeria), M. O. Oriafor (DPR, Nigeria) Pius Ogunjiafor (Agip Petroleum, Nigeria) and Seplat Petroleum Nigeria for finding time to grant me an interview, Mrs Maseli (DPR, Nigeria) Mrs Elizabeth Akah (my ever dependable boss and colleague at DPR, Nigeria), Mr Andrew Obaje (former Director of DPR, Nigeria) and Mr George Osahon (current Director of DPR) for their immense moral support and contributions.

Moreover, I would like to acknowledge with thanks all institutions especially, libraries, research institutes and companies around the globe that sent to me materials and books for the writing of the thesis.

I am most grateful to my sponsors, the Petroleum Technology Development Fund (PTDF) for funding the research degree and my employer, the Department of Petroleum Resources for releasing me for the period of the programme, without which it would have remained a pipe dream.

I am grateful to my parents, His Royal Highness Oba S. S. Tolorunse and Olori (Mrs) Rachael Tolorunse for their fervent support and prayers throughout the period of the PhD programme. I owe a debt of gratitude to my wife, Catherine and children, Tosin, Adeola and Timi for their prayers, love, care, support, patience and understanding. They suffered tremendous neglect in the course of my study at CEPMLP.

Finally, I thank God Almighty for endowing me the grace to bring this book into fruition.

CHAPTER 1

General Introduction

1. INTRODUCTION

Forming part of the current petroleum property system in the Common law countries that we have examined in this book is the Rule of Capture (ROC). This has encouraged unilateral capture or production of petroleum from straddling reservoirs. Unilateral capture (UC) of petroleum occurs where a landowner or lessee embarks upon independent drilling of wells on his land or lease area and takes from the underneath, petroleum[1] that he is able to move into his well including that coming from the land or lease area of his neighbour. UC, which traditionally emanated from the United States' petroleum industry, has been posing very serious legal challenge to the industry since the inception of petroleum production in 1850s because it resulted into oil allocation problems between two adjoining licensees that have a common petroleum reservoir. The legal issue was as to which property rule will apply once this happens. This was no doubt a difficult nut for the American Judges to crack as there was no precedent to follow. In trying to solve the difficult ownership or property problems, UC has been held by the courts to be legally permissible and that the adjoining landowner or leaseholder has no remedy other than to 'do likewise'. The legal protection accorded a landowner or lessee that engaged in UC is called the ROC. This is an indication that there is no protection or secured property right to underground petroleum resources.[2]

The ROC was traditionally applicable to things un-owned such as wild animals and percolating or subterranean waters but was imported to oil and gas industry to resolve difficult ownership claims. The rationale for the adoption of the ROC was attributed to lack of legislation on the subject and inadequate knowledge of reservoirs'

1. The word 'petroleum' as used in this book means 'oil and gas'.
2. Note that the property rights advocated in this book means not 'ownership rights' but lesser 'interests' or 'rights' in a resource that is proprietary in character.

mechanics[3] on the part of the Judges on whose shoulders laid the responsibility to develop the law on the issue. The Judges adopted the ROC as a rule of necessity[4] as it was simply convenient for them to use the ROC to solve difficult ownership problems. As the ROC was being applied, those with financial muscles and technical know-how were racing against one another to produce oil. It is therefore, a reward for those that diligently seek the oil and could produce it. This has a positive effect on oil production to the economy because as the game of capture is to reward those that diligently captured other's petroleum, there was an incentive to quickly explore, discover new horizons and promptly produce the resource. Therefore, for a country that newly discovered petroleum resources, making the ROC part of its oil and gas property system could lead to earlier or speedy development and production of the resources and thus promotes public interests as it would fetch quick revenues for the country to meet its social and economic obligations to its people.

However, as shown by evidence in the US, the application of the ROC could also spell woes for such country as it could plunge its oil and gas industry into very serious problems. In the US, the physical and economic wastes emanating from competitive drilling and the ensuing reduction in total recovery and reservoirs rent were colossal. The companies recorded high cost of production and lost total recovery of oil by engaging in production profile that ran against maximum value for the resources. With the ROC, coupled with multiple companies holding production leases to common-reservoirs, competitive drilling became prevalent. The race to produce also creates a race to waste important resources. Excessive capital expenditures were incurred on drilling more wells that were technically unnecessary in order to drain as much oil as possible from adjacent leaseholders.

Consequently, building unnecessary surface storage facilities to store the oil was on the increase while little reservoir rents and royalties were recorded because markets were over flooded with oil produced without regards to market forces and price. Reservoir energy was quickly dissipated leading to loss of total recovery. This eventually had an increasing effect on production costs and the ultimate consumer had to suffer the price increase. The irony of it is that in the short run prices will be low because market will be over flooded with the commodity while at the long run prices will increase due to the investor holding back their investment as a result of low returns on investment. As a result of low prices, wastage occurs as consumers will put the resource into inferior uses.[5]

3. In the case of *Barnard v. Monongahela Natural Gas Co.*, 216 Pa. 362, 365, 65 A. 801, 802 (1907), the Pennsylvania Supreme Court declared that ' Exact Knowledge on this subject is not at present obtainable ... This may not be the best rule; but neither the Legislature nor our highest court has given us any better. No doubt many thousands of dollars have been expended 'in protecting lines' in oil and gas territory that would not have been expended if some rules had existed by which it could have been avoided'.
4. False analogies were made to subterranean waters, animal *ferae naturae* and solid minerals while failing to adopt the rules relating to them in totality.
5. For a detailed economic analysis of this long, intermediate and short run price effects, see Stephen L McDonald, 'Petroleum Conservation in the United States: An Economic Analysis' (Baltimore and London: Resources for the Future, Inc. by The John Hopkins Press, 1971) at pp. 96-105. He is of the view that the price of crude oil is more stable under unitisation than under the ROC.

Sound conservation practices were also affected by the application of the ROC. This is because the ROC had modified the existing ownership principles and created a property system that encouraged the race to produce oil and gas without regard to reservoir pressure that would have enhanced oil recovery. It therefore discourages producers to embark upon unitised development and provides 'element of chance for additional reward' as individual tries to maximise his gain through drainage.[6] The ROC has shown that where the law fails to protect investments, there will be increased efforts by individuals to protect their investments through self-help and this could result into over-investments and excessive wastes. This is counter-productive as investment expectations will be negatively affected.

Furthermore, the ROC discourages secondary and other enhanced recovery operations. For example in carrying out water flooding operations, water is pumped into one end of the field in order to push oil to producing wells at the other end. A single operator will disallow secondary recovery operations like water flooding and gas injection for pressure maintenance especially where it will affect his underlie reservoir. He may also benefit from such recovery operations if the well on his property is strategically positioned to drain oil from the property of the person carrying out secondary recovery operation. The party who intends to carry out the operation will be discouraged as the other party draining will not suspend capture activities owing to the ROC. Moreover, if individuals attempt to flood fields unilaterally, subsurface trespass may be committed because of water invasion.

The ROC subjected reservoir oil and gas to open access regime. Consequently, individual owners of the land overlying the reservoirs had attempted to maximise their individual gain to the detriment of the common resource and ultimately to the rest of the landowners whose properties overlie the reservoir. It therefore, destroys title (i.e., 'the bundle of rights' – right to possess, the right to use, the right to manage, the right to the income of the thing, the right to the capital) of the lessee to oil and gas in situ. It erodes the security of oil and gas title of the licensee both when it is under the ground and when it has been produced unilaterally by an adjoining licensee. The legitimate expectation of the licensee in the use and enjoyment of the resources and also against interfering forces in society at large are negatively impacted by the ROC. This has a wider implication on investment in the industry at the long run as part of what investors consider before investing in a particular country is the extent to which their petroleum laws and regulations encapsulate the ROC.

Apart from the problems caused by the application of the ROC in the US as specified above, the continued operation of the ROC in this modern era raises economic and policy issues concerning Energy conservation policies of both the producing and consuming countries which are to the effect that measures must be taken not only to make maximum efficient use of available energy so as to postpone exhaustion of the resource and to reduce energy scarcity, but also to adopt measures that will increase total supply of energy. This means that petroleum reservoirs should be developed in such a way that maximum recovery of the oil and gas resource is achieved.

6. Edward Pierce, 'Coordinated Reservoir Development – An Alternative to the Rule of Capture for the Ownership and Development of Oil and Gas', (1983) Journal of Energy Law and Policy 4: 31.

In spite of the above concerns, some States' Regulators have issued some policy guidelines to the effect that the ROC would be allowed to govern their petroleum extraction rather than delay field development where unitisation could not be reached on time. For example, in the UK, the Department of Trade and Industry Oil and Gas Directorate – Regulation Guidance Notes, paragraph 2.5.1 (a) provides:

> [T]he Secretary of State will not necessarily refuse to grant development consent to a particular group of Licensees who have not concluded an agreement with the Licensees of an adjacent block on the basis that they have not concluded unitisation agreement. The Department does not consider that powers to require unitisation extend to issues of fairness and equity between groups of licensees. The Department's position is that proprietary rights do not exist in un-extracted hydrocarbons under the UKCS and ownership of hydrocarbon arises only once they have been extracted under appropriate regulatory consent.

Thus, by this policy Statement (i.e., granting development approval even where licensees have not concluded agreement on unitisation) could it be said that the Department's aim is to set the ROC as a default rule to be applied should the licensees failed or could not reach agreement on unitisation? This policy statement seems to have disregarded an important attributes of the licence which contradicts the whole essence of risk taken by the investor and his legitimate expectation.

Another example is Nigeria where the problem arises from failure of the Regulatory Agency, the Department of Petroleum Resources (DPR) to enforce compulsory unitisation at the appropriate time where Licence holders could not agree on unitisation terms. This has resulted to a situation where one Licence holder produced from a reservoir that straddles a field operated by another Licence holder for about fifteen years without unitisation agreement in place. This problem has occurred with respect to several petroleum fields in which either UC has occurred (Brown–Green fields) or both licensees have engaged in competitive drilling and production (Brown–Brown fields).[7] In addressing the problem, the DPR issued Guidelines on Unitisation and made provisions allowing the ROC in some instances while in some others, it disallowed its application. However, in practice, the DPR has allowed the ROC even where the Guidelines prohibited the same. In Canada, the problem occurred in split title situation which is different from the set of facts in which the problem occurred in the US. Yet, the Canadian courts just like the US courts drew analogy from the common law rules on percolating or underground water.[8] In Australia, there had been conflicting interpretations of Unitisation clauses among eminent Jurists on

7. Out of the 138 Petroleum fields that require unitisation in Nigeria, 44 fields had engaged in UC, 36 fields engaged in competitive production while 54 fields are yet to be unitised or produced. The terms Brown fields and Green fields respectively denote producing and non-producing fields. *Source*: The Department of Petroleum Resources, Nigeria. See Tables 6.1-6.4 in Chapter 6 of this book and the discussion on the adequacy of the approach adopted by the Regulatory Authority and the Petroleum Companies in Nigeria.
8. An elaborate discussion on the analogy to subterranean water and wild animal is contained in Chapter 5. The differences in the application of ROC in Canada and US are also brought into limelight in that chapter.

whether there is a statutory codification of the ROC.[9] This has accounted for the argument as to whether or not the common law ROC has been given statutory teeth.

This book also examined the problem in Netherlands - a civil law country - as it has witnessed the re-emergence of the ROC. It is also as a result of the failure of the Regulator to enforce compulsory unitisation. In the case of *Unocal Netherlands B.V. v. Continental Netherlands Oil Co. (Conoco)*,[10] the court held that the ROC is not applicable as a valid rule of Dutch law to the production licence granted pursuant to the Continental Shelf Mining Act. According to the court, this is because the production licence gives the Licence holder the exclusive right to produce oil in its license area and that the removal of oil from another licence area to which another party is the holder of a production licence constitutes an infringement of the subjective right of that other party, provided the oil removed would have been economically extractable in some way for the other Licence holder.[11] Although, there had been a change in the law since the Judgment was passed that could prevent UC from taking place in certain condition, the problem may still happen if the condition does not take place. The modified law provides that a licensee shall not proceed with production from straddling reservoirs without unitisation agreement or cooperative exploitation except the Minister grants an exemption with respect to obligation to conclude agreement. Therefore, if the Minister grants such a waiver that has the implication of allowing drainage, would the rule of capture apply or not?

Moreover, in the Domanial regimes, the States have provided in their laws that ownership of minerals belong to the State and have also made provisions for Compulsory Unitisation. This is to avoid the ROC and the disastrous consequences it engendered. However, this goal may not be achieved because of the language of the unitisation clauses which the Regulators have misconstrued as giving them discretionary power to order unitisation. Consequently, the Regulators have failed to enforce unitisation or evinced an intention not to enforce it where it is necessary do so. As a result, the Conservation laws and the common law doctrine of Correlative rights[12] have not been able to prevent all times drainage.

Also as they were not designed to address the issue of protection for property rights to oil and gas while still in the reservoir they could not completely eliminate the Rule. The defect in Conservation laws stemmed from their failure to provide remedy like compensation where one party engages in unilateral production from straddling reservoirs without unitisation in spite of the huge amount of resources expended by the innocent party to discover a reservoir from which petroleum had been drained.[13] This

9. Sections 52 (a) and 127 (a) (b) of the Petroleum (submerged lands) Act 1967 (sections 161 and 285 of the Offshore Petroleum and Green House Gas Storage Act of 2006).
10. Case C-04/127 HR, 14 October 2005, Hoge Raad (H.C. of Netherlands).
11. The proviso added by the Justices to the effect that 'provided the oil removed would have been economically extractable in some way for the other licence holder' has the tendency of denying a licensee his property rights in the oil extracted by his neighbour if it would have been un-economically extractable by the licensee from his licence area or the adjoining licence area after unitisation. A detail critique of this proviso is contained in Chapter 6 of this book.
12. The conservation laws and the Correlative rights doctrine are discussed in detail in Chapter 5.
13. The Courts in the domanial ownership of petroleum regimes might follow the decisions of the US courts of no property rights in underground petroleum because of the bond of common legal

has created conflicts between not only the licensees inter se but also between the licensees and the State. Reconciling the conflicting interests of the licensees inter se on the one hand, and the interests of the State and the licensees on the other, is very difficult. In some jurisdictions like Nigeria, United Kingdom and Australia, the issue is yet to come before the court, while in others where it has comes up like US and Canada, conflicting decisions were the result of those cases. Also, because unilateral capture occurs as a consequence of failure to enforce Compulsory unitisation by the State, it raises investments and human rights concern especially where the party suffering drainage is a foreign investor. In the field of international laws, it may have consequence on the Host's State's international obligation under the BITs/MITs and Human rights instruments. This Book therefore, re-examines the ROC in light of the consequence it may have on the State and its adverse implications on the investments and rights of licensees. This is because in upstream oil and gas investment projects, certain species of property rights are at play which has been recognised as protectable property under investment treaty laws. For instance, oil and gas project infrastructures and equipment such as oil wells, platforms, pipelines and flow stations, petrol-physical and geo-physical data acquired would be of great concern for an investor. In addition, intangible assets such as contracts, licences, goodwill, technical resources (technical know-how, skills, specialisation), subsoil resources (minerals and discovered petroleum reservoir), exclusive right to produce from the reservoir, title to the petroleum produced, a twenty-year production term with renewable option (for as long as there may be production) and various choses in action made up of rights under various kinds of contracts or the one overriding royalty interest will also be paramount to an investor in making final investment decision.[14] Each of these attributes is associated with economic property right because each of them has value. However, because of the rule of capture, some of these rights (i.e., beneficial rights or interests of licensee to reservoir oil or discovered petroleum reservoir and the exclusive rights to produce from the reservoir) may be affected as they have not been adequately protected by the Judges in some of the common law countries examined in this book. This problem becomes real when petroleum has been unilaterally captured by one licensee from a straddling reservoir and the State did not halt unilateral drainage or enforce unitisation retroactively. This raises the question as to whether this kind of property right could have protection under International investment treaties (BIT and MIT) and Article 1 Protocol 1 (A1P1) of the European Convention for the Protection of Human rights and Fundamental Freedoms (ECHR)[15] and hence could attract State's responsibility if the

heritage existing between them and coupled with the fact that their petroleum laws or constitutions, have expressly provided that ownership of petroleum in situ is vested in the State. But it should be noted that this should not imply that Licensees has no proprietary rights to petroleum while still in the reservoir because the terms 'ownership' and 'property rights' under the common law are conceptually different from each other as shown in Chapter 2.

14. Lorenzo Cotula, 'Human Rights, Natural Resource and Investment Law in a Globalised World' (Routledge, 2012), at 12.
15. However, these questions are anchored upon our findings in Chapter 4 that Licensee has property rights or interests in un-extracted oil and gas resources underlying his acreage. Subsequent chapters would show whether or not licensee's property rights in un-extracted petroleum resources is adequately protected under domestic private law.

State fails to protect it. In addition, a Capture-based petroleum property system has the potential of causing conflicts of interests not only between adjoining licensees but also between licensees and the State.[16]

From the above instances, it is clear that UC could still occur in Domanial Jurisdictions either because the Regulators permitted it or because of their laxities. The policy Statement or laxity of the Regulators may have emanated from the language of the unitisation clause which appeared to have given them discretion in enforcing Compulsory unitisation. As a result, even though many States have adopted differing petroleum ownership regimes from what is obtainable in the US and have enacted Compulsory unitisation laws; unilateral withdrawal of petroleum from straddling fields has occurred and could happen in the countries that are yet to experience it. The oil operators as well have latched on to this attitude of the Regulators to abdicate their responsibilities of complying with their statutory obligations. The fundamental question that this book addresses is, given the aforesaid regulatory and institutional laxity, how unilateral capture of petroleum from straddling reservoirs can be prevented considering its engendered externalities that far more outweigh its positive effects.

The aim of this book therefore, is to investigate how UC can be averted so that party can cooperate to develop the fields as a single unit, given that the negative consequence of allowing the Rule to govern petroleum extraction outweighs its advantages. This main question requires two lines of inquiry – (1) what is the legal nature of the rights held by licensee in un-exploited petroleum reservoir?; and (2) can failure to enjoin unitisation at the appropriate time or retroactively amount to a breach of the State's international obligations under BITs/MITs and/or Human rights instruments?

The book identified and analysed the deficiencies in the property rule of capture in both Accession and Domanial ownership of petroleum regimes and argues that protectable 'Property Rights in Discovered Petroleum Reservoir' will prevent unilateral capture and that it will serve not only public interests but will also protect the interests of the licensees.

It therefore, gave a synchronic and diachronic analysis of property rights concepts with a view of determining the existence or otherwise of proprietary rights in petroleum reservoir (being an important attribute of a production licence) and as a solution to unilateral capture. The book further addresses the implication of failure by the Regulators to compel unitisation on the States' obligations under investment treaties and Human rights instruments. Moreover, it examines the inadequacy of the protection given to licensee's proprietary rights or interests in petroleum reservoir under domestic private laws and explored the plausibility of protection for the rights under modern Investment treaties and International human rights laws.

The book examines six countries – US, UK, Canada, Australia, Nigeria and Netherlands with regards to UC so as to gain wider insights into the problem being examined and as a means of comparing experiences. With the exemption of Netherlands, these countries were selected because of their similar legal concepts and close

16. This is exemplified in the cases discussed in subsequent chapters of this book.

judicial linkage and except US, ownership of petroleum in situ is vested in the State and Provincial or Federating Units. Netherlands was chosen in order to serve as a comparison between the civil law and common law countries and because it has experienced the problem of UC.

The comparative analysis illustrates the problems of UC and the approach adopted by the countries in tackling it. It helps to identify the country with a good approach to the problem and in determining whether there is commonality of approach to the solution of UC.

In addition, employing law as the main analytical tool, the book draws from the principles and rules of International Investment law, International human rights law, and Economic theories on concept of property, Petroleum geology, and Reservoir engineering as means of analysing the problem and for provision of practical answers where it is necessary to resolve particular problem.

The main issue addressed in this book has been causing disagreement and tension between the Licensees inter se on one hand and between the Licensees and the Host State/ Lessors on the other.[17] Table 1.1 explains succinctly the varied interests and arguments of the three parties in this problem. The argument of the party draining petroleum had been that there is a legitimate right to produce petroleum from straddling reservoir from his own licence area and that if parties could not reach unitisation agreements on time, he can as well go ahead and drill well in his own licence area even though such well has the potential to drain hydrocarbon from the straddling reservoir. On the contrary, the party suffering drainage had argued that such a unilateral action amounts to taking of property right and that both parties should cooperate to develop the fields as a single unit.

The Host State in most cases remains passive, in spite of the compulsory unitisation power of the Minister, until the other party suffering drainage has filed a notice requiring an order for unitisation and by which time, drainage would have occurred.[18] An attempt by the Regulatory Authority to enforce retroactive unitisation is often met with stiff opposition and could lead to court action.[19]

The contention at that point would turn to whether the order of the Regulatory Authority should be made retroactive or not and if at all made retroactive, which date should the order commence.

17. The earlier capture cases in the US as shown in Chapter 5 of this book were between the lessors and lessees. In those cases, the lessors took action in the court against their lessees for failure to protect the lease against drainage.
18. Figure 1.1 explain graphically the conflicting interests of the licensees inter se and the State.
19. See full discussion on this issue in Chapter 7.

Figure 1.1 Conflicting Interests of Licensees Inter Se and the Host State

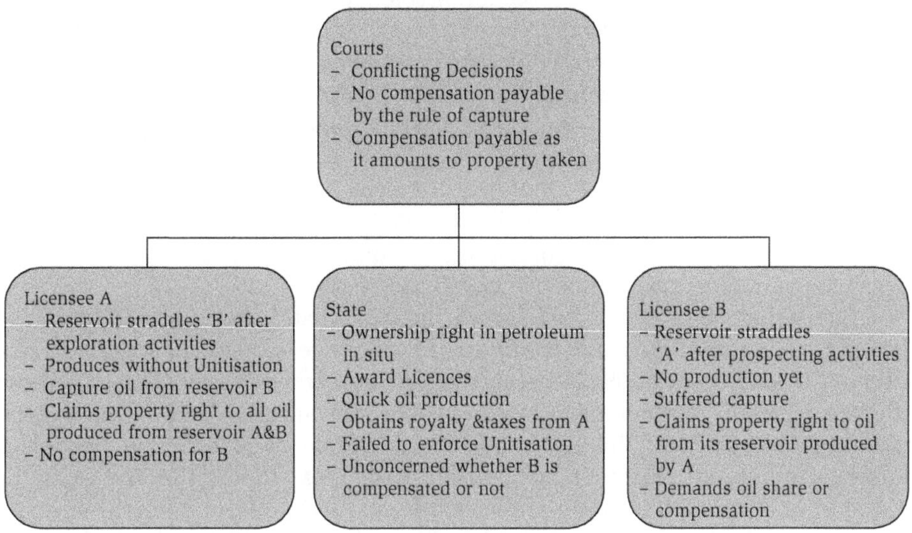

Therefore, the book is not a mere rhetoric or esoteric work but one with practical significance in that the result could serve as a verifiable tool of reconciling the interests of the Licensees inter se and the State, regulate and manage straddling petroleum resources, restore confidence and stimulate investments in the upstream petroleum sector since licensees will be ready to take up more exploration risks and be confident that they would have proprietary rights in any find. It will also enhance security of Licensee's title thereby enhancing access to finance of oil and gas projects.

Moreover, this book deals with a difficult practical and novel point especially in Nigeria where the Regulatory Authority, DPR, is currently facing critical challenge on how to handle the issue of whether to make unitisation order retroactive or not and if at all retroactive, to which date?

Potentially, this book has a lot of implications for the oil and gas industry. The lessors or Governments will have to wake up to both their domestic and international responsibilities as it will have significant impacts on the existing laws and regulations which will have to be modified. Oil companies, as well, will have to review their operational strategies as a result of the property rights concept that will emerge.

The result of this book will no doubt help to provide solution to this problem and also help in shaping Nigeria's legislative framework on unitisation, including that of all other countries' that are not robust enough to cater for all the legal issues identified above. It will lead to total optimisation of unitisation benefits that had hitherto eluded the companies and the State as it will curtail overreaching conduct of an aggressive resource driller. It will also help boost the goal of good oil field practice and sustainable resource management.

Even though substantial literatures have been written on the problems of unilateral capture and judicial decisions on the same are in abundance since its application to oil and gas in 1889, no enduring solution has been found for the problem. This is largely due to the conception that the fugacious nature of the oil and gas cannot yield it to the application of private property right unless and until it is extracted. It is largely seen as a problem common to common-pool natural resources. Most of the literatures have approached the issue in a descriptive manner, focusing on its historical background and its application to the oil and gas through the examination of the judicial decisions. For example, Professor Terrence Daintith[20] analysed the rule of capture from its historical background to its adoption and continued existence. The learned professor also examined the moves by some countries to avoid the Rule by towing the path of a unified State ownership and control.

One writer, D.E. Pierce[21] addressed the ROC and found out that legislative response to it in the United States has been inadequate. He suggested that Co-ordinated Reservoir Development (CDR) is the appropriate answer which according to him can either be achieved 'through judicial or legislative adjustment of the basic oil and gas ownership concepts' or 'through comprehensive State or federal unit operations statutes'. He concluded that for there to be effective conservation of the oil and gas, the ROC must be eliminated and surface owners' interest in the oil and gas in the reservoir must be recognised and protected. While this conclusion is quite sound and persuasive, Pierce's Article did not however address how the surface owners' interest in the oil and gas in the reservoir could be recognised and protected. It is not enough to peremptorily assume or conclude that it exists as it is not expressly stated in any statute. Therefore, it must be shown that it actually exists and that it is worthy of recognition and protection. This gap is one of the focal point of this book. Apart from this, Pierce's work was limited to private ownership of land and mineral rights in the US. This book is not only addressing the problem in the US but also focusing on countries where petroleum ownership rights are vested in the State by Statutes.

Moreover, none of the existing literature has approached the problem from the Property rights Jurisprudence, investment treaty law and International Human rights law perspectives. Also this book addressed comprehensively, the impacts of technological advances such as horizontal or directional well drilling, Hydraulic fracturing on the continued existence of the ROC. The courts have recognised liability for drainage arising from horizontal or directionally drilling while denying liability for drainage arising from 'Fracking'. These are drainages that happened in similar circumstances and also from similar technological innovations but attracting different legal effects and consequences. In the face of technological advances, the circumstances under which the court applied the ROC previously have now changed thus, questioning the continued adherence to this traditional common law rule of property right which might be unfit for modern oil and gas industry. This book therefore adopts a refreshing

20. Terrence Daintith, 'Finders Keepers? How the Law of Capture Shaped the World Oil Industry' (Washington, DC. London: RFF Press, 2010).
21. Pierce, 'Coordinated Reservoir Development – An Alternative to the Rule of Capture for the Ownership and Development of Oil andGas'.

approach to the problem of tackling the application of primordial legal concepts in modern industry practice. The common law, particularly, oil and gas property right needs to keep in step with the evolution of society in the field of technological innovations or improvements and economic thinking.

In addition, literature has shown that opinions are divided among the courts and eminent jurists in the United States on the issue of whether or not the unit order of the Regulatory Authority should be effective from the date the order was made or from the date of the application for Unitisation or from the date the first unilateral production occurred. In addressing this issue, Professor Owen Anderson asserts that a compulsory pooling order should normally be made retroactive from the date of first production.[22] In Oklahoma State for instance, pooling orders are made effective retroactively to the date an application for Unitisation is filed which is the date on which the adjacent landowner's right to drill is denied while applying the rule of capture to production had prior to the date of application. However, Stephen Schilde Williams in his article argued that 'retroactivity is not an option in Louisiana because based on the Louisiana's theory of mineral ownership, retroactivity takes the property of one individual and gives to another and that action has been interpreted as being unconstitutional'.[23] Why it is difficult to agree with this view is that the application of the rule of capture by the courts is not based on any ownership theory but rather on the physical nature or properties of petroleum. Besides, the question one will ask is what happened to the production before the filing of the application for unitisation? This is part of the gap that this book is set out to fill.

Other academic writers have focused on specific countries like United States, Canada and Australia. The writers have only analysed the various countries separately and not as a whole. This book is aimed at addressing the problem in these countries holistically. It also identifies the best standard or approach between the divergent practices on this issue and used the best practice to benchmark the standard expected from the Unitisation laws and guidelines of the selected countries.

2. SCOPE OF THE BOOK

The scope of this book is limited to common law countries selected from North America, Europe, Australia and West Africa where unilateral capture had occurred or has the potential to occur. A civil law country (Netherlands) was chosen to aid comparison with common law countries' approach to the problem because it has also experienced capture problem although, in a miniature way unlike Nigeria.

22. Anderson, 'Compulsory Pooling in North Dakota: Should Production Income and Expenses Be Divided from Date of Pooling, Spacing, or First Run?', (1982) N.D.L. Rev. 58: 537, 573.
23. Stephen Schilde Williams, 'Can A Louisiana Unit Order Be Effective Retroactively?', (1988-1989) La. L. Rev. 49: 1119.

The scope of this book is therefore limited to unilateral capture of petroleum from straddling fields within National borders and not between two countries.[24] This is why the solution to the problem was approached from the licensee's interests although it has the potential to ultimately cater for the States or public interest as well. Analysis of the Investment treaty laws and the Human rights instruments (particularly ECHR) was made in order to show the consequences on the State if proprietary rights of the licensee to reservoir oil are not protected by the State or that if domestic private law remedies are not available to the investor, avenue to vindicate such rights may be available through International tribunals. A brief outline of the book is given below:

Chapter 2 contains the Analytical framework. This chapter provides the foundation and the perspectives at which the problems were tackled. It sets out to analyse the legal, economic and philosophical perspectives on property rights in order to determine the basis for the respective legal rights of the States and the licensee over un-exploited petroleum resources.

This provides theoretical ground for conceptual framework applied in Chapter 4, to develop the concept of property rights in discovered petroleum reservoir. The chapter also examines the notion of property rights under International human rights law and investment treaty.

In Chapter 3, analysis of the nature of interests in Oil and Gas in Accession and Domanial Systems of Petroleum law was carried out. The legal nature of petroleum production licence is examined in relation to the domanial system of petroleum law. The chapter shows as clear as possible the development of the law of oil and gas and illustrates through the decisions of the courts, the influences that affected the adoption of the various theories of ownership as the basis of the rights or interests of the landowners and their lessees in the oil and gas in an Accession system of mining law. With respect to the nature of the property rights or interests created by petroleum production licence or lease in domanial regime of petroleum ownership, this chapter focuses on five countries – Nigeria, United Kingdom, Canada, Australia and Netherlands. The book first analyses the various laws of these States on ownership of petroleum and thereafter, the licence granting clauses. Comparison is made with the US ownership theories in order to determine whether there is any semblance between any of the US ownership theories and the domanial regime of ownership. In other words, the book determines where the domanial system of ownership is placed within the context of the US ownership theories. This analysis enables a determination of the approach to the issue of the nature of the interests of a leaseholder in domanial system.

Chapter 4, which also contains the Conceptual framework, uses property rights principles developed from the Analytical framework in Chapter 2 to see whether 'property rights in discovered petroleum reservoir' exists or could emerge with the capacity to tame the rule of capture and act as a standard against which the conflicting courts decisions could be resolved.

24. See Chapter 7 for discussion relating to the US which shows that opinions are divided as to whether or not the Unit order of the Regulatory Authority for pooling or unitisation should be effective from the date the order was made; or date of first production; or date of application for pooling or unitisation.

Chapter 5 examines the problem of unilateral capture of petroleum from straddling fields in Accession regime of petroleum ownership. It also examines the impact of technological advances on methods of well drilling on the continued existence of the ROC. The objectives here are to highlight the consequences of UC on the rights of the lessor or lessee to un-extracted petroleum resources in straddling petroleum fields, the various attempts made to solve the problem through regulations and the conflicting decisions of the courts arising from absence of standard rules and regulations.

Chapter 6 examines unilateral capture in domanial ownership of petroleum regime and the implication of the failure of the regulator to enforce unitisation at the appropriate time. It also analyses the regulatory provisions on Licence granting and Unitisation clauses of selected countries in order to determine whether they have capacities to prevent UC. It, therefore, examines whether or not there is protection for the licensee's right to un-exploited petroleum resources within national laws of the selected countries.

Chapter 7 examines the legal issues of retroactivity of costs and production and the legal implication of failure by the State to make unitisation order effective from date of first production. In addition, it examines whether there could be protection for this kind of property rights under international tribunals or courts in light of the jurisprudence of modern Investment treaties and International human rights norms. In this regard, it attempts to link cases of unilateral action taken by the licensees which captured petroleum from straddling reservoirs with the circumstances under which State's responsibility can be invoked in a legal relations between private persons, in order to determine whether a State can be held responsible for violating its international obligations to an investor's property rights as enshrined in Investment treaties and Human rights instruments.

Chapter 8 seeks to answer the questions raised in the book. It draws conclusions from all the lessons learnt, makes some recommendations and highlights areas for further research.

CHAPTER 2

Analytical Framework (The Nature of Property Right)

1. INTRODUCTION

In this chapter, an inquiry into whether a licensee could have a protectable property right in oil and gas in situ (Petroleum reservoir) will begin from an examination of the Philosophy of property which involves two key issues – (1) the nature of property and (2) the justifications for property.[1] The approach is therefore built on a 'two-pillar property matrix'. The first pillar is the perspectives on the conceptual meaning or nuances of property right (this comprises the legal, economic, investment and human rights perspectives) and the second pillar is the Justifications for property right (this comprises the legal, moral and economic justifications). The two pillars are intertwined in the sense that they hold the metaphor 'property.' They are significant because if an object cannot fall within the meaning of property and cannot be justified in any way by legal, moral and economic reasons, it cannot be property. However, our analysis in this chapter is restricted to the first pillar while the second pillar is dealt with in Chapter 4 because the second pillar provides theoretical justifications for the 'concept of property right in petroleum reservoir' discussed in that chapter.

1. In this context our focus is property theory and not property law. However, since it is difficult to divorce the property theory from property law because the former is built upon common law approach to property, reference to property law will be made where necessary. Our approach is pluralistic in that it sought to explain property right from legal, moral and economic perspectives. Even though an understanding of property requires a broader approach such as covering gender issues, cultural and social imperatives, the scope of this chapter is restricted to legal, moral, policy and economic perspectives of property. Though there may be some irreconcilable differences in the various theories, our objective is to synthesis them to construct a coherent concept of 'property rights in discovered petroleum reservoir'.

2. FIRST 'PILLAR': CONCEPTUAL MEANING OF PROPERTY

Our aim is to analyse how property has evolved and illustrate the legal, moral, policy and economic reasoning concerning the meaning of property.[2] Accordingly, the following questions are very important: What is property? In other words, what sorts of rights or entitlements in a thing constitute property and what can be objects of property? A number of studies have been carried out to conceptualise property after the classic work of Honore.[3] Even though there is wide divergence of opinion between the writers, their works have no doubt shed some lights on the concept of property.

2.1 Legal Perspectives[4]

The development of property began from the interaction of human beings with their physical environment. Since human beings live in a physical environment, their survival is dependent on the available resources in this environment. It is therefore, a necessity to have something that will link them to the resources existing in their physical environment. William Blackstone gave an idea of how the link was established.[5] He argued that just as occupancy gave temporary right of use of the soil; it was also by which permanent title in the substance of the earth itself was acquired to the exclusion of every other person except the owner.[6] Thus, a proprietary relationship between human beings and the physical resource in the environment was established. Competition for these resources among individuals is bound to happen as population increases. This could lead to conflicts among individuals as some individuals may want

2. The legal idea of property will examine the meaning of 'property' in both common law and civil law legal system. Under the Common law tradition, analysis will begin from the meaning of 'property' in property law as well as the western legal theorists' understanding of property right. The western legal Theorist's conception of property will start from the Blackstone running all through to the modern day meaning as exemplified by Honore. The various criticisms against them will also be examined and synthesised for application to the concept of property right in discovered petroleum reservoir.
3. See Lawrence C. Becker, 'Property Rights: Philosophic Foundations' (London: Routledge & Kegan Paul, 1977); Stephen R. Munzer, 'A Theory of Property' (Cambridge University Press, 1990), J.E. Penner, 'The Idea of Property in Law' (Oxford University Press, 1997), Margaret Davies, 'PROPERTY: Meanings, Histories, Theories' (Routledge, Cavendish, 2007); Jeremy Waldron, 'The Right to Private Property' (Oxford: Claredon Press, 1988); John Christman, 'The Myth of Property – Towards an Egalitarian Theory of Ownership' (New York: Oxford University Press, 1994); Thomas Merrill et al., 'What Happened to Property in Law and Economics?', (2001-2002) Yale L.J. 111: 357 at 360; Anthony Scott, 'The Evolution of Resource Property Rights' (Oxford University Press, 2008); Richard Barnes, 'Property Rights and Natural Resources' (Oxford and Portland, Oregon, 2009); Jonnette Watson Hamilton et al., 'Different Views of the Cathedral: The Literature on Property Law Theory', in Aileen Mcharg et al. (ed.) 'Property and the Law in Energy and Natural Resources' (Oxford University Press, 2010) at 35; J.E. Penner, 'The Bundle of Rights Picture of Property', (1995-1996) UCLA L. Rev. 43: 711.
4. As a preliminary, our objective is to give the meaning of property in the traditional real property law, the types and categories of property and the differences between the definitions of property in common law and civil law jurisdictions before we attempt to examine how property right is conceptualised by legal theorists.
5. Sir Williams Blackstone, 'Commentaries on the Laws of England', vol. 2 (1765) at pp. 3-4.
6. *Ibid.*, at p. 8.

to acquire resources more than the others. According to John Locke's account of property, men had introduced money device while still in the state of nature. This does not only make it morally right for unlimited appropriation but also removed all technical obstacles for anyone to appropriate such large and unequal amounts of property. In order to protect this unlimited appropriation, men agreed to establish civil society and government.[7] It then became necessary that property rules and norms be established to regulate the relationships between not only person and things but also between individuals with respect to things. The government is seen as coming into existence in order to provide protection for property. Property is therefore, the strand that link human beings to the resources and the government.

2.2 Meaning of 'Property' in Property Law

The traditional meaning of the term 'property' (i.e. under common law) is in two ways: (1) It denotes ownership of a 'thing' or an 'object'; (2) It also denotes ownership of the interest or estates a person has in a 'thing' or 'object'. With regards to the first meaning, a 'thing' could be tangible or intangible. Tangible things are: land, tenements or hereditaments. These are also referred to as real thing or corporeal because they carry the right of physical possession. Intangible things are invisible rights in land for examples, easement, lease and '*profit a prendre*'. They are referred to as personal or incorporeal because they carry the right to use the land only. Therefore both corporeal and incorporeal hereditaments are objects of real property.

As regards the second meaning, if the interest or estate a person has in land is for life or in perpetuity or freehold, the interests is classified as real property interests (or estates). While a lesser duration like a term of years is called personal property interest (or estates). Therefore, real property interests and personal property interests are both interests in real property. The difference lies in their duration.[8] Therefore, at common law, the concept of ownership has insignificant meaning when it concerns land. There is fragmentation of rights into bundles usually called interests such as fee simple, leasehold, *profit a prendre*, easement and rent. Ownership may have the highest interest but in common law jurisdictions, it is not absolute.

Under the civil law jurisdictions especially, Netherlands, property is said to comprise all 'things' and all proprietary rights and interests.[9] 'Things' include both immovable and movable. Immovable things are specified as 'land, un-extracted minerals, plants growing on land, buildings and works durably united with land, either

7. John Locke, 'Second Treatises on Government', edited with introduction by C.B. Macpherson (1980) at 19; John Locke, 'Two Treatises of Government', Mark Goldie ed. (EVERYMAN, 1993) at 157-158.
8. To analyse these terminologies further, if a person has complete ownership of tangible property, it can be said that the person has fee simple interests (or estate) in corporeal hereditaments. So also if he has complete ownership of intangible property, it can be said that he has fee simple interests (or estates) in incorporeal hereditaments. Similarly a person may have incomplete ownership, e.g., a term of years in either of these classes of real property objects. See Robert J. Blake, 'The Oil and Gas Lease', (1939-1940) S. Cal. L. Rev. 13: 304, at 308.
9. Book 3, section 1, Article 1 of the Civil Code of Netherlands, Hans Warendorf et al. (ed.) (Wolters Kluwer Law & Business, 2009).

directly or by incorporation with other buildings or works' while movable things are all other things that are not immovable.[10] These are household effects serving as household objects, upholstery or furniture in a dwelling. However, collections of books or of art and objects of a scientific or historical nature are exempted.[11] A right to any of these things vests in an individual, a property right[12] and such an individual is also regarded as the owner of the thing.[13] Thus, under the civil law, ownership is synonymous to property rights and is the most comprehensive right that a person can have in a thing.[14] This is unlike common law in which property rights and ownership is not the same thing. Though they are sometimes used interchangeably, property right is wider than ownership right as it also comprises 'lesser interests (i.e. non-ownership proprietary interests).'[15]

There are also marked differences between common law and civil law with regards to the scope of the entitlements or rights included in the concept of property and also the scope of what can be the objects of property. As has been noted above, property under common law regime comprises both ownership and lesser interests in resources. The varieties of things that could be objects of property are very wide. These are 'land, tangible and intangible, movable things such as chattels, debts, money in bank, shares in company, patents and copyrights.' The contrary is the case in some civil law countries like Netherlands, Germany and Turkey where the concept of property is used more restrictively as comprising ownership rights over only movable and immovable corporeal things.[16] It is however, significant to note that both legal systems recognised the traditional meaning of property as a right of a person with respect to a thing.

2.3 Categories of Property

The concept of property was broadly defined by Waldron as a system of rules governing access to and control of material resources.[17] It has significant role to play in the use and allocation of scarce material resources in the society. It follows that

10. *Ibid.*, Article 3 (1) (2).
11. *Ibid.*, Article 5.
12. *Ibid.*, Article 6 defines property right as 'any right of a proprietary nature which either separately with another right, are transferable; rights which are intended to procure a tangible benefit to their holder; or rights which have been acquired in exchange for actual or expected tangible nature'.
13. *Ibid.*, Book 5, Articles 4 and 5.
14. *Ibid.*, Article 1.
15. J.W. Harris (ed.) 'Property Problems: From Genes to Pension Funds' (Kluwer Law International, 1998), at p. 63 cited in Ali R. Coban, 'Protection of Property Rights within the European Convention on Human Rights', (2004) at 11.
16. *Ibid.*, p. 12 at n. 15 for provisions on Turkish Civil Code. The Netherlands Civil code provides in Book 3, (section 1, Article 2) that Corporeal objects are things which can be subject to human control.
17. Waldron, 'The Right to Private Property', at 31.

property, in performing the roles of material allocation and control, could place these resources in any of the following broad categories of property system:[18]

2.3.1 *Public Property*

This is a form of property owned or controlled by the State. The State holds title to the property and carries on operations on it or engages an individual or firm to extract the resources on its behalf subject to certain contractual arrangements.[19]

2.3.2 *Private Property*

This is a property owned by an individual or a firm.

The individual might have acquired the rights from another private individual by sale or contract. Therefore, the supplier of the rights to private property is a private individual unlike public property in which the supplier of the right is the State.[20] Excludability may also be possible depending on the physical nature of the resource. Where the resource is fluid in character, e.g., oil and gas resource, excludability is very contentious.[21]

In law relating to marine fisheries, where physical excludability is not feasible, legal mechanism was developed to permit physical excludability.[22]

2.3.3 *Common Property*

Common property is the most pertinent to fugacious resources like marine fisheries, oil and gas, etc. This is a property held in common by a group of people. According to Becker, there is a difference between cases in which property is held in common positively and cases where it is held in common negatively. In the former case, the property is jointly owned and everyone has a well-defined share in it. In the latter case, it is owned by no one but is equally available to everyone.[23] Becker argues that where property is jointly owned, an individual cannot dispose of the thing without the consent of the other owners even if such individual has not taken more than his share.

18. Hamilton et al., 'Different Views of the Cathedral: The Literature on Property Law Theory', in Aileen Mcharg et al. (ed.) 'Property and the Law in Energy and Natural Resources', at 35 notes 94, 95 & 96. She said that additional categories are still possible such as anti-commons, semi-commons and liberal commons.
19. Excludability is also possible here just like in the case of private property. This means that the government like a private individual can exclude all but a designated class from the resource. The designated class could be the firm or an individual engaged by the State to exploit the resource (e.g., minerals, water, oil and gas, geothermal resources etc.) See Scott, 'The Evolution of Resource Property Rights', at 56.
20. *Ibid.*
21. This is one of the focal point of this book. A detail discussion on this is in Chapter 4.
22. Barnes, 'Property Rights and Natural Resources', at pp. 26-27.
23. Becker, 'Property Rights: Philosophic Foundations', at 25 citing Samuel Pufendorf, De Jure Naturae et Gentium, translation of 1688 ed. by C.H. and W. A. Oldfather (Oxford: Claredon Press, 1934), bk IV, iv, 2-6.

This is because joint ownership presupposes joint management and capital. On the other hand where a thing is held in common but owned by no one, a valid appropriation by one person without the consent of the others can take place.[24]

This latter case is a classic example of open access commons, i.e., where resources are held in common but owned by no one but are equally available to all. Examples of Common pool natural resources are straddling oil and gas reservoirs, marine fisheries (ocean space) and even atmosphere.[25]

3. THEORETICAL MEANING OF PROPERTY RIGHTS

3.1 Property as a 'Thing'

Traditionally, a person is said to have a property right if he stands in a particular relationship to a 'thing' and by virtue of that relationship, he is able to exclude every other persons from the thing. This has been regarded as in rem rights as distinct from right in personam in which the right is personal to that person and can only be exercised against one or a group of persons.[26] This view of property was held by property theorists like Sir William Blackstone, Adam Smith, Jeremy Bentham and John Austin. Blackstone defined property as 'that sole and despotic dominion which one man claims and exercise over the external things of the world to the total exclusion of the right of any other individual in the universe'.[27] This means that property is a 'thing'. He argued that the objects of property are 'things' and that 'things' are divided into two - 'real things' and 'personal things'. Real things are lands, tenements or hereditaments, which are permanent, fixed and immovable.[28] Personal 'things' (property) comprise Chattel personal in possession and Chattel personal in action (*choses in action*). He defined hereditaments as comprising 'not only lands and tenements but whatsoever may be inherited be it corporeal, or incorporeal, real, personal or mixed'.[29]

24. *Ibid.*
25. A robust discussion on problems associated with common property that is held in common negatively is undertaken in Chapter 4 of this book.
26. Thomas W. Merrill et al., 'What Happened to Property in Law and Economics?', at p. 360.
27. Sir William Blackstone, 'Commentaries on the Laws of England', vol. 2 (1765), at 2.
28. *Ibid.*
29. *Ibid.*, at 17. Blackstone's conception of property as a 'thing' suffers some conceptual problem with regards to incorporeal hereditaments classification because a holder of such property held no 'thing' but a right only. Nevertheless, Blackstone made these rights 'real things' by calling them 'things' that 'exist only in contemplation. Also the idea that property rights are absolute could not explain certain limitations or restrictions that the State through the law may place on the use and enjoyment of property. Property owners are always subject not only to taxation and zoning restrictions of the Government, but the rights they enjoyed are also tied up to the economic policies of the State. In addition the courts have discovered that they could not protect certain interest absolutely even though such interest deserved protection because protecting such interest will unduly restrict the activities of others.

Various questions have resonated in property rights discourse concerning Blackstone definition of property. Blackstone has been criticised by some writers as a distortion of the common law.[30]

Adam Smith[31] conceived of estate (property) as either: real rights (rights to a particular thing) or personal right (a right against particular person).[32] Thus, like Blackstone, Smith also defined property as real rights or right to a particular thing. Smith however went further by making allusion to the civil law in distinguishing between personal rights and real rights. Thus, like Blackstone, Smith brought into limelight the evolution and functions of in rem *rights.* Smith emphasised the importance of property (in rem rights) as the society moved from one age to the other, e.g., from age of hunters to the age of shepherds, to the age of agriculture and to the age of commerce. As the society moved through these ages, so also the regulation of property varies.[33] Both Smith and Blackstone conceived property as a foundation for exchange and as basis for proving or enforcement of the legitimate expectation of the holder.[34]

Jeremy Bentham also recognised and gave vivid description of the in rem nature of property rights noting that 'in conveyances ... the parties bound ... are almost numerous and indeterminate. This at least is the case of those conveyances of which the possible subjects, the *proprietary subjects* as they may be called, are *things.* To give a man a property, if it be an exclusive property, in a thing, there must be ... a mandate prohibiting persons at large from meddling with it'[35] He emphasised the functional significance of property and that it creates security of expectation in the future control

30. Among such questions are whether or not the liberal western system is so obsessed with property in this manner and whether or not it is only 'external things' that can be property. What about 'internal things' like ourselves or body? Also can we really exercise dominion over things to the total exclusion of others; what about other limitations to the use of property? See Margaret Davies, *supra* n. 3, at pp. 1-2; see also John Christman, *supra* n. 3 at 22. He said that 'the idea that property rights comprise absolute dominion is not only historically parochial and ideologically contentious but also obviously false'; Jonnette Watson Hamilton et al., *supra* n. 3 at p. 23 referring in nn. 15 and 16 to D. Schorr, 'How Blackstone Became a Blackstonian', (2008) Theoretical Inquiries in Law 10: 103 and C.M. Rose, 'Cannons of Property Talk, or, Blackstone's Anxiety', (1998) Yale LJ 108: 601 at 604 (who described Blackstone's talk of an absolute right to property as 'a trope, a rhetorical figure describing an extreme or ideal type rather than reality').
31. Adam Smith, 'Lectures on Jurisprudence', Meek Raphael and Stein (eds) (1978) at 8. He was a professor of Moral Philosophy who delivered series of lectures on Jurisprudence at the University of Glasgow in the years 1762 to 1766. He started his works on Justice and Rights by considering first, rights that belong to a man as a man. As a man, he can be injured in three respects, viz: – in his person; or in his reputation; or in his estate. However, in this book our discussion is limited to estate. This is because we are concerned with the rights that are proprietary in nature e.g., rights to property. Becker defines property rights as follows: 'The term property rights refer to "one's proprietary rights (as opposed to personal rights) whether in rem, in personam, over either corporeal or incorporeal things".' See Becker, 'Property Rights: Philosophic Foundations', at 22.
32. *Ibid.*, at p. 9. He defined Real rights as what a man 'has in his immediate possession, not only what he has about his own person as his clothes, etc.', but whatever he has a claim to and can take possession of in whatever place or condition he finds it while personal rights is 'what is due to him either by loan or by contract of whatever sort, as sales etc.'
33. *Ibid.*, at p. 14.
34. Thomas Merril et al., 'What Happened to Property in Law and Economics?', at p. 362 n. 20.
35. Jeremy Bentham, 'The Limits of Jurisprudence Defined' (Charles Warren Everett ed., 1945), at 164. He is regarded as the founder of Utilitarian school of thoughts. This means that because of the relationship a person has with the thing he possessed, an expectation of deriving some

of a particular resource.[36] To Bentham, property consists in an established expectation of being able to draw some advantages from the thing we possessed.[37] In explaining the relationship between the law and property, he argued that the enjoyment of one's property can only be guaranteed by the law. It is through the protection of the law that one can freely utilise his property in any way that one likes and also being able to reap the fruits there from.[38]

This traditional account of property was subsequently elaborated upon by John Austin.[39] John Austin defined property or dominium as 'any right which gives the entitled party an indefinite power or liberty of using or disposing of the subject'.[40] He however, conceded that the power or liberty is limited by the rights of the others and the duty incumbent on the owner.

3.2 Property as a 'Bundle of Rights'

The modern approach to the understanding of the concept of property rights is as exemplified by Wesley Newcomb Hohfeld[41] and Honore.[42] The combined works of these two great scholars in this field can be classified as the 'Bundle of Rights' conceptualism of property rights. Property as a 'bundle of rights' can be viewed in three ways – aggregate version, dis-aggregate version and conceptual version.

3.2.1 *Aggregate Version*

The aggregate version was given by Wesley Newcomb Hohfeld (hereinafter 'Hohfeld'). He regards property as an aggregate of jural relations and that it is the assemblage and extent of those relations that endows it the character of 'property' not reference to some 'objects of ownership.' This version viewed 'property' as a legal complex that consists of an aggregate of rights, privileges, powers, and immunities which are all multital jural

---

advantages in the thing arises. It is this expectation that Bentham refers to as property or that the property is based on that expectation.

36. *Ibid.*, at 82; see also Jeremy Bentham, 'Theory of Legislation' (Richard Hildreth ed., 1975), at 68. He posited that property is nothing more than a basis of expectation, 'the expectation of deriving advantages from the thing in future in consequence of being already so situated with relation to it'.
37. *Ibid.*, he said that 'there is no image no painting, no visible trait, which can express the relation that constitutes property. It is not material, It is metaphysical; it is a mere conception of the mind.'
38. *Ibid.*, at p. 69. He said that 'Property and law are born together, and die together. Before laws were made there was no property: take away laws, and property ceases.' He defended property when he said that it is a means of stimulating industry and cultivation it affords and commended the legislator who protects the security of this expectation (property rights).
39. John Austin, 'Lectures on Jurisprudence or the Philosophy of Positive Law' (Robert Campbell ed., London: J. Murray 1885).
40. *Ibid.*, at 794.
41. Wesley Newcomb Hohfeld, 'Some Fundamental Legal Conceptions as Applied in Judicial Reasoning', (1913) Yale L.J. 23: 16; Wesley Newcomb Hohfeld, 'Some Fundamental Legal Conceptions as Applied in Judicial Reasoning', (1917) Yale L.J. 26: 710.
42. A. M. Honore, 'Ownership', in 'Oxford Essays in Jurisprudence' 107 (A.G. Guest ed., 1961).

relations. This complex aggregate does not necessarily (though it may) relate to some tangible objects.

In his 1913 Article, he exhibited all the eight fundamental legal relations in a scheme of 'opposites' and 'correlatives' and which he said are the elements of property. He afterwards dealt with their individual scope, their interrelations and then applied them to concrete cases.

In his theory of jural opposites (and correlatives), he paired rights, privileges, powers and immunities with no-rights, duties, disabilities and liabilities.[43]

His account of legal relations has provided a good aid to the understanding of property rights in Anglo-American jurisprudence of property rights. Although, Hohfeld did not use the metaphor 'bundle of rights', it has been argued by Merrill that his theory of jural opposites and correlatives, coupled with his effort 'to reduce *in rem* rights to clusters of *in personam* rights' justifies the metaphor.[44] Thus, it could be said that Hohfeld's theory conceived property relationship as a bundle of rights (bundle of legal relations) in which the incidents are claim-rights, privilege, power, immunity or duty. Each of these incidents is one stick in the aggregate bundle that constitutes property.[45]

Hohfeld's argument was that rights in rem cannot be properly conceived as 'rights to things' but that it is a jural relation existing between persons since jural relation takes significance from the law and the purpose of the law is to regulate the conduct of human beings.[46] In his view, all rights are against persons and not things and that whether the right is an in rem or in personam one depends on the number of people affected.[47]

43. Hohfeld summarised his theory as follows 'Suppose for example that A is fee simple owner of Black acre. His 'legal interests' or 'property' relating to the tangible object that we called land consists of a complex aggregate of rights (or claims); privileges, powers and immunities. First, A has multital legal *rights, or claims*, that others, respectively, shall not enter on the land, that they shall not cause physical harm to the land, etc.... Second, A has an indefinite number of legal *privileges* of entering on the land, using the land, farming the land, etc.... Third, A has the *power* to alienate his legal interest to another, ... to create a life estate in another ... to create a privilege of entrance in any other person by giving 'leave and licence' ... Fourth, A has an indefinite number of legal *immunities* ... Thus A has immunity that no ordinary person can alienate A's legal interest or aggregate of jural relations to another person... correlative to all these immunities are the respective legal disabilities of other persons in general'. See Hohfeld, 'Some Fundamental Legal Conceptions as Applied in Judicial Reasoning', (1917) at pp. 746-748.
44. Merril et al., 'What Happened to Property in Law and Economics?', at 365. Merrill however, argued that Hohfeld's view that in personam and in rem rights consist of exactly the same types of rights, privileges, duties etc., and only differ in the indefiniteness and the number of the persons who are bound by these relations, failed to recognise the fact that in rem rights attach to persons insofar as they have a certain relationship to some things (see p. 364).
45. Even though Hohfeld's second article did not focus on the meaning of property rights per se, his discussion of the difference between in rem rights and in personam right, couple with his treatment of property rights in the specific examples he gave, provides a platform upon which the 'Bundle of rights' metaphor was built.
46. Hohfeld, 'Some Fundamental Legal Conceptions as Applied in Judicial Reasoning' (1917) at 721.
47. *Ibid.*, at 718. He defined rights in personam and right in rem as follows: 'A paucital right, or claim, (right in personam) is either a unique right residing in a person (or group of persons) and availing against a single person (or a single group of persons) or else it is one of a few fundamentally similar, yet separate, rights availing respectively against a few define persons. A multital right, or claim, (right in rem) is always one of a large class of fundamentally similar yet

In reaction to Blackstone's equation of property with 'rights over things,' Hohfeld declared that legal relations are between persons and not between persons and things.[48]

This is because things are incapable of having rights or duties or be bound by or recognise by rules. Therefore, the legal relation involved must be a relation between persons.[49] Thus, Hohfeld has completely rejected Blackstone's definition of property either as 'things' or 'rights over things' and insisted that property could exist whether or not there is any tangible thing to serve as the object of the rights.[50]

3.2.2 *Disaggregate Version*

Disaggregate version is also a postulation of Hohfeld. His fundamental legal conceptions also looked at property as a disaggregated set of interpersonal relations. He contended that the above eight legal relations (i.e., the eight items in the Jural correlatives) are the lowest common denominators of the law, the sum or some combination of which can be used to express any legal relationship.[51]

The disaggregated version arises from the view that since property relationship is conceived as a bundle of rights (bundle of legal relations) in which the incidents are rights, privilege, power, immunity or duty, it follows that each of these incidents is one stick in the aggregate bundle that constitutes property.

The question to be asked is whether the absence of one or more of these sticks from the bundle will render the remainder of the sticks incapable of constituting a property? The answer to this question is likely to be negative. This is because each of the sticks in the bundle is regarded as a property. For instance, the right of use of one's property can form the subject of transactions in the market place. If 'A' sells his right to use his Generator to 'B' for a day, it means that 'A' is transferring one of the sticks of the bundle that forms his ownership of the Generator. This stick can be regarded as a property right.

Moreover, the disaggregated version is very relevant in the cases of tortuous 'Takings' of property. In such cases, to determine whether property rights have been materially interfered with, the court usually determines which sticks in the bundle is taken.[52]

---

separate rights, actual and potential, residing in a single person (or single group of persons) but availing respectively against persons constituting a very large and indefinite class of people.'

48. *Ibid.*, at 721.
49. *Ibid.*, at 738-739.
50. Jeremy Waldron, 'The Right to Private Property', at 27.
51. For good critics of Hohfeld on this point see generally Munzer, 'A Theory of Property', at pp. 19-20. See however, M.H. Kramer, 'Book Review of Harris', P&J (1997) Cambridge Law Journal 56: 642.
52. The court had declared in the case of *Andrus v. Allard* (444 U.S. 104 (1978) that 'the denial of one traditional property right does not always amount to a taking. At least where an owner possesses a full bundle of property rights, the destruction of one strand in the bundle is not a taking because the aggregate must be viewed in its entirety.'

Despite several criticisms[53] against Hohfeld's theory in property concept discourse, it has a strong appeal. His theory was warmly received in American legal Jurisprudence. This had led to the *Restatement of property* made by the American law Institute in 1936. Although the word property was not defined, the four constituent elements of property with their correlatives were defined in the Restatement. These are: rights, privileges, powers, and immunities. Their correlatives are - duties, no-rights, liabilities, and disabilities.[54] In the Legal circle, it also received wide acceptability. One commentator had, based on the Hohfeld's vocabulary, declared that:

> [O]ur concept of property has shifted; incorporeal right has become property. And finally, 'property' has ceased to describe any res, or object of sense at all, and has become merely a bundle of legal relations - rights, powers, privileges, immunities.[55]

In the Judicial circle, the theory had received accolade in the case of *People v. Warde*.[56] The court declared that:

> The word property as here used, is intended to embrace every species of valuable right and interest, and whatever tends in any degree, no matter how small, to deprive one of that right, or interest, deprives him of property.

By the end of the nineteenth century, Blackstone's physical and absolute concept of property became unpopular because of the above approach which conceived property as consisting of not rights over things, but of any valuable right. One Commentator had observed that the concept of non-physical and limited property would appear to be capable of recognising every valuable interest known to the law.[57] Property is seen not as an absolute or fixed assemblage of rights but a set of rights which are limited depending upon the circumstances. New kinds of property that have arisen during this period include trademarks, trade secrets, copyright, going value of businesses, franchise and equitable easements.[58] There were many property rights either created by the legislature or the courts that cannot be conjectured within the frame work of the Blackstone's physicality and absolutist conceptions of property.

53. Kenneth J. Vandevelde, 'The New Property of the Nineteenth Century: The Development of the Modern Concept of Property', (1980) Buff. L. Rev. 29: 325 at 362; Munzer, 'A Theory of Property' (at 20-21; Penner; 'The Bundle of Rights Picture of Property'; Penner, 'The idea of property in law'.
54. American Law institute, Restatement of property, sections 1-4 (1936).
55. A.L .Corbin, 'Comment, Taxation of Seats on the Stock Exchange', (1922) Yale L.J. 31: 429.
56. 145 A.D. 861, 863, 130 N.Y.S. 698, 700(1st Dep't 1911).
57. Dean G. Acheson, Book Review, (1919) Harv. L. Rev. 33: 329, 330. He said that the industrial revolution of the nineteenth century and the consequent material development made 'the all-absorbing legal conception of the nineteenth century that of the property right. Everything was thought of in terms of property - reputation, privacy, domestic relations - and as new interests required protection, their viability depends upon their ability to take on the protective coloring of property.'
58. Francis J. Swanyze, 'The Growing Law', (1915) Yale L.J. 25: 1, 10.

3.2.3 *Bundle of Rights Version*

The bundle of rights image of property was elaborated upon by Honore in his work titled 'Ownership.' He defined ownership as the 'greatest possible interest in a thing which a mature system of law recognises ...'[59] He indicated that 'ownership' consists of certain incidents. These are the right to possess, the right to use, the right to manage, the right to the income of the thing, the right to the capital, the right to security, the right or incidents of transmissibility and absence of term, the prohibition of harmful use, liability to execution, and the incident of residuarity[60] These incidents are the legal rights and duties which apply to the person who has the greatest interest in a thing. They are also regarded as standard incidents of ownership that do not vary from 'system to system' but remained constant from 'place to place and age to age.'[61] This is so even though different legal systems have different approaches to property especially on its importance and as to what could be the object. He further contended that the incidents may be regarded as necessary ingredients of ownership, but they are not individually necessary because all the incidents need not be present before a person can be designated an owner of a thing.[62]

The incidents can therefore be regarded as the 'criteria for the correct application of the term ownership in law.'[63] This means that the absence of one element would still render the holder of the others to be properly called the 'owner' of a thing. It is also to be noted that in his analysis of the concept of ownership he places reliance on the notion of a thing as he explained these incidents with respect to an owner's relation to a thing.

Furthermore, he noted that the standard incidents stated above applies to the holder of the greatest interest in a thing (ownership) as well as to the holder of the lesser interests such as easements, short leases, licences, special property and mere detention.[64] It follows therefore, that the holder of a lesser interest can also be regarded as the owner of the thing.[65] He argued unequivocally that the distinguishing criteria between greatest interest and lesser interest *may* be found in the last incident of ownership which is – Residuarity, as he doubted that the ultimate residuary can be regarded as 'owner.'[66]

59. Honore, 'Ownership', at 108.
60. *Ibid.*, at 113.
61. *Ibid.*
62. *Ibid.*, at 112-113.
63. Penner, 'The Bundle of Rights Picture of Property', at 737.
64. Honore, 'Ownership', at 124.
65. *Ibid.*, at 125.
66. *Ibid.*, at 127.This doubt arises because it is not in all cases that on the determination of a lesser interest, the corresponding rights will vests in or are exercisable by the owner of the thing. He argued that when a sub-lease determines, the rights in it becomes exercisable by the lessee and not by the owner of the property. Therefore, he concluded that Residuarity is a necessary but not sufficient condition of ownership and merely one of the standard incidents of ownership, though important but not to be accorded any special status.

The 'bundle of rights' theory of property which came out of Hohfeld - Honore analysis has been regarded by both the courts and academic writers as satisfactory explanation of the concept of property rights.[67]

4. EXCLUSIVITY AND EXCLUDABILITY CRITERIA OF PROPERTY

Exclusivity means non-interference, that is, non-owners may not trespass, take, handle, damage, or destroy the property in question. All the Honore's incidents of ownership depend on the elements of use and exclusion except the incidents of right to security, transmissibility and absence of terms, duty to prevent harms and liability to execution are not strictly incidents of ownership as they fell outside the exclusivity criteria of property rights. However, right of exclusive use has been adjudged insufficient criteria of property right unless it is coupled with right to alienate because property does not only protect exclusive use of the thing by the owner but also empowers him to alienate the same.[68]

Moreover, in evaluating Honore's incidents of ownership with regards to excludability criteria of ownership, some legal scholars have narrowed the range of incidents essential to ownership by looking at the relative quality of the incidents in practical terms.[69] Excludability means the power of the owner to exclude others from his property.

Richard Barnes defined property right in abstract legal terms as a 'state of affairs in which one party, the right holder, has a claim on an act or forbearance of another party, the right regarder, in respect of a thing'.[70]

Therefore, if property is regarded as claim right, the essential ingredients of property will only be limited to those incidents that comprise the claim, e.g., right to possess, right to use, right to manage, right to income of the thing and the right to capital of the thing. The only limits to the claim are those imposed by the right regarder, which are duty to prevent harm and liability to execution. These are regarded as external to the right.[71] Munzer contends that while claim rights are important, they are

67. Penner, 'The Bundle of Rights Picture of Property', at 33.
68. *Ibid.*, at 742. He defined 'exclusive use' as '[T]he right to property is the right to determine the use or disposition of an alienable thing in so far as that can be achieved or aided by others excluding themselves from it, and includes the right to abandon it, to share it, to licence it to others (either exclusively or not), and to give it to others in its entirety.'
69. Christman, 'The Myth of Property - Towards an Egalitarian Theory of Ownership', at 19. He listed the first five incidents of Honore as the essential incidents of ownership. These are right to possess, right to use, right to capital, right to manage and the right to income. He regarded the incidents such as right to security, transmission and absence of terms as adjuncts to the core incidents. Just as the incident of prohibition of harmful use is rejected as an essential incident of ownership, the residuary character of ownership is regarded as structural necessity of the legal system that protects ownership and as such not an element of ownership; see also Waldron, 'The Right to Private Property', at pp. 32-33, who argued that the incident of prohibition of harmful use places a limit on what a person can do with an object whether it is his property or not.
70. Barnes, 'Property Rights and Natural Resources', at 23.
71. *Ibid.*

neither the sole nor the most important elements of property rights. He regarded power to exclude and the power to alienate as the weightiest components of property rights.[72]

Thus, by the above reasoning, the whole essence of property has been reduced to excludability. Excludability as a pure view of property signifies the idea that property involves the protection of individual interest against collective power.[73] However, it is instructive to note that the power of excludability of the owner in all legal systems is not absolute. To claim otherwise, will mean that when exclusive control cannot be established over a resource, then it cannot be reduced to private property.[74]

For moral considerations, the State may justifiably impose certain duties upon the right holder or modify his rights even without his consent. Moreover, legal limitations on the exclusive use of a thing may be imposed by the State, e.g., where a State reduces property rights to bundle of entitlements and then by instrumentality of the law reserves certain of these entitlements from the owner of the property for overridden public interests. Also, because of the physical nature of a particular resource, excludability may not be possible, e.g., spectacle of sporting event, beam of light, wild animal and Marine fishery. Therefore, physical excludability exists only where it is reasonably practicable to exclude others from the benefit of the resource in its existing form.[75]

It has been suggested by Barnes that where it is impossible or impracticable to physically exclude, the law may be used to secure exclusion. Hitherto, fish were adjudged incapable of physical exclusion and so incapable of been an object of property right. Now the situation has changed as Individual Quotas have been developed by law which has facilitated exclusion, thus giving rise to property right in fisheries.[76] Thus, where 'proprietary interest is ephemeral or not easily susceptible to physical exclusion such legal excludability is absolutely crucial.'[77]

72. Munzer, 'A Theory of Property', at 25.
73. Barnes, 'Property Rights and Natural Resources', at 25. Barnes however argued that this pure view of property does not capture the whole essence of property because rights in general and property rights in particular are relational constructs that are contingent upon social institutions for their meaning and operation. Therefore, from the position that sees property as a social institution that is responsive to the societal needs, it follows from there that it is the society that will determine the scope and limits of that institutions.
74. *Ibid.*, at 26.
75. *Ibid.*
76. *Ibid.*, at 27.
77. *Ibid.*, but see Penner, 'The Bundle of Rights Picture of Property', at 743. He contended that 'the right to property itself is a right that correlates to a general duty that all others have to exclude themselves from the property of others. The owner does not have to physically or by court order exclude others from his property. It is on this premise that in some cases in which the court has to determine property in news, sporting events, or information, they did not concern themselves with the question as to whether the plaintiff has a right to exclude the trespasser or thief from the property, by not publishing the news stories, or by building a fence to prevent the viewing of an event, or by keeping information secret. The court only concerned itself with the question of whether the trespasser or the thief has duty to exclude himself from it. See the cases of *International News Service v. Associated press*, 248 U.S. 215 (1918) and *Victoria Park Racing & Rec. Grounds Co. v. Taylor* (1937) 58 C.L.R. 479.

5. ECONOMIC PERSPECTIVE

5.1 Property as a 'List of Circumscribed Use Rights' (Bundle of Rights)

Economists have taken the realists ideas about property a step further by conceiving property as a list of use rights that a person has in a given resource. To the Economists, property institution exercises the role of promoting utility or welfare and establishes the rules that define or delimit the type of benefits or privileges the owners, users and other persons can receive from a particular resource.

R.H. Coase[78] conceived of property as a bundle of rights to carry out certain actions with respect to resources. Thus, he sees property as a bundle of rights rather than physical entities. His Statement that portrayed his understanding of property rights in this manner can be found towards the end of his article where he stated that:

> [W]e may speak of a person owning a land and using it as a factor of production but what the land owner in fact possesses is the right to carry out a circumscribed list of actions.[79]

From this statement, it means that resources that firm owns are not the physical resources but rather are the property rights.[80] This is unlike the traditional Theorists who conceived of property as a distinctive right to a thing good against the world.

In his analysis of social costs – the harmful effects of a firm's activities on others – he used decided authorities especially nuisance cases and grouped his analysis into where transaction cost is zero, and in real world scenario, where it is positive. In both instances, he showed that the significance of property rights is no more than a collection or bundle of rights arising from judicial resolution of disputes over resource use.

The nuisance cases he used in his analysis of problem of apportionment of resource use rights and liability for social costs relate to two incompatible uses of a resource by two individuals. He pointed out that in making a choice between the different ways of coordinating economic activities, comparative efficiency is desirable. One of the cases is between a medical doctor and a confectioner.[81] The facts of the case was that the confectioner, in the course of operating his machinery, produces noise and vibration that made it difficult for the doctor who occupies the adjoining premises, to use his consulting room. The doctor instituted an action in the court to restrain the confectioner from operating his machinery. The court granted the injunction on the reasoning that allowing the confectioner to continue to operate will cause hardship to

78. R.H. Coase, 'Problem of Social Cost' (1960) JL & Econ. 3: 1. His work represents a modern discussion on the economics of property rights. Although he did not define property in his analysis of the influence of the law on the working of the economic system, however property was the background to his analysis.
79. *Ibid.*, at 44.
80. Jongwook Kim et al., 'Resource-Based and Property Rights Perspectives on Value Creation: The Case of Oil Field Unitisation', (2002) Manage. Decis. Econ 23: 225-245, at 226.
81. *Sturges v. Bridgeman* (1879) 11.ch. D. 852.

the doctor and will also have prejudicial effect upon the development of land for residential purposes.

Coase is of the view that the legal rules upon which use rights were apportioned in this case as well as the other cases discussed in his article were fairly wrong or arbitrary and that the reasoning of the court behind the resolution of those cases is strange to an Economist.

He argued that it would have been possible to modify the arrangement envisaged in the court's judgment by means of a bargain between the doctor and the confectioner.[82] An economic approach to the resolution of the conflicts would have depended on whether the continued use of the machinery adds to the confectioner's income than it subtracts from the doctor's income. If it does, the confectioner will offer to pay, and the Doctor will accept compensation for the surrender of his rights thereby optimising the welfare of both parties. As a result of this bargain, the right of the Doctor to be free from noise and vibration would be transferred to the confectioner and which means the confectioner will have the right to emit noise and vibration in continuing his work while the Doctor will move his consulting room from there. In this case, it is assumed there is no transaction cost. In his view, the decision reached by the court in this case would have been appropriate in a situation where the transaction costs exceed the gains which might be achieved by the rearrangement of rights.

Coase based his other analysis on a real world situation in which the Transaction cost is positive. In this instance, the costs of rearrangement of legal rights (transaction cost) will often exceed the gains from such transactions. However, where transaction cost is positive, he is of the view that the initial delimitation of legal rights would have an effect on efficiency with which the economic system operates. He concludes by proposing that it would be desirable:

> [T]hat the courts should understand the economic consequences of their decisions and should, insofar as this is possible without creating too much uncertainty about the legal position itself, take these consequences into account when making their decision.[83]

What this means is that court should adopt a solution through legal rules that will establish use rights in a way that promotes efficiency. Efficient allocation of resources can only come about if the courts adopt a legal rule that provides incentives to both parties to a dispute to take efficient precautions to minimise social costs.[84] This has seen property in the light of bundle of use rights imposed by the court arising from the resolution of a resource use dispute. This view however, have neglected to take into account the in rem aspect of property, but have seen each use conflict as a stand-alone problem whose resolution brings about the insertion or removal of one stick from the bundle of use rights.[85]

82. Coase, 'Problem of Social Cost', at 9.
83. *Ibid.*, at 19.
84. Robert Cooter, 'Unity in Tort, Contract and Property: The Model of Precaution', (1985) Cal. L. Rev. 73: 1 at 4.
85. Thomas W. Merril et al., 'What Happened to Property in Law and Economics?', at 379.

5.2 Property as 'Entitlements'

This perspective viewed property rights as entitlements. This view did not rely on any of the notions of property as right to a thing or as bundle of rights but rather on the rules by which an entitlement may be protected and enforced. Therefore, it ignored the in rem nature of property rights. A classic work on this view is the article written by Guido Calabresi and Douglas Melamed.[86] They referred to all allocated use rights as 'entitlements'. The State decides whom to entitle and the manner in which the entitlements are protected.[87] However, the type of protection to be granted depends on the type of entitlement involved. Entitlements are grouped into three in accordance with how they are protected by the State namely, property rule entitlements, liability rule entitlements and entitlements protected by inalienability rule. Entitlement protected by property rules can only be taken from the owner with his consent. This means that the value of the entitlement is negotiated and agreed to by the seller voluntarily. State's intervention here is minimal because once the initial entitlement is decided upon; the State does not concern itself with the value.[88] Entitlement protected by liability rule arises where the initial entitlement is taken from the holder upon payment of an objectively determined compensation. The value of the entitlement is objectively determined by the State's organ in a situation where the holder of the entitlement complained that the amount of compensation is insufficient.[89] Entitlement protected by inalienability rule is not permitted to be transferred. The State's role here is wider. It determines – (1) who is initially entitled, (2) the compensation to be paid should the entitlement be taken or destroyed, and (3) forbids its sale in some or all circumstances. Therefore, inalienability rules do not only protect the entitlement but also limits or regulate its transfer.[90]

86. Guido Calabresi & Douglas Melamed, 'Property Rules, Liability Rules, and Inalienability Rules: One View of the Cathedral', (1972) Harv. L. Rev. 85: 1089. They set out a framework with which variety of legal problems can be approached. Although they used nuisance and pollution as examples in their analysis, they thought that the framework may be applied in different areas of the law. Their framework, even though presents an understanding of property right, it however neglected the in rem nature of property rights, i.e. right of a person in a thing that excludes every other person in the world.
87. That is, the State decides not only which side wins but also the kind of protection to grant. State's intervention is necessary in order to protect the reign of the 'might over the weaklings'.
88. Calabresi and Melamed, 'Property rules, Liability rules, and inalienability rules: One view of the Cathedral' at 1092. The decision as to the value is left for the parties but the seller has an overridden decision if the buyer does not offer a good price. *'Property rules involve a collective decision as to who is to be given an initial entitlement but not as to the value of the entitlement.'* Most property rights are enforced by this rule and the holder of the entitlement are generally entitled to the remedy of injunction, e.g., cases of trespass are usually enforced through injunctive relief.
89. *Ibid.* Here State's intervention is not limited to entitlement protection only but extends to an objective determination through its organ, of its value whenever it is transferred or destroyed. The determination of the value is not done by the parties.
90. *Ibid.*, at 1092-1093. According to Calebresi, some entitlements to some goods are mixed in that they can possibly be enforced by the three rules. For example an owner of a house may be protected by property rules where another person is willing to buy it, by a liability rule where the government decide to expropriate it and by alienability rule where the owner suffers contractual incapacity.

He explained further the circumstances in which a particular entitlement should be granted and when it should be protected by using the three rules Stated above. In tackling the first issue, he is of the opinion that economic efficiency, distributional goals and other justice reasons should be the yardsticks.[91]

The bulk of his analysis is devoted to the reason why liability rule should be adopted in situations where there is high transaction cost. In such cases where negotiation is not feasible liability rule is appropriate. e.g., accident and pollution cases. On the other hand, property rule is appropriate in situations of no transaction cost (where there is room for negotiation between the parties). However, their analysis also overlooked the in rem nature of property right just as Coarse did in his analysis of social cost.[92]

One other Economist that is worth mentioning is Yoram Barzel. In his work,[93] he distinguished between legal property right and Economic property right. Legal property right is defined as 'the rights recognised and enforced, in part, by the government.' It is what the State transfers to a person. Economic property right on the other hand, is the ability to enjoy a piece of property. In other words, the Economic property rights that an individual has over a commodity or assets is the 'individual's ability, in expected terms, to consume the good or the services of the asset directly or indirectly through exchange.[94] The role of the legal rights is to enhance, enforce and protect the economic rights. Therefore, where economic property right to a resource has not been properly defined and enforced, there will be increased efforts to capture the value of such resource especially as the potential value of the resource increases.[95]

Modern economic discourse on property rights is to the effect that property has a distinctive in rem character that enhances security in the use and enjoyment of a particular resource.[96] For example Posner defines property as a:

91. *Ibid.*, at 1098-1105. See also Merril et al., 'What Happened to Property in Law and Economics?' at 380. He opined that the court should asks itself that: 'Taking into account economic efficiency goals, distributional goals, and other justice reasons, what is the allocation of use rights that will provide the correct baseline, against which the process of contractual exchange can proceed, or against which we can decide who must compensate whom in the event that forced exchange is appropriate'.
92. Merril et al., 'What Happened to Property in Law and Economics?' at 382. Although, he referred to situations involving large number of claimants, he nevertheless, uses these cases to illustrate the need for liability rules rather than using it to discuss the in rem nature of property rights. In those cases for example, where there is difficulty in reaching voluntary agreement between 1000 owners to transfer their property for use as a park, the impossibility of reaching agreement in advance between the perpetrators and victims of an accident and the problem of pollution that affects large numbers of persons, liability rule is required to protect entitlement because it permits forced exchange in return for the payment of just compensation.
93. Yoram Barzel, 'Economic Analysis of property rights' (1997) 2nd (ed.).
94. *Ibid.*, at 3.
95. Guilherme Fowler de Avilla Monteiro, 'Property rights strategy: Market Structure and Competition in Brazilian Soybean Seed Industry' at p. 5.
96. Merril et al., 'What Happened to Property in Law and Economics?' at 381. He pointed out that Calabresi's discussion of property rules as a device for facilitating contractual exchange and for protecting entitlements alone inadvertently overlooked this modern economic view of property.

> [R]ight that excludes the whole rest of the world from the use of a thing except on the owner's terms. A contract right excludes only the other party to the contract.[97]

Notwithstanding the above however, the whole bulk of economist tend to view property institution from the perspective of in personam right rather that in rem rights. This appears to have been borne out of Hohfeld's conception of property that recognised that in rem rights and in personam rights though, quantitatively different they are qualitatively the same.

6. CONCEPT OF PROPERTY UNDER INVESTMENT LAWS

Before attempting the conception of property under international investments law, it is instructive to note that neither international law nor investment treaties provide substantive rules on the scope or mode of acquiring property whether tangibles or intangibles. Such matter falls within the purview of domestic law of Host States. Therefore, in dispute concerning the scope of the property rights comprising the investment or to whom such an entitlement is given, reference is made to the domestic law of property.[98] This means that in an investment dispute, the treaty tribunal must first determine whether a right of 'property' which comprises the investments exists under the domestic law of the Host State before proceeding to determine whether that right of property constitutes an investment as defined by the investment treaty.[99] If the tribunal established that the domestic law of the Host State recognises such right as proprietary and that it fell within the confines of the definition of an investment as stipulated in the relevant treaty, then the protection afforded by the investment treaty is triggered.[100] The objective of this section is to consider what constitutes a protected

97. Richard.A. Posner, 'Economic Analysis of Law' (1998) 5th (ed.) at 74; see also Oliver Hart and John Moore, 'Property Rights and the Nature of the Firm' (1990) 98 J. Pol. Econ. 1119 at 1121. He defines property right as the 'right ... to exclude others from the use of an asset'; See Richard.A. Posner, 'Economic Analysis of Law' (1986) 3rd (ed.) at 34. Posner has argued that if property right is given to an individual in respect of a valuable resource (scarce and desired resource) with excludability and transferability power, value will be maximised as this will lead to efficient use of resources. Referring to the reasons for the difference in legal treatment between the domestic and wild animals, he argued that property right cannot arise in respect of a resource where it will be both difficult to enforce against every one and the resource is worthless. This is because there will be nothing to gain from creating incentive to invest in a valueless resource. He said that there is no property right in wild animals unlike the domestic ones because it is not only difficult to enforce property right in them but also because they are not valuable. Therefore, incentive to create property right in them is absent.
98. Zachary Douglas, 'The International law of Investment Claims' (Cambridge University press, 2009) at 52.
99. Campbell Mclachlan QC, et al., 'International Investment Arbitration: Substantive principles' (Oxford University press, 2007) at 183 quoting Zachary Douglas, 'The Hybrid Foundations of Investment Treaty Arbitration' (2003) 74 BYIL 151 at 211.
100. Douglas, 'The International law of Investment Claims' at 53. See *EnCana v. Ecuador* (Merits) 12 ICSID 427. See also *Thunderbird v. Mexico (Merits)*. The tribunal was of the view that the claimant will not be entitled to payment of compensation where it is established that he did not enjoy vested right in the business activity that was taken. See also the case of *Generation Ukraine Inc v. Ukraine*, (Award) (2005) 44 ILM 404 (ICSID, 2003, Paulson P, Salpius & Voss) and *William Nagel v. Czech Republic*, (Award) SCC Case 49/2002 (SCC, 2003). In the Generation Ukraine case, the tribunal first of all determined the exact nature of the various

investment under National and International investment laws, Investment Treaties (BITs & MITs) and the International Centre for Settlement of Investment Dispute Convention (ICSID) so as to throw some light on how the term 'property' comprising the investment is conceptualised. An analysis of the meaning of 'investment' is necessary because modern treaties do not define the term 'property rights' and 'interests.' They are however, built upon the narrower term 'investment'. Therefore, since property comprises an investment, the definition of investment in national and international investment laws will provide an insight to the conception of property in investment laws. The concept of investment, though an economic terminology, has to be defined as a legal concept as it is used in investment laws and agreements.

Under National laws, the approach adopted by State to the definition of investment is either transactions-oriented approach or an enterprise-oriented approach.[101] For example, in Nigeria, section 17 of the Nigerian Investment Promotion Commission Act[102] provides that a non-Nigerian may invest and participate in the operation of any enterprise in Nigeria. This provision is however limited by the provision of section 31 which contains negative list of those sectors in which investment is prohibited to both foreign and Nigerian investors.[103] Furthermore, the section interprets the term investment to mean 'investment made to acquire an interest in an enterprise operating within and outside the economy of Nigeria.'[104] Portfolio investment, i.e. investment in shares and other securities traded on the Nigerian Stock Exchange are also included in the definition of investment under the law.[105] This is a clear indication that investment under the Nigerian law is based on an enterprise-oriented approach since it permits investment in purchase of shares in an existing Nigerian Companies and for establishment in Nigeria, of a wholly owned foreign enterprise provided it is incorporated in

rights, permits, protocols and agreements involved in the dispute using Ukrainian law before setting out to decide whether they fell within the definition of investment as provided in the relevant BIT. In the Nagel case, the tribunal emphasised the need to refer to the municipal laws in determining the words 'asset' and 'investment' under the BIT (pp.72-73). But see M. Sornarajah. 'The International Law on Foreign Investment' 3rd (ed.) (Cambridge University Press, 2010) at 192. He pointed out that the Australian and Indonesian treaty represents attempt by Host States to overcome this problem by restricting the investments that are protected by treaty to investments made in accordance with their investment laws and regulations. The resultant effect is that treaty obligations could be rendered impotent if the Host State changes its laws and regulations.

101. Engela C. Schlemmer, 'Investment, Investor, Nationality, and Shareholders' in Peter Muchlinski, et al. (ed.) 'International Investment Law' (Oxford University press, 2008) at 52.
102. Cap. N117 Vol. 13 Laws of the Federation of Nigeria, 2004.
103. These sectors are production of and dealing in arms and ammunition, narcotics and psychotropic substances, military and paramilitary wears accoutrement and such other items as the Federal executive Council may from time to time, determine.
104. Enterprise is defined in the same section to mean 'an industry, project, undertaking or business to which this Act applies or an expansion of that industry, undertaking, project or business or any part of that industry, undertaking, project or business and, where there is foreign participation, means such an enterprise duly registered with the Commission'.
105. Section 21 of the Nigerian Investment Promotion Commission Act.

Nigeria.[106] Such an enterprise can carry on any type of business except those contained in the negative list.[107]

Modern Investment treaties usually contain the definition of 'investment'. They sometimes define 'investments' in broad terms, e.g., 'all assets' with illustrative lists of categories of such assets which is indicative but not exhaustive or definitive. This is normally referred to as the broad and open ended approach. For example, the United Kingdom Model Agreement provides in Article 1 that:[108]

> [F]or the purposes of this Agreement:
>
> (a) 'investments' means every kind of asset and in particular, though not exclusively, includes:
>   (i) movable and immovable property and any other property rights such as mortgages, liens or pledges;
>   (ii) shares in and stock and debentures of a company and any other form of participation in a company;
>   (iii) claims to money or to any performance under contract having financial value;
>   (iv) intellectual property rights, goodwill, technical processes and know-how; and
>   (v) business concessions conferred by law or under contract, including concessions to search for, cultivate, extract or exploit natural resources.

Other BITs adopted a narrower approach. This was done by either excluding certain types of investment[109] or assets of less than certain amount in order to reserve for domestic investor requiring small investment[110] or limiting the parts of the economy to which the agreement applies.[111]

---

106. *Ibid.*, section 19.
107. See also Schlemmer, 'Investment, Investor, Nationality, and Shareholders' in Peter Muchlinski et al. (ed.) 'International Investment Law' at pp. 53-54 for a similar approach to the definition of investment under the Namibian and Tanzanian Investment laws. He also referred to the law of Albania on Foreign Investment No. 7764 of 2 November 1993, Article 1(3) which defines investment in broad terms to include amongst other things, real and personal property, tangible and intangible or any other kind of property, every right recognised by law or contract, and every licence or permission given in accordance with the laws.
108. R. Dolzer et al., 'Bilateral Investment Treaties' at pp.228-229. See also the U.S. M odel BIT which defines 'Investment' to mean every kind of investment ... such as equity, debt, and service investment contracts; and includes without limitation: tangible and intangible property, including rights, such as mortgages, liens and pledges.... Any right conferred by law or contract, and any licenses and permits issued pursuant to law, including those issued for manufacture and sale of products' ... and 'any right conferred by law or contract, including rights to search for or utilise natural resources, and rights to manufacture, use and sell products'; the BIT between Ukraine and Denmark (1992) which provides that the term investment shall mean every kind of asset connected with economic activities acquired for the purpose of establishing lasting economic relations ...'.
109. See the 1998 ASEAN Framework Agreement on investment Area, Article 2 which expressly excluded portfolio investment from its coverage (available at http://www.aseansec.org) and Article 1139 of NAFTA which included portfolio investment but excluded debt security and loans and other type of commercial contract.
110. Article 15 of the community investment code of Economic Community of Great Lakes Countries provides for minimum of USD 1 million or equivalent.
111. Article 1 of ECT refers to 'investment' as an investment associated with an economic activity in Energy Sector. It defines investments in Article 1 (6) to mean every kind of asset, owned or

However, in spite of the fact that most BITs contained the definition of an investment, the Treaty tribunal particularly the ICSID have, in most cases interpreted investments independently of the treaty definition. This stemmed from the fact that Article 25 (1) of the ICSID Convention[112] did not contain the definition of investment. As a result of this, Arbitrators have resorted to the use of traditional definition as well as to modern definition of investment.[113] This is usually referred to as the objective approach. Therefore, where the contract satisfy the definition of an investment under the BIT but failed to satisfy the objective criteria of an investment within the meaning of Article 25 of ICSID, the tribunal will not assume jurisdiction.[114]

The other approach relied on the Report of the Executive Directors and the preamble to the ICSID Convention. The ICSID tribunals have by this, given the term investment a broad definition.[115] In the case of *Tradex Hellas SA v. Republic of Albania*,[116] the ICSID tribunal considered the broad interpretation given in international law to "property" or "investment" as the possible object of an expropriation.[117] In its examination of a possible foreign investment by Tradex in Albania, the tribunal

controlled (directly or indirectly) by an investor and includes: 'tangible and intangible, and movable and immovable, property, and any property rights such as leases, mortgages, and pledges; ... shares, stock or other form of equity participation in a company or business enterprise, ... claims to money and claims to performance pursuant to contract having economic value and associated with investment; ... and any right conferred by law or contract or by virtue of any licence and permits granted pursuant to the law to undertake any Economic Activity in the Energy Sector.

112. Article 25 (1) provides that the Jurisdiction of the Centre shall relates to any legal dispute arising directly out of an investment between a contracting State ... and a national of another contracting State which, the parties to the dispute consent in writing to submit to the centre.
113. Schlemmer, 'Investment, Investor, Nationality, and Shareholders' in Peter Muchlinski et al. (ed.) 'International Investment Law' at 63. Quoting David Lopina, she said that traditional forms of investments are 'concessions, establishment agreements, joint ventures, loans made by private financial institutions to foreign public entities, the arrangements concerning industrial property rights' Lopina, 'The International Centre for settlement of investment Disputes: Investment Arbitration for the 1990s' Ohio State Journal on Dispute Resolution 107 (1988) at 114-115. She also said that Lopina gave the list of modern forms of investment as 'profit sharing, service and management contracts, contracts for the sale and erection of industrial plants, turn-key contracts, international leasing arrangements and agreements for the transfer of know-how and technology'.
114. *Joy Mining v. Egypt* ICSID Case No. ARB/03/11, 6 August 2004, 44 ILM 7 (2005) where the tribunal opined that 'the parties to a dispute cannot by contract or treaty define an investment for the purpose of ICSID jurisdiction something which does not satisfy the objective criterion of *Article 25* of the convention. Otherwise Article 25 and its reliance on the concept of investment even if not specifically defined would be turned to a meaningless provision'.
115. This is often referred to as the subjective approach: – The consent of the parties in a particular case implies their recognition that investment criterion has been met. The Report of the Executive Directors (paragraph 23) states that consent of the parties is the cornerstone of the jurisdiction of the Centre. Paragraph 27 states that no attempt was made to define the term investment. This affords the parties to determine the classes of dispute they would or would not consider submitting to the Centre. This approach was adopted by the tribunal in *Goetz v. Burundi* – shares owned by the claimant in a locally registered corporation are protected investment within the meaning of Article 25 (1) of ICSID because under Article 8.6 of the BIT in question shares is included in the definition of Investment.
116. ICSID Case No. Arb/94/2, 24 December 1996, 14 ICSID Review-FILJ 197 (1999).
117. See also the decision of the ICSID Tribunal in the *Case of Fedax v. Venezuela*: Decision on Jurisdiction of 11 July 1997, ILM XXXVII, 1998, p. 1378 at sections 31 to 43; Award of 9 March 1998, ILM XXXVII, 1998, p. 1391 at section 29.

took into account the broad interpretation provided by the applicable law in this context.[118]

The ICSID tribunal has over the years developed specific criteria for determining whether a transaction constitutes investments. These are: 'the existence of substantial contribution; that the project should have certain duration; participation in the risks of the transaction for both parties; and the operation should be significant for the Host State's development.[119]

Since the decision of the tribunal in the case of *Fedax v. Venezuela*,[120] the above criteria have always been considered in addition to the requirements in a BIT or another instrument containing consent to ICSID jurisdiction. These criteria were considered to be embodied in Article 25 of ICSID Convention and were applied in several cases.[121] In each of these cases, the tribunal has held that construction contracts for highway, dam and investment-related promissory notes qualify as an investment to be protected by the investment laws. It is to be noted however, that it is yet to be clarified whether and to what extent all four criteria will have to be satisfied in each case. The four elements must be reviewed in their totality and assessed in the light of the circumstances of each case.

Similarly, the Iran-U.S. Claims Tribunal have also held in many cases that property includes both tangible and intangible rights. In *Amoco International Finance corporation v. Iran*,[122] the tribunal stated that 'expropriation defined as 'a compulsory transfer of property rights', extends to 'any right' which can be the object of a commercial transaction, i.e. freely sold and bought and thus has monetary value'. In this case, the claimant's oil exploration and exploitation agreement (Khemco agreement) was cancelled by decree and thus, prevented the claimant from producing and exporting oil. Also in *Starret Housing Corporation v. Iran*,[123] property was held to include assets and contractual rights and the right to complete the projects and earn

118. See also *CSOB V. Slovak Republic* ICSID Case No. Arb/97/4, 24 May 1999, 14 ICSID Rev-FILJ 251 (1999). But see the separate opinion of Ian Brownlie in *CME Czech Republic SA v. Czech Republic* Final award of 13 March 2003 where he said that investment should include only 'legal entitlements' and not 'mere expectations'.
119. Schlemmer 'Investment, Investor, Nationality, and Shareholders' in Peter Muchlinski et al. (ed.) 'International Investment Law' at 65. See also the definition proffered by Schreuer C, 'The ICSID Convention: A Commentary' in para. 122 at 140. He included regularity of profits and return i.e. there should be reasonable substantiated belief that profit will result.
120. Decision on jurisdiction, 11 June 1997, 31 ILM 1378 (1998).
121. See *Salini Costruttori SPA and Italstrade SPA v. Kingdom of Morocco* decision on Jurisdiction, 23 July 2001, *Journal de Droit Intenational* 196 (2002) 42 ILM 609 (2003) and also in subsequent cases of *Salini Costruttori SPA and Italstrade SPA v. The Hashemite Kingdom of Jordan*, decision on Jurisdiction of 29 November 2004, 44 ILM 573 (2005*). Fedax NV v. Republic of Venezuela* (*supra*). It is generally referred to as the Salini test. However, these cases can be contrasted with the case of *Joy Mining Machinery Ltd. V. Arab Republic of Egypt*, ICSID Case No. ARB/03/11, 6 August 2004, 44 ILM 7 (2005) published at www.ita.law.uvic.ca where the tribunal ruled that the giving of certain performance guarantees does not constitute an investment mainly because there was no risk involved and that the duration was too short. For a critic of this case, see Schlemmer, 'Investment, Investor, Nationality, and Shareholders' in Peter Muchlinski, et al. (ed.) 'International Investment Law' 102, at 68.
122. 15 Iran-US CTR 189.
123. 4 Iran-US CTR 122.

reasonable profits. The tribunal's decisions also demonstrate that interests in companies such as shares or stock and other shareholders rights and interests are included within the scope of property right. In *Philips Petroleum Company Iran v. The Islamic Republic of Iran,*[124] the plaintiff entered into a Joint Structure Agreement (JSA) with the National Iranian Oil Company to produce oil in the Persian Gulf. They both formed Non-profit Iranian Joint Stock Company (IMINOCO) to carry out the operation of JSA. During the unrest, IMINOCO's operations were shut down. After the success of the Revolution, IMINOCO resumed production but the claimants were not allowed to lift oil. Held – that the claimant was deprived of its property by conduct attributable to the government of Iran.

The following rights were held as constituting property rights under Article II, paragraph 1 of the Claims Settlement Declaration: right to receive dividend payment, right attendant to share ownership such as management rights, right to participate in decision making of the enterprise and rights to receive report and notices – these are recognised as compensable property rights. Also partnership interests and right to receive repayment of loans both generally and when they constitute long time investments.

The cases above have shown the modern conception of property as rights rather than things under international law. It emphasised the functionality of property and its ability to generate profits.[125]

Modern BITs or Multilateral Investment Treaties (MITs) broadly define 'property' or 'investment' to include shares, patents or trademarks and licenses to exploit natural resources and contract rights. Thus, they are included in the list of protected property or investments because of their ability to confer on their holders rights which are of economic and commercial value.[126] Investment treaties therefore, see property not

124. 21 Iran-US CTR 79.
125. Thomas Walde & Abba Kolo, 'Environmental Regulation, Investment Protection and 'Regulatory Taking' in International law' (2001) 50 International and Comparative Law Quarterly at 835. They argued that '[I]n modern understanding, the key function of property is less the tangibility of "things", but rather the capability of a combination of rights in a commercial and corporate setting and under a regulatory regime to earn a commercial rate of return'. Similarly in p. 843 at n. 140, Walde & Abba Kolo quoted Professor Grey as having observed that 'under the classical conception, actual dispossession was required before ownership rights were violated and property was taken. By contrast, modern lawyers – and multilateral treaties – are nominalists about "ownership"; they see property in resources as consisting of the infinitely divisible claims to possession, use, disposition, and profit that the people might have with respect to those things' T. Grey, 'The Malthusian Constitution' (1986) 41 U Miami L. Rev. 21 at 30.
126. See the NAFTA case of *Pope & Talbot Inc v. Canada*, Interim Award, Ad hoc—UNCITRAL Arbitration Rules, IIC 192 of 26 June 2000, where the tribunal held that 'the Investment's access to the US market is a property interest subject to protection under Article 1110' (Available at www.naftaclaims.com). See also Abba Kolo, 'Fat Cats and 'Windfall Taxes in the Natural Resources Industry: Legal and Policy Analysis in the light of Modern Investment Treaties' in 'A Liber Amicorum: Thomas Walde' at 103 referring to the observation of the tribunal in *Nagel v. Czech Republic* to the effect that the terms 'asset' and 'investment' means rights and claims which have financial value for the holder especially where the claim is well-founded or at least creates a legitimate expectation of performance in the future (SCC 49/2002 (2004), 1.

Stockholm Arb. Rep. 145 at 158, available at: http://ita.law.univ.ca. However, in *Methanex v. U.S.* award of 3 August 2005, Part IV, Ch. D, para. 17, the claim that access to

only in terms of physical assets or chattels, e.g., land, machinery and equipment but also in terms of its functional use. The type of the assets is less important. What is important is the ability of the asset to generate profit.[127]

Arguing in the context of windfall tax, Kolo have rightly pointed out that the assets that are of economic value for private investor 'includes not only profits and returns earned from investment but also reasonable legitimate expectation of gain or profit' and that 'the right to benefit from such profits are fundamental strands in the investor's bundle of proprietary rights which should constitute a protected investment'.[128]

Thus, in National investment laws, BITs and MITs, there have been an expansive interpretation of the notion of protected 'investment' or 'property'. This has been made to cover three particular categories: (1) physical property of foreign investors, (2) intangible rights, and (3) administrative rights (also an intangible right) that are needed to carry on the investment projects.[129] The latter rights which are often referred to as licences, leases, permits, concessions, production sharing agreements, joint venture agreements, service contracts, etc., especially in the field of natural resources are the vehicle of foreign investment. They have been variously described as proprietary, *'profit a prendre'* or contractual rights.[130] Some treaties have expressly recognised these rights as protected property in investment laws.[131] This is because these intangible rights that are granted to an investor by the Host State are often more valuable than the physical assets that he brought into the venture in that they enable an investor to carry out the activities in the Host State. If such rights are withdrawn by the Host States or its agency, the investment will cease to be of any value to the investor. Therefore, the

market and goodwill amounts to investment was rejected by the tribunal. But the tribunal accepted that a restrictive notion of property as material 'thing' is obsolete and has given way to a modern conception of property which includes 'managerial control over components of a process that is wealth producing'. For a good critic of this case see Kolo, (Fat Cats and windfall Taxes) *supra* n. 127, at p. 104 n. 15.

127. Abba Kolo, 'Legal issues arising from the termination of oil prospecting licences by the Nigerian Government' (2001) 19, No.2 JENRL 164 at 168.
128. Kolo, (Fat Cats and windfall Taxes) *supra* n. 127, at p. 104. To buttress this point, he relied on the dissenting opinion of Arbitrator Naon in *EnCana v. Ecuador* (*supra*) which was that the investor's legitimate return expectations (Tax refund) constitute an interest or ownership rights which should be protected and that it should not be based on the Host State's law once the investment that comprise the right to obtain returns has been made in accordance with the law of the Host State.
129. Sornarajah, 'The International Law on Foreign Investment' 3rd (ed.), at 16. He argued that administrative rights though, as a grant of the State that can be technically withdrawn by the State, can be lifted from the province of the State through treaty so that a withdrawal of the rights by the State can attract State responsibility. Administrative rights however must comply with the conditions stipulated for its grant otherwise treaty violations cannot be successfully invoked.
130. See Chapter 3 below for detailed analysis of the legal nature of these Administrative rights.
131. See the model UK BIT and the U.S. BIT *supra* n. 109. See also Sornarajah, *supra* n. 101, at 191 n. 73 for the Australia – Vietnam treaty which includes contractual rights in the list of protected property – '... rights to search for, extract or exploit natural resources ...'.

treaty has technically removed the discretionary powers of the Host State to interfere with these intangible rights throughout the duration of the treaty.[132]

From the above, it has been shown that intangible rights such as contractual right to 'search for, bore and get petroleum' granted by the Host State to an investor are protected property under international investment law. The question to be asked is what happens if after exercising the right to 'search for, bore and get petroleum' an investor is prevented from extracting discovered resources either by the State or an individual whose acts is attributable to the State? Would Treaty protect the investor if an individual interferes with or 'recovers' all or part of the discovered un-extracted resources and the Host State or its agency fails to prevent such action as provided by the Host State's law and regulations?[133] It could be argued that failure by the Host State to protect the investor from such 'conversion' or interference' could be because the Host State only recognises the investor's 'right to search for, bore and get petroleum' as proprietary but denies recognition of the rights of the investor to the underlying un-extracted resources as proprietary. If this is the case, such position of the Host State will make the proprietary rights to search for, bore and get petroleum' granted to the investor meaningless. Could this position of the Host State create dual investments – one in which the treaty will protect because the State recognised it and another which is not protected because it lacks recognition by the State? The jurisprudence of the investment tribunals as well as the US-Iran claims tribunal has shown that the State's position in this regard will not create dual investments. It is regarded as one investment in which the grant of proprietary rights to search for, bore and get petroleum by the Host State to the investor encompasses his rights to the underlying resources or assets discovered, but yet untapped.[134] Analogy could also be drawn from a situation in which the Host State denied the investor rights to export his products or repatriate profits after granting him administrative permits to carry out approved activities or where the Host State changes its law to impose punitive tax on the income of the investor.[135] By such action, the investor's licence to carry out the approved activities will be rendered useless.

7. CONCEPT OF PROPERTY UNDER HUMAN RIGHT LAWS

In the later part of the twentieth century, property right was incorporated into the international human rights instruments.[136] It can therefore, be said to have assumed

132. For the legal implication of including these public law rights granted by Host States in the international treaty, see Sornarajah, 'The International Law on Foreign Investment' 3rd (ed.) at 192–193.
133. This question is considered in Chapter 7 of this book.
134. *Starret Housing v. Iran (supra); Philips Petroleum v. Iran (supra); Amco v. Indonesia (supra)* and *CMS V. Argentina* (*supra*). See Chapter 4 for a discussion of these cases in relation to the valuation method for expropriated contractual rights.
135. Kolo, 'Fat Cats and 'Windfall Taxes in the Natural Resources Industry: Legal and Policy Analysis in the light of Modern Investment Treaties' in 'A Liber Amicorum: Thomas Walde.'
136. However, since the Magna Carta, right to property has been recognised as providing guarantee of individual freedom. Section 39 provides that 'no man shall be ... disseized of any tenement... except by lawful judgment of his peers or by the law of the land'. See also Article 2 of the

the status of a human right.[137] Its significance lies in its ability to foster individual's freedom, economic independence and personality development in a democratic society.[138]

The Universal Declaration of Human Rights[139] represents an important legal document at the international level that provides for right to property. It provides in Article 17 (1) and (2) that 'everyone has the right to own property alone or as well as in association with others'. It further provides that 'no one shall be arbitrarily deprived of his property'.

It has been argued that this declaration though has some intuitive moral value, its legal value remains relative as it has no legal force. In spite of this however, it has tremendous influence on national legislators and has been relied upon by private individual in cases where legislation was insufficient.[140] The fact that right to property was relegated to the background at the Global treaty level was apparent in the subsequent United Nations human rights documents in which there was no mention of property rights.[141] The infirmity above was however addressed at the regional level in which private patrimonial rights have been given prominent attention in the human rights instruments.[142]

Declaration of the Rights of Man of 1789 which stated that the right to property is a 'natural and imprescriptible right of man' and Article 17 which provides that 'since property is an inviolable and sacred right, no one shall be deprived thereof except where public necessity, legally determined, shall clearly demand it, and then only on condition that the owner shall have been previously and equitably indemnified'.

137. But see Loucaides, L.G. Nijhoff Law Specials, vol. 70 'European Convention on Human Rights: Collected Essays.' (2007) at p. 121. See also Alberto M. Aronovitz, 'Individual Patrimonial Rights under the European Human Rights System: Some reflections on the Concept of Possession and Dispossession of Property' (1997) 25 Int'l L. J. Legal Info at 89-90 who argued that rights to property has been relegated to a secondary background in the Global Human rights instruments.
138. *Ibid.*
139. UN Doc. GA Res. 217A (III), UN Doc. A/810 (1948) 71.
140. Aronovitz, 'Individual Patrimonial Rights under the European Human Rights System: Some reflections on the Concept of Possession and Dispossession of Property' at 89.
141. Articles 1, 55 and 56 of the Charter of United Nations, the International Covenant on Civil and Political rights (ICCPR) (999 UNTS 171 in force on 24 March 1976) and the International Covenant on Economic, Social, and Cultural Rights (993 UNTS 3, 16 December 1966).
142. Notable among them are as follows:(1) The *American Declaration of the Rights and Duties of Man* (Article XXXIII of American Declaration of the Rights and Duties of Man.) provides that ' every person has a right to own such private property as meets the essential needs of decent living and helps to maintain the dignity of the individual and of the home' (2) *American Convention on Human Rights* (Article 21, OAS Treaty Series No. 36, 1144 UNTS 123 in force 18 July 1978) provides that 'everyone has the right to the use and enjoyment of his property'. It however adds a proviso that 'the law may subordinate such use and enjoyment to the interests of the society'. Furthermore, it states that 'no one shall be deprived of his property except upon payment of just compensation for reasons of public utility or social interest and in the cases and according to the forms established by law' (3) The American Bill of Rights also emphasised the protection of property rights. In the *Fourteenth Amendment to the Constitution*, it provides that 'no person shall ... be deprived of ... property, without due process of law; nor shall private property be taken for public use, without just compensation.' (4) *The African Charter on Human and Peoples' Rights (ACHPR)* provides in Article 14 that 'the right to property shall be guaranteed. It may only be encroached upon in the interest of the public need or in general interest of the community and in accordance with the provisions of appropriate laws'. See

The European Convention for the Protection of Human Rights and Fundamental Freedoms (ECHR) which came into force in 1953 provides in Article 1 of Protocol 1 (A1P1) that:

> [E]very natural or legal person is entitled to the peaceful enjoyment of his possessions. No one shall be deprived of his possessions except in the public interest and subject to the conditions provided for by law and by the general principles of international law.[143]

This right however, is not absolute. The A1P1 further provides that:

> [T]he preceding provisions shall not, however, in any way impair the right of a State to enforce such laws as it deems necessary to control the use of property according to the general interest or to secure the payment of taxes or other contributions or penalties.

For the purpose of this book, it will be necessary to examine some fundamental issues that have arisen from the foregoing human rights protection instruments. These are: (1) what constitutes property rights? (2) What is the nature of State's responsibility in property rights protection – whether the responsibility is limited to negative obligations to abstain from interference or it includes positive obligation to protect property rights. Implicit in the second question is the issue as to whether it is only the acts or omissions of the public bodies that can be attributed to the State or the acts of private individuals can also be attributed. (3) Can the property rights encapsulated in these instruments be applied and enforced against private individuals at both the National and International levels?

The issues above shall be addressed using the jurisprudence of ECHR and where necessary, references will be made to its domestic counterpart, the English Human rights Act of 1998. This is not only because of its well-developed case law but also as a result of its overwhelming influence on all the State parties to the Convention as well as other legal orders.[144] It could therefore, be said to be the most important and effective regional instruments on human rights in the world. It is replete with well-reasoned decisions as to its operation in practice over the last fifty years.[145]

Malcom Evans et al. 'The African Charter on Human and Peoples' Rights: The system of practice, 1986-2000 (Cambridge University Press).

143. Protocol 2VE 213 UNTS 22, 262; ECHRFF.

144. Andrew Clapham, 'Human Rights in the Private Sphere' (Clarendon Press. Oxford, 1993) at 3. For example Articles 60 and 61 of the ACHPR provides that its monitoring institutions should 'draw inspiration' from the UN human rights instruments and to 'take into consideration as subsidiary measures other international rules and principles recognised by African States. Article 3 (1) of the African Court Protocol, 1998 defines jurisdiction with regard to the interpretation and application not only of the ACHPR, but also of other relevant human rights treaties ratified by the States concerned. Article 7 (1) of the Protocol also empowers the Court to apply the ACHPR as well as other relevant human rights treaties. Therefore, the ECHR applies indirectly to Africa. In fact, the African Commission of Human and People's Rights has referred to the judgments of the ECHR and the Inter-American Courts of Human Rights in its judgment in the case of *SERAC and CESR v. Nigeria*, Communication No. 155/96, 27 October 2001, African Commission on Human and Peoples' Rights, (2001) AHRLR 60 (ACHPR 2001).

145. Loucaides et al., *supra* n. 138, at 127.

7.1 What Constitutes Property Rights under ECHR?

A1P1 provides that 'every natural or legal person is entitled to the peaceful enjoyment of his possessions ...' Even though there is no mention of the words 'right to property' in the above provisions of the ECHR, it has been held by the court that the provision guarantee the right to property.[146] Therefore, under the Convention, protection over a wide range of proprietary interests are guaranteed, e.g., moveable and immoveable, corporeal and incorporeal interests such as shares[147] and patents, contractual rights including leases and judgment debts.[148] The term 'possession' has been interpreted to mean that other economic interests will be protected by the right.[149] This represents an autonomous definition of 'possession' because it is not based on the definition of property from any jurisdiction that are parties to the Convention as the concept of property is defined in different ways among the European countries.[150] The approach the Convention Organs and the Courts have adopted was to use constitutional law definition of property which is broader than the private law definition.[151]

It must be noted that the right is not a right to acquire property but a right to the protection of an individual's existing property.[152] Moreover, A1P1 does not recognise property as a bundle of rights but rather as a single use right. Therefore, each use right is not treated as independent property, but as a form of using property.[153] The implication of this is that an interference with any of the use right without taking the

146. *Marckx v.Belgium* (1979) 2 EHRR 330, para. 16.
147. *Bramelid and Malmstriom v. Sweden* (1982) 29 DR 64.
148. Loucaides, 'European Convention on Human Rights: Collected Essays.', at 127; Aronovitz, Individual Patrimonial Rights under the European Human Rights System: Some reflections on the Concept of Possession and Dispossession of Property' borrowed the French term 'biens' instead of 'possession' which defines property in wider terms to include personal or corporal things (such as clothes jewels, the lady's handbags or the gentleman's wallets), as well as material and immaterial things. Material things are either movable things (such as cars, books, pencil, biro etc.) or immovable things such as lands, houses etc.) while immaterial things are intellectual property like patents, designs, copy rights, trade marks, publisher's rights and shares, etc.
149. *Gasus Dosier-und Fordertechnik GmbH v. Netherlands,* Series A no. 306-B (1995), 20 EHRR 403, para. 53 where the court observed that 'possession' is not limited to ownership of physical goods: other rights and interests constituting assets can also be regarded as property. The court held that it was immaterial whether the claimant right to the concrete mixer was a right of ownership or as a security right in rem. In whichever way it was considered, it constitutes possession.
150. Ali Riza Coban, 'Protecting property rights within the European Convention on Human Rights' (ASHGATE, 2004) at 145 citing Samuel G, 'Are property Rights So Simple in Europe? In P. Jackson and D. C. Wilde (ed.) 'Property Law: Current Issues and Debates' (Ashgate: Dartmouth, 1999) p. 161.
151. *Ibid.*
152. D. Rook, 'Property Law and Human Rights (London Blackstone, 2001) at 60-61. See also Marckx's case, *supra* n. 170. The court held that expectation of inheritance did not constitute possession. But in the case of *Inze v. Austria,* (1987) Series A no 126, the Court held that on the death of the deceased, ownership of the estate vests jointly on his heirs and that will constitute possession even if the estate has not been shared.
153. *Mellacher and others v. Austria* App. No.10522/83, 11011/84, 11070/84 Op.Com Publ. Court A, 169. See also Coban, *supra* n. 151, at 146. He opined that property under the convention protocol is a 'single right which gives owners different use rights, rather than a bundle of rights.'

title of the claimant away will not be considered as deprivation of property. In the case of *Chassagnou and others v. France*, the court held that the claimant has not been deprived of their rights where the hunting rights over their lands were compulsorily transferred since they still retain title to the lands.[154] The court therefore, considered it as a control of use of property. This shows that the court may consider a single use right as possession but not as a separate property.[155]

It has also been argued that since the court defined possession independent of the national laws, a right or interests may be considered as 'possession' within the context of A1P1 even if the national law in question does not regard such right or interest as property.[156]

Several cases of the Court support this assertion.[157] In the Beyeler's case,[158] the court in rejecting the Government's argument that the applicant had not fully acquired an in rem right over a painting work since the contract upon which his claim was based was automatically null and void, the court held that 'the concept of possession' has an autonomous meaning which is not limited to ownership of physical goods and is independent from formal classification in domestic law and that certain other rights and interests consisting assets can also be regarded as property rights, and thus, as possession for the purposes of A1P1.

7.1.1 *Licences*

The court has held that rights to property falls within the scope of civil rights under Article 6, paragraph 1 of the Convention and have construed cases bothering on administrative licenses as such. The court has held that licences will constitute possession under A1P1 where the holder derives economic benefit from the licence. In the case of *Tre Traktorer Aktiebolag v. Sweden*,[159] the Swedish government withdrew the applicant's licence to sell beer, wine and other alcoholic drinks in a restaurant. The European Court after examining the legality of the licence revocation held that the licence constitutes 'possession' because the economic interests connected with the running of the restaurant were possession. The court was of the view that the withdrawal of the licence concerned had jeopardised the legitimate economic interests of the owners of the restaurant. The withdrawal was held to have constituted

154. Judgment of 29 April 1999, Reports, 1999-III. See also the case of *Lena Aschan & Others v. Finland*, Admissibility decision of the Court, 15 February 2001, App. No. 37858/97. Here the exclusive fishing rights of the applicant was considered as possession but there is no deprivation of that rights where the law was amended that deprived them of their exclusive right to sell fishing licences to their water areas and thus was unable to control fishing activities in their area.
155. Coban, 'Protecting property rights within the European Convention on Human Rights' at 147.
156. *Ibid.*, at 148.
157. *Ibid.*, see *Matos v. Silva, Lda., and others v. Portugal*, Judgment of 27 August 1996 (R 1996-IV) section 75; *Papamichalopoulos v. Greece*, Judgment of 24 June 1993, Series A no. 260-B and The Former *King of Greece and others v. Greece*, Judgment 23 November 2000 at 60-66.
158. *Beyeler v. Italy*, Judgment of 5 January 2000.
159. Judgment of 7 July 1989, 13 EHRR 309 para. 53. See also *Mimer v. Moldova*, Judgment of 10 July 2007 (licence to operate duty free shop).

interference with the peaceful enjoyment of the applicant's possession despite the fact that the licence conferred no rights under the Swedish law. This is because without the licence the owner of the restaurant will be unable to conduct the business. The withdrawal of the licence therefore, adversely impacts on the goodwill and value of the business. In the case of *Benthem v. Netherlands*, the court also established that a license to exploit and deliver liquid petroleum gas is a property and therefore civil rights for the purposes of Article 6 (1) of the convention. The court noted that such a licence is proprietary in nature as it can be assigned to third parties.[160] Also in the case of *Fredin v. Sweden*, the Court held that licence to extract and commercially exploit gravels from a certain piece of land could be considered as a possession if the cancellation of such licence renders the property in question valueless.[161]

The court has however, devised a limitation to this rule. A licence will not be protected under A1P1 where the holder has no legitimate expectation as to the lasting nature of the licence. For example, a provisional licence will not constitute possession and as such where it is withdrawn for failure to comply with the conditions of its grant, no protection will be granted by the court.[162] So also where it is withdrawn in accordance with the provisions of the law in which it was granted.[163] The important test to be applied according to the commission is as to whether the licence creates in the holder a reasonable and legitimate expectation as to the lasting nature of the licence and whether it is possible for the holder to continue to draw benefits from the licence activity. From this test, it could be argued that an oil and gas production licence is proprietary in character and it covers or encompasses the economic interest in the underlying assets with respect to which the licence was granted. Furthermore, in light of the economic value criterion used by the Convention organs to determine 'possession' within the meaning of A1P1, coupled with the licence holder's legitimate expectation in the benefits derivable from the said assets, such underlying assets should be recognised as 'possession' within the meaning of the A1P1. Since such licence constitutes 'possession', the economic interests (Reservoir oil and gas) connected with the operation of the licence could be regarded as 'possession' such that an interference with the Reservoir oil could be regarded as an interference with peaceful enjoyment of 'possession'.

In addition, under domestic law, personal rights arising from relationship between persons (rights in personam) are not regarded as property. However, under the Convention, A1P1 has been held to cover in personam rights.[164] Therefore, claims arising from contracts or tort or unjust enrichment are covered by A1P1. The important test is that the interest acquired by the individual must have economic value and not a claim based on mere expectation.[165] In this regard, pecuniary assets such as Judgment

160. *Benthem v. Netherlands*, No.1 (1991) 13 EHRR, 784 para. 53.
161. No. 1 (1991) 13 EHRR, 784 para. 53.
162. *Pudas v. Sweden* (1984) 20 DR 234.
163. *Gudmunsson v. Iceland* (1996) 21 EHRR CD 89.
164. Coban, 'Protecting property rights within the European Convention on Human Rights', at 150.
165. *Ibid.*

debts[166] and restitutions of property wrongly confiscated by the State[167] are covered by A1P1. Where the claim is based on mere expectation, e.g., where a Notary public based his claim on the expectation that the law on notarial fees were not going to be changed, it will not constitute possession because it is not a claim based on services rendered.[168]

Moreover, even if a claim or interest is not recognised by a National law as a legal right, it could still be regarded as a 'possession' under the A1P1. For example, where a claimant obtained an award in arbitration proceedings against the government which was subsequently confirmed by judicial proceedings, the Commission and the European court have held that the arbitration award constitutes 'possession'. The argument of the government that there was no 'possession' on the ground that the award and the arbitration clause under which the award was made have been voided by a National law was rejected by the court.[169]

According to the Commission, shares in a company have economic value in that the holder possesses some rights and a claim over the company assets. On this basis, a share is held as constituting 'possession'.[170] Also future income will constitute possession if the income has been earned or where an enforceable claim to it existed.[171]

From the above, wide range of economic interests arising from the relations of individual will be founded upon as 'possession' as long as it is an existing interest and not based on mere expectations.[172] For example mere expectation about income or profitability of a business does not constitute possession but 'good will' of a business or profession will grant possession.

7.2 The Nature of State's Responsibility in Property Rights Protection

Under the ECHR, it is very obvious that both natural and artificial persons are explicitly protected.[173] Therefore, either a corporation or an individual whose property rights has been allegedly violated can bring an application to the Court for redress. The ECHR imposes certain obligations on the State parties to the convention with respect to the rights and freedoms stipulated in the Convention.[174] The question is whether the responsibility is limited to negative obligations to abstain from interference or included

166. Admissibility Decision of the Commission App. No. 3039/67, Yearbook X, pp.516; 5479/72, 10 July 1997 Coll. 44 p. 53.
167. *Kopecky v. Slovakia* (2005) 41 EHCRR 43 (GC).
168. *X v. Germany* App. No. 8410/78, 13 December 1979, 18 DR 216. Here legislation was made by parliament to reduce Notaries' fees by between 50% and 80%. The expectation of the Notaries that their Fees will not change does not constitute possession.
169. *Stran Greek Refineries and Stratis Andreadis v. Greece* (1994) 19 EHRR 301, para. 31. See also *Van Marle & others v. Netherlands* (1986) 8 EHRR 483, paras 39-41.
170. *Bramelid and Malmstrom v. Sweden* (1982) 29 DR 64; *Lithgow & others v. UK*, Judgment of 8 July 1986, Series A no. 102.
171. *Van der Mussele v. Belgium*, Judgment of 23 November 1983, Series A no. 70.
172. Coban, *supra* n. 151, at 152.
173. First sentence of A1P1.
174. Article 1 of ECHR. The rights stipulated in the convention are: Right to life (Article 2 (1), provision of prison conditions that is not inhuman (Article 3), provision of courts, legal aid and translators (Article 6), (Right to respect for family life (Article 8), Right to education (P1-2), right to join trade unions (Article 11).

positive obligation to protect property rights. From the wordings of Article 1 of the Convention, it has been said that the nature of the State's obligation is both positive and negative.[175]

These obligations apply also to the rights and freedoms stipulated in protocols 1, 4, 6, and 7 of the convention.[176] Positive obligation requires the State to secure or protect these rights to 'everyone within their jurisdiction' regardless of their nationality or status. This obligation also covered nationals of the State concerned, the nationals of other contracting States, and the nationals of States not parties to the Convention and Stateless persons.[177]

The victims who are neither national of the State concerned nor of the other contracting States, would be covered if they can show that they are in some respect subject to the jurisdiction of the State concerned.[178] Residency in the State concerned is also not essential and the State concerned could still be held responsible where the alleged violation happened outside its territory.[179]

The State's positive obligations in some cases relate to the State's relation with individual while in some other cases, it is centered on the relation between private persons. In the latter case, the State's responsibility emanated from its failure either by acts or omission to secure the Convention rights against interference from other private persons.

With regards to right to property under the A1P1, there is also a positive obligation on the State to protect enjoyment of property. It is however essential to note that right to property even though has economic characteristics, is a liberty right under the ECHR as opposed to other economic and social rights which are claim rights. It does not guarantee a right to acquire property. Therefore, the positive obligation of the State under A1P1 is limited to the protection or preservation of existing property. Thus, the court held that the State must ensure that the owner of real property can obtain access to the property[180] or to take practical steps to avoid the destruction of the claimant's home.[181] The court observed in this case that:

> Genuine, effective exercise of the protected by that provision does not depend merely on the State's duty not to interfere, but may require positive measures of protection, particularly where there is a direct link between the measures which an applicant may legitimately expect from the authorities and his effective enjoyment of his possessions.[182]

175. Harris et al., 'Law of the European Convention on Human Rights (Butterworths: London, 1995) at 19 cited by Ali Coban, *supra* n. 174 at 163.
176. P. Van Dijik et al. 'The Theory and Practice of the European Convention On Human Rights' (Kluwer Law International, 3rd (ed.), (1998) at 3.
177. *Ibid.*
178. *Ibid.*, see notes 6 and 7 thereof.
179. *Ibid.*
180. *Loizidou v. Turkey* (1996) 23 EHRR 513. The applicant was denied access to her property for a period of sixteen years. The court held that Article 1 Protocol 1 is applicable.
181. *Neryildiz v. Tukey* (2005) 41 EHRR 20 paras 133-138.
182. *Ibid.*, at para. 34.

The positive obligation of the State extends to both damage caused by man-made and natural hazards. However, the extent of the State's response differs in both respects.

With respect to damage caused by man-made hazard, State has a wider margin of appreciation to prevent harm to property than when the hazard is natural.[183]

The positive obligation also requires the State to carry out prompt, impartial and attentive investigation of interference with property (e.g., disappearance of goods), provide police assistance to execute a judgment for possession of property and to provide judicial procedures that enables domestic court to adjudicate effectively and fairly in property matters. State's failure in this direction may constitute a form of 'private expropriation' and thus, a violation of A1P1.[184]

In the case of *Cyprus v. Turkey*,[185] it could be inferred from the judgment of the court that the State is required to protect the property against interference from private persons where there is evidence of practice of denying individual's access to court for redress. The Court in this case dismissed the claim because there was no evidence of such practice.

7.3 Applicability and Enforcement of Property Right under the ECHR

The question that has resonated in the enforcement of the Convention rights is as to whether the rights (e.g., property rights) encapsulated in the ECHR will be applicable and enforceable as between private individuals at both the National and International levels.[186] This is what has been referred to as the horizontal effects of the Convention rights. This section will be divided into two parts. The first part will examine the horizontal effects of the convention rights at the International level while the second part will look at it at the National level.

183. Richard Clayton QC et al., 'The law of Human Rights' (Oxford University Press, 2009) para. 18.96. He pointed out that the 'positive obligation of the State does not require it to compensate the property owners to the full market value of destroyed property'.
184. *Ibid.*, see the cases of *Mathew v. France*, Judgment of 31 March 2005; *Bistrovic v. Croatia*, Judgment of 31 May 2007, para. 33; *Novokeletski v. Ukraine* (2006) 43 EHRR 53, para. 100; *Gustasson v. Sweden* (1996) 22 EHRR 409 para. 60; *Immobiliare Saffi v. Italy*, Judgment of 28 July 1999; *A.O. v. Italy*, Judgment of 30 May 2000.
185. Judgment of 10 May 2001.
186. On this debate, see Sir William Wade Q.C., 'Horizons of Horizontality' (2000) 116 L.Q.R. 217.; Murray Hunt, 'The 'Horizontal effect' of the Human Rights Act' (1998) Public Law 423, available at https//login.westlaw.co.uk; Nicholas Bamforth, The true 'Horizontal effect' of the Human Rights Act 1998' (2001) (Jan) Law Quarterly Review at 117; Van Dijk et al., 'The theory and practice of the European Convention on Human rights' (Kluwer Law Int., London, 1998 3rd (ed.) pp. 22-26; Clapham, A, 'Human Rights in Private Sphere' (Oxford: Claredon Press, 1993); Thomas D.C. Bennett, 'Horizontality's new horizons – re-examining horizontal effect: privacy, defamation and the human rights Act: Part 1'; Thomas D.C. Bennett, 'Horizontality's new horizons – re-examining horizontal effect: privacy, defamation and the human rights Act: Part 2 (2010) Entertainment Law review', 21(3) 96-104.

7.3.1 *Horizontal Effects of Convention Rights at the International Level*

The concept of Horizontal effect of fundamental rights can be viewed in two ways. First, it means that human rights provisions are applicable to legal relations between not only private party and public bodies, but also between private parties. Second, it means the enforceability of the fundamental human rights by one individual against another individual.[187] This concept in German law is also called *'Drittwirkung'*, meaning that an individual could rely on national bill of rights to bring a claim of violation of his rights against the private person who violated the rights through the court or other procedure. With regards to the second meaning of horizontal effect, by virtue of the provisions of some Articles of the Human rights Convention and the decisions of the court, it has been contended that direct enforcement of human rights violation by one individual against another individual is not possible.[188] This is because the convention only imposes obligations on the contracting States and not on an individual. It follows from there that compliant against an individual cannot be entertained by the court as this will be contrary to the Convention *ratione personae*.[189] However, indirect enforcement of human rights violation by one individual against another is possible where the State can be held responsible for the violation in one way or another. But even in this instance, the investigation is said to concern the responsibility of the State involved and not that of the individual.[190] This indirect enforceability stems from the provisions of the Convention which imposes positive obligations on the States to take measures in order to make the rights inferred for individuals under Articles 3, 10 and 11 to be enforced 'vis-à-vis third private parties'.[191] Therefore, State's responsibility is engaged where the contracting State failed to protect the convention rights against interference by other private persons. The Convention organs have held that under A1P1, a State is responsible in certain specific circumstances for interferences with property rights resulting from transactions between private persons.[192] However, a State is not responsible where the facts in issue emanated purely from contractual relationship between individuals and in which the State has not exercised any governmental authority.[193] Exercise of governmental authority could either be in legislative or executive capacity and if it interfered in the

187. Van Dijik et al., 'The Theory and Practice of the European Convention On Human Rights', at 23.
188. *Ibid.*, citing Articles 19, 24, 25, 31, 32, 50 and the cases of Appl. 6956/75, *X v. United Kingdom*, D&R 8 (1978),at 103; Appl. 19217, *Durini v. Italy*, D7R 76-A (1994), p. 76.
189. *Ibid.*, at pp. 23, 119.
190. *Ibid.*
191. *Ibid.*
192. *MN v. Bulgaria* App. No. 29785/96 Decision 4 September 1996; See also *Arrondelle v. United Kingdom* (1983) 5 E.H.R.R 118 where the ECtHR held that the State was sufficiently connected to the noise generated by private aircraft in the Gartwick airport since it was being operated by a public airport authority and the State had assisted in the airport's location and development. Thus Article 8 of the Convention was used to prevent interference with private home by private party when the State is connected one way or the other to the activity causing the interference.
193. *Gustafsson v. Sweden, Judgment* of 25 April 1996 at 60.

civil relationship between private individuals to the extent that one of the parties suffers deprivation, State's responsibility will be engaged.[194]

On the other hand, exercise of judicial power has been held not to amount to interference by State in property right. This is because the court is merely providing an avenue through which resolution of private disputes can be carried out.[195] Positive obligation of the State to protect property rights of an individual does not arise in the context of ensuring that all argument concerning the dispute between individuals will be fully considered by the courts.[196] The exception to this rule is that State's responsibility will be incurred where the decision of the court in a dispute between private persons contravenes the right to fair trial provisions in section 6 of the Convention.[197] Coban has argued that on the ground of fairness, public authorities and judicial bodies should not force some individuals to bear a loss in favour of other individuals. Where this is lacking, then State's responsibility should be incurred. This is in consonance with the decision of the Commission in *Bramelid and Malmstrom v. Sweden*[198] where it held that State organs - public authorities and judicial bodies - must ensure that in the determination of the legal relations between individuals the 'law did not create such an inequality that one person could be arbitrarily and unjustly deprived of property in favour of another.'[199]

7.3.2 *Horizontal Effects of Convention Rights at the National Level*

At the National level, different countries apply different systems of Horizontality of fundamental rights. In the United Kingdom, several writers have proposed different systems before the Human Rights Act of 1998 (HRA) came to force.[200] The first writer that set the stage for the debate was Sir William wade Q.C. who argued that the HRA would make the rights Stated in the ECHR applicable and enforceable as between private individuals in the United Kingdom. That is, the HRA would have direct horizontal effects.[201] In the same year of Sir Williams Article, Sir Richard Buxton also wrote and argued that the HRA cannot have horizontal effect whenever it takes effect.[202] In this debate the provisions of sections 3 and 6 of the HRA are very important. Section 3 provides that courts should interpret statutes as far as possible in the light of the convention rights while section 6 provides that it is unlawful for public

194. *James and others v. UK*, Judgment of 21 February 1986, Serial A no. 98; *Hipakka and others v. Finland* App. No. 29069/95, 15 May 1996 here an individual suffered deprivation as a result of the actions of the Forestry board and though it did not result in transfer of property from the individual to the State, the court held that the deprivation has incurred State responsibility.
195. Coban, 'Protecting Property Rights within the European Convention on Human Rights', at 168 n. 138.
196. *Ibid.*
197. *Ibid.*, at 169. See also the cases of *Estima Jorge v. Portugal, Judgment* of 21 April 1998 (Reports 1998- II, P.762 contrast, *O.N. v. Bulgaria* (App. No. 35221/97) Decision 6 April 2000.
198. App. Nos. 8588/79, 29 DR 64; App. No. 12462/86, 13 July 1987, 53 DR 234.
199. Coban, 'Protecting Property Rights within the European Convention on Human Rights', at 169.
200. The Human Rights Act domesticated the European Convention on Human Rights law.
201. Sir William Wade Q.C., 'Horizons of Horizontality' (2000) 116 L.Q.R. 217.
202. Sir Richard Buxton, 'The Human Rights Act and Private Law' (2000) L.Q.R. 116: 48.

authorities to act in contravention of the Convention. There is no such duty imposed on private individuals or organisation.

The planks of the argument against horizontality are that:[203]

(1) Convention rights are rights only against the government or public bodies and not rights against individuals.
(2) Convention rights can only be asserted against the government before the European Court of Human Rights at Strasbourg and judging from the contents of the convention rights, it can only be effective against the government and public authorities but not against private individuals.
(3) Public authorities or national governments are permitted to interfere with conventions rights in certain circumstances but there is no mention of private individuals other than as right holders.
(4) The grounds upon which derogation from convention rights are permitted - such as national security, public safety, or prevention of disorder or crime - can only apply to acts done by public, not by private interests.
(5) Human Rights Act imported the exact contents of the Convention rights and since the Convention right cannot be enforced against private party, the HRA must therefore not be applied against private persons in a matter before the national court. ECHR imposed no positive obligations on individuals to respect each other's Convention rights. Therefore, the HRA cannot transfer such rights into UK law since they are non-existent in the first place.

Those who are in support of horizontality premised their arguments on the following grounds:[204]

(1) A literal interpretation of section 6 (3) of the HRA shows that a court is deemed to constitute 'public authority' and since section 6 (1) makes it unlawful for public authority to act in a way that is incompatible with a convention right, court must determine both horizontal and vertical cases in accordance with convention rights since section 6 does not confine this duty to the vertical cases. This in effect means that court must apply convention rights in all cases whether the claim is brought against the public authority or against an individual.[205]
(2) Even though the spirit of the HRA is to counter human right violation by the State, human rights can be regarded as 'general principles of justice' which have a universal and fundamental character which ought to be operative *erga*

203. Nicholas Bamforth, 'The True "Horizontal Effect" of the Human Rights Act 1998' (2001) L.Q.R 117: 34-41; Buxton, 'The Human Rights Act and Private Law', at 50-51.
204. Wade, 'Horizons of Horizontality', at 220-224; see also Bamforth, supra n. 204, at 35. Horizontal cases are cases between private individuals while vertical cases are those between individual and public authorities or the State.
205. Section 6(1) provides that 'it is unlawful for a public authority to act in a way which is incompatible with a Convention right'.

omnes' so that citizen's rights should be respected by other individuals as much as by the State.

(3) The court is required by[206] section 3 (1) of the HRA to read and give effect to primary and subordinate legislation 'in a way which is compatible with ... Convention rights'. This suggests that courts are required by HRA to apply convention rights through statutory interpretation to not only vertical cases but also to horizontal cases. Moreover, in a horizontal dispute that involves purely common law issues, the court can under this section apply convention rights by way of analogy.

(4) Judicial attitude at present have shown that courts are prepared to apply convention rights in both 'horizontal and vertical cases when interpreting the law and when exercising judicial discretion'.[207]

Between the two positions above, were those who favoured indirect horizontal application of the HRA. The argument in support of indirect horizontality was premised on the grounds that it is a position that comfortably located in the middle ground and that courts have shown an indication that this was the approach that the judges would take. In addition, they contended that there is no positive obligation upon the courts to act in accordance with Convention rights since there is no sanction to punish the courts if they failed to act compatibly.[208] They concluded that indirect horizontality comes solely from section 3 which enjoins the court to interpret the statutes in accordance with the Convention rights as 'far as possible.' Yet another School of thought proposed a position between indirect and direct horizontal effect.[209] Hunt relied on the dissenting judgment of Kriegler J. in the South African case of *Du Plessis v. De Klerk*,[210] a case bordering on private action of defamation between private parties. Here the judge posited that fundamental rights in the constitution governed 'not only the relationship between the State and the individual, but also governed relations between private individuals wherever law is involved.' This means that where private relationships are not regulated by law, constitutional rights will not apply but once law is involved in regulating those relationships, the private nature of those relationships is lost. The 'State as the maker, administrator, the interpreter and the applier of the law that governs those relationships' is bound to step in and protect the fundamental rights.[211] Hunt therefore, concluded that the HRA will not have direct horizontal effect but since it will be regarded as 'applying to all law', it will be relevant in proceedings between private parties. The HRA will also not confer a new private cause of action against

206. Bamforth, 'The True "Horizontal Effect" of the Human Rights Act 1998', at 35.
207. *Ibid.*, at 36. See the cases of *Middlebrook Mushrooms v. Transport and General Workers Union* (1993) I.C.R. 612 at 620; *Rantzen v. Mirror Group Newspapers* (1986) Ltd (1994) Q.B. 670 at pp. 690-692; *Associated Newspapers Group Ltd v. Wade* (1979) 1 W.L.R. 570, Lord Denning remarked at p. 709 that 'if there is to be no interference (with the right) by public authority, all the more so there should be no interference by private individuals'.
208. Bamforth, 'The True "Horizontal Effect" of the Human Rights Act 1998, at 34.
209. Murray Hunt, 'The "Horizontal Effect" of the Human Rights Act', (1998) P.L, Aut, at 423-443.
210. [1996] (3) S.A. 850 cited by Hunt, *ibid.*, at 434.
211. Hunt, 'The "Horizontal Effect" of the Human Rights Act', at 435.

private person in respect of breach of Convention rights.[212] He gave example of an all-male club which does not allow women guests into its bar. He said that the HRA will not confer any new cause of action on women who complained of discrimination under Articles 11 and 14 but that a woman who is physically ejected from the premises may sue for assault. He argued that the common law of trespass cannot provide the club with a defence of lawful ejection. The court cannot also accede to such defence without making itself in breach of the Convention. The club, by the defence, will also be seen as entreating the court to preserve its present freedom to discriminate which section 6 of that HRA does not allow the courts to do.[213]

However, as one commentator has pointed out, the courts neither adopt the *indirect horizontal effect* nor the position *between indirect and direct horizontal effect* canvassed by Hunt as shown in some recent cases bordering on Privacy law and Defamation but rather *direct horizontal* effect.[214] *In Campbell v. MGN Ltd*[215] the photograph of a model, Naomi Campbell was taken by the defendant and subsequently published in their Newspapers with information relating to the whereabouts of the treatment she was receiving for drug addiction. The House of Lord held that the publication exceeded the margin of appreciation to which the press is entitled under Article 10 of the ECHR and so disproportionately infringed her right under Article 8 of the ECHR. This case created a new tort of privacy in that to be successful in such an action, the claimant must show that she had a reasonable expectation of privacy regarding the facts that were published. The new tort created by this case in Privacy law has been called 'misuse of private information' which differs from the old common law 'breach of confidence.'[216] Other cases on law of privacy followed this new tort created by the Campbell case thus, constituting a confirmation that Article 8 of the convention are directly horizontally enforceable.[217] It can therefore, be concluded that

212. *Ibid.*, at 442. Hunt declared that 'Law which already exists and governs private relationships must be interpreted, applied and if necessary developed so as to achieve compatibility with the Convention. But where no cause of action exists, and there is therefore no law to apply, the courts cannot invent new causes of action, as that would be to embrace full horizontality which has clearly been precluded by parliament.'
213. *Ibid.*
214. Thomas D.C. Bennett, 'Horizontality's New Horizons – Re-examining Horizontal Effect: Privacy, Defamation and the Human Rights Act: Part 1' (2010) Ent. L.R 21(3): at 96-104; see also Garvin Philipson, 'Clarity Postponed: Horizontal Effect after Campbell and Re. S', in Fenwick, Masterman & Pililipson (eds), 'Judicial Reasoning under the UK Human Rights Act' (Cambridge University Press, 2007). He clearly ruled out any direct horizontal effects and courts developing a new causes of action and instead postulated two possible types of indirect effect – 'weak' and 'strong' indirect effect.
215. [2004] 2 A.C. 457. See also Richard Clayton, 'Developing Principles For Human Rights', 2 HER.L.R 175, 182 (2002) where he cited two cases of *Wilson v. First County Trust* and *Wilson v. First County Trust (No. 2)* to show that Courts are by section 3 requires to interpret statutes in private party disputes in a manner consistent with the Convention.
216. *Ibid.*, at 101.
217. *Mosley v. NGN Ltd* (2008) EWHC 1777, Q.B. 7; *Murray v. Express Newspapers Plc.* [2008] EWCA Civ. 446 [27], where the Court of Appeal in reversing the decision of the high court and holding that the case is arguable and should be tried, observed that Articles 8 and 10 of ECHR are now the new content of the domestic tort that the English law must enforce. The court applied the Convention in a direct horizontal manner. See also the case of *Applause Store Productions Ltd. v. Raphael* (Facebook case) [2008] EWHC 1781, Q.B. 81; *Arrondelle v. United Kingdom* (1983)

in cases of fundamental rights in UK, direct horizontal effects will be given to the HRA so that Convention rights will be applied in both vertical and horizontal cases.

Some other countries apply constitutional rights (fundamental rights) vertically, that is only in relation between public bodies and an individual. They only apply constitutional rights horizontally (i.e., in relation between private individuals) where State action is involved. Example of such country is United States (US). The US constitutional law requires the presence of 'State action' in a dispute between individuals in order for the constitutional protections in the Bill of right to apply. This means that the constitutional rights will not apply or be enforced in a relation between private parties unless it can be established that the activities of the private party alleged to have violated constitutional right are sufficiently connected to the government to constitute 'State action' to which the constitution applies.[218] An opposite approach to the US 'State action' requirements is the direct horizontality adopted by the Ireland Republic. Judicial authorities have shown that direct enforceability of constitutional rights by one individual against another is permitted.[219]

In Canada, indirect horizontality appears to have been adopted going by the Supreme Court cases of *Dolphin* Delivery[220] and *Manning v. Hill.*[221] The courts have held that element of 'governmental action' is required before the Canadian Charter of Rights and Freedoms can apply but a degree of horizontal application is also allowed in litigation between private parties. This means that in private litigation, courts ought to develop and apply common law principles consistently with the provisions of the Charter values even though individual cannot raise constitutional provision directly against another individual. It is within the inherent powers of the court to 'modify or extend the common law in order to comply with the prevailing social conditions and charter values'.

From the above, the direct horizontal approach adopted by the English and Irish courts is preferable to the practice in the US and Canada because it enables an aggrieved person to vindicate his rights directly against another individual even if State's action is not connected to the violation of his right. The English system endows an aggrieved private person a direct cause of action even where State's action is not involved. That is not to say however that avenue for a private person to have his property right vindicated whenever violated by another private person is totally lost in US and Canada. Where the acts or omission of a government body contributed to the

5 E.H.R.R 118 where the ECtHR held that the State was sufficiently connected to the noise generated by private aircraft in the Gartwick airport since it was being operated by a public airport authority and the State had assisted in the airport's location and development. Thus Article 8 of the Convention was used to prevent interference with private home.

218. Hunt, *supra* n. 210 at 427.
219. *Ibid.*, at 428 citing the cases of *Meskell v. Coras Iompair Eireann* [1973] I.R. 121 at 132-133; *Lovett v. Gogan* [1995] I.L.R.M. 12 at 20 and *Parsons v. Kavanagh* [1990] I.L.R.M. 560.
220. *Retail, Wholesale & Department Store Union, Local 580 v. Dolphin Delivery Ltd.* [1986] 2 S.C.R 573.
221. [1995] 126 D.L.R. (4th) 129 cited by Hunt at pp 430-432.

breach of the right by private person, access to court on the bill of rights is still possible.[222]

8. CONCLUSION

The different perspectives to the concept of property have helped us to understand the dynamic nature of property right. How property is understood conceptually among the common law theorists differs from one and another. But there is a commonality among them particularly on the evolutionary trends of property. The concept of property keeps evolving as the society changes. We have seen from the works of traditional property right theorists that as the society moved from one age to the other, e.g., from age of hunters to the age of shepherds, to the age of agriculture and to the age of commerce, so also what constitutes property keeps changing. Blackstone had presented property as absolute domination of external things and total exclusion of others from any control over the use to which such property is put.[223]

But by the end of the twentieth century, this physical and absolute view of property has been overtaken by the realists (These include both legal and economic property Theorists) who saw property in a different way. The Realists view is that property did not precede the law but rather it is a legal construct. It is a 'consequence of the significance attached by law to the relationships between legal persons.'[224] In essence, it is not a relationship between person and a thing but as legal relation between persons with respect to a thing. Property rights theories have also helped in understanding that technically, property is not an 'object' or 'thing' but rather the 'rights' which a person has over the 'object'. That was why Hohfeld contended that there is no difference between the quality of the rights in rem (property) and the rights in personam (contract). Their difference only lies in the quantity of people they bind or apply to. Rights in rem only give rise to multitude of rights and correlative duties while rights in personam are confined to the parties. Both are all rights against persons. What is also common to the Realists' perception of property is that property no longer has a distinctive character but varies according to the context and the object which is at stake. Therefore, property is essentially a separable bundle of rights subsisting between persons with respect to thing. The bundle of rights comprises right to use, possess, income, capital, manage, power to alienate and exclude others. This shows that property has no essential character as it is flexible and can accommodate wide range of rights and responsibilities in different ways and in different context. That is why some

222. See further discussion on this issue in Chapter 7 of this book. See also *Shelley v. Kraemer*, 33 US 1 (1948) where there was a dispute between two private parties regarding the use of a racially restrictive covenants. Because the property owner sought to use the court to enforce the discriminatory covenant against the other party, the Supreme Court held that there was a sufficient State action to trigger consideration of the constitutional rights of the disadvantaged party.
223. Davies, 'PROPERTY: Meanings, Histories, Theories', at 20.
224. *Ibid.*

theorists contended that property has disintegrated[225] in that the whole concept of property is flexible so that increasing range of things can become property. This means that if property does not consist a definite set of rights (such as the incidents mentioned above), but includes different rights for different contexts, more resources might likely fall within the concept of property. For example, it has been judicially recognised that an individual possesses property rights in his own tissues and that it is possible to enjoy property rights in tissues of others that have been separated from the body.[226]

Moreover, in the fields of modern investment and human rights laws, we have witnessed an expansive definition of property rights. It covers wide range of interests both tangibles and intangible rights, including expectations of profits. Property includes all interests and rights which may be evaluated in financial and economic terms. Also of commonality between investment law and human rights law is that every legal claim that has economic value is regarded as property and that other economic interests will be protected. In both laws therefore, the notion of property as a material thing is out of fashion. It has been replaced by the modern conception which includes managerial control over components of a process that is wealth producing. This view of property is also in accord with the Realist's conception of property.

One striking lesson learnt from the analysis of the concept of property is its relational dimension. This described property as right exercised with obligations towards others and not just a right exercised in total exclusion of them. The owner of property may enjoy the dignity, welfare and self-fulfillment that the property affords him but the very essence of property requires that certain obligations should be imposed on him to use his property in a way that will not injure the legitimate interests of others.[227] Property is not limited to situation where an individual exercises dominion over things and others but is also all about 'individuals and communities: how they are formed, how they live together, and how they use their resources'.[228] By this, property will bring orderliness in the society. This means that property can develop into more socially responsive concept.[229]

The use of property right theory would help in understanding that the common law judges adopted the rule of capture at a time when property was regarded as absolute dominion of a person over things and not right against persons with respect to things. The focus of the Common law Judges was all about the 'ownership of the quantity of the oil' taken rather than the 'right' which the affected licensee has over the oil to deny him any remedy for the oil taken. If their focus had been on the right, they would probably have reached a different conclusion. The Judges held on tenaciously to this view perhaps because of the strict adherence to precedents and were not ready to change even when property perception changes.

225. See T. Grey 'The Disintegration of Property' (Nomos, 1980), 22 at 69-85; K. Gray 'Property in Thin Air', Cambridge Law Journal 50: 252-307.
226. *Moore v. Regents of the University of California* 703 P.2d 479 (Cal. 1990).
227. J.W. Singer, 'Entitlement: The Paradoxes of Property' (Yale University Press, 2000), at 204.
228. Davies, 'PROPERTY: Meanings, Histories, Theories', at 2.
229. *Ibid.*, at 21.

The conceptual meaning of property as analysed above shall resonate through our subsequent chapters and shall form the backdrop against which the chapters shall be analysed more thoroughly to show why the licensee's property rights to petroleum reservoir should be recognised and protected.

CHAPTER 3

Analysis of the Nature of Interests in Oil and Gas in Accession and Domanial Systems of Mining Law

1. INTRODUCTION

This chapter will analyse the nature of interests in Oil and Gas in Accession and Domanial or Regalia Systems of Mining law. The objective of this chapter is to show as clear as possible the development of the law of oil and gas and to illustrate through the decisions of the courts, the influences which account for the adoption of the various theories of ownership as the basis of the rights or interests of the landowners and their lessees in oil and gas rights in Accession systems of mining laws (e.g., United States and Canada). With respect to the domanial system of mining law, the nature of the property rights or interests created by Petroleum production licence or lease will be analysed. Six countries will be our focus in this chapter. These countries are - United States, Nigeria, United Kingdom, Canada, Australia and Netherlands. The research will first analyse the various laws of these States on ownership of petroleum and thereafter, the licence granting clauses. Comparison will then be made with the US ownership theories in order to determine whether there is any semblance between any of the US ownership theories and the domanial regime of petroleum ownership. This will help to determine where the domanial system of ownership can be placed within the context of the US ownership theories. The analysis will be useful in the determination of the appropriate legal character of the petroleum licence in the domanial system.

2. ACCESSION SYSTEMS

Accession system of Mining law denotes Jurisdiction in which there is private ownership of land in fee simple absolute and the underneath minerals is regarded as accessory to ownership of the land (The system recognises landowners' ownership of both the land surface and the mineral rights in fee simple absolute). Also in this system, the hydrocarbon in place accedes to someone who has been granted mineral lease by the surface owner. The system is currently in practice in the US and to some extent, Canada and Netherlands.

The landowner possesses a bundle of rights, powers, privileges and immunities in his relations with other persons over the particular piece of land. This bundle of rights includes right to drill well, produce oil from the discovered reservoir, dispose of the oil produced for his own benefit, and he may exclude other persons from sharing in the oil produced from the well,[1] etc. According to Honore's vocabulary, each of these rights is a property.[2] He can also alienate by deed or a lease or reserve to himself certain of these rights, powers, privileges and immunities by separating them from the estate in fee simple absolute in the land. These interests are variously described as Leasehold interest,[3] Mineral interest[4] and Royalty interest.[5] He will be able to prosecute unauthorised persons who entered his land for the same purpose or who interfere with any of the sticks that make up the bundle of rights.

However this right is not absolute in that legislation may be made to restrict his operations and under the private and public law of nuisance, the adjoining land owner may also be protected from activities that may be injurious to the enjoyment of his land. The interests of the owners of the tracts overlying the producing formations may also restrict his operations.

2.1 Nature of Landowner's Interest in Oil and Gas *In Situ*

Under the common law, the legal maxims '*cujus est solum, ejus est usque ad coelum et ad infernos*'[6] (hereinafter '*ad coelum et ad infernos*') was the applicable norm in any ownership of mineral's discourse. Thus, before the discovery of oil and gas in the US, it was a settled law that the owner of the land also owns the solid minerals under his land. However, in order to give 'a just and equitable right to the landowner in respect to lateral support, light, air, and water on the surface, it became necessary to qualify the principles of absolute ownership. Another legal maxim *sic utere tuo ut alienum non laedas* was thus evoked by the court to qualify the principle of absolute ownership.[7] This is 'positive qualification' in that it added some other rights to the bundle of rights enjoyed by the owner of the land. However, the court had refused to apply the principles of absolute ownership to substances of wandering nature on the surface of

1. Williams & Meyers, 'Oil and Gas Laws', vol. 1 (2004), Chapter 2, pp. 17-18.
2. See Chapter 2 at p. 34.
3. Eugene Kuntz et al. 'Cases and Materials on Oil and Gas Law', 2nd edn (1992), at p. 138; John S. Lowe, 'Oil and Gas Law in a Nutshell', 5th edn (2009), at pp. 21 and 43.
4. Williams & Meyers, 'Oil and Gas Laws', at 25.
5. *Ibid.*
6. Means that to whomsoever the soil belongs, he owns also to the sky and to the depths. This was further consolidated by the Blackstone's book to the effect that 'Lands hath also, in its legal signification, an indefinite extent, upwards as well as downwards ... if a man grants all his lands, he grants thereby all his mines of metals and fossils, his woods, his waters, and his houses, as well as his fields and meadows.'
7. W.L. Summers, 'Property in Oil and Gas', (1919-1920) Yale L.J. 175, at p. 174.

the earth such as wild animals, birds and fishes. Also subterranean substances (such as water, oil and gas), presented serious problem for the court to decide what qualification should be made to the absolute ownership doctrine because of their wandering and fugitive nature at the subsurface.

As regards landowner's right to underground percolating water, the first English case that the issue arose was the case of *Acton v. Bludell.*[8] In this case, a coal mining company dug coal pits to such depth as to deprive the neighbouring cotton mill owner of his supply of well water. In formulating what can be regarded as the first groundwater law opinion, the court held that:

> [T]he case was not to be governed by the law which applies to rivers and flowing streams, but that it rather falls within that principle, which gives to the owner of the soil all that lies beneath his surface; that the land immediately below is his property, whether it is solid rock, or porous ground, or venous earth, or part soil, part water; that the person who owns the surface may dig therein, and apply all that is there found to his own purposes at his free will and pleasure; and that if, in the exercise of such right, he intercepts or drains off the water collected from underground springs in his neighbour's well, this inconvenience to his neighbour falls within the description of '*damnum absque injuria*', which cannot become the ground of an action.

In recognition of the fact that the absolute ownership doctrine may result into an unjust outcome in percolating water cases, exception to the theory was developed in latter cases to the effect that the landowner cannot intercept and use all of the water of underground stream or maliciously divert percolating water or appropriate such water in a manner that injure a flowing stream. In the case of *Bassett v. Salisbury Manufacturing Co.*[9] the Supreme Court applied the correlative rights doctrine to percolating water based on the maxim, '*sic utere tuo ut alienum non laedas*'. This decision was equally approved in the subsequent decisions of the courts on this issue.[10]

When oil and gas was discovered in great quantity in the US, there was social and economic need to produce oil and gas as fast as possible to meet the fast growing economy. However, in doing so, it was practically impossible for drainage of oil from an adjacent tract to the well bore on the adjoining land not to occur. This has somewhat led to a conflict between social and economic imperatives and the legal theory of '... *ad coelum et ad infernos*'. In trying to strike a balance between these conflicting interests, there arose irreconcilable conflicts among the oil and gas producing States in the US and hence conflicting court decisions as regard the nature of interest held by landowner in the oil and gas in situ and the interests he gives to others by contract. Thus, the questions that arose were whether the land owner possesses absolute ownership to oil and gas in place just like the solid minerals. Second, whether absolute ownership principle should apply to oil and gas in exact manner as it has been applied to solid

8. (1843) Exch. 12 M. & W. 324.
9. (1862) 43 N.H. 569.
10. See also *Swett v. Cutts* (1870) 50 N.H. 493 and *Kathy v. Walkinsshaw* (1903) 141 Calif. 116, 70 Pac. 663.

minerals. The argument rested upon three ownership of oil and gas theories viz:- Non-ownership theory, Ownership in place theory and Qualified ownership theory (This third one falls in between the two, but more like the Non- ownership theory).[11]

Under the Non-ownership theory, a landowner does not own the oil and gas underneath his land until they are produced and reduced to possession. It means that any other person, i.e., an adjacent land owner could capture the oil and gas through a well bore on his land before he exercises his right without incurring any liability. The adoption of this theory stemmed from the emphasis placed by the courts on the fugacious character of oil and gas and its comparison with subterranean waters and wild animals (*ferae naturae*).

By this, landowner has no property right in oil and gas underneath his land.[12] Many States in the US have adopted the Non-ownership theory although it is sometimes uncertain which particular ownership theory the court had applied.[13]

The Ownership in place theory is to the effect that the land owner owns the oil and gas in place beneath his land and that the ownership of such minerals may be severed from the surface of the land just as the ownership of solid minerals may be severed by conveyance from that of the soil. The first proposition the courts established clearly was that oil and gas are minerals since the term 'Minerals' denote inorganic substances in or under the surface of the earth. Therefore, it was conceded that any component part of the surface or the strata underneath it was part of the land. So it was thought as well that a disposition of any of these is a disposition of a part of the land. Hence an ordinary lease of the land cannot authorise mining of oil and gas from the land and certain category of persons e.g., executors and guardian *ad litem* cannot grant power to extract oil and gas even though they possessed power to lease in the instrument appointing them.[14]

Ownership in place theory has gained more popularity than the Non-ownership theory as it has been adopted in the majority of States in the United States.[15] Several cases have also recognised and approved this theory.[16]

In Canada, judicial pronouncements in some cases have shown that ownership in place theory has been finally adopted exactly as practised in the US This means that a fee simple owner of land owns the oil and gas in place especially in cases where the

11. See Chapter 5 for detailed discussion on ownership theories.
12. *Ohio Oil Co. v. Indiana* (1899) 177 U.S. 190, 209.
13. Williams & Meyers, 'Oil and Gas Laws', at pp. 33-39. The States are - Alabama, California, Illinois, Indiana, Kentucky, Louisiana, New York, Ohio and Wyoming. See also Robert J. Blake, 'The Oil and Gas Lease', (1939-1940) S. Cal L. Rev. 13: 305, at p. 306.
14. D. Edward Greer, 'The Ownership of Petroleum Oil and Natural Gas in Place', (1922-1923) Tex. L. Rev. 1: 162 at p. 162 n. 1.
15. See generally Williams & Meyers, 'Oil and Gas Laws', at pp. 44-50. The States are Arkansas, Colorado, Kansas, Maryland, Michigan, Mississippi, Montana, New Mexico, North Dakota, Pennsylvania, Tennessee, Texas, Washington and West Virginia.
16. *County v. Mid-Kansas Oil & Gas Co. 113* Tex. 160, 254 S.W. 290, 29 A.L.R. 566 (1923); *Attorney General v. Pere Marquette* 263 Mich. 431, 268 N.W. 860 (1933); *Ross v. Damm* 278 Mich. 388, 270 N.W. 722 (1936); *Murray v. Allard,* 100 Tenn. 100. 43 S.W. 355 (1897); *Hamilton v. Forster,* 272 Pa. 95, 116 A. 50 (1922); *United States Steel Corp. V. Hoge,* 503 Pa. 140, 468 A.2d 1380, 79 O.&G.R. 96 (1983).

crown had not reserved oil and gas rights in the grant of the land.[17] These cases also alluded to the possibility of landowner's ownership rights to in situ oil and gas to be defeated by the rule of capture as modified by the conservation laws.

The basic conceptual difference between the two ownership theories is that in ownership in place States, legal title to oil and gas vests upon conveyance of fee title to the realty while in the Non-ownership in place States, conveyance in fee title merely gives the owner the right to drill; title to oil and gas only vests when reduced to actual physical possession through production. The latter system seems to be more in accord with the principles of the rule of capture while the former appears to be a contradiction of the principle, as it does not fit within the Rule's framework.

The Qualified ownership theory is to the effect that each of the owners of the tracts of land overlying a producing formation has correlative rights and duties to one and another in respect of the oil and gas underneath. Each of the tract owners has a right to produce and may take as much oil and gas from the common-pool even though the oil and gas might have come from the land of his neighbour. There is, however, a corresponding duty not to waste the oil and gas or to damage the producing formation in the course of such production. The theory departed from the ownership in place theory when the Pennsylvania Supreme Court analogised the principles of animals '*ferae naturae*', in the case of *Westmoreland Natural Gas Company v. DeWitt* (*supra*) and declared that:

> Oil and gas belong to the owner of the land so long as they are in it or on it, but when they escape, and go into other land, or come under another's control, the title of the former owner is gone.

But the United States Supreme Court disagreed with the analogy made to the animals '*ferae naturae*' and declared in the case *Ohio Oil Company v. Indiana*[18] as follows:

> But it cannot be that property to a specified thing vests in one who has no right to prevent any other person from taking or destroying the object which is asserted to be the subject of the right of property.

Consequently, the court declared that the landowner has no property interest in the oil and gas in place and can acquire no title to them until he reduces them to possession and that in doing so, he can reduce to possession all or every part, if possible, of the deposits without violating the rights of other surface owners. The court also introduced the correlative right doctrine in the case and declared that there is a co-equal right in them (surface proprietors) to take from a common source of supply.

Subsequently, the court having realised the problem its earlier decisions of no ownership in oil and gas will cause, quickly qualified it by ruling that the landowner

17. *Boris v. Canadian Pacific Railway and Imperia oil* (1953) 7 W.W.R. (NS) 546 (PC) at 559; See also Stratton J.A. in the case of *Prism Petroleum v. Omega Hydrocarbons* (1994) 4 W.W.R. 585 (Alta. C.A.) at 594; Fruman J. in *Anderson v. Amoco Oil & Gas* (1999) 3 W.W.R. 225 (Alta. SC.) at 293. These cases approved the pronouncement in Boris case to the effect that the petroleum reserved is owned as a fee simple interest by the landowner. This clearly indicates that oil and gas while in place is capable of ownership.
18. 177 U.S. 190 (1899).

has exclusive right to mine oil and gas underneath his land and that in itself is a property right.[19]

Yet, in another case, *Manufacturer's Gas Co v. Indiana Gas Co*[20] (*supra*), the court though, agreed with the reasoning of the Supreme Court in the case of *Ohio Oil Co v. Indiana* (*supra*) which rejected both the absolute ownership doctrine as applied to percolating water and the animal '*ferae naturae*' however, declared that the owners of oil and gas lands are *common owners of the oil and gas beneath* and that in the exercise of the right to take from the common source, neither of the owners could destroy the common source. As a result, either of the owners could bring an action to enjoin the acts of the other that would materially injure or destroy the common property source. This case appeared to have departed from the extreme position taken by the court in the case of *Ohio Oil Co. v. Indiana* (*supra*) which held that the landowner has no property right in oil and gas in situ.

Following the court's decision in *Ohio Oil Co v. Indiana's* case (*supra*), many other jurisdictions including the Non-ownership States accepted the correlative right concept thus eliminating in practice, the dichotomy between the qualified ownership and non- ownership theories.[21]

2.2 The Legal Nature of the Oil and Gas Lease and the Lessee's Interest in Accession Systems

2.2.1 *Legal Nature of Oil and Gas Lease*

We are concerned in this section, with the legal character of the 'Lease' and the nature of interest that lessee holds over the Mineral interest granted to him by the Landowner.

The instrument by which the transfer of mineral interest to the lessee is carried out is called a 'Lease'. A lease has been described by an eminent American author as:

> [N]ot only the legal act, the conveyance, by which a lesser estate is vested in another, but in addition, the legal act or acts by which various contractual obligations are created in connection with such conveyance.[22]

Various courts' decisions have recognised an oil and gas lease to have dual character, that is, it is a conveyance of an interest in real property, and a contract between the lessor and lessee.[23]

The word 'lease' given to the instrument by which the transfer is carried out has been described as unfortunate because it might by that, be confused with the

19. *Richmond National Gas Co. v. Davenport* (1905) 37 Ind. App. 25, 76 N.E. 525; *Manufacturer's Gas Co. v. Indiana Gas Co.* (1900) 155 Ind.451, 57 N.E. 912.
20. *Ibid.*
21. Walker, 'The Nature of the Property Interest Created by an Oil and Gas Lease in Texas', (1928) Texas L. Rev. 7: 1 at 2 n. 3.
22. 1 Tiffany, 'Real Property', 3rd edn (1939) 110 at 74 referred to by Robert J. Blake, *supra* n. 13 at 312; See also Megarry & Wade, 'The Law of Real Property' 7th edn (Sweet & Maxwell, 2008), at 729.
23. See the California case of *Samuels v. Ottinger*, 169 Cal. 209, 146 Pac. 1024 (1921); *Bickett v. City of Paris Dry Goods Co.* 98 Cal. Dec. 450, 96 Pac. 2d 122 (1939).

conventional lease between landlord and tenants.[24] Even though the instrument is called a 'lease' in that it conveys to the lessee the use of that portion of the surface of the land to carry out drilling operations, it is primarily a 'grant' of the exclusive rights to extract the oil and gas in situ.[25] Therefore, Professor Lowe gave three significant distinguishing features of oil and gas leases from ordinary leases of real property. Those features signified that they are more of deeds of easement, or mineral deeds, or deeds creating a *profit a prendre* than an ordinary lease of real property.[26]

Generally therefore, it has been settled that the leasehold interest is more like property right created by a Deed of real property rather than a Lease of real property.[27]

2.2.2 *Nature of Lessee's Interest Created by Oil and Gas Lease*

There are divergent opinions among the courts in the US on the classification of the rights or interests created by the oil and gas lease because of two principal reasons: (1) there was no direct precedent for the court to follow (2) adequate knowledge of the nature of oil and gas in their natural habitat was lacking on the part of the common law Judges. As a result of these, laws relating to solid minerals, water and wild animals were analogised thus giving rise to varied property terminologies devised by the courts with regards to the nature of the lessee's interest in oil and gas lease.

It is necessary to examine the nature of the lessee's interest in oil and gas in relation to the type of ownership theory adopted by the State (which is invariably tied to the nature of the lessor's interest in oil and gas in situ). In those States that adopted ownership in place theory, the lessee's interest has been classified as a '*fee simple determinable estate*'. It is fee simple because the duration of the lease has been expressed to continue indefinitely after the primary term i.e. 'as long as there is production.' It is determinable because it may be terminated by the lessor if the lessee fails to pay delay rentals, to commence operations or produce petroleum by the end of the primary term, or the cessation of production at the end of the secondary term.[28]

Again opinions are divided among the ownership in place States as to whether the granting clause is significant in determining the nature of interest created by oil and gas lease. Majority of the ownership in place States have held that the granting clause is not important and that irrespective of the type of granting clause, the oil and gas lease operates as a conveyance of title to '*in situ*' oil and gas,[29] while the minority ownership

24. Williams & Meyers, 'Oil and Gas Laws', at 23.
25. Professor James W. Simonton, 'The Nature of the Interest of the Grantee under an Oil and Gas Lease', (1917-1918) W. Va. L. Q. 25: 295. See also the case of *Rich v. Doneghey* 71 Okla. 207, 177 Pac. 86, 90, 3 A.L.R. 352, 357 (1918) where the court observed that 'though denominated a lease ... the instrument before us, strictly speaking, is not such, but it is in effect a grant in "*praesenti*" of all the right to the oil and gas to be found in the lands described'.
26. Lowe, 'Oil and Gas Law in a Nutshell', at 65.
27. Kuntz et al., 'Cases and Materials on Oil and Gas Law', 2nd edn at 140.
28. *Ibid.*, at 140.
29. In the Texas case of *Stephens County v. Mid Kansa Oil & Gas Co.* 113 Tex. 160, 254 S.W. 290 A.L.R. 566 (1923), the Supreme Court declared that 'Notwithstanding the distinctions attempted to be drawn in the decisions, we cannot conclude otherwise than that there is no real difference in the title conveyed whether an instrument takes the form of a grant of the exclusive right to

in place States placed emphasis on the granting clause. The latter States contended that where the granting clause purportedly conveyed the oil and gas in place, it will be regarded as creating a *fee simple interest* and therefore the nature of rights or interest of the lessee is *corporeal*, but where it merely grants an exclusive right to search, develop and produce, *an irrevocable licence or a* 'profit a prendre' is created and the nature of the rights or interests of the lessee is *incorporeal*.

In this respect three general types of granting clauses are found in the ownership in place States which gave rise to differing legal effects and consequences. The first is where the lease purports to '*grant to the lessee … exclusive rights to mine and produce.… petroleum and natural gas …*' the court has held that the lease grants no estate or property either in the soil or oil and gas in place.[30] The second is where the granting clause of the lease provides that '*the lessor grants, demise, lease, and let, for the sole and only purpose of mining and operating for oil and gas … all that certain tract of land …*' Again, opinions of the courts are divided on the issue of the extent of the rights or interests of lessee in the oil and gas in place. The majority of the courts have held this type of granting clause as conveying no title to the oil and gas in place but corporeal leasehold of the surface estate with an exclusive right to take the oil and gas.[31]

The minority have held that such a granting clause conveys not only the right of possession of the surface but also title to the oil and gas in place or such part as he may be able to remove during his tenancy.[32] The third type of granting clause is where the lease purports to '*grant, lease and let to the lessee … all the oil and gas in and under the following described tract of land …*' The courts have held that this granting clause grants oil and gas in place to the lessee together with the necessary right to use the

---

mine and appropriate all of certain minerals, or takes the form of a demise of the land, for the sole purpose of mining operations, coupled with a grant of the exclusive right to produce and dispose of the mineral, or takes the form of a grant of the mineral with the exclusive right to mine for, produce and dispose thereof. The results are substantially the same to all parties in interest, whether the one or the other form of instrument is used. Why should that instruments in different forms create different estates, where there is no difference in fact with respect to that of which each divests the grantor, his heirs or assigns, nor with respect to that with which each invests the grantee, his heirs or assigns.' See also *Texas Co. v. Dougherty* (*supra*).

30. *Funk v. Haldeman* 53 Pa. 229 (1866) In this Pennsylvania case, the granting clause in a lease provides that 'the lessor hereby grants to the lessee, his heirs and assigns, the exclusive right to mine and produce from the following described tract of land petroleum and natural gas, with possession of so much of the land as might be necessary for such purposes'. The court held that the interests granted was not a part of the corporeal estate, but a right issuing out of a thing corporeal. The court concluded that it is a profit a prendre in gross and may be held and assigned apart from the possession of the land. See also John N. Sawyer 'Interests created by oil and gas leases in Pennsylvania', 4 U. Pitt. L. Rev. 274 (1937-1938) at 277.
31. *Duke v. Hague,* 107 Pa. 57 (1884) at 66 'the lessee is vested with an interest in the land. His interest is that of a tenant for years for the purpose of mining, he has an absolute right of possession of the entire surface necessary, and no one else can rightfully take out oil during the term, save under him. The whole of the oil, or only a part, may be taken under the lease, but whatever shall be taken is of the substance of the realty. He is not an absolute owner of the whole of the oil as he would be were all the oil in place conveyed to him in fee.' See also *Westmorland Gas Co v. Dewitt* (*supra*), *Kitchen v. Smith,* 101 Pa. 452 (1882), *Chicago and Allegheny Oil and Mining Co v. U. S. Petroleum Co.*, 57 Pa. 83 (1868).
32. *Barnsdall v. Bradford Gas Co*, 225 Pa. 338; 74 Alt. 207 (1909).

surface for the purpose of developing and extracting the substances.[33] In this instance, the courts have construed the words '*grant, demise, lease and let of all oil and gas*' in a lease as effecting a sale or a grant of all the oil and gas in place in fee from the remainder of the land.[34] Although this 'fee' has been held to be conditional or determinable, it has all the incidents of a fee simple title in the land.[35]

The Courts of the Non-ownership States (Qualified ownership) have however held the nature of lessee interest as an irrevocable licence or a '*profit a prendre*' determinable and that the granting clause is not important since a conveyance of oil and gas in place is not possible. In these States, the nature of the lessee's interest in the oil and gas in their natural State is restricted to the incorporeal hereditament classification. A very significant champion of this view is the decision of the Supreme Court of California State in the case of *Callahan v. Martin*[36] which after reviewing the two ownership theories, rejected the ownership in place theory for the following reasons: (1) ownership in place theory fails to take cognizance of the fact that oil and gas actually brought to the surface may include both oil and gas underneath the leased area and those drawn from underneath adjoining lands (2) ownership in place theory 'implies a present transfer of definite corporeal property when the operating oil lease is not for unlimited duration or for so long as oil shall be produced in paying quantities, but for a fixed period of years which may not exhaust the oil.'[37] The court therefore, accepted the non-ownership theory as the correct principles to be applied in determining the lessee's interest created by oil and gas lease. The court further analysed the right to extract oil and gas and the interest or estate which could be created by this right and concluded that the interest or estate created is a '*profit a prendre*' in gross. In its analysis, the court defined the term 'property' in two senses: (1) the rights or estates a man may have in property and (2) the objects of these rights or estates. The objects of property estate include land, tenements and hereditaments. Hereditaments may be either corporeal or incorporeal. Corporeal applies to lands and tenements while incorporeal applies to any subject of property which is inheritable and not tangible or visible, e.g., an easement and a '*profit a prendre*.'[38] The court further said that since

33. *Hamilton v. Forster*, 272 Pa. 95, 116 Alt. 50 (1922); *Caldwell v. Copeland*, 37 Pa. 427 (1861); *In Re: Prager's Estate*, 74 Pa. Super. 592 at 595 (1920), The court declared that 'while owing to the migratory or fugacious character of oil and gas there are certain distinctions existing between them and fixed minerals, there is no difference as respects the interest or estate conveyed ...'.
34. *Ibid.*, see also *Blakely v. Marshall*, 174 Pa. 425, 429, 34 Alt. 564, 565 (1896), the court declared that 'an oil lease, investing the lessee with the right to remove all the oil in place, in the premises, in consideration of his giving to the lessors a certain per centum thereof, is in legal effect a sale of a portion of the land ...'.
35. Sawyer, 'Interests Created by Oil and Gas Leases in Pennsylvania', at 283 n. 50.
36. 3 Cal. 2d. 110, 43 Pac. 2d. 788, 101 A.L.R. 871 (1935).
37. *Ibid.*, at 117, 792, 877.
38. Blake, 'The Oil and Gas Lease', at 327 referring to 11 Halsbury Laws of England (1910) 336, at 656 'The subject matter of a profit a prendre, i. e. the substance which the owner of the right is by virtue of the right entitled to take, may consists of ... any part of the soil itself, including mineral accretions to the soil by natural forces... The right constituting the profit a prendre may be exercised to the exclusion of all other persons, in which case it is said to be a right in severalty or a several profit a prendre; or it may be exercisable in common with one or more persons, including the owner of the land.... A profit a prendre may be created for an estate in perpetuity analogous to an estate in fee simple, or for any less period or interest such as a term for years....

'under the usual oil and gas lease the owner-lessor transfers to his lessee his right to drill for and produce oil and other substances, the rights of the lessee present a clear case of a '*profit a prendre*' in gross. ...' The court concluded that looking at the incidents of a *profit a prendre* as stated by Lord Halsbury's Laws of England; it appeared that the use of the term *profit a prendre* has properly classified the nature of the lessee's interest in oil and gas lease.

In Canada it has been held by the court that the standard oil and gas lease grants a *profit a prendre* for an uncertain term.[39] The conclusion in this case is in tandem with the ownership in place theory adopted in the *Boris and Prism cases* (*supra*) so that it can be said that oil and gas lease in Canada grants a *profit a prendre* which is a real right or an interest in land.

However, in the case of *Hamilton Bros Corporation v. Royal Trust Corp of Canada*,[40] where the court was called upon to determine legal characterisation of a working interest in some (79) oil and gas leases in Alberta and an interest in one gross overriding royalty in order to determine the extent to which extra judicial process can be made against the interests, the learned judge held that:

> [O]n the basis of these authorities and the legal nature and characteristics of petroleum and natural gas lease as a *profit a prendre* for a term certain together with earned working interests therein which also depend upon the term of the lease and production under the lease, it is my conclusion that Jennifer interests are chattel real.

The case illustrated what kind of property is the 'the right to earn win and take petroleum and natural gas and what kind of property is an earned working interest in such right. The Judge in this case appeared to have overlooked the possibility of an oil and gas lease to create a *profit a prendre* for an uncertain term. He rather focused its decision upon the 'certain' primary term of a lease and neglected to view the continuation of petroleum and gas lease that may occur for an indefinite period (which would continue so long as the lease continue to produce petroleum and gas) as creating an uncertain term required to pass beyond chattel real and into realty. The Judge therefore failed to evaluate properly the decision of the Supreme Court in the case of *Berkheiser V. Berkheiser*.[41] The majority decision in this case relied on the authority of Halsbury's law of England and held that a '*profit a prendre* may be created for an estate in perpetuity analogous to an estate in fee simple, or for any less period or interest such as term of years.' Particularly, Kellock J. Stated that:

Profits a prendre, though sometimes called licences, must be carefully distinguished from mere licences which are not tenements and do not pass any interest or alter or transfer property in anything, but merely make an act lawful which would have otherwise been unlawful . ...'

39. See *Kellock J. in Berkheiser v. Berkheiser* (1957) S.C.R. 387.
40. (1991) 70 ALTA. (Q. B.).
41. *Berkheiser v. Berkheiser* (1957) 7 DLR (2D) 721.

> In my opinion, the instrument is to be construed as a grant of a profit a prendre for an uncertain term which might be brought to an end upon the happening of any of the various contingencies for which it provides.

It is very clear from the above that the Supreme Court did not quite characterise the lease as a 'profit a prendre' for a term certain but for an uncertain term. The trial Judge in the Hamilton's case failed to decide whether the level of uncertainty of term described by Kellock J. in Berkheiser's case is sufficient that the oil and gas lease creates 'realty' as opposed to a 'chattel real'. The usual or traditional lease is a chattel real as it does not have the continuation aspect of oil and gas lease.

3. DOMANIAL AND REGALIA SYSTEMS

The Domanial mining law system denotes jurisdictions in which ownership of minerals is vested in the Sovereign.[42] Sovereign rights are exercised by the States to regulate and control activities relating to exploration, exploitation and production of the minerals within their jurisdictions through their Constitutions and Petroleum laws and regulations.[43] Some legislations expressly stipulate the stage in which ownership passes to the licensee while some others are silent on the issue.

The Regalia System of Mining law is based on the principle that minerals are '*res nullius*'. They are neither owned by the States nor by private individual. This means that they are owned by the person who first discovered them. The role of the State in this regard is to stipulate by law the methods of acquiring its ownership or its exploitation.[44]

In this regard there are two methods for the acquisition of ownership right. These are: first, by 'Occupancy of the mineral' and second, by granting 'exploration and exploitation rights.'[45]

42. See Claude Duval et al., 'International Petroleum Exploration and Exploitation Agreements: Legal, Economic & Policy Aspects', 2nd edn (2009), at p. 17; Martha Roggenkamp, 'Oil & Gas: Netherlands Law and Practice' (1991) at p. 20.
43. Through the instrumentality of these laws, some States have exercised their sovereign rights in monopolistic and expropriatory (Nationalisation) manners while some other States have exercised such power to grant concessions, licences, leases and other contractual arrangements for the exploitation of the oil and gas. In some instances, the States have sought participation in the development of these minerals by entering into various types of agreements with the International oil Companies e.g., Joint Venture, Production sharing contracts, Risk service or Service contract, etc.
44. Duval et al., 'International Petroleum Exploration and Exploitation Agreements: Legal, Economic & Policy Aspects', at 18.
45. Roggenkamp, 'Oil & Gas: Netherlands Law and Practice', at p. 20.

3.1 Ownership of Petroleum and the Nature of Property Rights Created in Petroleum Licences

3.1.1 *Ownership of Petroleum in Domanial Regimes*[46]

In the United Kingdom, property in all petroleum existing in its natural condition in strata in Great Britain is vested in the Crown.[47] Section 2 (1) (2) of the Petroleum Act 1998 (the 1998 Act) provides that Her Majesty has the exclusive right of searching and boring for and getting petroleum from onshore or beneath the territorial sea adjacent to the United Kingdom. In the offshore, the Crown exercises sovereign rights over the natural resources of the United Kingdom Continental Shelf.[48] The Crown now exercises power to grant oil and gas licences to companies to 'search and bore for and get' petroleum within the onshore, territorial sea and the United Kingdom Continental Shelf (UKCS) under the 1998 Act.[49]

In Nigeria the Constitution vests:

> ...the entire property in and control of all minerals, mineral oils and natural gas in, under or upon any land in Nigeria or, in, under or upon the territorial waters and the Exclusive Economic Zone (EEZ) of Nigeria in the Government of the Federation ... .

The Petroleum Act of 1969 as amended by the Petroleum (Amendment) Act of 1998 contains identical provisions with the Constitution.[50]

The land refers to includes all land covered by water which is in Nigeria or is under the territorial waters of Nigeria, or forms part of the Continental shelf (CS) or the EEZ. In the EEZ the Federal Republic of Nigeria (FRN) has sovereign and exclusive rights to exploit the natural resources of the sea-bed, the subsoil and superjacent

46. For the purpose of this book, the Domanial and Regalia systems of mining law are regarded as the same in our analysis of the nature of the interests of the holder of a licence or lease granted by the respective State. Therefore, where Domanial system of mining law is mentioned, it also includes Regalia system.
47. Section 1 (1) of the Petroleum (Production) Act of 1934 (This Act applies to petroleum in the onshore). This legislation was amended by the Oil and Gas (Enterprise) Act 1982. Section 18 of this Act expressly vests in the Crown in situ oil and gas under the territorial sea as well as those in the onshore. The Petroleum Act of 1998 (1998 Act) repealed both legislations and re-enacted the provisions relating to licensing, together with some other provisions relating to oil and gas contained in the Petroleum Act of 1934 (1934 Act).
48. Section 1 (1) of the Continental Shelf Act of 1964 vests in the crown 'any rights exercisable by the United Kingdom outside territorial waters with respect to the sea bed and subsoil and their natural resources, except so far as they are exercisable in relation to coal, are hereby vested in Her Majesty.' This Act, unlike the 1934 Act, did not expressly grants property rights in petroleum in situ in the Crown.
49. Section 3 (1).
50. Section 44 (3) of the Constitution of the Federal Republic of Nigeria, 1999 (1999 Constitution); Section 1 (1) and (2) CAP P10, Laws of the Federation of Nigeria, 2004. See the case of *Attorney – General of the Federation v. Attorney General of Abia State (No. 2)* (2006) 6 NWLR Part 674, 542-905 where the Supreme Court of Nigeria held that as between the Federal Government, the States and the local Government in Nigeria, ownership of petroleum in or under any land is vested only in the Federal Government even where such resources are located under lands occupied by the States or Local governments.

waters of the EEZ. The provision of the EEZ Act conforms to the international law which gave coastal State 'sovereign rights' to exploit natural resources of the C.S and the EEZ.[51] There appears to be conflict between the Nigeria Constitutional provisions and the EEZ Act in that the constitution vests full ownership of petroleum in situ to the FRN whereas the EEZ confines such interests to 'sovereign rights.' Where there is such conflict, however, the provision of the constitution prevails because of its supremacy over all other laws in Nigeria.[52]

Therefore, by the combined effects of the 1999 Constitution and the Petroleum Act of 1969, ownership rights in respect of all minerals, mineral oils and natural gas in, under or upon any lands, Territorial sea, C.S and the EEZ are vested in the FGN.

In *Canada*, generally in areas of early settlement, ownership of mines, minerals, including petroleum and natural gas are concentrated in individuals who owned the land surface. Crown ownership of minerals is concentrated in the areas of latter settlement such as Alberta and Northwest Territories.[53] Also, Federal Parliament's proprietary interest in the oil and gas resources is negligible within the provinces but very extensive outside these provinces.[54] Therefore, in Canada there are privately owned minerals as well as those owned by the Crown in the right of the provinces and also in the rights of Canada.[55]

Section 109 of the Constitution Act of 1867 provides that all Lands, Mines, Minerals and Royalties... belonging to the several provinces shall remain with the provinces.

Several cases in Canada have held that the provision of this section 109 encompasses oil and gas resources.[56] Therefore, onshore petroleum resources belong to the Crown in the right of the province except few cases where those resources are privately owned as mentioned above.[57]

However, the case of *A.G. Ontario v. Mercer* (*supra*) has declared that the interest of the provincial legislature in the oil and gas is proprietary only.[58]

51. Article 2 (1) of the Convention on the Continental Shelf.
52. Section 3 (1) of 1999 Constitution of Nigeria.
53. D.E. Lewis, 'The Canadian Petroleum and Natural Gas Lease', (1952) 30 Can. Bar. Rev. at 965. Mineral substances held by the Crown in these areas are very high compared to the small amount of Crown's holding in the Eastern part of the country. Moreover, as time goes on, privately owned oil and gas property were re-vested in the Crown through legislation made by some provinces.
54. Brian W. Semkow, 'Energy and the New Constitution', (1985) Alta. L. Rev. 23: 134 at pp. 118-119. He opined that the areas covered by Canada Lands (i.e. Yukon and Northwest Territories and area off Canadian Coastlines) are twice as large as the area covered by the ten provinces with substantial oil and gas deposits.
55. See generally John Bishop Ballem, 'The Oil and Gas Lease in Canada', 2nd edn (University of Toronto Press, 1985), pp. 8-11.
56. *A.G. Ontario v. Mercer* (1883) 8 App. Cas. 767 at 775 and 776 (P.C.); *A.G. British Columbia v. A.G. Canada* (1889) 14 App. Cas. 295 (P.C.).
57. Ontario, Quebec, New Brunswick and Nova Scotia, British Columbia, Newfoundland and Prince Edward Island. It is to be noted that public ownership of oil and gas in Quebec, Ontario and the Eastern provinces are very limited because before 1887, the Dominion and Provincial lands that were granted by the Crown to individuals did not include a reservation of Minerals to the Crown. As a result, large junk of lands are still been held as freehold in these provinces. However, in the Alberta and Saskatchewan Provinces, about 80% of the mineral rights are owned by the public.
58. (1883), App. Cas. at 775 and 776.

In the offshore, the legislative and limited proprietary rights to explore and exploit the minerals in those portions of the C.S belong exclusively to the Government of Canada.[59] A political compromise was, however, reached between the Federal Government and the Provincial Government of Newfoundland after the decision of the Court which provides for the participation of the Provincial Government in the governance of the offshore areas.[60]

Australia, in a similar fashion like Canada, operates Federal system of government in which jurisdiction and ownership of petroleum resources are shared between the two levels of governments, Commonwealth and State (including the Northern Territory). Each State maintained jurisdiction and control over the petroleum resources within its boundary and as such there are separate regimes governing onshore petroleum extraction.[61] The first State to assert ownership and control of onshore petroleum in situ was the Queensland State.[62]

With respect to offshore petroleum resources, an agreement was reached in 1967 between the Commonwealth and all the States to resolve the issue of competing jurisdictional claims. By this agreement, a system of petroleum licensing was established through a device of 'mirror legislation' in which each State and the commonwealth enacted a uniform comprehensive legislation called Petroleum (Submerged Lands) Act 1967 (PSLA) to be administered by a Joint Commonwealth-State Authority.[63]

Thus, an identical PSLA with that of the Commonwealth was equally enacted by all the States. Another features of the agreement was that each State legislate on areas adjacent to that State while the Commonwealth's legislation applies to all of the various

59. Reference Re: The seabed and subsoil of the Continental Shelf Offshore Newfoundland (Hibernia Reference) (1984) S.C.R. 86; 5 D.L.R. (4th) 385 (S.C.C.).
60. This compromise was called *Canada-Newfoundland Accord on Joint Management of offshore oil and gas Resources off Newfoundland and Labrador (the Atlantic Accord).* In 1986, similar Accord was entered into between the Federal Government and the Provincial Government of Nova Scotia. Two laws made to implement the two Accords were, namely: The *Canada-Newfoundland Atlantic Accord Implementation Act*, S.C. 1987, C.3 *and the Canada – Nova Scotia offshore Petroleum Resources Accord Implementation Act*, S.C. 1988, C, 28. As a result of these Accords Implementation Acts, the Federal Government enacted a legislation extending federal and provincial laws into offshore. The Canadian Laws Offshore Application Act of 1990 extended federal laws in section 5 (1) (a) beyond the territorial sea to continental shelf. Section 7 (1) of this law extended the law of coastal provinces to two areas where such laws had not previously covered. These were the Territorial sea of Canada and the marine installations. These were previously under the sole jurisdiction of the federal government. However, provincial laws will only apply to this area in so far as there is no existing federal legislation. In the event of any conflict between the two laws, that of the federal Government will prevail.
61. Michael Crommelin, 'Legal Character of Petroleum Production Licences in Australia', in T. Daintith (ed.), 'The Legal Character of Petroleum Licences: A Comparative Study' (1981) 60.
62. The Queensland parliament enacted the Petroleum Act 1915 (as amended in 1923) to declare crown ownership of in situ petroleum irrespective of whether the crown had granted the land to private individual previously without petroleum reservation or not. This was followed by the remaining States. For example, section 13 of the 1998 Petroleum Act of Victoria State provides that 'the Crown owns all petroleum on or below the surface of any land in Victoria that came to be on or below that surface without human assistance'. See A G Lang & Michael Crommelin, 'Australian Mining and Petroleum Laws' (Butterworths Pty Ltd, 1979), at 20.
63. T. Daintith, 'A Critical Evaluation of the Petroleum (Submerged Lands) Act as a Regulatory Regime' (2000) AMPLA YEARBOOK, 91 at 93.

'adjacent areas'[64] This means that two levels of statutes governed all offshore petroleum activities in the area adjacent to each State and also two levels of licences for each offshore block.[65]

However, in 1973 the Commonwealth promulgated the Seas and Submerged Lands Act (SSLA) to vests in its self 'sovereign rights' over resources of the continental shelf, sovereignty over territorial sea and over internal waters.[66] This legislation was upheld by the High court of Australia in the case of *New South Wales v. Commonwealth.*[67] This means that it is the commonwealth legislation rather than the States' identical legislation that governs grant of petroleum licence in the offshore. The PSLA established a concessionary regime in which exclusive rights is granted by way of a licence, to a company to explore for and produce petroleum, which becomes the company's property and which it can dispose of on its own account.[68] It is to be noted that the PSLA has been repealed by the Offshore Petroleum and Greenhouse Gas Storage Act 2006[69] (as amended) (OPGGSA).

In *Netherlands*, the Mining Act of 1810[70] and Article 626 of the Dutch Civil Code of 1838 did not make very clear provisions on ownership of mines or minerals.[71] There was a limitation (i.e. 'with the exception of changes resulting from laws and police regulations relating to mines, turf-cutting and other such subjects') placed on ownership rights by Article 626 of the Dutch Civil Code. This has created confusion as it is capable of dual interpretation.[72] The provisions could be interpreted to mean that ownership of the topsoil also comprises ownership of what is on and in the land. Second, it is not clear whether mines are excluded from the landowner's ownership of topsoil and underground.

However, Article 5 of the Mining Act of 1810 provides that 'mines may be exploited only by virtue of a deed of concession'. This includes a landowner who

64. Crommelin, 'Legal Character of Petroleum Production Licences in Australia', in T. Daintith (ed.), The Legal Character of Petroleum Licences: A Comparative Study', at 63.
65. *Ibid.*
66. Section 11 provides that 'It is by this Act declared and enacted that the sovereign rights of Australia as a coastal State in respect of the continental shelf of Australia, for the purpose of exploring it and exploiting its natural resources, are vested in and exercisable by the Crown in right of the Commonwealth.' Section 6 provides that 'sovereignty in respect of the territorial sea is vested in and exercisable by the crown in right of the commonwealth'. Section 10 makes similar provisions in respect of the internal waters.
67. [1973] 135 CLR 337.
68. Daintith, 'A Critical Evaluation of the Petroleum (Submerged Lands) Act as a Regulatory Regime', at 93.
69. Act No. 14 of 2006. It added extensive provisions on carbon sequestration which were not in the PSLA.
70. This Act was drafted by Napoleon Bonaparte and introduced in the Netherlands by French. On the independence of Netherlands from French in 1813, the Act was retained provisionally but was never changed until about 200 years later.
71. Article 626 provides that 'the ownership of the land carries with it ownership of what is on and in the land. Underground, the landowner may, as he thinks fit, construct and dig, and remove all products from that excavation which are yielded by that same; with the exception of changes resulting from laws and police regulations relating to mines, turf-cutting and other such subjects.'
72. Martha Roggenkamp, 'Oil and Gas: Netherlands Law and Practice' (Chancery Law Publishing, 1991), at 23.

discovers minerals on his own land. Thus, the grants of the concession transferred ownership of the mines to the concessionaire.[73] Perpetual ownership of the minerals is conferred on the concessionaire when a deed of concession is executed in his favour and he has a right of occupation if it is necessary for exploitation.[74] The grant of concession creates a new property in the mineral underneath the land.[75] Some commentators have argued that the granting of concession merely gives the concessionaire a right in rem over the mine while others submitted that the granting of a concession gives the concessionaire a new property.[76] However, it is generally accepted that the grant of the concession gives the concessionaire ownership right over the mine and that the ownership of the mine is separate from the ownership of the surface. Moreover, the ownership would also be regarded as a 'new' ownership for a landowner who acquires a concession over the mine. This will entitle the landowner to payment of compensation.[77] Like in the offshore, three different licences are required for onshore petroleum operations - Reconnaissance work, exploration drilling and exploration of the minerals (production licence).[78]

In the offshore, the Continental Shelf Act of 1965 provides in Article 22 that 'the minerals present in or on the continental shelf are the property of the State.' Article 23 of the same Act provides that 'the ownership of the minerals produced under a production licence shall pass to the licence holder through the fact of being produced.' The combined effect of these sections is that domanial system of mining law is in full operation and that the grant of an exploration licence does not confer ownership of the minerals on the licensee with respect to Continental shelf.[79]

However, in 2003 a new Mining Act was made by the Dutch Government to replace the 1810 Mining Act, which now vests ownership of minerals in the State.[80] This Act applies to both onshore and offshore petroleum as well as geothermal energy activities.[81] Article 2 (2) of this Act applies to minerals situated at a depth of more than 100 metres below the surface of the earth. Therefore, State ownership is limited to

73. Articles 7 and 44.
74. Roggenkamp, 'Oil and Gas: Netherlands Law and Practice', at 23.
75. Article 19 of the Mining Act provides that 'from the moment that a concession has been granted, even to the landowner, this property shall be distinguished from that of the surface and shall further be considered as new property, on which new mortgages may be taken, without prejudice to those which may have been or shall be taken out on the land and the royalty as determined in the preceding article ... .'
76. Roggenkamp, 'Oil and Gas: Netherlands Law and Practice', at 24-25.
77. *Ibid.*, at 25, referring to the Supreme Court case of *Weekblad van het Recht*, No. 8606 of 25 October 1907.
78. *Ibid.*, at 200. He recalled that before the Mining Act of 1903 was enacted to empower the crown to revoke a concession and to make regulations regarding safety matters, the grant of concession meant that the crown has relinquished all control over mining activities. The Mineral exploration Act of 1967 was enacted to enable exploration licence to be granted for onshore exploration activities especially drilling. This system replaced the system whereby, the landowner's consent is paramount before a concessionaire can enter upon his land for exploration activities.
79. Roggenkamp, 'Oil and Gas: Netherlands Law and Practice', at 26.
80. Article 3 (1) of the Act provides that 'Minerals are the property of the State'.
81. The Act also applies to mining activities such as salt, production of marl and supervision of pitholes. Geothermal energy is the subsoil heat that has its source from natural causes located in 500 metres or more beneath the earth surface.

minerals located beyond this depth. Ownership rights of landowners are preserved in respect of minerals located above 100 metres.[82] This Act has resolved the lingering problems of ownership of minerals before the grant of a concession as the 1810 Mining Act did not expressly provides for such. Article 3 of the 2003 Mining Act also provides that 'ownership of the petroleum produced under a production licence is transferred to the licence-holder by the production of the said minerals.' A very important chapter is the transitional provisions contained in Article 143 (2) (4) which provides that the owner of the previously held onshore concessions shall now hold it as a production licence and shall continue to own the mines underlying its licence area for the duration of the licence.

In summary, it is clear that in the domanial system of Mining law, ownership of the oil and gas in situ vests in the States through the instrumentality of the law or the Constitutions of the States even though the surface land might be the property of an individual. The State has through the law practically severed the mineral interests or estate from the land in order to vest same in itself.[83] This system can be said to have located domanial regime in the US ownership of oil and gas in place theory in which oil and gas in situ is capable of ownership. The follow up discussion will determine whether the State has by the issuance of various explorations and production licences grants or conveys this severed Mineral interest to the licensee. This will entail an analysis of the legal character of the licence and the nature of the interests it confers on a licence holder.

3.2 Legal Character of Petroleum Licence

The legal character of the right that a licensee might be vested to carry out oil and gas exploration and exploitation activities may vary from country to country. The right granted by the Host States to the companies also comes in varied labels and often coined for political, economic or legal reasons.[84]

In the *United Kingdom*, there are four standard types of licences granted namely,[85] (1) the Seaward production licence, (2) Exploration licences – seaward areas and landward areas below low water mark, (3) Landward exploration and development licences, and (4) Methane drainage licence. For the purpose of this book, we are

82. See Martha Roggenkamp, 'A New Mining Act for the Netherlands – The End of a 200 – Year Debate' [2003] I.E.L.T.R. at pp. 185-186. See also Land Clearing Act of 1996 (as amended). The normal accession rule of the Civil Code applies. Minerals accede to the ownership of the land.
83. See *Bocardo SA v. Star Energy UK Onshore Ltd* (2008) EWHC 1756 (ch); [2008] 2 P. &C.R. 23. Peter Smith J. declared that 'when the minerals become vested either in the Crown or somebody else (say for example by virtue of an exception and reservation on conveyance) the land in question is therefore, severed so that the surface and the mineral rights become in separate ownership'.
84. They are sometimes coined as Permit, Licence, Work contract, Production sharing contract, Joint venture, Concession, Lease etc. Their legal effects could vary in accordance with the terminology used.
85. T. Daintith & G. Willoughby, 'U.K. Oil and Gas Law' 3rd edn (2000), para. 1-311 at p. 1052. However other variants of licences includes the 'promote licence' granted for two years to companies who cannot undertake full scale funding of exploration work in a block (s) so that such companies will be able to attract investor who will be ready to fund full scale work

however concerned with number (1) and (3) types licences. This is because both licences confer the exclusive right to search and bore for and get petroleum on the licensee in the offshore and onshore respectively. Therefore both licences will hereafter be jointly referred to as Production licence.

The legal character or form of Production licence with regards to both the landward areas and seaward areas is the same. Their differences appeared to be with regards to the nature of interests of the licensee under those licences. As regards to the form and character of production licence, it has been generally regarded as contractual. The mere fact that the document is coined a 'licence' as opposed to 'lease' does not really matter. What matters is the substance of the document and not its form. The contractual nature stems from the fact that the licence takes the form of a Deed executed between the Minister (representing the Crown) and the licensee by which, certain rights are transferred from the Crown to the licensee for a specified period, in consideration of payment of premium or royalty and tax.[86] Therefore, both in form (deed) and in substance (transfer of valuable rights from the Crown to the licensee for payment of certain consideration) a production licence has been regarded as contractual in nature.[87] However, the production licence has also been regarded as regulatory in nature. This latter view is as a result of the numerous controls exercised by the Crown over the licensee's operations throughout the entire life span of the licence and the fact that the Minister is required by the legislature to enact model clauses. These controls are contained in the various rules in the regulations and model clauses made by the minister from time to time. These controls ranged from technical matters such as exploration, drilling, safety and environment to commercial matters such as royalties, rents and assignment of interest, etc.[88]

It is to be noted that under section 4 (1) of the Petroleum Act, 1998, the Minister is empowered by the Parliament to make regulations prescribing model clauses which shall be incorporated in the licence.[89] The Minister exercises this power at his discretion as he can modify or exclude them in any particular case as he deems fit.

---

programme for the remaining life span of the licence and Frontier licence granted to encourage exploration work in difficult deep water areas. Supplementary seismic survey licences are also granted.

86. *Ibid.*, at 1063.
87. R. Higgins, 'Ten Years of State Involvement in the Petroleum Industry: The U.K. Experience', in International Bar Association, Energy Law Seminar, vol. 2 (1979), paper R-1, at p. 6.
88. Although safety issues has been removed from the model clauses and licenses by virtue of the offshore safety Act, 1992 because health and safety matters has been removed from the Department of Energy and transferred to the Health and Safety Commission and Executive. Also Royalty payment has been stopped since 1 January 2003 by the Government. However, other countries like Nigeria, Canada, Australia and Netherlands are still charging royalty and safety matters remained an integral part of the licence conditions. See Daintith & Willoughby, 'U.K. Oil and Gas Law', at 1063.
89. The model clauses are contained in the following current regulations: The Petroleum licensing (Production) (Seaward Areas) Regulation 2008 (SI 2008/225), Petroleum (Production) (Landward Areas) Regulation 1995 (SI 1995/ 1436 Sch. 5 – Methane drainage licences); Petroleum Licensing (Exploration and Production) (Seaward and Landward Areas) Regulation 2004 (SI 2004/352); the Offshore Exploration (Petroleum, and Gas Storage and unloading) (Model Clauses) Regulations 2009 (SI 2009/2814); Petroleum (Production) (Landward Areas) Regulation 1995 (SI 1995/ 1436 Sch. 4 – Supplementary seismic survey licences).

Thus, it is evidently clear that much power of control is exercised by the Minister over the licensee by virtue of the model clauses and the regulations. Moreover, though the licence confers rights to explore and exploit hydrocarbons on the licensee, the degree of statutory obligations imposed on him at the same time is enormous. However, as pointed out by Professor Daintith, in spite of the importation of substantial regulatory flavour into the licence, the contractual element of the licence has not been displaced.[90]

However, the ability of the Minister to alter the terms of the licence unilaterally (which negates the general principles of contract law that requires mutual consent of parties to the contract before such alteration can be validly made) is detrimental to the contractual picture of a Production licence.[91] The unilateral alteration has pointed irresistibly to the fact that 'the obligations of some of the model clauses, while contractual in form, were regulatory in function'[92] In view of the above, it is arguable that a unilateral amendment of production licence may erode its contractual character even though it remains contractual in form.[93]

In *Nigeria*, the Petroleum Act of 1969 provides for a three stage rights system in respect of upstream petroleum operations. First, Oil exploration licence (OEL), second, Oil prospecting licence (OPL), and third, Oil mining lease (OML).[94] The focus of this research is on OML.[95] There is no difference between the rights granted by the OPL and

---

90. T. Daintith, 'The Petroleum Production Licence in the United Kingdom', in T. Daintith (ed.), 'The Legal Character of Petroleum Licences: A Comparative Study' (1981) 200 at 217.
91. In 1975 the UK Government enacted the Petroleum and Submarine Pipeline Act to secure unilateral alteration of the provisions of the existing production licences. Substantial alterations were made by introducing new obligations without compensation in regards to development programmes and depletion, and stricter limitations on assignments. In addition, in 1982 and 1987, the Oil and Gas (Enterprise) Act and the Petroleum Act were made respectively to amend the terms of existing licences. Several other unilateral changes ranging from administrative matters to matters of technical nature were also made in 1992, 1998 and 2008. Even though these later alterations imposed little or no burdens on the licensees, the contractual character of licenses requires that there should be 'bi-partisan acceptance of the legitimacy of unilateral alteration of licences'. See Daintith & Willoughby, *supra* n. 88 at 1071.
92. Daintith & Willoughby, 'U.K. Oil and Gas Law', at 1070.
93. Daintith, 'The Petroleum Production Licence in the United Kingdom', in T. Daintith (ed.), 'The Legal Character of Petroleum Licences: A Comparative Study', at 217.
94. Section 2 (1) Petroleum Act, 1969. Oil Exploration Licence (OEL) is granted for one year duration to company to explore for petroleum in areas where there is no existing Oil Prospecting License (OPL) or Oil Mining Lease (OML). The Licence confers no exclusive rights over the areas granted to the Licensee in that other companies can be granted OEL or OPL or OML over the same concession area already granted to the Licensee. It does not confer any right to the grant of an OPL or OML. OPL on the other hand confers exclusive rights of surface and subsurface exploration for the production of petroleum in an area not more than 2,590 sq. km. (1,000 sq. miles) in size. The duration of an OPL is five years including any periods of renewal. For the Deep water blocks and Frontier Basins, the exploration period is 10 years, broken into two 5 years. The holder of an OPL may carry away and dispose of petroleum won during prospecting operations, subject to the fulfillment of obligations imposed upon him by or under the Petroleum Act (including any special terms or conditions imposed under para. 34 of the 1st Schedule to the Petroleum Act) or by the Petroleum Profits Tax Act or any other law imposing taxation in respect of petroleum.
95. This is because OEL neither confers on the licensee exclusive right nor right to get petroleum. In addition, it has become unnecessary to grant OEL to any company again in Nigeria since virtually all the Petroleum potential areas in Nigeria has been fully explored and seismic data has been generated over them. For OPL, even though it confers on its holder exclusive right to carry out exploration activities at the subsurface and the right to produce and dispose of petroleum

the OML except that the latter is granted for production purposes and for a longer duration. Consequently, our analysis will centre on the legal character and the nature of interest of the holder of an OML.[96] The Act provides[97] that the Minister may grant a lease, to be known as an oil mining lease, 'to search for, win, work, carry away and dispose of petroleum.' It further provides that an OML may be granted only to the holder of an oil prospecting licence who has – (a) satisfied all the conditions imposed on the licence or otherwise imposed on him by this Act, and (b) discovered oil in commercial quantities.[98]

The term of an oil mining lease is twenty years, but may be renewed in accordance with the petroleum Act. The holder of an OML has 'the exclusive right within the leased area to conduct exploration and prospecting operations and to win, get, work, store, carry away, transport, export or otherwise treat petroleum discovered in or under the leased area.' A renewal of an OML is granted by the Minister upon the application of the holder 'made not less than 12 months before the expiration of the lease either in respect of the whole of the leased area or any particular part if the lessee has paid all rent and royalties due and has also performed all obligations under the lease.'

The legal character of the OML and the nature of interests of its holder are not defined in the Petroleum Act. The authorisation granted for production operations is called a 'lease'. It applies to both onshore and offshore including deep offshore petroleum operations in Nigeria. Under the common law, a 'lease is both a contract and, in most cases, an estate.'[99] It is as an agreement between two or more persons creating or granting an interest in land for a fixed period (usually but not necessarily) in consideration of rent. The lessee enjoys the use and occupation of the land and exclusive possession thereof. The OML granted by the Petroleum Act, however differs from the Common law lease. This is because the grant of an OML creates a mineral lease which permits the holder to use the land to explore, win and dispose of the petroleum discovered under the lease area for a definite term subject to the payment of rents, royalty and profits tax.[100]

---

worn and saved in the process, it is usually granted for a short period of five years (including any period of renewal) except for the deep water blocks and frontier basins which period is 10 years, broken into two 5 years. See Deep Offshore and Inland Basin Production Sharing Contract Decree, 1994.

96. However, it must be noted that the offshore and onshore licensing regime are the same in Nigeria. The three types of licences apply to both areas and the rights granted by the licences are the same for both areas.
97. Paragraphs 8, 9,10, 11 and 13 (1) of the first schedule to the Petroleum Act, 1969.
98. Oil is deemed to have been discovered in commercial quantities by the holder of an oil prospecting licence if the Minister, upon evidence adduced by the licensee, is satisfied that the licensee is capable of producing at least 10,000 barrels per day of crude oil from the licensed area. Production of 25,000 barrels per day will be required as the minimum commercial production level for conversion of a Deep offshore OPL to OML.
99. Megarry & Wade, 'The Law of Real Property', 7th edn (Sweet & Maxwell, 2008), at 729. See also pp. 76-77 above for a discussion on the legal nature of oil and gas lease in US.
100. It may be renewed by the minister. The term of the renewal is not however provided anywhere in the Petroleum laws. It is submitted that as long as the lessee pay rents and royalties and performed all obligations under the lease, the lease will continue indefinitely until when production ceased or when it becomes uneconomical to produce.

The form of the lease is usually by deed granted by the minister to the company lessee and signed by both of them. The form is provided in the schedule to the Petroleum (Drilling & Production) Regulations of 1969 as 'Form D'.[101] The 'Form D' provides that:

> This Oil Mining Lease is granted to ... of... for a term of ...years commencing on the...day of... to search for, win, work, carry away and dispose of all petroleum in, under or throughout the lands described in the schedule hereto and delineated in red in the plan attached.

In form and substance, reinforced by the term used ('lease'), it can be concluded that, like the production licence in UK, an OML in Nigeria creates a contract between the Minister and the lessee. However, wide regulatory powers are granted by the Act to the Minister. Specifically the Act empowers the Minister in sections 8 and 9 to supervise all operations carried on under the licences and leases which include powers of summons or arrest of offenders of the Act, suspension of operations for breach of the provisions of the laws and good oil field practice, and to make regulations prescribing anything requiring to be prescribed for the purposes of the Act including matters dealing with safety, conservation, environmental, crude oil measurements, construction, maintenance and operations of installation used in petroleum operations. The Minister under this section regulates and prescribes fees, rents and royalties payable by the licensees or lessees. All these matters are not incorporated in the lease unlike the repealed Mineral oils Act of 1914 in which all the contractual and regulatory terms are set out in the lease or licence documents itself. These matters are subject of separate regulations made by the Minister under the Petroleum Act of 1969. Therefore, contractual matters are separated from regulatory matters with respect to OPL and OML in Nigeria. This is contrary to the practice in UK where the Petroleum Act of 1998 empowers the minister to incorporate directly the model clauses contained in the regulations to the production licence. In spite of this difference however, the fact that the acreage is awarded and subsequently confirmed by a grant of licence or lease pursuant to an Act of parliament, is ample evidence that an OML is a contract with statutory flavour. This is further reinforced by the fact that matters concerning its renewal, assignment, surrender, relinquishment and terminations are governed by statutory provisions. The lease is also granted subject to the Petroleum Act and the regulations in force or which may come into force throughout the duration of the lease.[102]

Some decided cases on cancellation of Petroleum licences in Nigeria have pointed to this assertion even though the legal character of the licences was not directly in issue.[103]

In *FGN & Others v. Zebra Energy Ltd.*,[104] the FGN offered OPL 248 to the respondent in accordance with the Indigenous Exploration Programme initiated by the FGN in 1991 by virtue of the Petroleum Act of 1969. The offer was subject to certain

101. Cap P10 LFN, 2004.
102. Form 'D' of the Petroleum (Drilling and Production) Regulations 1969, Cap P10 LFN, 2004.
103. In May 1999, the FGN cancelled eleven OPLs issued by the previous Military regime to private companies. Some of the affected companies went to court to challenge the cancellation.
104. [2002] 12 S.C (Pt. II) 136.

conditions specified in the letter of award. These conditions, payment of the application fees of (N50,000), bidding fees (USD 10,000) and signature bonus (USD 20 million), amongst other things were to be satisfied within a given period of time. The respondent accepted the offer and commenced performance of these 'conditions' by paying fully the application and bidding fees. The respondent however made part payment of USD 1 million leaving a balance of USD 19 million. The respondent had seven days left to comply fully with the conditions of the offer (i.e., payment of the USD 19 million) when the FGN cancelled the Licence. The Supreme Court, confirming the judgment of both the High court and Court of Appeal held that there was a binding contract between the FGN and the respondent since the respondent has accepted the offer of the Licence and has commenced performance of the 'conditions' of the offer. (The court interpreted the 'conditions' as 'terms' of the contract). Both the Court of Appeal and the Supreme Court declared that:

> There is no doubt that the granting of an OPL by the Government is governed by statute; the Petroleum Act Cap. 350 LFN, 1990 .... There is no doubt that the contractual relation created by the parties herein is statutory and the appellant are bound to comply with the statutory provisions which apply to govern the contract.[105]

From this dictum, it can be argued that where the legal character of an OPL or OML is directly in issue, the court would most likely construe it as creating contractual relation between the FGN and the Licensee and that such contractual relationship is governed by the Petroleum Act. Similarly in the case of *Oil and Gas Ltd v. Ministry of Petroleum Resources*,[106] the plaintiff complied with and performed fully the conditions of the award of OPL 249 within the time stipulated in the letter of award. The plaintiff was thereafter issued the OPL (Exhibit 'H') and was directed by the regulatory authority to mobilise resources and start operations on the block. The licence was thereafter cancelled by the government. The Federal high court had no difficulty in finding that there exists a valid contract between the FGN and the plaintiff in respect of OPL 249. The court further declared that:

> on the proposition of the law which I have referred to above, as well as legal authorities, 'Exhibit H' (the oil prospecting Licence No. 249) is the contract between the plaintiff and the first defendant herein and it is that which spells out the rights and liabilities of the parties to the contract. It is pertinent to state here that 'Exhibit H' is granted subject to the petroleum Act 1969 and the regulations thereunder, then in force and which come to force during the continuance of the licence. The legal effect of this provision therefore, is that the provisions of the petroleum Act 1969 and any regulations made thereunder shall be read into the contract – 'Exhibit H'.[107]

105. *Ibid.*, at pp. 152-153.
106. Unreported suit no. FHC/L/CS/481/2000. See also *NNPC & Anor v. Famfa Oil Ltd* (2012) 17 NWLR at 148 the acquisition by Government of the 5/6 of the 50% participating interests of Famfa in OML 127 was declared null and void and contrary to sections 44 (1) of the Constitution because of failure of the Governement to negotiate with Famfa and pay compensation before it exercised its right of acquisition under the Petroleum laws and regulations.
107. *Ibid.*, at 46 of the Judgment.

In *Canada*, licences, leases and permits are granted by the Canadian Government to companies to prospect for petroleum resources owned by the Government. For example the Canada Oil and Gas Land Regulations, 1961(Federal) and also the Newfoundland and Labrador Petroleum Regulations 1977 (Newfoundland) provided for a two stage rights system – first, exploration permit and second, oil and gas lease. They are granted by the Minister by virtue of the power conferred on him by an enabling legislation and regulation made thereunder. The term upon which such interests are granted is generally spelt out in the legislation and the regulations.[108]

Some decided cases have however, shown that Petroleum licence creates contractual relationship with the crown, the nature of which depends on the terms of the individual licences and the legislation under which it was granted.[109] Harrison has argued that in Canada, interests in crown petroleum arise from contract and do give rise to vested or acquired interests.[110] He contended further that the wordings of the instruments, e.g., the Alberta Crown petroleum and natural gas lease showed that they are contracts. As regards Permits, he argued that the Federal and Newfoundland permits do create contractual rights.[111] He said that a permit is an option to acquire a lease and since a lease granted by the crown is a contract, it follows that an option to acquire contractual interest can be characterised as contractual.[112] Furthermore, since the legislation under which a permit is granted, imposes contractual obligations on the permittee (e.g., the obligation to carry out a work programme set out in the Schedule attached to the permit), and becomes contractually binding on the permittee, it means that the obligation flows from the permit and not the regulation. Moreover, the permit contains several stipulations especially in Newfoundland that the permittee undertakes to carry out a particular work programme, to relinquish certain areas covered by the permit, and to spend fixed sum of money in training research and development programmes. If these undertakings constitute contractual obligation binding on the permittee, it then follows that there must be a correlative contractual rights binding on the crown as the other contracting party.[113]

Above are very compelling reasons that support an argument in favour of the contractual form and character of petroleum licences – permits and leases – granted by the crown in Canada in respect of onshore oil and gas resources.

108. Rowland J. Harrison, 'The Legal Character of Petroleum Production Licences in Canada', in T. Daintith (ed.) The Legal Character of Petroleum Licensing: A Comparative Study' (1981) at 129.
109. *Ibid.*, at 102 and 131 citing *Spooner Oils Ltd. v. Turner valley Gas conservation Board* [1933] 4 DLR 545; *In re Timber Regulations* [1935] 1 WWR 607.
110. *Ibid.*, at 133. He cited the cases of *Spooner oil Ltd v. Turner Valley Gas Conservation Board* [1893] 4 DLR 545 and the cases following it to show that the rights conferred by petroleum and natural gas lease were contractual right. Also in the case of *In Re Timber Regulations* [1935] 1 WWR 607 at 613, the permittee's rights was regarded as arising from its consensual arrangement with the crown rather than from an exercise of legislative capacity by the crown. Also the permittee's right to cut for sale and sell timber off the land was itself not merely a licence, but an interest in lands. Moreover, the wordings of the instruments in some cases show that they are contract e. g. the Alberta crown petroleum and natural gas lease.
111. *Ibid.*, 140.
112. *Ibid.*, at 136.
113. *Ibid.*, at 139.

In *Australia*, under the Offshore Petroleum and Greenhouse Gas Storage Act 2006[114] (as amended) (OPGGSA), three types of licences are granted to companies in respect of offshore petroleum operations, namely Petroleum Exploration Permits (PEP), Petroleum Retention Lease (PRL) and Petroleum Production Licence (PPL).

The PEP authorises the permittee, to explore for petroleum in the permit area; to recover petroleum on an appraisal basis in the permit area; and to carry on such operations, and execute such works, in the permit area as are necessary for those purposes.[115] The rights conferred on the permittee are subject to the provisions of the Act and the regulations. It is a criminal offence to explore for petroleum in the offshore areas without such permit and the penalty for such offence is five years imprisonment.[116]

The PRL confers the same rights like PEP on the permittee except that PRL will only be granted to a holder of PEL or a holder of a life-of-field production licence over the block. Moreover, it will only be granted over a block if the block contains petroleum though, the recovery of petroleum is not currently commercially viable, but is likely to become commercially viable within fifteen years.[117] The rights conferred on the lessee by the PRL are subject to the Act and the regulations.[118]

The PPL authorises the licensee, to recover petroleum in the licence area; to recover petroleum from the licence area in another area to which the licensee has lawful access for that purpose; and to explore for petroleum in the licence area; and to carry on such operations, and execute such works, in the licence area as are necessary for those purposes.[119] The rights conferred on the licensee by or under the licence are subject to the Act and the regulations. It is a criminal offence to carry out petroleum recovery operations in the offshore areas without such licence and the penalty for such offence is five years imprisonment.[120]

It is to be noted that the licensing regime and the granting clause under the PSLA are the same with that of the OPGGSA. They both contain a two- stage system of rights - exploration permits and production licence except that petroleum retention lease has been added in the OPGGSA. This is unlike UK and US but it is similar to the position in Nigeria, Netherlands and Canada. The rights and obligations of a permittee, lessee or licensee are well spelt out in OPGGSA as have been shown above. They are neither contained in contract nor regulations made by the minister. The provisions making it a criminal offence to engage in exploration or production of petroleum without a license, and the circumstances under which PSLA was enacted shows that PSLA is a system of authorisations rather than a system based on property and contract.[121] They

114. Act No. 14 of 2006. It added extensive provisions on carbon sequestration which were not in the PSLA.
115. *Ibid.*, section 98 (1).
116. *Ibid.*, section 97 (1).
117. *Ibid.*, section 136. This lease allows retention of gas field without development pending when lessee is able to find market for the gas.
118. *Ibid.*, section 135.
119. *Ibid.*, section 161.
120. *Ibid.*, section 160.
121. Daintith, 'A Critical Evaluation of the Petroleum (Submerged Lands) Act as a Regulatory Regime', at 95.

are also granted subject to the terms and conditions as the designated Authority thinks fit and specifies in the permit or licence. The granting clauses of the permit, lease or licence also made the rights conferred on the holder subject to the provisions of the Act. The contractual character of the production licence has not been judicially determined in Australia unlike the exploration permit. On the contrary, court's decisions are numerous with regards to the legal nature of mineral lease.[122] Therefore, the legal character of the permits and licences should be decided by interpreting the relevant provisions of the PSLA (OPGGSA).[123] After reviewing the provisions of the PSLA, Professor Crommelin had argued that the Act gives no power to the Designated Authority to conclude contracts with prospective licensee or permittee and as such the rights and obligations conferred under the Act are statutory rather than contractual. However, he expressed doubt in this conclusion given the lack of decided authority on the issue.[124] In spite of this flaw however, a permittee or licensee may still be able to resist administrative interference with his rights. The legal character of the rights will only determine the types of remedies he may claim from the court.[125]

In *Netherlands*, under the Mining Act of 1810, exploration for oil and gas or coal (mine) is permitted only under a concession. However with the passage of the Mineral exploration Act of 1967, three different licences are required for upstream petroleum operations - Reconnaissance work, Exploration drilling and Exploration of the minerals.[126]

The legal character of the concession granted under the Mining Act 1810 can be regarded as a conveyance of the oil and gas in situ to the concessionaire by virtue of section 19 of the Act.[127] These concessions have been converted to production licences under the Mineral Act of 2003 and ownership rights of the licensee to the mine are preserved. This means that the converted production licence still operates as a conveyance of the oil and gas in place.

A two stage licensing regime applies under the new Mining Act of 2003. The first is exploration licence and the second, production licence. The grant of a production licence extinguishes exploration licence even if the latter has not expired at the time of the grant.[128] By virtue of Article 7 (1) both licences are exclusive in the sense that no other licence will be granted at the same time in respect of the same areas covered by the licences. It is also prohibited to carry out without licence any activities for which these licences are required.[129] Exploration licence is awarded through competitive and transparent procedures while Production licence is granted to a holder of exploration

122. *Cudgen Rutile No. 2 Pty Ltd v. Chalk* [1975] A.C. 520.
123. Crommelin, 'Legal Character of Petroleum Production Licences in Australia', in T. Daintith (ed.), The Legal Character of Petroleum Licences: A Comparative Study', at 74.
124. *Ibid.*, at 75.
125. *Ibid.*, at 77. He opined that if the legal character of the licence is contractual, damages and specific performance will be the appropriate remedy but if it is statutory, it could be one of mandamus, certiorarai or prohibition or declaration or injunction.
126. Martha Roggenkamp, 'The Award of Concessions for Onshore Petroleum Operations in the Netherlands', [1987/88] 7 OGLTR 199 at 200.
127. See p. 88 above for a discussion on the interpretation of section 19.
128. Section 10 Mining Act 2003 as amended.
129. *Ibid.*, section 6.

licence who has discovered petroleum that is exploitable economically.[130] Though this exploitability criterion is not defined in the Act, the provisions of the previous Act may be of guidance. The criteria provided by the previous Act include price of oil, the dollar and the distance to the existing infrastructures. It is submitted that the quantity of the petroleum in place will be considered as well. The licence will specify the activities, the period of its validity and the areas for which it is applicable. The areas delineated shall specify the limits of the surface area and unless otherwise stated in the licence, the area shall consist of the surface area indicated and its subsoil.[131] This is important because where the limits of surface area have been specified; the limitation shall equally apply to its subsoil except if the licence states otherwise. The holder of a licence can assign the whole or part of the licence to another party subject however to the permission of the Minister.[132] The minister may also withdraw a licence on ground stipulated in Section 21 of the Act. The licence may be withdrawn if the licensee is carrying out activities without conforming to the licence or not observing the rules applying to him. Before withdrawal on these grounds however, the minister must have issued warnings to the licensee and there must have been repeated infringements in spite of such warnings.[133] A holder of production licence may also request a withdrawal of his licence and so also a holder of exploration licence can surrender his licence.[134] The State, through its Agent (usually a company) can participate in the upstream activities (both in onshore and offshore). This will give rise to a joint venture agreement between the State company and the licensee. Here the State is not a licence holder but a shareholder. The Act provides that the participating interest shall be 40/60 in favour of the licence holder.[135] The participation could either be at exploration or production stage or both. However, State participation at exploration stage in the offshore has to be at the request of the licence holder, which request the State will normally accept in practice.

From the wordings of section 6 – without permission from Our Minister, it is prohibited to explore for minerals; to produce minerals – it is clear that exploration and production of minerals are allowed by permission or licence. What is the legal character of such licence? It is instructive to note that the minister cannot amend the licence unilaterally once granted. It can only be amended at the request of the licensee.[136] This has pointed irresistibly to their contractual nature. The argument canvassed by Rowland J Harrison in support of the contractual nature of the oil and gas permits issued by the Canadian Government is also very relevant to the question of the legal character of an exploration licence or production licence.[137]

130. *Ibid.*, sections 7 and 15.
131. *Ibid.*, section 11 (1) (2) (3).
132. *Ibid.*, section 20.
133. *Ibid.*, section 21 (1) (2).
134. *Ibid.*, section 21(3) (4).
135. *Ibid.*, section 82.
136. *Ibid.*, Article 18 (1).
137. Harrison, 'The Legal Character of Petroleum Production Licences in Canada', in T. Daintith (ed.), The Legal Character of Petroleum Licensing: A Comparative Study', at 129.

3.3 The Nature of Interests Granted by Petroleum Production Licence

The nature of interests conferred on licensee by the petroleum production licence in the onshore and offshore areas will be considered separately

3.3.1 *Onshore*

In the UK, the Petroleum Act of 1998 empowers the Crown to grant oil and gas licences 'to search and bore for and get' petroleum within the on shore, territorial sea and the United Kingdom Continental Shelf (UKCS). Clause 2 of the Petroleum (Production) (Seaward Areas) Regulation 1998 (as amended) provides that:

> Minister, in exercise of the powers conferred upon him by the Act hereby grants to the licensee exclusive licence and liberty during the continuance of this licence and subject to the provisions hereof *to search and bore for, and get, Petroleum* in the sea bed and subsoil under the seaward area.

This granting clause is identical to the one in the landward exploration and development licences that applies to the landward areas. With respect to the Onshore and Territorial sea, it is very clear that the Crown has ownership right to the petroleum in situ. The landward petroleum licences granted by the Crown in consequent of this can be said to be proprietary.[138] It can be logically deduced that the crown can by the licence transfer all of her rights or limited property rights to the licensee.

In *Nigeria* the granting clause of an OML provides that:

> This Oil Mining Lease is granted to ... of... for a term of... years commencing on the... day of ... to search for, win, work, carry away and dispose of all petroleum in, under or throughout the lands described in the schedule hereto and delineated in red in the plan attached.[139]

It is to be noted that the granting clause of the OML is the same for both the onshore and the offshore leases. It is also to be noted that the interests of the FRN in respect of both situations are full ownership by the combined effect of the provisions of the Constitution, and the Petroleum Act. The FRN, having vests in its self, ownership rights of all minerals, mineral oils and natural gas under the lands in Nigeria, could be said to have severed these resources from the land. This negates in practical terms the argument that oil under the ground is incapable of ownership because of its fugacious character. With respect to the onshore, ownership of the surface and the underneath minerals is thus separated. The surface belongs to the land owner which in most cases in Nigeria are the communities while the underneath minerals belong to the FRN. In the Territorial sea, the subsoil minerals, the sea bed and the waters belong to the FRN. This scenario is similar to the ownership in place theory as practiced in majority of States in the US. Similarly in the offshore (EEZ), the minerals in the subsoil have been severed

138. Greg Gordon, 'Petroleum Licensing', in Gregg Gordon, et al., 'Oil and Gas Law: Current Practice and Emerging Trends' (Dundee University Press, 2007), at 30.
139. See section 1 (2) of the Petroleum Act, 1969 and Form 'D' in the Schedule to the Petroleum (Drilling and Production) Regulations, 1969.

from the sea bed and same vested in the FRN by virtue of the provisions of the laws mentioned above.[140]

The question that arises is whether by the above granting clause in the OML, the FRN could be said to have conveyed to the lessee, the same interest it has in the resources or a lesser interest. If it is a lesser interest, what is the nature of such interest, is it proprietary or otherwise? There is no judicial decision yet on this issue apart from the licence revocation cases referred to above and from which we have seen that the legal character of the licence could be said to be contractual although regulated by statute.

One thing that is clear is that it is neither a bare licence nor an ordinary lease between landlord and tenant. The provisions of paragraphs 8, (a) (b) and 11 of the first Schedule to the Petroleum Act 1969 are very instructive here. They provide that an OML may be granted only to the holder of an oil prospecting licence who has satisfied all the conditions imposed on the licence or otherwise imposed on him by the Act, and have *discovered oil in commercial quantities*. Also, that the lessee of an oil mining lease shall have the exclusive right within the leased area to conduct exploration and prospecting operations and to '*win, get, work, store, carry away, transport, export or otherwise treat petroleum discovered in or under the leased area*'. The term of an OML is twenty years which may continue thereafter indefinitely so long as the lessee continues to pay rents and royalties and as long as commercial production is possible.

The provisions above clearly showed that an OML is granted to a licensee who has discovered oil in commercial quantity. In other words, the lessee must show that a given quantity of petroleum that is commercially exploitable exists underneath the licence area before OML can be granted. The grant of an OML therefore, confirms that a commercially exploitable hydrocarbon exists underneath lessee's lease area. It is in respect of this quantity of petroleum that the OML is granted to enable the lessee to 'win, work, store and carry away ...' etc. The discovered petroleum while still under the ground qualifies as a real interest as it is connected to land.[141] The OML is therefore

140. One other thing that needs to be mentioned is the fact that the wordings of the granting clause above is slightly different from the one contained in the leases granted pursuant to the repealed Mineral Oils Act of 1914. The granting clause of these leases confers on the lessees 'all or any petroleum lying or being within or under the leased areas described in the lease'. This could be said to have granted to the lessee ownership right to petroleum in situ. Some of these leases are still subsisting as they have been saved by the Savings and Transitional provisions contained in the Fourth Schedule to the Petroleum Act. However, the leases are now to be governed by the provisions of the Petroleum Act and to any regulations made thereunder except matters relating to their duration, rents and royalties and terms and conditions which the Minister in his discretion certifies that should continue. The implication of this is that the terms and conditions contained in those leases granted pursuant to the 1914 Act (with the exemption of the terms mentioned in the Transitions and Savings provision above) are to be read in line with the provisions of the 1969 Act and regulations made thereunder. The Minister has made a new regulation providing for a new granting clause as contained in Form 'D' of the Schedule to the Petroleum (Drilling and Production) Regulations of 1969. It is submitted that the granting clause of the subsisting leases of the pre-1969 Act will have to be read in line with the granting clause specified in the 1969 regulations.

141. Roderick Paisley, 'Aspects of Land Law Relative to the Transportation of Oil and Gas in Scotland', in Gordon et al., 'Petroleum Licensing', in Gregg Gordon et al., 'Oil and Gas Law:

a conveyance to the licensee of the petroleum discovered by him at the time of the grant.

This is more than a *profit a prendre.*[142] Thus, from the wordings of the granting clause, a full ownership interests can be said to have been granted to the holder of an OML and such interest is an interest in land. The duration is also indefinite as it is renewed as long as commercial production of oil continues and the licensee pays rents and royalties. In the *Oil and Gas Nig. Ltd.'s case* (*supra*), the court regarded the OPL 249 granted to the plaintiff as property and that before such property is taken away by the government, the licensee must be given fair hearing. Also in the *NNPC & Anor v. Famfa Oil Ltd* (*supra*) the acquisition by Government of the 5/6 of the 50% participating interests of Famfa in OML 127 was declared null and void and contrary to sections 44 (1) of the Constitution because of failure to negotiate with Famfa and compensation paid before the Government exercise its right under the Petroleum laws and regulations.

In *Netherlands*, under Article 5 of the Mining Act of 1810, Mines can only be exploited by a deed of concession. Article 19 provides that the grant of a concession creates a new property different from the surface and on which new mortgages may be taken. This provision has been interpreted as granting concessionaires ownership rights to the mines. This has been confirmed by virtue of the combined provisions of Articles 143 (2) (a) and 143 (4) of the 2003 Mining Act which after converting the previously held concessions to production licences also provides that the holders of such converted production licences shall continue to be the owner of the mines throughout the duration of the licence. This means that the nature of the interests of the holder of a production licence granted under the 1810 Mining Act in Netherlands as regards onshore minerals is full ownership. However, the production licence granted after 2003 Mining Act might attract different interests especially with regards to minerals situated at a depth of more than 100 metres. Article 3 (1) of the Mining Act, 2003 vests ownership of minerals beyond that depth in the State and that petroleum produced at the depth under a production licence is transferred to the licence-holder at the moment of production. It is also prohibited to carry out without licence any activities for which these licences are required. In spite of this provision however, there are other provisions of the Act which showed that the production licence is not a bare licence or merely statutory. By virtue of Article 7 (1) both licences are exclusive in the sense that no other licence will be granted at the same time in respect of the same areas covered by the licences. Exploration licence is awarded through competitive and transparent procedures while Production licence is granted to a holder of exploration licence who has discovered petroleum that is exploitable economically.[143] The grant of production licence confirms that economically exploitable oil has been discovered by

Current Practice and Emerging Trends', at 412. He listed the three most suitable real rights in Scotland and most legal systems as (a) ownership, (b) lease and (c) Praedial Sevitude.

142. Defined as 'an incorporeal interest in land authorising entry upon a tract of land and severance and removal of a part of the corpus of the land'. See Williams & Meyers, *supra* n. 1 at 18; see also Megarry & Wade, 'The Law of Real Property', at 729. See the Nigerian case of *NNPC &Anor v. Famfa Oil Ltd* (2012) 17 NWLR 148 at paras H p. 196 – A p. 197.

143. Articles 7 and 15 of Mining Act 2003.

the licensee. This means that an economic and legal (real) interest connected to land and associated with licensee has been identified to be present. The production licence can therefore be regarded as conveying an interest in land. Even if not full ownership, it is proprietary in the nature of *profit a prendre*. However, under the Civil law the definition of property is limited to movable and immovable things. Therefore, a production licence or lease is not regarded as property but contractual rights. As has been held in the *Unocal's case* (*supra*), it confers subjective right to the licensee in respect of the petroleum underlying his licence. This right can be enforced against third party and hence it qualifies as an in rem right and as such analogous to a proprietary right under the common law.

3.3.2 *Offshore*

3.3.2.1 Theoretical Analysis

International law[144] confers 'sovereign right' on the State to explore and exploit the resources of the Continental Shelf (C.S.) rather than 'sovereignty'. As a result, controversy has mounted on the precise nature of not only the rights of the State but also the rights the State can confer on a licensee through production licence. The question one may ask is what is the composition of the above 'sovereign rights' given to the coastal State by these Conventions especially with regards to the non-living resources? In other words, is there a limit to the coastal States power of granting property rights in the continental shelf?

Since the time of Grotius's Mare Liberum of 1609, the idea that the high seas belong to no one and therefore were beyond the jurisdiction of any nation had gained momentum. Spanish and other nations' claim to exclusive rights of ownership and navigation in large portions of the world's oceans were supported by the Selden's Mare Clausum of 1631. The concept of the freedom of the high seas gained serious support by the end of the eighteenth century and by the beginning of the twentieth century, a successful campaign was launched in support of the concept. This was as a result of new technical innovations in the areas of exploitation of the resources of the Continental shelf.[145] In September 1945, President Harry Truman made a Proclamation that attracted the attention of the International community to the concept of national

144. Article 2 (1) of United Nation Conference on the Law of the Sea 1958 (1958 Geneva Convention) provides that: 'The coastal State exercises over the continental shelf sovereign rights for the purpose of exploring it and exploiting its natural resources' (2) 'the rights referred to in paragraph 1 of the Article are exclusive in the sense that if the coastal State does not explore the continental shelf or exploit its natural resources, no one may undertake these activities, or make a claim to the continental shelf, without the express consent of the Coastal State' (3) 'The rights of the coastal State over the continental shelf do not depend on the occupation, effective or notional, or on any express proclamation'. Article 77(1) (2) (3) of the United Nation Law of the Sea Convention contain identical provisions with Article 2(1) (2) (3) of 1958 Geneva Convention.

145. Van Penick, 'Legal Framework in the Canadian Offshore', (2001) Dalhousie L.J. 24: 5 at p. 5 citing P.C. Jessup, 'The Law of Territorial Waters and Maritime Jurisdiction' (New York: G. A. Jennings Co., 1927), ch. 1.

jurisdiction over the C.S.[146] He claimed a limited jurisdiction over the Us's C.S in order to preserve the principle of the freedom of the high sea hence the addition of the phrase to the proclamation '... *The character as high seas of the waters above the continental shelf and the right to their free and unimpeded navigation are in no way thus affected'*. The United States who had canvassed the use of the word 'exclusive' to qualify the nature of the State's rights to explore its C.S was persuaded by international community to accept the word 'sovereign' when there was an express provision confirming freedom of the high seas.

Furthermore, at the drafting stage of the provisions the adoption of the word 'Sovereign rights' as opposed to 'sovereignty' was a compromise position. Some States favour the territoriality of the C.S in order to avoid it being adjudged *res nullius* and to prevent non-coastal States from laying claim to it. For example, the UK government had argued that its rights over the C.S were the same as its rights over land Territory.[147] These States preferred to give rights of sovereignty to coastal States over the C.S.[148]

Some commentators have also remarked that these rights belonged to coastal State *ipso jure* and as such the terminology used is inconsequential.[149] Only one State, Denmark was said to have objected to the term sovereignty.[150] Subsequently, at the drafting stage opinion were divided into two camps. One was in favour of the term sovereignty and the other was in favour of the word 'control' and 'jurisdiction'. 'Sovereign rights' was however adopted as compromise to diffuse tension between the two opposing camps. Moreover, it was noted that the expression 'sovereign rights' should be adopted because it gave coastal State property rights over the C.S and because it avoided the ambiguity that the words 'control' and 'jurisdiction' might create in the future.[151] The term 'sovereign right' was finally adopted after much debate at the Geneva conference.[152]

With this right, a coastal State can exercise the power of granting petroleum licences, construction of artificial islands and drilling for purposes of production of petroleum.[153]

The exercise of these rights with respect to the C.S does not depend on occupation or proclamation. It automatically attaches to the coastal State.[154] These rights exist *ab initio* and it is also exclusive to Coastal State. This means no other State may claim to

146. See 4 Whiteman, 'Digest of International Law', 75 at 756 (Washington, D.C., 1968). He declared that 'Having concern for the urgency of conserving and prudently utilizing its natural resources, the Government of the United States regards the natural resources of the subsoil and sea bed of the continental shelf beneath the high seas but contiguous to the coasts of the United States as appertaining to the united States, subject to its jurisdiction and control ... .'
147. Barnes, 'Property Rights and Natural Resources' (Oxford and Portland, Oregon, 2009), at 273 citing 1953 Ybk ILC, vol. II, 13.
148. *Ibid.*, referring to 1950 Ybk ILC, vol. I, 214-5.
149. *Ibid.*, referring to (1950) Ybk ILC, vol. I, 214-5.
150. O'Connell, 'The International Law of the Sea' (Oxford: Clarendon Press, 1982) at 479.
151. Barnes, 'Property Rights and Natural Resources', at p. 273 referring to (1956) Ybk ILC, vol. I, 140.
152. See UNCLOS 1, Official Records, vol. 1, 14.
153. Articles 60, 80 and 81 of UNLOSC.
154. Articles 2 (3) of Geneva Convention; 77(3) of UNLOSC.

exercise rights to exploration and exploitation over the shelf without the consent of the coastal State even if the coastal State does not make a claim to it.[155]

Therefore, the use of the word 'sovereign rights' as opposed to 'sovereignty' cannot limit coastal State's right or power to implement or grant property rights in the C.S areas. It is also from these rights that the Coastal State derives its power to regulate the terms and conditions upon which exploration and exploitation of petroleum are conducted and standards and safety rules enforced.

It can therefore, be inferred that the use of the word 'sovereign' to qualify the coastal State's rights in the natural resources of its C.S was intended not to restrict its power to develop the natural resources but confine the power to the resources alone as well as to preserve the principle of the freedom of high seas, the water column and the superjacent air space. This restriction does not change its essential character as even restrictions on property use are also common within the domestic sphere.[156]

It is therefore, arguable that the use of the wider word 'sovereign' as opposed to the narrower word 'exclusive' has given a coastal State the power needed to develop the natural resources contained in its C.S. Thus International law could be said to have accorded a Coastal State real property rights in oil and Gas in situ in its C.S as long as the coastal State preserves the freedom of the high sea, the water column and the superjacent air space.[157] This principle of Coastal State rights over its continental shelf received Judicial accolade in the *North Sea Continental Shelf Cases*[158] and was followed in the case of *Aegean Sea Continental Shelf.*[159] This was why one commentator has rightly pointed out that the 'ICJ has endorsed the propensity of 'sovereign rights' to crystallise as 'sovereignty'[160]

There is evidence that some other countries have even claimed greater rights over their C.S and even sovereignty over the Shelf, water column, the submarine areas, and

155. Articles 2 (2) of Geneva Convention; 77(2) of UNLOSC.
156. T. Daintith, 'Correlative Rights in Oil Reservoirs on the United Kingdom Continental Shelf', in 'European Offshore Petroleum Conference and Exhibition' (1978), at p. 74.
157. F.V.W. (Van) Penick, 'Offshore Financing: The Nature of Security Interests in Oil and Gas Projects on the Continental Shelf', (1985) Alta L. Rev. 23: 33, at p. 33.
158. (1969) ICJ Rep. 3 19 at 23. The court stated that:

> the right of the coastal State in respect of the area of continental shelf that constitutes a natural prolongation of its land territory into and under the sea exist ipso facto and *abinitio* by virtue of its sovereignty over the land, and as an extension of it in an exercise of sovereign rights for the purpose of exploring the sea bed and exploiting its natural resources. In short there is an inherent right'. The court further observed that 'the submarine areas concerned may be deemed to be actually part of the territory over which the coastal State already has dominion.

159. (1978) ICJ Rep.3, at 36. Here the court stated that 'legally the coastal State's rights over the continental shelf are both appurtenant to and directly derived from State's sovereignty over the territory abutting on that continental shelf. ...In short, continental shelf rights are legally both an emanation from and automatic adjunct of the territorial sovereignty of the coastal State. It follows that the territorial regime – the territorial status – of a coastal State comprises, "ipso jure", the rights of exploration and exploitation over the continental shelf to which it is entitled under international law. A dispute regarding those rights would, therefore, appear to be one which may be said to relate to the territorial status of the coastal State.'
160. O'Connel, 'The International Law of the Sea', at 481.

the superjacent air space. Some Latin American countries even extended their claims beyond the Shelf to the superjacent waters and the air space above those waters. For example Brazil claimed exclusive rights to control marine scientific research and environmental protection.[161] Yugoslavia claimed sovereignty over other resources in addition to natural resources including archaeological and other submerged objects.[162] Some States have by their constitutions or legislation claimed full ownership rights over the mineral resources, including oil and gas in the seabed and subsoil of their C.S.[163] This shows that Coastal States in their practices have demonstrated their strong intention to territorialise the C.S in order to maintain complete regulatory control over same.

From the above analysis, it can be said that the term 'sovereign rights' amounts to much the same thing as the term 'sovereignty' although, sovereign rights are limited under international law in that coastal State is prohibited from exercising any rights over C.S in such a way that it will amount to an unjustifiable interference with navigation and the rights and freedom of other States.[164]

Richard Barnes however, expressed doubt as to whether the coastal State can exercise any regime of property rights in the C.S in view of the fact that the authority of a coastal State over the C.S is functional and not plenary in that it will be affected by other activities of other users of the same space. A c c or di ng to him, this may undermine any property rights provided for in the C.S as this will require 'limits on any private property rights, especially in respect of management incidents and the extent of the prohibition on harmful use so that other legitimate activities on the C.S are protected'.[165]

As persuasive as this argument might seem, it has not completely displaced the argument that ownership of petroleum in place has been conferred on the coastal State by international law and States practices, even though it is not expressly stated in the 1958 Geneva Convention. The critical question to be asked is whether the State can divest itself of ownership of petroleum or create protectable petroleum property in favour of a person in the C.S. Assuming a coastal State can do that, at what stage would property in petroleum passes? Is it when petroleum has been discovered or when it has been evacuated from the reservoir and captured at the wellhead?.

These are the critical questions that have assumed a high volatile academic debate profile among eminent jurists and industry practitioners.[166]

With this theoretical analysis in place, we shall now begin to address the nature of interest created by offshore oil and gas production licence in our selected jurisdictions. In the *United Kingdom*, the crown has a sovereign right over the resources of the

161. Article 13 of law no. 8617 of 4 January 1983.
162. Article 24 of the 1987 law on the coastal sea and continental shelf.
163. See pp. 83-89 above for discussion on the Nigerian Constitution of 1999, the Petroleum Act of 1969 and the Netherlands Mineral Act of 2003 and the Continental shelf Act of 1965.
164. Articles 78 (2) and 79 of UNLOSC.
165. Barnes, 'Property Rights and Natural Resources', at 275.
166. These are some of the main planks of this study that will be dealt with in more detail in Chapter 4.

Continental shelf.[167] Several authors have argued that the nature of the crown's rights in the resources of the Continental shelf is proprietary in character and can no longer be regarded as *res nullius* because under section 1 (1) of the Continental shelf Act of 1964, the crown has a right to reduce them to possession and to exclude every other persons from doing so. They argued further that the proprietary character of the Crown's right is akin to the 'qualified ownership' of onshore oil adopted by the Pennsylvania and California States in US, the *profit a prendre*[168] in English law or the lease of mineral rights in Scots law.[169] Therefore, the provision is sufficient to give a coastal State right of property in the oil and gas resources of the continental shelf. This has also given the UK power to exclude anyone else from exploring and exploiting the Shelf without having to enact separate criminal prohibitions. Some other commentators have argued that full ownership of petroleum in situ is vested in the Crown in the C.S as much as within Great Britain.[170] On the other hand Marriage and Greg Gordon have argued that oil and gas in strata in the UKCS is *res nullius*.[171] This matter is yet to be settled as there is no judicial authority on the issue. However, going by the debate that surrounds the adoption of the term 'sovereign rights' at the drafting stage of the Convention, this book is inclined towards the view expressed by professor Daintith. This means that the Crown can pass proprietary rights to the licensee. However, the extent to which she has done so could only be known by looking at the substance of the licensee's right. This can only be determined by examining the words contained in the granting clause.

In the United Kingdom, Professor Daintith interpreted the granting clause contained in the model clause of a standard production licence as conferring exclusive rights on the licensee and that it is coupled with a grant of the petroleum which the licensee may get under the licence. In this sense, the licence closely resembles the mining lease in Scotland and the *profit a prendre* in England and therefore, should produce similar effects especially as regards the licensee's rights with third parties.[172] According to him, the analogies to these property rights or real rights are appropriate considering the massive investments the licensee will incur in the working of the acreage and also the fact that the controls imposed on the licensee, even though

167. Section 1 (1) of the Continental shelf Act 1964.
168. '*Profit a prendre*' is a right given to one person to take something off another person's land. For the right taken to be profit, the thing taken must either be part of the land or existing on it and must at the time of being taken, capable of ownership, e. g. minerals, crops, wild animals and fish. See Megarry & Wade, *supra* n. 102 at 1230.
169. Daintith & Willoughby, 'U.K. Oil and Gas Law', at 1078/4. See also R. Higgins, 'Ten Years of State Involvement in the Offshore Petroleum Industry-The U.K. Experience', in 'Proceedings of the Energy Law Seminar', vol. 1-2 (1979), paper R1.1 at P. R1.5 who opined that the resources of the Shelf are not to be regarded as *res nullius* having regard to customary international law, judicial decisions and emerging international treaty law as well as State practice.
170. Taverne, 'Petroleum, Industry and Governments', (1999) at para. 6.3.1.
171. Gordon, et al., *supra* n. 141 at 33 citing P. Marriage, 'North Sea Continental Sea Petroleum Financing in the United Kingdom', (1977) Int. Bus Lawyer 5: 207 at 209.
172. *Ibid.* See also Daintith, 'Correlative Rights in Oil Reservoirs on the United Kingdom Continental Shelf', at 75. He cited the decision of the House of Lord which had ruled that a mineral lease that entitles its holder to exhaust rather than use the leased property amounts to a sale of the minerals in situ. See *Gowans v. Christie* (1873)11 M. (H.L) 1. Accordingly, a grant of petroleum production licence secures the same effect as it is akin to a *profit a prendre* in English law.

stringent, are normal as they would not be different from those which a prudent landowner would insert in the mining lease or *profit a prendre*. In agreement with this view, Higgins also argued that the licence operates to pass a property right in the nature of a '*profit a prendre*'.[173]

In *Canada*, there is a three stage petroleum licensing regime in the offshore provided under both the Canada-Nova Scotia Offshore Accord Implementation Act of 1988 and the Canada-Newfoundland Offshore Accord Implementation Act of 1987[174] (Accord Implementation Acts). These are exploration licences, significant discovery licences and production licences.[175]

The legal nature of the interest granted by these licences will depend on whether the crown enjoys real property right or not in the offshore and whether from the language of the Accord Acts, an interest in land is conferred on the holder of these licences.

In the case of *Reference Re: The seabed and subsoil of the Continental Shelf Offshore Newfoundland (Hibernia Reference)*,[176] the Supreme Court held that the right conferred on the Federal Government was not the right of full sovereignty over the Shelf. According to the court, even though the right was an extension of a coastal State's sovereignty, 'it is an extension in the form of something less than full sovereignty ... the continental shelf is not part of a coastal State's territory ... and therefore the coastal State cannot 'own' the continental shelf as it can 'own' its land territory.'[177] The court said further that:

> We do not think continental shelf rights are proprietary in the ordinary sense...In pith and substance they are an extra-territorial manifestation of, and an incident of, the external sovereignty of a coastal State.[178]

One commentator on the legal nature of these licences submitted that because Canada's rights in the CS is restricted in that it has no full ownership rights to the resources of the CS coupled with the fact that the Accord Acts used the term 'licences' instead of the term 'grant' and also because the production licence only grants title to produced petroleum rather than in situ petroleum, offshore licences, and the royalties which the licensee may grant to third party, can be regarded as personal rights.[179]

The question of whether Canadian law recognises absolute ownership of oil and gas in situ within the continental shelf or not has not been addressed directly by any case law apart from the references made indirectly to the issue in the above named case.[180]

173. Higgins, 'Ten Years of State Involvement in the Offshore Petroleum Industry - The U.K. Experience', in Proceedings of the Energy Law Seminar, at R1.5.
174. Both Acts contained identical provisions. Therefore, the Canada-Nova Scotia Offshore Accord Implementation Act of 1988 will be our reference point in this book.
175. Section 68 Canada-Nova Scotia Offshore Accord Implementation Act of 1988.
176. (1984) S.C.R. 86; 5 D.L.R. (4th) 385 (S.C.C.).
177. *Ibid.*, at p. 96.
178. *Ibid.*, at 396.
179. Van Penick, 'Legal Framework in the Canadian Offshore', (2001) Dalhousie L.J. 24: at 19.
180. The issue in the said case was as to which level of government has jurisdiction over the oil and gas resources of the Shelf as between the Federal and Provincial Governments in Canada. The

It is submitted that the fact that international law grants 'sovereign rights' (even if regarded as less than full ownership) to coastal State over the Continental shelf does not deprive coastal State's interest over the resources of the CS as proprietary given our theoretical analysis of the regime of CS herein. The mere fact that the Accord Acts used the term 'licence' rather than the term 'grant' does not really matter. What is important is the substance of the right conferred and not its form. The licences are not bare licences or administrative permits. An examination of the rights conferred by the licences would lend support to this assertion.

A holder of exploration licence is vested with the right to explore, exclusive right to drill, exclusive right to develop and exclusive right to obtain production licence over a defined area of the offshore to which the licence applies. The terms and conditions of the licence may be prescribed and may contain such other terms and conditions agreed between the Canada-Nova Scotia Offshore Petroleum Board (Board) and the licence holder subject however to the provisions of the Act or Regulations made by the Governor in Council.[181]

The Board may amend an exploration licence but such amendment must be with the agreement of the interest or licence holder.[182] The life span of an exploration licence is nine years but may be continued if exploration drilling has commenced prior to the expiration of the licence in order to determine significant petroleum discovery.[183]

Where a significant discovery is made on any portion of the offshore area to which the exploration licence applies, the Board shall make a declaration of significant discovery on its own volition or on the application of the interest holder. A significant discovery licence is thereafter granted to holder of exploration licence.[184] A significant discovery licence continues indefinitely subject to certain requirements and it confers the same rights as exploration licence.[185] It continues in force as long as the significant discovery declaration issued by the Board is in force.[186] The duration of the significant discovery declaration is however not stated. It will likely terminate on the issuance of a production licence in respect of the areas of which the significant discovery licence or declaration applies.[187] A significant discovery licence shall be in the form prescribed and may contain terms and conditions as may be agreed between the Board and the licence holder subject however to the provisions of the Act or regulations made by the Governor in Council.[188] An exploration licence ceased to exist on the issuance of a discovery licence.

Where a commercial discovery is made on any portion of the offshore area that is subject to an interest or a share in it, the Board shall make a declaration of commercial

court held that the Federal Government (Canada) and not the Province (Newfoundland) has the right to explore and exploit the natural resources of the seabed and subsoil of the CS.

181. Section 70 (1) (2) of Canada-Nova Scotia Offshore Accord Implementation Act of 1988.
182. *Ibid.*, section 71.
183. *Ibid.*, sections 72 and 73.
184. *Ibid.*, sections 74 (1) (2) and 76.
185. *Ibid.*, section 75.
186. *Ibid.*, section 78 (3).
187. *Ibid.*, section 88.
188. *Ibid.*, section 76 (4).

discovery on its own volition or on the application of the interest holder.[189] A production licence is thereafter granted to an interest owner in respect of any one commercial discovery area to which an exploration licence or discovery licence applies. Subject to some terms and conditions, a production licence could also be granted to one interest owner in respect of two or more commercial discovery areas that are subject to an exploration licence or discovery licence. Production licence could also be granted jointly to two or more interest owners in respect of two or more commercial discovery areas that are subject to an exploration licence or a discovery licence.[190]

A production licence entitles the holder, within the portions of the offshore areas to which the licence applies, exclusive right to explore for, to drill and test for petroleum, to develop, to produce petroleum and title to petroleum so produced.[191] Rights conferred on a production licensee are identical to those conferred on the holders of exploration and significant discovery licences except that the production licence confers title to the petroleum produced on the holder of the licence. The production licence is in accordance with a prescribed form and may contain terms and conditions as agreed between the Board and the licence holder subject however to the Act and Regulations made there-under.[192] The duration of a production licence is twenty-five years but is automatically extended for as long as production continues or if at the expiration of the initial term commercial production continues.[193] The Board also has discretionary power to extend the initial term of the licence if it has reasonable ground to believe that commercial production will recommence where production has ceased before or after the twenty -five years.[194]

Section 88 provides that the interests held prior to the issuance of production licence ceased to exist on the grant of a production licence in respect of the portion of the offshore areas to which the production licence was issued otherwise, such interests shall continue to have effects subject to their terms and provisions of the Act. This section is particularly striking because a significant discovery licence has no duration under the Act. Its term supposed to cease when production licence is issued. Where the production licence does not terminate it, then it continues indefinitely.

The crown has a reversionary interest at the expiration of all or any of these licences. The portion of the offshore areas to which the licences apply become Crown reserve areas.[195]

The Board is vested with the power to cancel rights of any interest owner who fails to comply with the provisions of the Act or regulations. Before issuing order for cancellation, the interest holder is entitled to fair hearing before the Oil and Gas

189. *Ibid.*, section 81 (1) (2).
190. *Ibid.*, section 84 (1) (a) (b).
191. *Ibid.*, section 83.
192. *Ibid.*, section 84(4).
193. *Ibid.*, section 87 (1) (3).
194. *Ibid.*, section 87 (4).
195. *Ibid.*, sections 72 (4), 78(4) and 88(2).

committee set up for that purpose. The order of cancellation is subject to judicial review by the Supreme Court.[196]

All the above features of the licences (Significant discovery and production licences) - right to produce petroleum, indefinite duration, exclusivity and the facts that their terms are to be agreed between the minister and the licensee - showed that they are not bare licences. They are irrevocable licences coupled with interests or a *profit a prendre* within the common law classification of property interests.

In Australia, in order to determine whether the exploration permit and production licence creates a proprietary interest in the grantee, an interpretation of the granting clause is required. Legal characterisation of permits was determined in Australia in the case of *Commonwealth of Australia v. Western Mining Corporation Ltd.*[197] The respondent (WMC) was a holder of exploration permits under the PSLA in respect of disputed area between Australia and Indonesia. A Treaty was subsequently entered into by the two countries which created a Zone of Cooperation for the exploitation of petroleum resources in the disputed offshore area called Timor Gap. The treaty was domesticated by the enactment of two legislations by the Commonwealth parliament.[198] Section 24 of one of the Enactments, the CP Act, provides that compensation should be paid by the Commonwealth for acquisition of property from any person. Consequently, certain blocks were removed from exploration permits granted under the PSLA so as to comply with the Treaty. The WMC's blocks held under its exploration permit were affected along with some others. WMC instituted an action before the Federal Court claiming compensation and declaratory relief under the Act.

Held - The Federal court held that the removal of the blocks from the WMC permit constitutes acquisition of property otherwise than on just terms and consequently, Commonwealth was liable to pay compensation. An appeal to the Full court of the Federal Court was unanimously dismissed by the court. The Justices held that there was an acquisition of property within the meaning of section 51 (xxxi) of the Constitution. The interests of WMC in the permit under the PSLA were held to constitute property because it was an *exclusive, identifiable, and assignable and subject to the question of defeasibility, they are stable rights.*[199] On further appeal to the High Court, the majority of the Justices accepted the argument of the appellant that the rights were such that their termination did not constitute an acquisition within the section 51 (xxxi) of the constitution. (Four judges concurred while two dissented). The reasons given for their decisions were as follows:

> The permit concerned offshore areas in the continental shelf where according to the Justices, the Commonwealth has no proprietary interest, contending that the term sovereignty is stronger than the term sovereign rights used in respect of exploration and exploitation of resources of Continental shelf. According to them, since the commonwealth does not have absolute title to the resources of the C.S,

196. *Ibid.*, sections 126 and 127.
197. (1998) 194 CLR 1.
198. Petroleum (Australia-Indonesia Zone of Cooperation) Act 1990 (ZOC Act); and the Petroleum (Australian -Indonesia Zone of Cooperation) (Consequential Provisions) Act 1990 (CP Act).
199. The indicia of property as stated by Lord Wilberforce in the case *National Provincial Bank Ltd v. Ainsworth* [1965] AC 1175 at 1247 to 1248 were followed with approval by the Justices.

> the permit was regarded as a creation of the commonwealth statute and that the rights conferred by the statute are inherently defeasible. However, there was no unanimity between the four concurring justices on this issue. Two of them held the view that the *commonwealth had a vested interest in the resources of the C.S and so the permittee.* The quality or character of the permittee's right is derived from the PSLA which created them and not from the SSLA though they agreed that the permit were defeasible for different reasons. The reasons were based on the provisions of the PSLA e.g. sections 5 (8) and 28. The combined effects of which makes the permit susceptible to modification by the parliament from time to time in response to changing circumstances or policy. The provisions of section 19 which makes it unlawful for anyone to explore without a licence, was also conceived as reminiscent of a bare licence which creates no interest in land. The provision that the permittee cannot conduct recovery of petroleum except with a production licence was also an added reason. For these reasons, it was held that no interest or estate was created by the commonwealth in the blocks removed from the permit but only a right to explore for petroleum, supporting that right by making it a criminal offence for anyone else to do so. The permit to them is statutory and hence can be modified or extinguished at any time without incurring the wrath of the constitutional provisions.

The reasons given by the dissenting judges for their opinion were that: PSLA conferred substantial rights and obligations upon the holder of the permit, e.g., right to production licence upon discovery of petroleum. The offshore legislative regime is expected to attract high risk capital. Part of the permit was acquired in order for the commonwealth itself to prospect for petroleum and as such it confers benefit on it. That the rights conferred though statutory, were not transient and defeasible but rather to provide security for those prepared to explore and develop offshore petroleum resources.

From the above decision, the entire statutory regime for offshore petroleum resources in Australia has been thrown into serious turmoil. The quality of the rights conferred on the permittee by the legislation are no more than the rights obtained under a bare licence that can be withdrawn by the grantor at any time. The quality does not represent a fair balance between the huge capital investment and the associated high risk that an investor would undertake in petroleum operations. This has wider implication for the security of offshore petroleum titles and investment on one hand and legislative framework for the efficient management of the resources by the government on the other.[200]

The comments of professor Crommelin on this case are very instructive. He is of the opinion that the 'congenial infirmity' suffered by the offshore permits would also apply to the lease and licences granted under the PSLA, an infirmity that stems not from the status of these rights in international law but from the manner in which the rights granted by international law were received into the domestic law of Australia.[201] In spite of this however, he argued strongly that sovereign rights and sovereignty though are jurisdictional concepts, property may flow from jurisdiction. Therefore, since radical title flows from sovereignty that is exercised in the territorial sea and land

200. Michael Crommelin, 'The Legal Character of Resource Titles', (1998) AMPLJ 17: 57 at 68.
201. *Ibid.*

territory, qualified title should equally flow from sovereign rights enjoyed by the commonwealth in the continental shelf. He argued further that the State's sovereign rights to explore and exploit the resources of the CS is similar to the common law concept of *profit a prendre* which confers right to extract resources from the land belonging to another. This analogy is strong enough to allow much flexibility so that proprietary interests can be attached to Australian sovereign rights over the resources of the C.S. In conclusion he called for the amendment of the afflicting provisions of the PSLA and an assertion of limited title to the seabed of the CS so as to save the offshore petroleum titles of the 'congenital infirmity' of defeasance.[202]

It is submitted that though the right conferred may be statutory in nature, the other characteristics of the rights such as permanence, stability and long duration and transferability coupled with the economic value of the permits should have been taken into consideration by the majority judges in their judgment. The views of the dissenting judges are thus preferable as it accords with modern meaning of a protectable property especially under the International Human rights laws and investment treaties. It is not likely that the majority's decision would stand the tests laid down in the jurisprudence of those two regimes. What is trickling about the case also is the observation of Brennan CJ that the permit possesses proprietary character (as it can be traded among private parties) and yet, he held that it transferred no property back to the commonwealth when it was excised.[203] If it was regarded as property in the real sense, an acquisition by the commonwealth for the purpose of exploring the blocks itself should have been regarded as a re-transfer of property. A refusal to see the permit in this light will mean that the permit was not even a property of any kind. This will have a wider negative implication for the upstream petroleum investments. If it is just an administrative authorisation to engage in otherwise prohibited conduct, then revoking it will not be tantamount to acquisition. The majority decision ignores section 11 of the SSLA and failed to interpret the term 'sovereign right' as given proprietary interest to the commonwealth (contrary to the interpretation given to the term in the English CS Act, 1964) which could have been seen to have modified the afflicting provisions of the PSLA.[204] Professor Daintith disagreed with the reasoning of the judges to the effect that because the permits can be modified by subsequent legislation it has thereby suffered congenital infirmity. He argued that the legislative expression that the terms of the permits should be read subject to the Act is common to all petroleum regimes with a proprietary basis. He suggested that the criminal provisions of the PSLA should be scrapped so that civil remedies can be provided for both or either of the Joint Authority and the title holder as appropriate. Furthermore, he suggested that the licensing powers of the PSLA should be grounded on Section 11 of SSLA indicating their origin in proprietary rights.[205]

202. *Ibid.*, 70.
203. Brennan CJ, at para. 9.
204. Daintith, 'A Critical Evaluation of the Petroleum (Submerged Lands) Act as a Regulatory Regime', at 99.
205. *Ibid.*, at 99.

In spite of the strong arguments of professors Crommelin and Daintith, the wordings of the granting clause of the permits and licences have not changed under the new legislation (OPGSSA).

It is instructive to note that court in the above case refused to follow their earlier decision on mineral lease even though their facts are very similar. In the case of *Newcrest Mining (WA) Ltd. v. The Commonwealth*[206] the Commonwealth extended a National park to include land in respect of which the respondent had twenty-five mineral leases and as a result of which he could not continue his mining operations because such activities is prohibited by an Act of parliament in the National park. The respondent was not paid compensation. The court held that the action of commonwealth amounted to acquisition of property without just terms under the constitution. The court quoted with approval the earlier cases of *Gowan v. Christie*,[207] (Lord Cairn's dictum) and *Wade v. New South Wales Rutile Mining Co. Ltd.*[208] which were to the effect that a 'mining lease ...is really a sale by the Crown of minerals reserved to the Crown to be taken by the lessee at a price payable over a period of years royalties.' The court therefore, concluded that the affected mineral leases were property within the meaning of the term property in the Constitution.

Opinions are divided as to whether the Mineral lease principles can be applied to oil and gas. Some Judicial authorities are of the view that because petroleum is fugacious, it cannot be subject of property right until reduced to possession.[209] This has been conceived as flowing from false analogies between petroleum deposits and either underground waters or wild animals.

Also international law provisions with regards to offshore regimes posed some difficulties. Professor Crommelin contends that it may be said that the provisions represent customary international law and that obviously the concepts of sovereign rights relate to the idea of 'imperium' rather than 'dominion' but nevertheless, it is not conclusive against the existence of property right. This is because the matter in this context is one of international law and not domestic law. For example, UK, US, Canada and even Australia declared sovereignty over territorial sea. If sovereignty can be argued to incorporate property rights, sovereign right can as well be considered akin to a *profit a prendre*.

Therefore, statutory rights and obligations should be characterised in terms of common law proprietary interests. The importance of permits and licences should be taken into consideration in classifying their legal character.

206. (1997) 71 ALJR 1346.
207. (1873) LR 2 Sc & Div 273, 284.
208. (1969) 121 CLR 177, 192-193.
209. See American cases and the English case of *U Po Naing v. Burma Oil Company* 91929) LR 16 Ind. App 140 (PC). However see contrary case of *Trinidad Asphalt v. Ambard* [1899] AC 594 9PC) and *Berkhesier v. Berkheiser* [1957] SCR 387 (SCC).

3.4 Evaluation of the Nature of Oil and Gas Lease or Production Licence and the Interest Granted

In the Accession system of mining law, the nature of the landowner's interest in the oil and gas in situ could be rationalised within the context of the ownership in place and the Non-ownership (qualified ownership) theories.

The ownership in place theory regards the owner of the land as an absolute owner of the oil and gas in place and that he may take all the oil and gas he finds beneath his land through a well bore on his own land even if it is shown that part of the oil comes from adjacent land. From the decisions of the courts as stated above, it is clear that the court did not apply absolute ownership principles to oil and gas exactly as applied to solid minerals. The absolute ownership principle applied was qualified by the rule of capture. This is a negative qualification in that it subtracts from the bundle of rights of the owner of tract of land unlike the positive qualification applied by the courts to solid minerals. This has produced an awkward situation. Here the landowner is given an absolute ownership of oil and gas in place with right to take oil and gas beneath his land even if in doing so his neighbour's substances are drained. On the other hand, the same principle of absolute ownership was not recognised in enforcing or protecting the ownership of one whose oil or gas is drained. The principle does not also recognise the remedy available to the landowner if his oil or gas is drained by his neighbour. This means that the law did not protect him from drainage even though he is proclaimed to be the absolute owner of oil and gas in place.

The qualified ownership principle introduced correlative rights doctrine to the effect that the adjoining landowners have property rights to the oil and gas in the common reservoir – in that they respectively have exclusive right to take them – and that in exercising this right, either of them must so act as not to unreasonably injure the other. This shows that qualified ownership principle has also been expressed in terms of the possibility for the land owner's title to oil and gas in place to be defeated by the operation of the rule of capture.

The basic difference between the absolute ownership theory as propounded by Pennsylvanian courts and the qualified ownership propounded by the Indiana courts is that, while the absolute ownership defines property right, but fails to protect it, the qualified ownership denies any right of property in one whose oil or gas is taken. What is common to both theories, is the existence of the rule of capture as both of them allow its operation albeit, in different manners.

From the above analysis, the factors that have influenced and shaped the nature of the land owner's interest in oil and gas in place and the development of oil and gas in Accession Systems, appeared to be the fugacious or migratory nature of the oil and gas and the real property principles of the common law as applied by the courts. The existing real property principles as applied to solid minerals were not applied in exact manner to oil and gas.

Majority of States that adopted ownership in place theory classified the lessee's interest as fee simple determinable estate and they insisted that the granting clause is unimportant. Irrespective of the type of granting clause, the oil and gas lease operates as a conveyance of title to '*in situ*' oil and gas. The minority of the ownership in place

States insisted that the granting clause is the determinant factor. Where the granting clause purportedly conveyed the oil and gas in place, it will be regarded as creating a fee simple interest and therefore, the nature of rights or interest of the lessee is corporeal but where it merely grants an exclusive right to search, develop and produce, an irrevocable licence or a '*profit a prendre*' is created and the nature of the rights or interests of the lessee is incorporeal.

The Courts of the Non-ownership States (Qualified ownership) have however held the nature of lessee interest as an irrevocable licence or a '*profit a prendre*' determinable and that the granting clause is not important since a conveyance of oil and gas in place is not possible. In these States, the nature of the lessee's interest in the oil and gas in their natural state is restricted to the incorporeal hereditament classification.

The lesson learnt from the above analysis is that the practical difference between the various ownership regimes is inconsequential with regards to the nature of lessee's interest created by the oil and gas lease because whether the nature of the lessee's interest in oil and gas is classified as corporeal or incorporeal, real or personal, the lessee's interests is in real property object within the meaning of common law classification. It is an interest in land.[210] The difference between corporeal or incorporeal, real or personal property therefore, could be said to lie in duration of the lease and not on any ownership theory.[211]

In Chapter 2 of this book, we have shown that the traditional common law meaning of property is in two ways which is very relevant here.[212] A reasonable conclusion is that the nature of the lessee interests created by oil and gas lease in Accession system of mining law is an interest in real property and therefore, qualified to be regarded as a property within our theoretical analysis in Chapter 2.

In the Domanial systems of mining law, there is clear provision on the ownerships rights of all the States we have studied with respect to the oil and gas resources located at the onshore and territorial sea. In these areas, the State, either the Federal government or Provincial government, owns the oil and gas resources. Currently in practice in the Netherlands, is the concessionary system in which a landowner or the person to whom a deed of concession has been granted by the government is vested with the full ownership of the oil and gas underneath the concession at the time of the grant. With respect to offshore (the Continental shelf) some States, e.g., UK, Canada and Australia claimed only sovereign rights to the oil and gas resources located in that area. Other States like Netherlands and Nigeria provided by legislations that full ownership rights in those resources vest in their respective governments.

210. See above decision of the Supreme Court of Canada in the case of *Bank of Montreal v. Dynex Petroleum Ltd* (2002) S.C.C. 7 File No. 27766 which held that an interest in land could be created from an incorporeal hereditament depending on the language of the grant and the intention of the parties. Overriding royalty was classified as an interest in land.

211. Blake, 'The Oil and Gas Lease', at p. 309. See also the case of *Dabney v. Edwards*, 5 Cal. 2d. 1 53 Pac. 2d. 964 (1935) where the court declared that lease for years is personal property while a lease in perpetuity is real property.

212. See Chapter 2, pp. 25-26 for further classifications of property.

Also of commonality among our selected jurisdictions is the legal character of production rights whether coined as a licence or a permit or a lease. It may generally be regarded as a contract with statutory flavour. In Australia however, there is a judicial authority to the effect that an exploration licence is sui generis and that it is only statutory in nature. The reason being that the rights conferred on the licensee under the licence are made subject to the Act and the regulations, backed up by a provision that makes it a criminal offence to carry out petroleum recovery operations without such licence with five years imprisonment as penalty for such offence. The court was of the view that such a provision is reminiscent of a statutory permit. As pointed out by Professor Crommelin however, whether a licence is contractual or statutory in nature does not really matter as it is only relevant to the type of judicial remedies that a party may validly claim in the court. However, as the case of *Commonwealth of Australia v. Western Mining Corporation Ltd* (*supra*) has shown in Australia, a permit that is regarded as statutory only can be modified or extinguished by the government unilaterally. It is no more than a bare licence. It means that it cannot even create in the holder an interest that is proprietary. This decision might apply to production licence as well since the rights conferred by it under the law are identical to that of the exploration licence. In Netherlands, a deed of concession granted under the Mining Act of 1810 can be regarded as contractual and a conveyance while production licence granted under new Mining Act of 2003 can be regarded as contractual and regulatory in nature.

With regard to the nature of the interests of the licensee in a production licence, we have found that they are reminiscent of the legal character of those licences and which in turn based on the interests of the State grantor in the underlie petroleum. It appears that they have no much bearing with the terrain of the applicability of the licence, i.e. whether based on the onshore or offshore. This is reinforced by the findings from our theoretical analysis of the nature of rights granted to coastal State in the oil and gas resources of the C.S. In this instance, we found that the 'sovereign rights' purportedly granted by international law could be construed as ownership or at least proprietary rights to the oil and gas resources of the seabed and subsoil of the C.S.

In all the States that we have examined, full ownership of petroleum in situ is claimed onshore and it is logical to infer that the State can transfer by licence such interests to the licensee except otherwise stated in the licence granting clause. In the UK, we have seen that the licence granting clause in both onshore and offshore are the same and yet full ownership is claimed in the onshore whereas sovereign rights is claimed in the offshore. The licence granting clause has been interpreted as conveying a proprietary interest in the nature of a *profit a prendre* under English law or mineral lease under Scots law.

In Nigeria however, the OML granting clause which States that *'[T]his Oil Mining Lease is granted to… search for, win, work, carry away and dispose of all petroleum in, under or throughout the lands described …'* is akin to the private lease granting clause in the U.S. lease which purports to *'grant, lease and let to the lessee … all the oil and gas in and under the following described tract of land….'* The courts have held that this granting clause grants oil and gas in place to the lessee together with the necessary right to use the surface for the purpose of developing and extracting the substances.

Therefore, an OML in Nigeria could be said to have conveyed mineral in place to the lessee (corporeal interest). This assertion is reinforced by the fact that the operating oil mining lease is for unlimited duration or for so long as oil shall be produced in paying quantities and the lessee pays rents and royalties. This granting clause applies to OML granted in both onshore and offshore in Nigeria.

In Netherlands the nature of the interests of the holder of a production licence granted under the 1810 Mining Act with regards to onshore minerals is full ownership (concession) while in the offshore the production licence can be regarded as conveying a proprietary interest in land. Even if not full ownership, it is proprietary in the nature of profit a prendre. This is because in the offshore, property in petroleum vests in the State.

In the offshore of Canada, certain features of the licences (Significant discovery and production licences) such as indefinite duration, exclusivity and the facts that their terms are to be agreed between the minister and the licensee showed that they are not bare licences. They are irrevocable licences coupled with interests or a *profit a prendre* within the common law classification of property interests and as such, convey such interests to the holder of the licence. In Australia, though there is no judicial decision on the issue with respect to production licence, an exploration licence has been held to convey no proprietary interests in the licensee. This decision as has been shown above is very controversial even among the judges as there was no unanimity as to the reasons given for their judgment.

Another lesson learnt is that in those countries where a two or more stage rights system is adopted, e.g., Nigeria, Canada, Netherlands and Australia, a production licence can be regarded as conveying real interests to the licensee as the licence is often granted where commercial discovery of petroleum has been made.

The next chapter will examine the issue as to whether since the production licence is granted to enable the licensee to mine the resources discovered by him, the resources while still forming part of the land, vests in him an interest in land under the common law classification of property. It is to be noted that some of these countries (e.g., Netherlands and Australia) specified in their legislations that property in the petroleum passes to the licensee when produced while others are silent on the issue. The question is whether this could preclude an inference, from the licence granting clauses, that the licensee has a proprietary interest in the petroleum before production. The next chapter is then aimed at examining whether protectable property rights in unexploited petroleum could be said to have emerged or exists given that it is an important or valuable attribute of a production licence.

CHAPTER 4
Property Rights in Discovered Petroleum Reservoir?

1. INTRODUCTION

This chapter examines whether protectable 'property rights in petroleum reservoir' exists with capacity to tame the rule of capture and act as standard against which the conflicting courts' decisions could be resolved. It uses the analytical framework developed in Chapter 2 and the analysis of nature of oil and gas interests in Chapter 3 as guide. It also provides on a theoretical level, legal, economic and moral justifications for this new property right concept.

2. PETROLEUM LICENCE OR LEASE AS PROPERTY

2.1 Accession Systems

Chapter 3 has shown that in Accession systems of mining law, the instrument by which the transfer of mineral interest to the lessee is carried out is called a 'Lease'.[1] Various courts decisions have recognised an oil and gas lease to have dual character, i.e. it is a conveyance of an interest in real property, and a contract between the lessor and lessee.[2] As a result of this dual character, an oil and gas lease goes beyond in personam right to qualify as an in rem right. This is one of the ways in which the conception of property in the common law tradition differs from the civil law tradition. Under the

1. See the definition of a Lease in Chapter 3 p. 80. See also Megarry & Wade, 'The Law of Real Property', at 729.
2. See the California case of *Samuels v. Ottinger*, 169 Cal. 209, 146 Pac. 1024 (1921); *Bickett v. City of Paris Dry Goods Co.*, 98 Cal. Dec. 450, 96 Pac. 2d 122 (1939).

former tradition, leasehold is part of the law of property while it is regarded as a contractual relationship in the latter tradition.[3]

The analysis of the legal nature of the interests created in the lessee also discussed in Chapter 3 has shown that the lessee's interests are in real property object within the common law classification of property. It is an interest in land.[4] A reasonable conclusion therefore is that an oil and gas lease in Accession system of mining law is a property and the nature of the lessee's interests in oil and gas lease is an interest in real property. It can therefore be qualified as 'property' within our analytical framework in Chapter 2.

2.2 Domanial Systems

Chapter 3 has shown that, with the exception of Australia,[5] there is commonality among the selected common law countries as regards the legal character of offshore production rights whether coined as a licence or a permit or a lease. It may generally be regarded as a contract with statutory flavour but the regulatory aspect of the licence cannot displace its contractual element. In Australia however, there is a judicial authority to the effect that an exploration licence is sui generis and that it is only statutory in nature.[6]

The nature of the interests of the licensee in a production licence is reminiscent of the legal character of the licence and on the interests of the State grantor in the underlie petroleum. Also we found in Chapter 3 that it has no much bearing with the terrain of the applicability of the licence, i.e. whether based on the onshore or offshore. Having regard to the licence granting clauses in both terrains, the lessee's interest has been found to be either a *profit a prendre* or Mineral lease (UK and offshore Netherlands), or an irrevocable licence coupled with interests or a *profit a prendre* (offshore Canada), or a conveyance of the oil and gas in place (Nigeria and onshore Netherlands). However, In Australia, though there is no judicial decision on the issue with respect to production licence, an exploration licence has been held to convey no proprietary interests to the licensee in the *WMC case* (*supra*) while a contrary decision was reached in *Westover Holdings Pty Ltd case* (*supra*). The decision in WMC case, as

3. Cotula, 'Human Rights, Natural Resource and Investment Law in a Globalised World', at 13 citing U. Mattei, 'Basic Principles of Property Law: A Comparative Legal and Economic Introduction' (Westport, CT/London: Greenwood Press, 2000), at p. 12.
4. See Chapter 3 p. 127, and n. 213 above.
5. There are conflicting judicial authorities and opinions of renowned publicists differ as to the legal nature of Offshore Exploration Licence. See Chapter 3, pp. 119-123 of this book for a discussion of the case of *Commonwealth v. W.M.C Resources Limited* (1998) 194 CLR 1, per Gummow J. at 73-74 *contrast Westover Holdings Pty. Ltd v. BHP Billiton Minerals Pty Ltd & Others.* [2004] WAMW 12 (2005) 24 ARELJ 295 Per Calder SM at 63.
6. The reason being that the rights conferred on the licensee under the licence are made subject to the Act and the Regulations, backed up by a provision that makes it a criminal offence to carry out petroleum recovery operations without such licence. The court was of the view that such a provision is reminiscent of a statutory permit. This decision might apply to production licence as well since the rights conferred by it under the law are identical to that of the exploration licence.

has been shown in Chapter 3, is very controversial even among the judges as there was no unanimity in the reasons given for their judgment.

As a result of this dual character (i.e., a 'Contract' and a 'Conveyance' of an interest in land), a production licence, lease or permit in a domanial regime also goes beyond in personam right to qualify as an in rem right. It is proprietary in character and therefore conveys proprietary interest in the holder of the licence.

3. INCIDENTS OF PETROLEUM PRODUCTION LICENCE / LEASE AS PROPERTY

Having found that petroleum production licence, lease or permit is regarded as property right, then it is necessary to examine the incidents of such property right because it is the quality of the incidents bestowed by the law on the right that is significant. It must be noted that the traditional property right which is a product of property law derives its source from common law while petroleum production licence derives its source from the statute. Could the fact that a production licence derives its source from the statute renders the rights granted by it non-proprietary?

Even though the differences here may go to the root of the quality of the right, one commentator has argued that the legal source of a property right does not determine its status but that the effectiveness of a property right depends on the strength of each of the incidents that make up the right.[7]

The legal incidents of a petroleum production licence must be analysed in the context of the incidents of exclusive right to possess, use, manage and enjoy income and capital of a thing. However, as stated in Chapter 2, it is not mandatory that the full extent of these incidents be present before legal ownership can take place. Therefore, the quality of a petroleum production licence as a property right can be measured in terms of its duration, flexibility, exclusivity, quality of title, transferability and divisibility.[8] A petroleum production licensee obtains a right to search, bore and get petroleum that includes greater proportion of these incidents. The licensee possesses the petroleum production licence in order to search, bore and get petroleum. The holder of the licence can assign the whole or part of the licence and may enjoy income rights from the licence. The licensee may even create an interest out of the licence thus

7. Barnes, 'Property Rights and Natural Resources', at pp. 325-326 citing also R. Arnarson, 'Property Rights as a Means of Economic Organisation', in Shotton (ed.), 'Use of Property Rights in Fisheries Management. Proceedings of the Fish Rights 99 Conference.' Fremantle, Western Australia, 11-19 November 1999. Barnes considered the quality of the property incidents of Individual transferable Quotas (ITQs) in fisheries. This bears great semblance with the Property incidents of a Production licence in oil and gas.
8. See the case of *National Provincial Bank v. Ainsworth* [1965] AC. 1175 at pp. 1247-1248 where Lord Wilberforce declared that '[B]efore a right or an interest can be admitted into the category of property, or a right affecting property, it must be definable, identifiable by third parties, capable in its nature of assumption by third parties and have some degree of permanence and stability.' See also Blackburn J in *Millirpum v. Nabalco* (1971) 17 FLR 141 at 269 where he declared that 'property in its many forms generally implies the right to use and enjoy the right to exclude others and the right to alienate. I do not say that all these rights must co-exist before there can be a proprietary interests or deny that each of them may be subject to qualifications.'

making the licence divisible, assignable and transferable.[9] Generally, a licensee may consume, waste or destroy the licence in the sense that he may decide on what to do with the petroleum produced or decide the time to produce or not to even produce at all. Judging by the quality of the property incidents of petroleum production licence, it will not be out of place to conclude that it is a property right. The only limitation arises in respect of the right to manage. Although the holder of a petroleum production licence enjoys the right to manage how and when he produces petroleum, in the broader management scheme, will have little or no say in how the petroleum industry is managed unless he is consulted as a stakeholder. This overall management function is performed by the State. The State determines conservation, environmental, technical and other management measures pertaining to the petroleum industry. The holder of the licence must comply with all these measures as established by the State. Also, the State exercises controlling interest in petroleum production licence with respect to its duration. The quality of a property right especially its economic value can be undermined by any uncertainty as to the duration of the right. The duration of a petroleum production licence is usually twenty years in most jurisdictions which is renewable as long as there is production and the licensee continues to fulfil its obligations under the licence. This feature has made some commentators to conclude that the continuation of petroleum production licence that may occur for an indefinite period (which would continue so long as the lease continues to produce petroleum and gas) as creating an uncertain term required to pass beyond chattel real and into realty. As petroleum production licence or lease is realty, thus, it passed the test of a traditional property rights. Therefore, there is a security of title and also the presence of term which further enhances its quality and value as economic property right. Moreover, petroleum production licence satisfies the requirement of excludability because only the licence holder can undertake the development of the licensed area. In fact, a petroleum production licence is granted over an exclusive area meaning that once it is granted to a person, it cannot be granted to another person while the licence is still valid. This makes the licensee de facto owner of the petroleum underneath its licence area. Even though a licensee may, in the exercise of his rights, have those rights restricted by the State, such restrictions would not necessarily deny existence of property right per se.[10]

4. PROPERTY RIGHTS IN 'DISCOVERED PETROLEUM RESERVOIR'?

The analysis above have shown that an oil and gas lease, permit or production licence is a property right and that it conveys proprietary interests to the Licensee or lessee within the common law classification of property interests. The follow up question is

9. In May, 2010, it was reported in Nigeria that Shell Petroleum Development Company (SPDC) assigned all its 45% equity interests in OML 30 to Consolidated Oil Ltd. for the sum USD 1.3 billion. Also in the same year, SPDC assigned all its 45% equity interests in OML 34 to Niger Delta Energy and Petroleum Company for the sum of USD 600 million. See 'Last minutes Oil deals that cost Nigeria dear' available at http://234next.com/csp/cms/sites/Next/Home/5713375-146/last_minute_oil_deals_that_cost.csp.
10. Barnes, 'Property Rights and Natural Resources', at 328.

whether, by virtue of such fact, a licensee or lessee can be said to have a property interest that is protectable in the discovered petroleum resources underlying his licence area. This is the most controversial legal question in the entire oil and gas exploration and production phases. The intensity of the controversy is much where the underlie petroleum resource lies across licence boundaries. This question takes us to the problems or challenges of regulating cross-licence petroleum resources which we shall discuss below. Therefore, before addressing the question, we shall examine the challenges and how the challenges can be overcome.

4.1 Challenges in Regulating Straddling Petroleum Reservoirs

Apportionment of ownership rights to fugacious resources like oil and gas present a difficult problem for the courts as we have pointed out in Chapter 3 and which is further discussed fully in Chapters 5 and 6. This is because unlike solid minerals, they cannot 'easily or cheaply be bounded spatially, into private estates.'[11] According to the courts, the existing property rules relating to solid minerals were not suitable for application to oil and gas. As a result, rules originally applying to ownership of wild animals and percolating waters were applied to the effect that property rights to oil and gas were conferred on the lessee when he captures or reduces them into possession. The settled principles of the law relating to subterranean waters was applied because, oil and gas, like subterranean waters, was regarded as incapable of stabilising under a single tract of land for any definite period, but constantly wandering at the subsurface and because of its wandering nature, it can flow from one tract of land to another, thus rendering it capable of capture from beneath the surrounding land. In their believe, oil and gas in the underground behave like a free flowing underground river without regards to surface boundaries and cannot be quantified or allocated among surface owners.[12] This attitude stems from improper judicial understanding of the nature of reservoir structure, its mechanics and the behaviour of oil and gas in the reservoir.

The perceived ambulatory or fugacious nature of oil and gas in the reservoir has wider implications for the lessee. It means that his efforts at capturing it can be thwarted by his rival if the latter gets there before him by diverting or taking the resource, thereby leaving little or nothing for him. It also means that the resource may not be available for him if it migrates from beneath his land before he captures it.[13] As a result of perceived notion of the natural feature of oil and gas, it has been said that fugacious resources lacked exclusivity, an essential incident of property rights.[14] Common-pool oil and gas resources have therefore, been regarded as open access as there are no holders of the resources. Anthony Scott has argued strenuously that the absence of rights over fluid and common property resources, e.g., underground petroleum is because of lack of demand and supply. He said that the drillers for oil and gas had failed to demand from the court for changes in the characteristics of

11. Scott, 'The Evolution of Resource Property Rights', at 55.
12. *Hail v. Reed*, 54 Ky. 383 (15 B. Mon. 479) (1854).
13. Scott, 'The Evolution of Resource Property Rights', at 56.
14. *Ibid.*

pre-existing but imperfect property rights.[15] On the supply side, he contended that the suppliers of rights, e.g., courts, did not give because they were hampered by their own precedents such as the adoption of the law of capture to oil rights.[16] This has prevented gradual evolution of property rights to fluid resources like oil and gas. Although, government through unitisation legislation have supplied property rights with a measure of exclusivity characteristic, it has not supplied 'property-like rights to individuals who would share and independently draw from common-pool resource.'[17]

As persuasive as this view might seems, judging from the numerous cases that were decided by the courts in the US on drainage of oil and gas, it is difficult to agree with Scott on his lack of demand argument. The problem is more of sticking to precedents by the court even when it became apparent that the property rules developed from analogy to water and wild animal cases resulted into injustice. Therefore, his argument with regards to lack of supply of rights is well founded. Consequently, the law of capture has continued to dominate legislative and judge-made rules (correlative rights) on entitlements to underground oil and gas.

4.2 Overcoming the Challenges

4.2.1 *Judicial Understanding of Scientific Advances*

4.2.1.1 Petroleum Geology

The above challenges are not insurmountable considering the current state of scientific advances in petroleum geology and reservoir engineering. Scientifically, it has been proved that petroleum is found in Reservoir rocks and not in caverns or lakes underground as previously thought by the common law judges. Reservoir is a connected bed of rock that is both porous and permeable.[18] The reservoir contains 'minute holes, gaps or pores' between the grains of sands or sandstones. This is what makes the rock pervious or permeable and hence able to contain petroleum accumulation.[19] However, for petroleum to be formed, it needs a source rock that is oxygen free.[20] After formation in the Source rock, the petroleum then migrates from the source rock into the reservoir rock. Where there is absence of petroleum trap at the top layer of the reservoir rock, further migration could take place from the reservoir rock to the surface earth because of its porosity and permeability. However, where petroleum trap

15. *Ibid.*, at 58.
16. *Ibid.*
17. *Ibid.*, at 59.
18. Sandstone or Limestone (also called sedimentary rock) is a good example of reservoir rock.
19. Robert Stoneley, 'Introduction to Petroleum Exploration for Non-Geologists' (Oxford University Press, 1995), at 36.
20. *Ibid.*, at 27, he stated that this is usually achieved where the sediment is impervious clay. Examples of such Source rocks are Mudstones and Shale. It has generally been accepted that petroleum is formed from microscopic organisms like marine plankton and also from plant material that have been preserved in certain sediments. Having been buried deeper and deeper in the earth, it is gently cooked by exposure to the heat from the earth crust. This organic matter is then interred in the source rock from where petroleum is formed.

is present at the top layer of the reservoir rock, upward percolation of petroleum through the reservoir is blocked and petroleum will 'start to accumulate in the fine pore spaces of the reservoir rock layer.'[21]

Therefore, oil and gas is usually found in the reservoir that is confined within natural barriers (called traps). Traps are impermeable rocks which locked oil and gas into the porous and permeable rock called reservoir. Traps are normally classified under four headings – Structural, Stratigraphic, Combination trap and Hydrodynamic trap.[22]

This means that oil and gas in reservoirs are capable of bounds and do not move freely like underground water. As a result, it can be quantified and appropriated to surface owners even while still in underground. Unless there is an intervention, it will remain confined to the reservoir rock.

4.2.1.2 Reservoir Engineering

Reservoir engineering is a branch of science that uses proven engineering techniques to develop a reservoir to achieve maximum or optimum recovery of petroleum.[23] A typical petroleum reservoir contains three substances. These are – gas cap at the top, oil in the middle and water at the bottom. Water being heavier than the other substances is displaced by oil and gas and the force of gravity will cause it to settle at the lower floor of the reservoir. Gas may also be assimilated into the oil when the reservoir is under pressure. For efficient recovery to take place, the mechanics of the particular reservoir must first be understood. The drive mechanism of the reservoir is determined so that the engineer can appropriately place his wells and determine the depth at which they should be completed in the reservoir. There are three main drive mechanisms which may operate to create the reservoir pressure necessary to move petroleum towards the well bored. These are dissolved gas expansion, gas cap expansion and water encroachment.[24] Since the reservoir in its natural state is constantly under pressure, prior to drilling into the reservoir, the reservoir pressure and the substances within it are static or stable.[25] Once drilling is made into the reservoir, the pressure is released. The pressure release will create pressure gradient within the reservoir towards the bottom of the well bored. The oil and gas under pressure will move through the permeable rock towards the low pressure zone at the well bored and there they will enter the well for onward collection at the surface.[26] Energy needed to push the oil and gas through the permeable rock is provided by the force of gravity and any of the three drive mechanisms stated above.

21. *Ibid.*
22. *Ibid.*, at 45, See also Pierce, 'Coordinated Reservoir Development – An Alternative to the Rule of Capture for the Ownership and Development of Oil and Gas', citing in note 8 'Interstate Oil Compact Commission, Oil and Gas Production' 15-16 (1951).
23. Pierce, *ibid.*, at 12.
24. *Ibid.*, at pp. 9-11. He gave detailed explanation of how this drive mechanism operates in order to achieve maximum oil and gas recovery.
25. *Ibid.*, at 8.
26. *Ibid.*, at n. 25.

In order to ensure maximum use of reservoir energy, after well drilling and completion, the rate of production is controlled. Excessive well drilling or rates of production allow water or other less viscous fluid to break into the producing formation, thereby bypassing pockets of oil and leaving significant quantities of oil to be trapped in the reservoir.[27]

Therefore, where a reservoir is not produced in accordance with its assigned Maximum Efficient Rate (MER),[28] it can lead to loss of oil during primary phase of production. Where production is not controlled, it can also lead to production of excessive amounts of gas in proportion to oil and since oil is what the company wants to produce, the well will have to be abandoned while production may take place from the one with lower ratio. Uncontrolled production rates can also convert efficient drive mechanisms to less efficient mechanisms.[29]

The adoption of the law of capture as oil and gas property rights by the judges failed to take into consideration the above nature of reservoir structure and its mechanisms. This prevented good production practices and encourages production in accordance with artificial surface boundaries instead of natural subsurface boundaries that could promote rational development. The current oil and gas property law of capture promotes competitive drilling, excessive production and significant wastes. With the current scientific development or discovery in the field of petroleum geology and engineering as analysed above, the insistence of the judges on the rule of capture as the basic oil and gas property rules is anachronistic and should therefore be jettisoned. Understanding this basic oil and gas science will no doubt help the judges and legislatures to overcome the challenges highlighted above.

4.2.2 *Petroleum Development Phases*

The stages of petroleum development can be grouped into preliminary investigation activities, exploration surveying, exploratory and appraisal wells drilling, development and production, and decommissioning. Each of these stages will be examined in order to determine whether it is possible for a licensee to start production without having knowledge of the size and extent of the reservoir beneath his licence area.

4.2.2.1 Preliminary Investigation Activities

An oil and gas company would have to carry out preliminary investigations about petroleum potentials of a particular country before deciding to apply for exploration rights. This involves information sourcing from both published and unpublished literature about the country of interest. It also involves purchase of data generated from geological investigations (i.e., satellite images and aerial photographs) already carried

27. *Ibid.*, at 11.
28. *Ibid.*, citing 'American Institute of Mining and Metallurgical Engineers, Petroleum Conservation, 71 (1951) at 151; Bruce, 'Maximum Efficient Rate' – Its Use and Misuse in Production Regulation', (1976) Nat. Resources L. 9: 441.
29. *Ibid.*, at 12.

out for scientific purposes as well as in search for oil over the years.[30] This information is analysed in order to determine whether or not the area of interest contains sedimentary basins. The results of their analysis will enable them to decide whether to obtain a licence in the country or not. If the results are positive, the company will then obtain concession or exploration licence to explore for petroleum in that country.

4.2.2.2 The Exploration Surveying

This involves Geological survey done by mapping the surface geology and then extrapolates downwards to the subsurface. Certain information is gathered through this process. These include the thickness of the successive beds, the ages and nature of the sediments in the basin, the environment of deposition of the various sedimentary layers, the structure of the beds and oil or gas natural seepages in the area.[31] Geophysical survey is also carried out at this stage. This involves a study of the subsurface geology of the concession through seismic reflection, gravity and magnetic surveys. By this process data are generated, processed and interpreted to enable the company to know the nature of the rocks and their distribution.[32] The depth of the basement, i.e., the total thickness of sediments in the sedimentary basin and the major structural features within it will be known as well. Through the interpretation of the seismic data acquired, structural traps and potential drilling locations are identified.

4.2.2.3 Exploratory and Appraisal Wells Drilling

Drilling of exploratory well will help the company to obtain information regarding the petroleum geology of the strata drilled through. The wells will enable the company to determine the type of rock, the porosity of the potential reservoirs and the nature of the fluids in the reservoir. Appraisal wells are thereafter drilled to determine the size and extent of the field. The information obtained at this stage will enable the company to build a model or picture of subsurface geology layer by layer and bed by bed so as to predict where oil or gas will be encountered during drilling. After the geological or basin model and the prediction about the petroleum history has been carried out, evaluation of the volume or quantity of the petroleum is made.[33] But before this, prospect evaluation is carried out to determine whether there is petroleum accumulation or not. This involves an assessment in turn of the five essential requirements that has to be met for there to be an 'accumulation awaiting discovery.'[34] Once a discovery has been made – which is known after prospect evaluation – and the decision to drill

30. Stoneley, 'Introduction to Petroleum Exploration for Non-Geologists', at 67.
31. *Ibid.*, at 68-71.
32. *Ibid.*, at 71-80.
33. *Ibid.*, 81-95.
34. *Ibid.*, these are –generating source rock (its thickness and richness in petroleum), reservoir's porosity and permeability and the extent to which it extends laterally, existence of cap rock or seal and whether they are strong enough to contain the high pressures of oil or gas in an underlying reservoir, and presence of traps at depth. The results of these parameters are pulled together in order to inform a decision of whether to drill or not.

is established, the quantity of the resource is evaluated or estimated. This involves quantitative assessments of the petroleum found or hope to find. The normal way of estimating how much oil has been found or discovered is by eliminating everything that is not oil from the bulk volume of the reservoir within the closure of the trap. This process is not an easy one for the geologists as it involves complex mathematical calculations using computer simulation. But at the end of their calculations, they will be able to determine proven, probable and possible reserves. Proven reserves are those reserves that the company believes to be present in the reservoir with 85% or 95% degree of confidence or statistical probability.[35]

Probable is with 50% degree of confidence or probability while possible is with 15% or 10%. Other terminologies include recoverable reserves (which is the volume of oil that can be actually produced to surface from an accumulation), and original and remaining reserves (refers to what was there before start of production and what is still there for the taking at a future or given date respectively).[36]

4.2.2.4 Development and Production

After discovery has been made and evaluated, the next phase is development and production. Here a detailed study of the reservoir is carried out to understand the distribution of the petroleum in the subsurface. In this regard, evaluation of the amounts of oil present coupled with how they underlie individual licence areas is also carried out. Many accumulations extend under more than one licence block, and therefore will be partly owned by individual licence area. The proportion of the field belonging to each company is determined by the volume of oil in place beneath its block.[37] Also, optimum number of appraisal and production wells and their respective best locations are determined. The production well should be well positioned to ensure maximum recovery for as long as possible. At this stage also, control of production is carried out to ensure that early water or gas production is avoided. Otherwise, much of the oil may be trapped or by-passed irretrievably in the reservoir. Therefore, the oil should not be allowed to flow indiscriminately from the reservoir. Enhanced oil recovery programmes may also be used at this stage to assist the oil in getting to flow through the reservoir and into the production wells.[38]

4.2.2.5 Decommissioning

This happens at the end of the life span of the field. Here production has ceased and the production site will have to be abandoned. It involves plugging of wells down-hole and near the surface and the removal of the surface structures. It is usually a complex operation depending on whether the terrain is offshore or onshore.

35. *Ibid.*
36. For the importance of oil and gas 'Reserves' to a company, see *infra* p. 150.
37. Stoneley, 'Introduction to Petroleum Exploration for Non-geologists', at 96-97.
38. *Ibid.*

From the analysis of the petroleum production phases above, it is very obvious that a licensee cannot claim ignorance of the fact that his discovery extends beyond his licence area, the extent of the extension and to a certain degree, the quantity of oil underlying his licence area and that of the extension. It is also clear that production from a field requires control in order to achieve optimum recovery. Unilateral capture militates against this rational development of straddling fields as explained further in Chapters 5 and 6 of this book. The analysis above has also helped in understanding the structure of the natural habitat of oil and gas at the subsurface and its mechanics.

4.3 Production Licence as Symbol of Overlying Proprietary Rights

Comparing the property rights regime in fisheries with bill of lading, Barnes stated that:

[B]ills of lading are widely regarded as amounting to constructive possession of goods in transit in order that certain commercial needs are met. Both a bill of lading and an Individual transferable quota (ITQ) are symbols of overlying proprietary interests. Whereas the title function of a bill of lading is a legal construct necessary to facilitate international trade, the title function of an ITQ is a legal construct necessary to overcome the physical impediments of allocating ownership to fish in the natural State.[39]

An ITQ has been defined as a paradigmatic property rights-based mechanism used as a form of output control to grant individual harvesting rights to a set amount of an overall quota of a fish as set by a national fishing authority.[40] Barnes argued that even though an ITQ holder merely enjoys the right to catch rather than ownership of any actual fish until they are caught, this does not prevent the ITQ being examined in proprietary terms.[41]

The relationship between ITQ and the fish in its natural state in fisheries regime is very similar to the relationship existing between a petroleum production licence and the petroleum in its natural state in petroleum extraction regime. Therefore, by way of analogy, a Petroleum Licence is a 'symbol of underlying proprietary interests, the title functions of which can be regarded as a legal construct necessary to overcome the physical impediments of allocating ownership to petroleum in the natural state.'[42] Furthermore, Barnes contended that a plausible argument that could be canvassed is that because an ITQ is wholly dependent on regulatory measures, they cannot amount to property rights and as such remains as regulatory entitlements.[43] Similar argument has been canvassed by some commentators with respect to petroleum licence. It has been argued that as a result of the various forms of regulatory controls exercised by the State on the petroleum licence, it has defeated its claim as a property right. However, relying on the authority of Bentham, such a legal contingency has been regarded as a quality of all property rights. Bentham had opined that '*Till law existed, property could*

39. Barnes, 'Property Rights and Natural Resources', at 325.
40. *Ibid.*, at 324.
41. *Ibid.*
42. *Ibid.*, at 325.
43. *Ibid.*

scarcely be said to exist. Property and law were born and die together. Till there was law there was no such thing as property: take away law and property is at an end.'[44] Therefore, issuance of production licence is another way in which the challenges of allocating property rights to petroleum reservoir has been or could be overcome.

Having examined the challenges inherent in regulating cross-licence petroleum resources and how the challenges can be overcome, we can now turn to the question of whether rights of licensee to Petroleum Reservoir discovered by him is proprietary or not. A conceptual framework will be sieved from the analytical framework in Chapter 2 to answer this question. The conceptual framework will then be contextualised for application to un-exploited oil and gas resources.

4.3.1 *Conceptual Analysis*

From the analytical framework in Chapter 2, we have seen that the traditional account of property places emphasis on property as 'things'. It emphasises the 'thing hood' of property, its in rem character, as well as its functional role. As an in rem right, it empowers the right holder to exclude all other persons from the thing. This means that property is a power against others in the society and the State and it gives the holder an aura of freedom against the State. It emphasises the relationship between a person and a thing. In this relationship, the person (the right holder) has the right to use, right to enjoy and power to alienate the thing. The functional role of property in this regard also means that property provides a security of expectation in the use and enjoyment of resources and also against interfering forces in society at large. As a security of expectation, property will give legal protection to the holder of the right to a thing to the exclusion of all others in the society. This therefore, guarantees that a person will reap the fruits of his labour. However, by the end of the nineteenth century, the traditional conception of property became unpopular because of its failure to conceive property as consisting of not only rights over things, but of any valuable right. The concept of physical and absolute property is incapable of recognising every valuable interest or property such as trademarks, trade secrets, copyright, going value of businesses, franchise and equitable easements, etc. These are property rights either created by the legislature or the courts that cannot be conjectured within the frame work of the Blackstone's physical and absolutist conceptions of property.

The modern approach as exemplified by Hohfeld's theory is to the effect that property is a relation between persons that concerns things.[45] It is no longer a relation between person and object. Property is characterised as a complex aggregate of jural relations. It is the combination or some of those relations that endows it with the

44. Bentham J, 'The Limits of Jurisprudence Defined' (Charles warren Everett ed. 1945) at p. 85; Jeremy Bentham, 'Theory of Legislation' (Richard Hildreth ed. 1975) at 69.
45. This relational concept of property is widely acknowledged by other legal theorists (Munzer) and legal anthropologists (Von Benda-Beckmann). For example Munzer defines property rights as 'relations, usually legal relations, among persons or other entities with respect to things' while Von Beckmann also defined property rights in relational terms. See Munzer, 'A Theory of Property', at 16; F. Von Benda-Beckmann, 'Anthropological Approaches to Property Law and Economics', (1995) European Journal of law and Economics 2: 309-336 at 311.

character of property and not any reference to some object of ownership. He sees property as a way of defining our relationship with other people. Property involves not just about controlling a 'thing' but also about one's relationship with every other person in the world.[46]

The combination of Hohfeld's and Honore's theories (Holfedian elements, correlatives, opposites and Honore's standard incidents of ownership) plus other related but less powerful incidents; and the subjects of these incidents (tangible and intangible 'things') provide a good picture of property. These incidents are the relations that constitute property. They can also be regarded as the 'sticks' in the bundle called property. Furthermore, property also includes less powerful collections of incidents that do not rise to the level of ownership. For example, a holder of an easement has a claim-right and privilege to use the land of another and also a power to compel enforcement of that claim-right and privilege. Therefore, easement can be regarded as property or property interest, even though it does not amount to ownership. Bailment, Franchises and some Licences also fall into this category of property called limited property. In this respect, property rights encompass not only ownership but also a much wider range of rights or interests.

Economists have taken the realists ideas about property a step further by conceiving, property as a list of use rights that a person has in a resource. Thus, property is seen as a bundle of rights rather than physical entities. According to Economists, property institution exercises the role of promoting utility or welfare and establishes the rules that define or delimit the type of benefits or privileges the owners, users and other persons can receive from a particular resource.[47] Other economists' perspectives conceived of property rights (or use rights) as entitlements to a 'thing'. They see property as revolving around the desire for resources and to control other's access to those resources. Property serves the role of settling people's conflicts about resources. This is done by allocating exclusive rights. This gave a sense of security to each owner so that he can invest more in the production of resources.[48] Yet, other economist's view of property did not rely on any of the notions of property as right to a thing or as bundle of rights but rather on the rules by which an entitlement may be protected and enforced.[49] Majority of Economists have viewed property rights as any legal entitlement that has monetary value.[50] This is in line with the public law approach to property rights which does not make a distinction between in rem rights and in

46. See also Carol Rose, 'Property as Story Telling: Perspectives from Game Theory, Narrative Theory and Feminist Theory', (1990) 2 Yale J. L. & Human at 42-49.
47. Legal theorists, anthropologists, law and economic scholars also accepted the economic roles of property rights. They agreed that it is the mechanism by which allocation of scarce resources among multiple users in the society are regulated. This is done through market or non-market allocations and exchanges. See Waldron, 'The Right to Private Property', at 31-32; Von Benda-Beckmann, 'Anthropological Approaches to Property Law and Economics', 310-311 and R.A. Posner, 'Economic Analysis of Law', 4th edn (Boston, MA: Little, Brown, 1992), at 32.
48. Rose, 'Property as Story Telling: Perspectives from Game Theory, Narrative Theory and Feminist Theory', at 43.
49. Calabresi & Melamed, 'Property Rules, Liability Rules, and Inalienability Rules: One View of the Cathedral'.
50. Cotula, 'Human Rights, Natural Resource and Investment Law in a Globalised World', at 14 citing Candian et al., 'Property-Propriete-Eigentum: Corso di Diritto Privato Comparato, Padova'

personam rights. However, modern economic discourse on property rights is to the effect that property has a distinctive in rem character that enhances security in the use and enjoyment of a particular resource.

Economists have also distinguished between legal property right and economic property right. Legal property right is what the State transfers to a person while economic property right is the ability to enjoy or consume the good or the services of the assets directly or indirectly through exchange. The role of the legal rights is to enhance, enforce and protect the economic rights.

International investment laws -BITs and MITs -have given protected 'investment' or 'property' an expansive definition. The definition has been made to cover three particular categories: (1) physical property of foreign investors, (2) intangible rights, and (3) administrative rights (also an intangible right) that are needed to carry on the investment projects.[51] The Administrative rights are often referred to as licences, leases, permits, concessions, production sharing agreements, joint venture agreements and service contracts in the field of natural resources. They are the vehicle of foreign investment. They have been variously described as proprietary, *'profit a prendre'* or contractual rights.[52] Some treaties have expressly recognised these rights as protected property in investment laws.[53] This is because these intangible rights that are granted to an investor by the Host State are often more valuable than the physical assets that are brought into the venture in that they enable an investor to carry out the activities in the Host State. If such rights are withdrawn by the Host States or its agency, the investment will cease to be of any value to the investor. Therefore, in oil and gas investment projects certain species of property rights are at play. An investor would be more interested in the subsoil resources (e.g., minerals and discovered petroleum reservoir), project infrastructures and equipment (e.g., oil wells, platforms, pipelines and flow stations, petrol-physical and geo-physical data acquired) and in intangible assets such as contracts, licences, goodwill, technical resources (technical know-how, skills, specialisation), exclusive right to produce from the reservoir, title to the petroleum produced and a twenty-year production term with renewable option (for as long as there may be production), various choses in action made up of rights under various kinds of contracts or the one overriding royalty interest. Each of these attributes is associated with economic property right because each of these attributes has value. This value has to be maximised by the possessor of the asset in that if unused by the possessor, no one else has legal capacity to do so except if the rights of value maximisation is extinguished by the State with payment of compensation. The Licensee therefore, must be able to maximise the value of its asset through consumption, sale or exchange.[54] This is why property rights have been given expansive

(CEDAM, 1992), at 164. See also Walde & Kolo, 'Environmental Regulation, Investment Protection and "Regulatory Taking" in International Law'.

51. Sornarajah, 'The International Law on Foreign Investments', at 16.
52. See Chapter 3 above for detailed analysis of the legal nature of these administrative rights.
53. See the model UK BIT and the U.S. BIT above. See also. Sornaraja, The International Law on Foreign Investments', at 191 n. 73 for the Australia – Vietnam treaty which includes contractual rights and the list of protected property …'.
54. Barzel, 'Economic Analysis of Property Rights', at p. 3.

definition under international investment law. Investment treaty tribunals have not restricted application of takings law to cases of Host State's interferences with ownership of physical assets such as land but have extended it to cover cases of interferences with 'all interests and rights which ... may be evaluated in financial and economic terms'.[55] It goes beyond in rem rights to include rights derived from natural resources concessions and other government contracts. Therefore, investor's contractual rights have been treated as property and any breach thereof by the Host State (through the exercise of its sovereign authority as opposed to purely commercial conduct) is tantamount to expropriation.[56] Thus, in international investment law, any legal claim that has economic value that is related to investments is regarded as property. In addition, expectation linked to market access has been treated as property interests and respect for the investor's 'legitimate expectations' has been regarded as a pillar of the standard of fair and equitable treatment to which an investor may be entitled under applicable BITs.'[57]

Under A1P1 of ECHR, the term 'possession' has been given an expansive interpretation that covers a wide range of proprietary interests, e. g. moveable and immoveable, corporeal and incorporeal interests such as shares and patents, contractual rights including leases or licences, welfare benefits and judgment debts or tort compensation. Effectively, the term 'possession' has been interpreted to mean that other economic interests or things which have economic value will be protected by the right. Therefore, the definition of 'property rights' or 'possessions' go beyond ownership of physical goods. It has been interpreted to cover certain other rights and interests constituting assets. Under A1P1 Jurisprudence, in conceptualising property rights, emphasis is placed on economic expectation and the ability of the assets to generate income.[58]

Consequently, the ECtHR has held that 'possessions' cover not only existing possession, but also 'assets, including claims, in respect of which an applicant can argue that he has at least a 'legitimate expectation that they will be realised'.[59] This represents an autonomous definition of 'possession' because it is not based on the definition of property from any jurisdiction that is party to the Convention. The approach the Convention Organs and the Court have adopted was to use constitutional law definition of property which is broader than the private law definition. Thus, like the investment law, the distinction between in rem rights and in personam rights has been eroded in the Human rights law approach to the definition of property rights. This is unlike private law approach in which such distinction is held sacrosanct.

Similarly, Inter-American Commission and Court of Human Rights (ICCHR) accepted the notion of autonomous meaning of property rights and have therefore, held

55. *Libyan American Oil Company (Liamco) v. The Government of the Libyan Arab Republic*, at 189. See also *Amoco Finance Corp. v. Iran* (*supra*).
56. *Compania de Aguas del Aconquija S.A. and Vivendi Universal v. Argentine Republic*, [7.5.4]; *Parkins-Compagniet AS v. Lithuania* (*supra*); *Azurix v. Argentina (Merits)* (*supra*).
57. Cotula, 'Human Rights, Natural Resource and Investment Law in a Globalised World' at 14.
58. Walde & Kolo, 'Environmental Regulation, Investment Protection and "Regulatory Taking" in International Law'.
59. *Gratzinger and Gratzingerova v. Czech Republic* (*supra*).

that customary rights of the indigenous and tribal groups over their ancestral territories should be protected even where such rights are not formally recognised by national laws and irrespective of any evidence of the monetary value of the resources found in those territories.[60] The ICCHR has also defined property rights as 'any ...object capable of having value.'[61] Following the jurisprudence of the European and Inter-American courts, the African commission on Human and People's Rights has also held that the rights to property includes the traditional possession of land by indigenous peoples, even where these people no longer hold that land due to historical injustices.[62]

4.3.2 *Conceptual Analysis Contextualised: To Determine Whether Discovered Petroleum Reservoir Is a Property Right*

In those countries where a two or more stage rights system is adopted, e.g., Nigeria, Canada, Netherlands and Australia, it can be argued that a production licence can be regarded as conveying proprietary interests in the underground petroleum to the licensee. The licence is often granted where commercial discovery of petroleum has been made. The production licence is granted to enable the licensee to mine the resources discovered in his licence area. The resources discovered, while still forming part of the land at the time the production licence is granted, is an interest in land which is a property under the common law classification. It is to be noted that some of these countries (e.g., Netherlands and Australia) specified in their legislations that property in the petroleum passes to the licensee when produced while others are silent on the issue. It is submitted that this will not preclude an inference from the licence granting clauses, that the licensee has a proprietary interest in the petroleum before production. From the theoretical or conceptual analysis above, and within the context of the modern conceptions of property by the legal and economic theorists, international investments and human rights laws, it is submitted that oil and gas in the reservoir qualifies as a protectable property interests or rights in favour of the Licensee. It is an entitlement that has economic value. If property right is anything that is 'valuable', discovered oil and gas in the reservoir constitutes property right as it is an asset that is valuable. It qualifies as an investment and it represents the value of the production licence. As stated above, when a licensee discovers oil and gas under the ground, reserves are estimated. The reserves can be categorised into proven, probable and possible. Each of these categories has value in the company's records and it constitutes an asset that enhances the stock value of the company. The importance of the

60. Cotula 'Human Rights, Natural Resource and Investment Law in a Globalised World', at 13 citing the case of *Maya Indigenous Communities of the Toledo District v. Belize*, Report No. 40/04, 12 October 2004, ICCHR, Case 12.053, available online at http://www1.umn.edu/humanrts/cases/40-04.html.
61. *Ibid.*
62. *Ibid.*, at 14 citing the case of *CEMIRIDE and Minority Rights Group International v. Kenya*, Communication No. 276/2003, African commission on Human and People's Rights, available online at http://www.minorityrights.org/9587/press-releases/landmark-decision-rules-kenyas-removal-of-indigenous-people-from-ancestral-land-illegal.html.

company's reserves is aptly demonstrated when Shell Petroleum Development Company (SPDC), downgraded its proven reserves estimates for the years 2002 and 2003 to probable category. Though, reserves estimates could differ or vary considerably depending on how they are defined, reserves booking is very important because the calculation of the future cash flow of the company is based on its reserves by applying year-end oil and gas prices, current tax rates and a 10% annual discount factor. It also plays crucial role in determining the value of oil stocks and enables benchmarking of companies against their peers. Most importantly, it provides a more comprehensive picture of the asset value of an oil company which ultimately reflects the value of the shares of the company at the stock market. The economic and market value of such reserves is an important factor considered in the valuation of the company. Such reserves or discoveries boost the market value of the company on the stock market and in some cases expose the company to hostile takeovers or voluntary transfer of assets (at huge profits) to third parties.[63] This aptly demonstrates the role of the market in establishing property rights, perhaps ahead of or without State intervention in the form of legislation.[64]

The economic value of the company's reserves also affects the company's rating. For example, the Standard and Poor's rating of shell dropped from its long time rating of AAA to AA+.[65] Therefore, part of what constitutes lessee's assets is the reservoir oil and gas. This will account for an economic argument in support of the assertion that Petroleum reservoir is equivalent to proprietary interest in that discovered oil in the reservoir is an asset that enhances the stock's value of a production company. Therefore, Law must have business sense when dealing with commercial matters. The stock value of an oil and gas companies in the capital market depends on their reserves. Since their reserves attract such value, it should be brought into law by recognising licensee's proprietary right to unexploited oil. There is a link between the stock value of an exploration and production companies and the unexploited reserves. Also, if there is legal recognition of the link between the stock value of a company and its unexploited reserves, the law should equally recognise the oil capture by the licensee from underneath the licence area of his neighbour as the property of the latter.

Following the above reasoning, the international investment arbitral tribunals have used modern valuation methods such as Discounted Cash Flow (DCF) to calculate damages payable to an investor for expropriated upstream petroleum property.[66] This

63. As was the case with Tullor oil Plc. in Ghana and Heritage Oil in Uganda. See also the cases of SPDC's divestment of assets in Nigeria n. 9 at p. 133 above. See also Chapter 7 *infra* the discussion on the case between *Shell Nigeria Ultra Deep Ltd v. Federal Republic of Nigeria* (ICSID Case No. ARB/107/18. After the case was discontinued by the tribunal in 1 August 2011 based on the parties' request, SNUD negotiated a take-over of the assets of Malabu Oil Company in OPL 245 for the sum of USD 1,092,000,000 and the OPL was transferred to SNUD and NAOC by Malabu Oil Company.
64. Andrzej Rapaczynski, 'The Roles of the State and the Market in Establishing Property Rights', (1992) Journal of Economic Perspectives 10(2): 87-90.
65. See 'Shell Hopes Worst Is Out of Way', *Petroleum Economist*, May 2004 at 13.
66. Rudolf Dolzer et al., 'Principles of International Investment Law' (Oxford University Press, 2008), at 274. See also V. Rajarao, 'Determining Damages in Cross-Border Disputes', (November, 2007) TDM 4(6): 3-10; W.H. Knull et al., 'Accounting for Uncertainty in Discounted Cash Flow Valuation of Upstream Oil and Gas Investments', (November, 2007) TDM 4(6): 10-15.

involves (1) calculation of the anticipated future cash flows to be generated from the enterprise for each year during the life of the enterprise, term of lease, etc. (2) calculation of the future costs, (3) determination of an appropriate discount rate to be applied to the future profits. It therefore, takes into account the amount of oil in reservoir and its market value under present market conditions discounted by inflation and price fluctuation, etc. factors. This shows that the licence and or the oil and gas reserves carries economic value in company's books since the tribunal's calculation of damages is not restricted to physical assets but also to estimated reserves, taking into consideration the number of years it will take to exploit the oil which is discounted at the end. All the above go to show that the licensee possesses proprietary interest in un-extracted petroleum.[67]

This method was applied in several Iran-U.S. Claim Tribunal cases such as *Starret Housing v. Iran (supra)*, *Philips Petroleum v. Iran (supra)*, *Amco v. Indonesia (supra)*, *Amoco v. Iran (supra)*, *Aminoil v. Kuwait* (1982) and Investment treaty case of *CMS v. Argentina (supra)*. In Philip's case, the plaintiff entered into a Joint Structure Agreement (JSA) with the National Iranian Oil Company to produce oil in the Persian Gulf. They both formed Non-profit Iranian Joint Stock Company (IMINOCO) to carry out the operation of JSA. During the unrest, IMINOCO operations were shut down. After the success of the revolution, IMINOCO resumed production but the claimants were not allowed to lift oil. The tribunal held that 'Taking' had occurred and that claimant was entitled to the Fair Market value of its JSA rights at the date of the 'Taking'. The tribunal relied on the DCF calculation by the Claimant with minor adjustments to arrive at the fair market value. This was 'calculated based on the projected amount of recoverable oil, future oil prices, projected costs of production and the appropriate risk.'

Furthermore, reference can be made to the nature of licensee's interest for security of loan to illustrate the economic property right associated with reservoir oil. The necessary question to be asked is what is the security a licensee can offer lenders for the huge indebtedness that will be incurred before production of oil and gas and achievement of cash flow from the project?

In a typical oil and gas project finance, the lender's right to repayment is dependent on the ability of the project to generate income. The lenders ensure that there is oil or gas to produce and therefore conduct an audit of the company's reserves base. Therefore, the security that a licensee would offer to the lender would be *the project's assets and receivables*. The nature, quality and enforceability of the security are also very important.[68] The nature of the security that a licensee can offer its creditors is tied to the nature of the rights acquired at the time of the loan. Principally, a licensee would seek funds for development when commercial discovery has been

67. For criticism of this method of valuation see Thomas W. Walde et al., 'Compensation, Damages, and Valuation', in Peter Muchlinski et al. (ed.) 'International Investment Law' (Oxford University Press, 2008) 1049 at 1074. Although this method of valuation has been criticised as not providing objective and predictable outcomes, this criticism does not go to the root of the proprietary character of the production licence or of its underlying value which is the oil in the reservoir.
68. See F.V.W. (Van) Penick, 'Offshore Financing: The Nature of Security Interests in Oil and Gas Projects on the Continental Shelf', (1985) Alta L. Rev. 23: 33.

made and a production licence or lease is obtained. This coincides with the appropriate time for unitisation because at the exploration stage, parties must have known that the reservoir straddles and would require unitised development. The nature of the rights acquired by the licensee at the production stage, as we have seen in Chapter 3 is proprietary in nature. It is this right that licensee assigns to a lender as security for loan. Since this right (Licence) contains some attributes (which discovered oil in the reservoir forms a part), the totality of which a licensee assigned to a lender as security for a Loan, it follows that in the event of default of repayment, the lender can obtain a writ of attachment of the asset in satisfaction of the debt. What the lender has is an assigned property right in the licence which as has been pointed out above, contains some attributes, including the oil in the reservoir.

It is submitted that since a production licence is an asset to the licensee and which forms part of the security that is offered to a lender in financing oil and gas projects, it follows that a licensee must have property right in the licence and hence the petroleum reservoir before a lender can have an enforceable security.

4.4 Evaluation of 'Discovered Petroleum Reservoir' as 'Property Rights'

This calls for an examination of the incidents of this economic property right. The incidents will include exclusive rights (the holder must have the right to control or limit access to the reservoir), the holder must be able to determine the amount and kind of use of the reservoir, the holder must be able to enjoy the benefits from the use of the reservoir, the holder should enjoy the right to future returns from the reservoir, there must be duration/terms of year within which the holder would capture/recoup satisfactory returns on any investments made. All these incidents are enjoyed by the holder of a production licence over discovered petroleum reservoir.

A very challenging issue could be how to ascribe excludability criterion to reservoir oil and gas. However, from the meaning of property rights and the incidents of ownership analysed in Chapter 2, we have seen that excludability incidents of ownership is determined by physical, legal and moral factors and hence the scope of private property rights. We have also seen that where a 'thing' is impossible to be physically excluded, legal factors must be responsive to it so that legal excludability would be made possible. As it has been pointed out, underground petroleum resources is contained in a reservoir bounded by traps either on the top or by the side or both thus, making it possible for the resources to be confined in a particular place unless intervening circumstances occur from the activities of either human being or natural forces. Therefore, physical excludability with respect to underground petroleum resources in a reservoir is possible. In addition, the use of licence by the Government is one of the legal means by which physical excludability has been achieved. An example could be drawn from the marine resources.

At the inception, because it was impossible of bounding the ocean, marine spaces and its resources were regarded as open access resource. However, with the designation of international boundaries across the ocean spaces and the enforcement of same through positive international law, the regime of open access has to change, thus culminating in the enjoyment of exclusive rights over wide areas of the world oceans.[69] It is instructive to note that with scientific and technological advancement in the modern world, many rules as to how property rights operate will have to change.[70]

In making a case for recognition and protection for proprietary rights in Discovered Petroleum Reservoir, reference could also be made to Chapter 2 in which we had examined the legal character of Petroleum production licence. It has been shown that property is in the licence and this could extrapolate downwards to encompass the petroleum in situ that is the object of the licence. The licence could be said to have been designed as one of the ways to overcome the difficulty in identifying the object of ownership or application of property regime to underground petroleum. In fact the overall object of the licence is to provide licensee with a pre-capture interest in the petroleum so as to prevent drilling race or competition. If the object of the licence, that is, the pre-capture petroleum is absent, the licence is useless as both economic and legal rights. It may be erroneous to conclude that licence comprises only rights to search, bore and get petroleum rather than ownership of the pre-capture petroleum. A right conferred by the licence on a licensee is more than a mere or bare licence to search, bore and get petroleum. It is a form of constructive possession of fugacious resources in their natural state which is converted to full ownership upon capture.[71] This is more in agreement with the value of the right (licence) which is the pre-capture petroleum.

4.5 Rule of Capture or Discovered Petroleum Reservoir as 'Property rights': Theoretical Comparison

The Common law rule of capture has been regarded as a property rule that allocates ownership of resource to whoever gets the resource first from straddling reservoir even if part of the resource comes from an adjoining land. Whereas the concept of property rights in petroleum reservoir has the potential to allocate resources to adjoining licensees based on volume of resources underlying their respective licence. The question is whether on a theoretical level, which of these two opposing property concepts can be properly justified as a property rights?

Theoretical justifications for property rights comprise legal, economic and moral justifications for property rights. However, as pointed out by Becker, justifications for property can be looked at from three different angles - general, specific and particular justifications. This will probably provide answers to three questions - (1) why there ought to be any property right, (2) why there ought to be any specific sort of property right, e.g., private property right (full liberal ownership) and (3) why a particular person ought to have a particular property right in a particular thing.[72]

69. Barnes, 'Property Rights and Natural Resources', at 314.
70. *Ibid.*, see generally pp. 314-316.
71. *Ibid.*, at 324.
72. Becker, 'Property Rights: Philosophic Foundations', at 23. These questions represent general, specific and particular justifications for property.

Our inquiry in this book is focused on the third question although implicitly, it includes the first and the second. However, one must bear in mind that much of the philosophical and political discussions on justification for property focused mainly on the first question and in the discussion of them, answers to the second and third questions can be discovered. Therefore, an inquiry into these theories will provide us with a tool (legal, economic and moral reasons) to evaluate why licensee should keep petroleum withdrawn from beneath his neighbour's land through a well lawfully drilled on his land. Our analysis will focus on the Natural right (or labour) /desert theory, the first appropriation theory and the Utilitarian theory. From the Economic angle, we shall be examining Utilitarian /Economic theories. However, the various constraints provided by these schools of thoughts are also examined against the background of our study.

4.5.1 *Natural Right (or Labour) Theory/Desert Theory*

The Labour theory was propounded by John Locke.[73] The essence of Locke's theory is the idea that since one's body is one's property (i.e., self-ownership) and the produce, i.e., labour is also one's property, it follows from there that the labour's product will also be one's property.

Several questions have been raised concerning this proposition. Amongst the questions are – Is it possible to have property in one's body? Is labour a commodity that can be an object of property right having regard to the fact that it cannot be separated from personality? Why is mixing of one's labour with a thing makes the thing one's own rather than a way of losing one's labour?[74] Also why should the labourer gain property to the whole object rather than the value his labour added? Is it possible for an action (labouring) to be mixed with a material?

Robert Norzick argued in support of self-ownership as justification for property. He is of the view that every individual has a natural right to the fruits of his labour and that if seized from him, it will be tantamount to forcing him to work for others which means slavery.[75] A counter argument to this was offered by Ali Coban. He said that since slavery has been abolished, an individual no longer has property rights over his body but rather personality rights.[76]

Waldron, in support of Locke's proposition of owning labour, remarked that if labour is regarded as expenditure of energy, it can be a subject-matter of property rights

73. John Locke, 'Second Treatises on Government' edited with introduction by C.B. Macpherson (1980), at 19. This is however contrary to views expressed earlier by Hugo Grotius, who contended that the original owner got his title from the first persons that received the property from God. Hugo Grotius, 'On the Law of War and Peace', bk. 2, Ch. 2, pp. 1, 4-5 (Kelsey Trans. 1925).
74. Robert Norzick, 'Anarchy, State and Utopia' (New York: Basic Books, 1974), 174-175.
75. *Ibid.*, at 174.
76. Coban, 'Protecting Property Rights within the European Convention on Human Rights', at 48.

and that just as energy is a property of electricity companies which can be purchased, energy can be regarded as the property of the labourer.[77]

Locke, in support of his proposition that mixing one's labour with a thing gives rise to property in the products of labour, gave an estimate that the value that labour produced is much more than the value that nature produced. According to his estimate, the proportion of the goods produced by labour is ratio 9/10 or 99/100. But this does not mean however that 'equal quantities of labour will generate equal quantities of value.'[78] It will appear that Locke used this proposition to support his claim that appropriation is legitimate without the consent of the rest commoners.[79] But still he needs to show that what labour contributed makes the greatest part of the value of the thing. It is only then that a complaint about being excluded by an appropriator can be tantamount to a desire to take the benefits of another's pain.[80]

One other commentator had remarked that on the basis of labour, occupants might likely claim rights to land they had appropriated and the produce thereof but that:

> ...it is not clear what, more than his labour, man can put into things he has not made, in order to appropriate them,' ... 'regardless of how they painted their usurpations, they remained just that, usurpations.[81]

The Lockean's provisos – 'enough and as good ...in common for others' and that one can acquire as much as one's use before it spoils – have also been criticised by some theorists, as meaningless. This is because if mixing one's labour creates property rights why should the person leave enough and as good for others be important or why should he be answerable to others for wasting or spoiling that which he owned.[82] The rationale for these provisos appear to be for the justification of act of appropriation without the consent of other commoners and that it will only be applicable where the things appropriated is common to all, e.g., land and other natural resources. It will not apply to creative works like arts, picture or songs which does not involve using natural resources.[83] Locke's theory is plausible if the act of unilateral appropriation is in respect of abundance resources like domain name on the Internet as opposed to scarce natural resources such as radio wave frequency. The former can be appropriated without the consent of other commoners, while the latter cannot be appropriated without consent of others in the form of licence.[84]

---

77. Waldron, 'The Right to Private Property' at 183. He also contends that ownership of one's body and its labour can be interpreted as one's personal liberty as this can be connected with the notion that a man is the master of himself.
78. *Ibid.*, at 192. Waldron is of the opinion that five minutes labour might account for nine-tenth of the value of an apple while one hour's labour accounts for nine-tenth of the value of the wooden staff and this does not mean the value of the wooden staff is ten times more than the apple.
79. *Ibid.*
80. Coban, 'Protecting Property Rights within the European Convention on Human Rights', at 49.
81. Jean-Jacques Rousseau, 'Discourse on the Origin of Inequality', Part II, 24 at 30.
82. Coban, 'Protecting Property Rights within the European Convention on Human Rights', at 50 citing J.W. Harris, P&J; J.W. Harris, 'Is Property a Human Right?', in Janet Mclean (ed.), 'Property and Constitution' (Oxford: Hart Pub., 1999), at 197.
83. *Ibid.*
84. *Ibid.*

Robert Norzick[85] however, noted that the proviso – 'enough and as good ...in common for others' – provided by Locke should be modified. A literal application of Locke's proviso will mean that cultivation of previously un-owned land will only generate property right if there were other land available for use by one who claims to be prejudiced by the acquisition. Therefore, if the proviso is not qualified, it will mean that in period of scarcity, no appropriation will be legitimate as there may not be 'enough and as good' left for others after the first appropriation.[86] As a result of this, Norzick suggested modification of the proviso to the effect that the situation of the others should not be worsened by the acquisition taking into account the indirect benefits that others might eventually derive from the acquisition.[87] If their situation is worsened, then they are either compensated or the resources acquired will be relinquished. If they are otherwise not made worse by the act of acquisition in that they receive other indirect benefits, then the acquisition is legitimate even though there is not 'enough and as good' left for them. This in effect protects the rights of the other persons and acts as a constraint on act of appropriation. Therefore, my act of appropriation is just if only it does not place others in a worse position than they would be if I had not appropriated the resource.[88]

4.5.2 *Desert Theory*

The desert principle is a variant of the labour theory. It arises as a result of the perception that Labour theory per se, does not cover all cases because some labour may yield property rights in the very thing laboured on while other labour may not.[89] In some cases, labour may deserve property in the thing laboured on while in other cases, it deserves property in the fee for the labour or even no property at all. In the last cases, it may simply deserve recognition, admiration or gratitude of other people.[90]

Becker asserted that a reformulation of the labour theory by the desert principle is necessary so that it can be determined when people deserve property right in the thing laboured on, i.e., the products of their labour. He therefore defined desert principle as follows: '[A] person who, in some morally permissible way, and without being morally required to do so, 'adds value' to others' life deserves some benefit.'[91]

This means that if a person performs some acts which added value or benefit to the rest of the world, then property right will be appropriate reward for the act based on desert principle.

According to Munzer 'Desert' means 'worthiness of some recompense because of some personal feature or action.'[92] He constructed his desert principle in two stages. In the first stage, which is very similar to the labour theory of John Locke, he is of the view

85. Norzick, 'Anarchy, State and Utopia', at 75.
86. Waldron, 'The Right to Private Property', at 281.
87. *Ibid.*
88. Barnes, 'Property Rights and Natural Resources', at 34.
89. Becker, 'Property Rights: Philosophic Foundations', at 47.
90. *Ibid.*
91. *Ibid.*, at 50-51.
92. Munzer, 'A Theory of Property' at 257.

that the labourer is entitled to moral property rights in the product of his labour not as a reward for his product benefiting the society at large but because of his labour. His belief is that man is an autonomous agent who merits reward for the changes he made to the world through his actions. Therefore, his argument is not based on whether the products benefit the society or on the notion of reward.

In the second stage of his desert principle, he canvassed limitations on the property right. In his view, it is the society that determines whether a person who performs some labour is worthy of recompense or not. This makes desert a socially constructed principle that is determined by the wider community.[93] Munzer was quick to set some qualifications to the desert theory.[94] He believed that on moral grounds, property right should be limited by utility and justice. This is to bring the principle in alignment with the cotemporary social and economic life. For example, in the modern world, a labourer deserves property right in their wages rather than in the product of his labour. In most cases there is even no product at all because in modern society, most property rights are acquired through exchange rather than by acquisition. However by virtue of this revised desert principle, the recompense received by the labourer should be proportional to the work done. He however expressed doubt as to the possibility of achieving commensurability because workers' recompense is not product-tied.[95] In modern society therefore, it is possible that worker's property right (wages) is not commensurate with the work done. He recommended that the value of labour should be determined by free market through contracts of service as formulation of wage policy by the government to deal with this issue might not be successful.[96]

According to Becker, the principle of Desert should be premised on four grounds. First, it must be morally permissible acts which both add and subtracts value. Inherent in this view is that if a benefit is due for adding value, presumably, a penalty is due for subtracting value.[97] This shows that the principle of desert is a double edged principle.[98]

This accounts for 'imposition of tax on companies whose activities depleted the community stocks of un-owned resources or limits the opportunity of others without their consent.' It also accounts for arguments on compensation to any persons who suffer a demonstrable personal loss. The size of the penalty may far outweigh the benefits.[99]

93. Barnes, 'Property Rights and Natural Resources', at 35.
94. Munzer, 'A Theory of Property', at 284. Labour/desert theory is qualified by the duty not to waste, spoil, or accumulate beyond one's needs, duty not to allow the effect of acquisition negatively impact others and that where resources are scarce, commensurate wages could be paid to labourers rather than rights to the resource.
95. *Ibid.*, at 280.
96. *Ibid.*, at 284.
97. Becker, 'Property Rights: Philosophic Foundations', at 51.
98. *Ibid.* He is of the view that some morally permissible acts will both add and subtract value – by improving lots of some at the expense of others – then it follows that both a benefit and a penalty are due.
99. *Ibid.*

Second, the action must be beyond what is morally required of them to do for others. Again, here 'people deserve some benefit for the value their labour produces and conversely they deserve penalty for the disvalue their labour produces.'

Third, principle of proportionality must apply. The benefit must be proportional to the value added by labour. Similarly, the penalty must be proportional to the value subtracted (loss produced) by labour. Therefore, an assessment of any diminution of value produced by the labour should be carried out for the purposes of penalty against the labourer.

Fourth, the type of benefit must fit the type of labour. In this respect, it is necessary to determine whether property right is the only or most fitting benefit for the labour produced. To determine the standard of fittingness, 'the nature of labour, the labourer or the products of labour' must be considered.[100] The purpose or goal of the labour is also paramount. The purpose must first be to 'get and keep' as property the product of the labour. If this is established, further hurdles to jump are - the labourer must deserve a benefit for his labour and the benefit (property right) must be proportional to the value added or produced by labour. It is only when these requirements are satisfied that property right can be the fitting benefit.

This yardstick - purpose or goal of labour - for measuring the fitness of benefits allows a determination of why or when money reward, or recognition, admiration or gratitude are more fitting than property rights to the thing produced.[101]

4.5.2.1 An Assessment of Labour Theory, Its Basis for Rule of Capture and Its Application to Oil and Gas Straddling Reservoir

An evaluation of the labour theory is necessary in order to determine whether it applies to oil and gas and whether it has the capacity to justify the property rule of capture or property rights in petroleum reservoir. Some legal theorists have contended that most of the standard incidents of ownership as exemplified by Honore could be sieved out of Locke's theory. This is because the premise upon which Locke's proposition was based can be said to have established security in the right to capital, right to possess, right to use, right to manage and right to income, absence of term and prohibition of harmful use. Also liability to execution could follow from power of alienation.[102]

100. *Ibid.*, at pp. 51-54.

101. *Ibid.*

102. *Ibid.*, at 36. Becker said that this is borne out of the two reasons he gave as entitling a person to property in the product of his labour. These are that because one has property right in one's body and in its labour, and that on ground of justice, property rights is required in return for his pain. See also Stephen Buckle, 'Natural Law and the Theory of Property' (Oxford: Clarendon Press, 1991) at 180 who said that the historical account of Locke's theory accepted the notion that property constitutes a cluster or bundle of rights. But see John Christman, 'Can Full Ownership Be Justified By Natural Right', (1986) Philosophy and Public Affairs 15: 156. Also referred to by Barnes, 'Property Rights and Natural Resources', at 33, He said that Locke's natural right to property only encompasses right to possess, use and manage the property laboured upon. In this regard, he contended that labour theory does not apply to the modern conception of property typified by Honore's incidents.

Labour theory could find strong appeal in morality. For if on the ground of morality, a person is responsible for his action, it follows that he should be entitled to property rights not only in the value addition he made to a thing but also in the thing so long as no one is wronged by his actions. Individual as an independent agent should be held responsible for his actions. If his action is praiseworthy, he should receive benefit for it. On the other hand if his action is blameworthy, he should be penalised. There is a correlative duty on others not to interfere with his rights to the product of his labour provided that there is no injury to others as a result of his actions. Therefore, this duty is restricted where the action of the labourer violates other's actual right.

The question as to whether it applies to other scarce natural resources such as mines and oil and gas has been raised. One commentator has said that it does not apply to Mines and lands since no body produced them.[103] Stephen Buckle however concedes that they can be object of property only that they can only be acquired by getting consent from the government on payment of tax. This is because it emphasised the virtues and liberty of individuals rather than those in power. It also enjoyed broad political legitimacy because it is based on social construct and encompasses the moral fabrics of the society. Its fundamental tenets that acquisition of resource should not be wasted or spoiled or that should not be accumulated beyond what is needed for usage will serve as control and management tools for natural resources.[104] As pointed out above, the labour theory says that ownership is established in the person who first commingles his labour with a thing common to everyone. Straddling Petroleum reservoir has over the years been regarded as common to every licensee whose licence area overlies the common reservoir. It has therefore been subjected to open access regime. Locke says that as a result of the mixture of his labour with the thing, ownership of the thing vests in him. This appropriation does not require the consent of the rest commoners. Application of the rule of capture to oil and gas straddling reservoirs could be said to have proceeded from this principle. Moreover, labour has to be expended before mineral resources are mined or extracted. Even after extraction, improvements would have to be made on them before they are usable. It is in this light that labour theory may be said to be applicable to mines, and oil and gas. A licensee, who expended heavy capital (both human, technical and financial) to acquire a concession, worked on the concession and discovered an oil and gas reservoir, has a legitimate expectation in the result of his labour. Property right ought to be ascribed to the result of the labour as pointed out by Locke that it is the expenditure of labour that reduces a thing to private property. As Stated by *Posner* 'no one would bother cultivate land, investing much time and effort, if others were free to help themselves to the product of the work.'[105]

Therefore, a plausible argument could be made that labour theory just like the first possession rule convincingly allocates property in oil and gas to the person who

103. Buckle, 'Natural Law and the Theory of Property', at 186. It is the view of this book that in spite of this, its basic principles are applicable to unilateral capture from common-pool petroleum resources.
104. Barnes, 'Property Rights and Natural Resources', at 36.
105. R. Posner, 'Economic Analysis of Law', 5th edn (New York: Aspen, 1998).

captured and reduced them to possession. On this note, the rule of capture may be said to have been justified by the labour theory. However, the proviso to the theory which states that '... at least where there is enough, and as good left in common for others' protects the rights of others and acts as an absolute constraint on acts of appropriation.

Thus, my act of acquisition is just only if it does not place others in a worse position than they would have been if I did not acquire the resource. This proviso therefore, questioned the legitimacy of such appropriation where the rule of capture left the other licensee with no economical quantity of oil in his reservoir.

The questions posed by Becker in this debate are well noted. He asked that 'How does a man's labour justify rights to what he produced? Naturally the answer will be the type of objections people may raise against producer – 'You have destroyed my opportunity for acquisition,' or 'you have put me at a disadvantage.'

He queried further that what if there are enough resources (initially) for each person to make full use of his or abilities? Assuming that people are equal in ability and are aware of the consequences for their own eventual opportunities and competitive positions if they allow others to 'get ahead', one might then ask the question – what is wrong with securing for the industrious the fruits of their labour in this sort of situation?. 'Surely they deserve it. And if their initial acquisitions make it possible for them to use more of the land, minerals, and other resources than they could initially, and the non-producers see this, but still do not care to appropriate (by their labour) their original 'shares', then what is unfair about letting the industrious take that too?[106] Furthermore, 'the slothful do not deserve the produce of others. Nor do they deserve to be protected from the consequences of their sloth' and so it will not be wrong to give property rights – including claim right to the industrious. Becker however, conceded that this argument even though a labour theory appeal, it is still too weak because at best one might be able to derive recipient right from it, and that is not a property right.[107] Also the person who came there first clearly leaves the remainder, no matter how industrious, with reduced opportunities.

Robert Norzick had argued that private property should only arise if it has been justly acquired. A licensee or lessee who legitimately acquired licence or lease from either the government or private individuals and has worked on the licence area to discover petroleum reservoir cannot be said to have unjustly acquired the right. On the other hand if the oil underneath his lease area is produced by his neighbour before he did, what his neighbour has acquired could be regarded as an unjust property. Moreover, the four principles upon which desert are premised by Becker also go to show that the first appropriator to be entitled to what he produced from the underneath adjacent land must be ready to jump all the hurdles.

The labour theory when complimented by the desert theory provides a good justificatory argument for property rights. Becker's desert principle is very instructive to our study. It says that people deserve some benefit for the value their labour produces and conversely they deserve penalty for the disvalue their labour produces. A licensee who unilaterally produced oil and gas from straddling petroleum reservoir

106. Becker, 'Property Rights: Philosophic Foundations', at 48.
107. *Ibid.*

and thereby drained his neighbour's resources obviously deserves penalty for the disvalue his labour produces. The principle of proportionality is also relevant here. The penalty must be proportional to the value subtracted by labour. It is on the strength of this that the rule of capture cannot be properly justified as property rights by the Labour theory. The proviso to the theory clearly supports argument for recognition of the concept of property rights in petroleum reservoir.

4.5.3 *First Occupation / First Possession Theories*

The theory of first Occupancy or first Possession is all about how a person came to own 'things'. The issue is no doubt a hard nut for legal theorists to crack.[108] First Occupancy theory is usually expressed in relation to acquisition of real property, e.g., land, while first possession theory is in respect of chattels. However, both theories are related to Labour and desert theory.

At common law, possession or occupancy has been regarded as the origin of property based on the Maxim, 'first possession is the root of title.'[109] The Maxim has been applied in a variety of cases dealing with capture of wild animals, oil and gas, underground water, the law of finders and the rule of free entry in mining law.[110]

First occupancy or first possession has been generally recognised as falling within the category of particular justification for property rather than general justification.[111]

An evaluation of this theory would show that even though it has a very strong appeal for justifying why a particular person should have a particular property right to a particular thing, it nevertheless provides no sound basis for ownership claims. This is because before it can justify title to property the object occupied must be un-owned. Second, the occupation must be actual and not intentional or declaratory. Third, actual occupation must define with reasonable clarity how much one can occupy. Lastly, occupier must claim no more than what has been defined.[112]

With regards to the first reason, first occupancy can only apply where the things are not owned by any one because such things are what Roman law regards as *res communes*, i.e. property belonging to everyone in common. Examples of *res communes* are air, running water, sea, or vacant seats in the public theatre. Pufendorf, however, is of the opinion that things held in common could either be jointly owned with everyone having a defined share or 'owned by no one but equally available to all.'[113] He argued that the first occupancy is only meaningful with respect to the latter category of

108. Carol M. Rose, 'Possession as the Origin of Property', (1985) U. Chi. L. Rev 52: at 73. She said that 'one buys things from other owners, to be sure, but how did the other owners get those things? Any chain of ownership or title must have a first link.'
109. *Ibid.*, at pp. 74-75.
110. A detailed discussion of these cases is contained in Chapters 5 and 6 of this book.
111. Lawrence Becker, 'Property Rights: Philosophic Foundations', at 23, Particular justification in its own, explains why a particular person should have a particular property right in a particular thing. See also Hamilton et al., 'Different Views of the Cathedral: The Literature on Property Law Theory', in Aileen Mcharg et al. (ed.) 'Property and the Law in Energy and Natural Resources', at 49, note 174.
112. Becker, 'Property Rights: Philosophic Foundations', at 24.
113. Samuel Pufendorf, 'De jure Naturae et Gentium Libri Octo,' bk 4, c 4 (Oldfather Trans., 1934).

things held in common. With respect to the former category, first occupation is not applicable because things jointly owned can neither be acquired nor disposed of by one person without the consent of the joint owners, even if the person has taken no more than his share.[114]

Becker contended further that since joint ownership involves joint management and joint right to capital, the decision to allocate a particular share must be a joint decision even where first occupier may constitute the only rational method for allocating specific shares among the joint owners.[115] This is very instructive when first occupancy or first possession is applied to oil and gas straddling resources. All the licensees of the leases overlying the common reservoir should have been regarded as joint owners of the reservoir but the application of the rule of capture has shown otherwise. The application of the rule of capture has shown that common reservoir is an asset owned by no one but equally available to all. The rule of first possession has thus been made applicable. This has been greatly criticised by some legal theorists as oil and gas in a private lands are not things un-owned. Application of first possession to oil and gas therefore, proceeded from false premise.

Argument based on distributive justice has also been proffered to question the rationale for giving everything to the first occupier while everyone else is left with nothing. Viewing property in this manner may mean that property is theft.[116]

4.5.4 *Utilitarian / Economic Theories*

4.5.4.1 Utilitarian

Utilitarian arguments[117] present a powerful justification for property rights in Western legal and political thinking. However, legal rules imposing restrictions on property have also been justified on utilitarian grounds as well. This is mostly done in the interest of the general society. It was developed from the criticism of the positivists school of thought championed by John Austin. The argument against the positivists is that their theory is unable to provide guidance on moral and political issues. It was

114. Becker, 'Property Rights: Philosophic Foundations', at 25.
115. *Ibid.*
116. Pierri Joseph Proudhorn, 'What Is Property?: An Inquiry into the Principle of Right and of Government', B. Tuker, Trans, cited by Hamilton et al., 'Different Views of the Cathedral: The Literature on Property Law Theory', at 50.
117. See David Hume, 'Treatise of Human Nature', vol. 2 (London: J.M. Dent & Sons Ltd, 1956), at 207; he is the first utilitarian theorist of property. He justified private property rights on the ground of stability of possessions; Aristotle, 'The Politics', Stephen Everson (ed.), Book II, Chapter 5 (Cambridge University Press, 1988); he remarked that private property promotes efficient, economical and careful use of resources than common. It eliminates the conflict and social disharmony prevailing amongst common users of resources. That means that private property promotes utility; J. Bentham, 'An Introduction to the Principles of Morals and Legislation', He is regarded as the father of modern utilitarianism. He espoused that we should 'order our lives so as to promote the greatest happiness of the greatest number; J. Bentham, 'Theory of Legislation', (1914), at 145, he posited that property 'is nothing more than a basis of expectation, the expectation of deriving advantages from the thing that we are said to possess, in consequence of the relation in which we stand towards it.

therefore, conceived that utility principles will provide proper guidance as to how the community will leave and the type of law to govern them. Utility argument is based on moral grounds and that the basic requirement of morality is that happiness should be maximised. Therefore, a moral or legal rule that does not promote average utility of the community is unacceptable to the utilitarian.[118] According to them; right actions are the one that promote utility for the generality of the community. However, controversy among the utilitarians is centered on what is utility. They see it differently as pleasure, happiness, welfare, preference satisfaction, etc.[119] The property rule of capture could promote public utility in the short run in that it may enable the State to realise its goal of early development of the resource and hence speedy revenues, but at the long run, the society may be made worse for it. The attendants competitive drilling that engendered grave wastes of the resources will adversely affect community's satisfaction.

The traditional Utilitarian argument for justification of private property is anchored on the claim that property maximises human happiness which have been defined broadly to include all sorts of human satisfactions.[120] They noted that private ownership embodies use, transfer and income rights. When an owner of resource enjoys the combination of these incidents, utility will be maximised as this will also act as impetus for people to work more effectively. A security in possession and use is therefore necessary. This, they argued, can be provided by a system of property rights.

Unlike Hume, Bentham defines property in terms of security of expectations. He said that human beings experience pleasure when their expectations are fulfilled and pains when they are disappointed. Therefore, if his theory regards utility as presence of pleasure and absence of pain, then utility will be promoted by securing persons' expectations with respect to things that they possess.[121]

Bentham abhorred an attempt by State to invade one's possession or holdings (e.g., through taxation) on ground of redistribution of wealth to achieve equality because that will be in violation of one's security of possession. A person should expect to derive some advantages from his possession. Such advantages according to him may come from trade, rent or productive development. Bentham however admitted that the State's wealth redistribution efforts through taxation should be made public, stable and consistent. It is only on this ground that security of possession can be gained as it enables prediction about one's present and future holdings.[122] Both Hume and Bentham seemed to have suggested that a man who first takes a resource into his possession would have formed an expectation to continue to hold and use the resource on long-term basis and that this natural expectation ought to be respected.

Utilitarian account of property rights suffered some internal inconsistencies. They are of the view that justice is measured by the determination of the greatest benefit for the greatest number and are also against State's invasion of one's possession

118. Munzer, 'A Theory of Property', at 193.
119. *Ibid.*
120. Becker, 'Property Rights: Philosophic Foundations' at 57.
121. Munzer, 'A Theory of Property'at 195.
122. *Ibid.*, at 102.

on ground of wealth redistribution. This view overlooked the possibility that the majority might benefit by the taking of property from an individual. Utilitarian may therefore, find it hard to identify inviolate human rights. Moreover, Utilitarian perspective has shown that since the marginal utility of wealth decreases as a person gets richer, a more equal distribution will likely increase overall satisfaction. However, one commentator has contended that if there is great disparity of wealth between a small number of rich and a large number of poor, there will be lower level of satisfaction.[123] Christman, is also of the view that security of expectation can also be derived from public institution of property and that since private property allows free market to emerge, the unpredictability in the market could make many people to be less secure in their possessions.[124]

In spite of the above criticisms, utilitarian arguments have been regarded as very important justification for private property and it is reputed for its 'directness and apparent simplicity.'[125] It is direct because it specifically postulates that private property is needed in some things to ensure security in possessions and to promote happiness which in turn gives incentive to labour to work more effectively. What people need to acquire, use and consume in order to optimise their happiness will determine the choice of the sort of property rights they should have. Utilitarian's view is that a denial of people's need or want without any moral justification is unacceptable.

4.5.4.2 Economic Justification

There is a link between Utilitarian perspective and economic justifications for allocation of property rights. The question to be asked is whether there is economic justification for allowing the property rule of capture to allocate resources between two competing claimants in oil and gas extraction from straddling fields. According to the Economists, the most efficient response to the problem of having insufficient resources is by promoting greater total welfare.[126] Economics' perspective is to the effect that property rights gives 'an incentive to productive labour and allows for an exchange via market mechanism where supply and demand can lead to the most efficient allocation of resources.'[127]

Economic efficiency argument has always been presented by the Economists as a justification for private property as the goal of economics is how efficiency can be

123. Jeff Waincymer, 'Balancing Property Rights and Human Rights in Expropriation', in Pierre-Marie Dupuy et al. (ed.) 'Human Rights in International Law and Arbitration' (Oxford University Press, 2009), at 282 citing Coban, 'Protection of Property Rights within the European Convention on Human Rights' at 42.
124. Christman, 'The Myth of Property – Towards an Egalitarian Theory of Ownership', at 103.
125. Becker, 'Property Rights: Philosophic Foundations', at 58. He noted that the argument is deductively valid and realistic than 'natural acquisition in some fictional state of nature'.
126. *Ibid.*
127. *Ibid.*

enhanced. Therefore, labour, desert, first occupation and first possession has been regarded as a subset of economic justification.[128]

The justification offered is to the effect that private property is the most efficient way of allocating resources. They argued that if full package private property rights are given to a person, efficient outcomes will be the result. Common property breeds inefficiency and leads to degradation of resources. It is always better to 'internalise some effect or factors i.e. give people property rights over it than to adopt some alternative system of use.'[129] However, they agreed that for economic efficiency to be achieved, existence of competitive market is necessary.[130] They also pointed out that there should be no transaction costs. Thus, transaction costs are assumed to be costless and any right obtained thereby can be enforced without cost.[131]

In advancing utility argument by economists, they noted that there are varieties of costs or dis-utilities associated with non-ownership use of scarce resources. This is because others will be free to interfere with one's uses and enjoyment of the resources which invariably resulted to over-accumulation of resources to offset anticipated losses.[132]

Private property right is necessary to address these external dis-utilities by minimising the costs. However, for considerations of economic utility, this will only be justified if the cost of establishing and maintaining the system of property rights is lower than the total costs of the dis-utilities created by the actions of others.[133]

Furthermore, there are concerns about the way an individual deals or transacts with the resources used in the production of goods (e.g., land, labour, etc.). Where there is no enforced property right to these resources, such dealings or transactions may be carried out among individuals based on custom and social pressure 'liberally laced with deceit, threats, and open force or violence.'[134] Becker is of the view that such transactions will not maximise the total satisfaction of such individuals. To ensure that such transaction maximise the total of satisfactions, the allocative transactions need to be stabilised by a system of ownership rights – 'a system which will give owners right to exclude others as well as to transfer their rights.'[135]

How can efficiency be applied as criterion for societal choice given that efficiency invokes individual's satisfaction or welfare rather than the societal welfare? Economists have however, believed that the yardsticks for determining efficiency are those concepts called pareto-optimality and pareto-superiority (first coined by Vilfredo Pareto) and Kaldor-Hicks efficiency.[136] Pareto superior situation arises if an increase in the welfare of a person does not lead to decrease in the welfare of any other person,

128. Hamilton et al., 'Different Views of the Cathedral: The Literature on Property Law Theory' at 50.
129. Barnes, 'Property Rights ...' at 42.
130. *Ibid.*, at 43.
131. *Ibid.*, at 44.
132. Becker, 'Property Rights: Philosophic Foundations', at 68.
133. *Ibid.*
134. *Ibid.* See generally Rapaczynski, 'The Roles of the State and the Market in Establishing Property Rights'.
135. *Ibid.*
136. Barnes, 'Property Rights and Natural Resources', at pp. 42-43.

while Pareto optimality arises where an allocation of goods does not make at least one person better off without making another person worse off. In other words, Pareto optimal has no Pareto superior. The Criticism against Pareto ranking is that it cannot apply where a person is made worse off, and since there are many situations in which persons are made worse off, Pareto ranking is defective.[137] Kaldor-Hicks test has been used to surmount this deficiency. The test states that a state of affair is superior to the other if those who gain in that state of affairs could compensate those who lose to the extent that make no one worse off by the change.[138] This means that those whose welfare has increased should compensate those whose welfare has decreased. The compensation needs only be hypothetical but Pareto improvement would be achieved if the payment is made.[139] The compensation is however dependent on willingness to pay and which in turn depends on how badly the person wants the thing. The 'intensity' of desires of people can thus be compared contrary to the notion that efficiency ranking avoids interpersonal comparison.[140] This willingness to pay measure of well-being is problematic because how much a person is willing to pay for something might be dependent on how much money a person has and not his evaluation of the thing itself.[141]

According to Munzer, it is possible and advantageous to combine principle of utility and efficiency. When combined, it means that property should be allocated so as to (1) maximise utility regarding use, possession, transfer, etc. of things and (2) to maximise efficiency regarding the use, possession, transfer, etc. of things.[142]

4.5.4.3 Evaluation of Economic Justifications for Rule of Capture: Transition from One Property System to Another

Based on the Non-ownership theory and qualified ownership theory, petroleum *in situ* belongs to no one (Non-ownership theory) or that it belongs to the two lessees as co-tenant or co-ownership (qualified ownership theory). In both ownership theories, straddling oil and gas reservoirs have been governed by open access regime through the application of the rule of capture, thus presenting a tragedy. This is the kind of situation which the rule of capture has entrenched. Therefore, one plausible explanation for why there should be a movement of open access regime to private property category is to avoid tragedy of the commons as propounded by Hardin.[143] Hardin is of the view that 'Freedom in the commons brings ruin to all.' In other words this will be avoided if the 'commons could be privatised or rights of entry and use could be

137. *Ibid.*
138. *Ibid.* See John Christman, 'The Myth of Property – Towards an Egalitarian Theory of Ownership', at 100.
139. *Ibid.*
140. *Ibid.*
141. *Ibid.*, at 101.
142. Munzer, 'A Theory of Property', at 202.
143. Hardin G. 'Tragedy of the Common', (1968) Science 162: 1243 at 1244-1245.

regulated.'[144] He stated that where resources are available to all without discreet property rights, tragedy of the common is expected to occur because there will be 'incentive for individual to exploit the resources for short-term gain and make no effort to prevent or counter long-term depletion in the value of the resources. For example, grazing will be over-grazed, Oceans will be over-fished, Air will be polluted to the detriment of all and Common-pool petroleum resources will be over-exploited.

This was also Demsetz's argument in his earlier work.[145] He argued that private property eliminates or reduces dissipation of rent commonly found in open access property regimes. This is very apposite in fishery and oil and gas straddling reservoir resources. If property is allocated to the first to grab or capture the resource, competition to secure the resource will ensue, thus leading to premature consumption and wasteful dissipation of resources. Therefore, externality is imposed by each consumer of resources on other potential consumers in an open access regime. This is eliminated with private property as it allows each consumer to determine the optimal timing and degree of consumption.[146]

Demsetz also gave evolutionary accounts of private property by addressing the factors that will determine the movement from one property rights regime to another. He said that 'private property should arise wherever the gains produced by internalisation exceeded the transaction costs involved in establishing the property right and the legal system protect that right.'[147] In other words private property rights evolved whenever there was need for changes for resource management.[148] Externalities are those effects borne by persons who are not party to the transaction. The parties whose actions produced externalities caused them without any intention and as such did not bargain for it. Therefore, Economists like Demsetz and Coase assumed that, because private property is best positioned or emerged to alleviate or internalise externalities, it promotes efficiency. For there to be efficient allocation of resources, there must be no externalities.[149] Property rule of capture will only aggravate these externalities, thereby inhibiting efficient allocation of resources. This property rule has become an archaic that is not justifiable economically in modern days as new property concepts have developed over the years in response to the relative change in the value of resources and technological change.[150]

With respect to evolution of property rights in response to technological change, oil and gas field straddling reservoirs presents a good example. In examining the evolution of property rights in the oil and gas extraction from straddling fields,

144. Hamilton et al., 'Different Views of the Cathedral: The Literature on Property Law Theory', in Aileen Mcharg et al. (ed.) 'Property and the Law in Energy and Natural Resources', at 52.
145. Harold Demsetz, 'Towards a Theory of Property Right', (1967) Am Econ Rev. 57: 347.
146. Thomas W. Merill, 'Introduction: The Demsetz Book and the Evolution of Property Rights', (2002) 31 at 332.
147. Hamilton et al., 'Different Views of the Cathedral: The Literature on Property Law Theory ...', at 53 referring to C.M. Carol Rose, 'Servitude', Arizona Legal Studies Discussion Paper No. 09-13, available at http://ssrn.com/absract=1371251.
148. *Ibid.*, at 53.
149. Barnes, 'Property Rights and Natural Resources', at 42.
150. Demsetz, 'Towards a Theory of Property Right', at 353.

Economists have found from the unitisation agreements, some evidence that substantiates Demsetz predictions that rights will be changed in response to relative prices and technological change.[151] In the US, property rights of rule of capture emerged as a result of inadequate knowledge of reservoirs mechanics to provide a technological framework that would have allowed lessees to negotiate a coordinated solution to the problem. With the technological advances into reservoir mechanics, scientific and technological reasons were produced to enable parties to negotiate agreement for coordinated development that could mitigate the effects of the externality. The property rights that developed in response to this technological change were production quotas (technically called 'allowables') and bundle of property rights to oil in situ is created through Unitisation principles. Thus, where a complete Unitisation is possible, a single bundle of property rights to oil in situ resources is created. On the other hand where there is incomplete Unitisation owing to the uncertain relative prices of different reservoir fluids (oil and gas), separate bundles of property rights within the reservoir is created by the parties. This shows that parties can by agreement create certain bundles of right within a reservoir that can move parties away from extractive anarchy.

It is submitted that even though unitisation could allow new bundle of property rights to be created within the reservoir, failure to reach agreement between the parties could prevent this from taking place. Therefore, the law should be made to recognise such bundle of rights so that even where unitisation agreement has not been reached by the parties, the bundle of rights can be preserved.

Consequently, in addition to the economic property rights mentioned above, it may be possible for a new petroleum property right (property right in discovered petroleum reservoir) to emerge in response to technological change as predicted by Demsetz.[152]

Technological changes such as the new ways of drilling wells, separation of commingle reservoirs substances, better information on reservoir mechanics and quality of seismic data to determine parties share, could pave way for this new property right to internalise some of the externalities produced by bargaining difficulty and extractive anarchy. This is because with the recognition of Licensee's property right to petroleum reservoir, the fear that unilateral production will give rise to civil action for trespass and conversion may mitigates hold-out and thereby reduces transaction or bargaining costs.[153] This will give rise to efficiency of private negotiations and thus strengthened unitisation as the parties already knew that neither of them can produce from common-pool without unitisation agreement. One of the policies behind the application of the rule of capture by the courts is that because the quantity of the oil drained is difficult to ascertain, the party who suffered drainage has no remedy. The new technological advances on commingling and method of calculating recoverable oil

151. Gary D. Libecap et al., 'The Economic Evolution of Petroleum Property Rights in the United States', paper prepared for the conference on the Evolution of Property rights, Northwestern University School of Law, 20-22 April 2001 at p. 4.
152. See further discussion on the impacts of Technological change in Chapter 5.
153. The impact of these technological development on the rule of capture and how new property right could emerge in response to them has been discussed above.

and gas in place using computer simulation will enable ascertainment of the quantity drained, thus accounting for a claim of property right by the licensee on the portion of the oil drained by his neighbour. Even if the exact quantity of oil drained cannot be ascertained, such issue should not prevent liability, at best it should only affect assessment of damages.

4.5.4.4 Shortcomings of Economic Justification

Economic arguments presented very formidable claims for the application of property rights to natural resources. However, as powerful as the economic justification for property right seems to be, there are certain criticisms. Reliance on efficiency and the idea that human beings are all rational utility maximisers as the reasons for the movement from common property regime (open access) to a private property regime has been questioned. Some Economists have argued that the solution to the tragedy of the common does not lie in the existence of private property but rather in the control of resource use. As pointed out by Carter, it was the private ownership of cow that caused overgrazing because if they were not individually owned, there would have been no need to increase grazing efforts.[154]

The assumptions that private property requires free market and that it leads to efficient allocation of resources has also been criticised on the ground that individuals are self-interested preference maximisers who will like to trade goods to increase their wealth.[155]

Besides, it has been contended that the existence of free market is unrealistic because most economies are mixed system and to a large degree imperfect, which means that allocations of resources may not be efficient as proposed.[156] In practical sense, perfect market does not exist because of the prevalence of monopolies and oligopolies whose activities can distort allocation of resources and thus, causing disutility. These entire reasons have created some doubts on the claim that private property rights enhance efficiency.

Demsetz's book has been criticised for its oversight of the historical accounts (e.g., property rights theories like Labour/desert first occupation/ possession) of movement from one system of property regime to another which is not as smooth as his theory portrayed.[157] From historical account, such movement is at times completed on a happy note but the processes of transitions are often more contentious or bloody than as simply suggested by Demsetz. Furthermore, Epstein contended that at other times, the transition are never undertaken or completed because of the mixed legal regimes or systems of common property which if clearly understood and regulated are, from

154. A. Carter, 'Philosophical Foundations of Property Rights' (London: Harvester Wheatsheaf, 1989), at 68, cited by Barnes, 'Property Rights and Natural Resources', at 48.
155. Barnes, 'Property Rights and Natural Resources', at 48.
156. *Ibid.*, at 49.
157. Richard A. Epstein, 'The Allocation of the Commons: Parking on Public Roads' (2002) 31 J. Legal Stud. p. 516.

efficiency standard, preferable to full liberal ownership regime.[158] Property transitions from one form of regime to another are dynamic. It could move back and forth between private and common property in response to the dynamic nature of public choices.[159]

Stuart Banner however, maintained a contrary view. He is of the view that from empirical evidence, transitions between property regimes generally seem to occur on efficiency grounds as proposed by Demsetz because there are examples of resources in which exclusive rights were created in response to increase in their value.[160] He however identified some obstacles to smooth transitions and how those obstacles could be surmounted.[161]

Other writers have suggested that transition from one property regime to another requires a political decision as well as concerted effort of the people to cooperate to set up the system rather than investing all of their efforts in their own harvesting activities. In other words, people need to get together, go to meetings, discuss the options, and figure out who gets what and how the entitlement will be protected either through parliament or courts actions.[162] This aspect of property marks the distinction between the kind of self-interested individual contemplated by the traditional property rights theory like John Locke, who needs exclusive property to induce him to labour.

5. CONCLUSION

In conclusion, we have seen that the examination of the challenges inherent in the regulation of straddling oil and gas reservoirs and how the challenges can be overcome has reinforced our assertion that proprietary rights in the unexploited oil and gas resources exists. It is only that it has not been recognised by the Courts having regards to the judicial authorities discussed in Chapter 5. The conceptual framework developed from our analytical framework in Chapter 2, when contextualised, has also helped us to understand that a petroleum production licensee has a proprietary right or interests in the discovered petroleum reservoir underlying his acreage. The various property justificatory arguments have further lend credence to our assertion that where such proprietary rights in unexploited petroleum resources have not been recognised, there

158. *Ibid.*
159. *Ibid.*
160. Stuart Banner, 'Transitions between Property Regimes' (2002) 31 J. Legal Stud. at 360. He however, identified some obstacles in transiting less efficient property regime to a more efficient one. He pointed out that it can only be done if there is a 'mechanism for translating the collective cost/benefit balance into a sufficiently large aggregate of individual cost/benefit balances.' He gave two reasons why such mechanism may not exist. First, there is likelihood of high cost of transiting from one property regime to another in that it will require valuation of rights under the old regime and assigning right under the new regime (i.e. re-distribution of rights). Second, there is a collective action problem inherent in the transition process. To him, these obstacles must be overcome before such transition can take place.
161. *Ibid.*, at pp. 369-370 he submitted that the first problem can be overcome by adopting measure that is not rigorous in the valuation and assignment of the property rights of the majority. The second problem of collective action can be overcome by skewing the payoffs in favour of the small number of powerful and rich in the society.
162. Carol M. Rose, 'Property as Storytelling: Perspectives from Game Theory, Narrative Theory, and Feminist Theory' (1990) Yale J Law & Humanities 2: 37 at 51.

are strong legal, economic and moral reasons for it to be so recognised and protected. An assessment of the property rule of capture against the backdrop of the property justificatory arguments reveals that its application has proceeded from false premise that could not stand the test of time and that explains why with new technology in the field of oil and gas it could be overtaken by new property concepts. The transition from open access regime as entrenched by the rule of capture to a regime of private property or joint property with respect to straddling petroleum reservoir canvassed herein could also arise through markets forces as the reserves value of the licensee is traded in the Stock market and during company merger, take-over and/or acquisition. As pointed out by Andrzej, creation of enforceable entitlements to diverse resources is a product of market forces rather than government fiat.[163] In modern economic system, institution of property rights cannot be left in the hands of the government alone as property rights, like most goods are produced in response to market demand.[164] Therefore, the appropriate medium by which the property right can be recognised and protected may not only be through the legislature or judiciary. For the legislature or judicial recognition of the property rights to be achieved, the stakeholders in the oil and gas operations need to converge and discuss how the entitlement will be protected either through parliament or courts.[165]

The subsequent chapters will show how and to what extent property rights in petroleum reservoir have been protected in the selected countries of our study.

163. Rapaczynski, 'The Roles of the State and the Market in Establishing Property Rights', at 87.
164. *Ibid.*, at 102.
165. See Rose, 'Property as Storytelling: Perspectives from Game Theory, Narrative Theory, and Feminist Theory', at 51.

CHAPTER 5
The Regime of Unilateral Capture I – Accession Jurisdiction

1. INTRODUCTION

This chapter analyses the problem of unilateral capture of petroleum from straddling fields within Accession jurisdiction (United States). The objectives of this chapter are to show the origin of the Rule and how it was imported to in situ oil and gas ownership disputes. It is also aimed at showing how the Rule has destroyed property rights to petroleum reservoir and to further highlight the challenges inherent in regulating cross-boundary petroleum fields, the conflicting decisions of the courts arising from absence of standard rules and regulations and the various attempt made to solve the problem through regulations.

2. HISTORICAL BACKGROUND

The Rule (Unilateral capture) of petroleum was sanctioned by the common law courts as a legitimate method of oil and gas extraction in the United States since the inception of commercial oil production in 1850s. This application of the Rule is to the effect that property rights to petroleum can only be acquired upon extraction.

The origin of the rule of capture could be traced to the Roman law on underground water. The development of the Roman water law was based on the writings of the eminent Roman jurists over 2,000 years ago. These writings have further served as the instruments through which the water laws of Europe and America were developed. An examination of the Roman writings on water law reveals that the common law judges did not apply the Rule exactly the same way it was applied under Roman water law.

Unlike the Common law, the Rule as applied under the Roman law has been described as a property right vesting at the moment of the ownership of property and not at the moment of capture.[1] This means that in water law cases, the rule of capture confers property right in the underground water on the owner of the surface land but with respect to oil and gas, it confers no property right in the oil and gas in situ on the owner of the surface land but on whoever captures it first. The rule as applied to oil and gas therefore proceeded from a false analogy and hence created serious anomalous situations.

An example of Roman Jurist whose writings formed the basis of the earlier decisions of the courts in water law cases and has been credited as the most direct source of the rule of capture is Marcus Claudius Marcellus. He wrote in the Digest that:

> [N]o action, not even the action for fraud, can be brought against a person who while digging on his land, diverts his neighbour's water supply. And of course the latter ought not to have even the action for fraud, assuming that the other person acted not with the intention of harming his neighbour, but with that of improving his own field.[2]

This excerpt written 2050 years ago has been considered to be very important as the development of an entire body of law was based on this reasoning.

This in effect means that no action could lie against a land owner who completely performed a kind of work that he has a right to do on his land without any defect. In other words, there will be no liability against landowner whose development of ground water causes another's landowner's well to become dry.

Similarly, Trebatius declared that:

> a land owner is not liable for injury to a neighbouring landowner due to work done on the original landowner's property, provided that the work was not defective nor was done pursuant to a right held by the original owner.[3]

---

1. Dylan O. Drummond et al., 'The Rule of Capture in Texas-Still So Misunderstood After All These Years', 2004-2005 Tex. L. Rev. 37(1): at p. 16. He gave classic examples of the writings of some notable Roman Jurists on water law such as Marcus Claudius Marcellus, a contemporary of Cicero who died in 45 B.C., Ulpian, Quintas Mucius, Pomponius, Trebatius and Proculus. *Ulpian* was interpreted to have declared that:

   > Suppose that I dig a well in my house and by so doing so I cut off the sources of your well. Am I liable? Trebatius says that I am not liable on a count of anticipated injury since I am not to be thought of as having caused you injury as a result of any defect in the work that I carried out, seeing that the matter is one in which I was exercising my rights. However, if I dig so deeply on my land that one of your walls cannot stand upright, a stipulation against anticipated injury will become operative.

   See Alan Watson, 'The Law of the Ancient Romans', (1970) 10: p. 93 cited in Dylan et al., *supra* at p. 23. See also DIG.39.2.24.12 (Ulpian, Ad Edict 81). Other notable Roman jurists are *Quintas Mucius and Trebatius. Quintas* propounded that 'a downstream property owner would have no recourse against a spring owner who diverts or uses the water before it reaches the downstream property owner's land', see DIG. 39.3.21 (Pomponius, Quintas Mucius 32) cited in Dylan et al., *supra* at p. 25 at n. 146. Quintas was a jurist who served as a Consul around 95 B.C.
2. DIG. 39.3.1.12 (Ulpian Ad Edict 53 (as translated in 3 The Digest of Justinian 396 (Theodor Mommsen).
3. DIG.39.2.24.12 (Ulpian, Ad Edict 81) cited in Dylan et al., 'The rule of capture in Texas-Still so misunderstood after all these years', at 26.

This is a non-liability rule propounded by Trebatius which is analogous to the non-liability rule availing a landowner under the rule of capture as currently applied to oil and gas.

Another Roman jurist, Pomponius[4] declared that:

> if water which has its sources on your land bursts onto my land and you cut off those sources with the result that the water ceases to reach my land, you will not be considered to have acted with force, provided that no servitude was owed to me in this connection, nor will you be liable to the interdict against force or stealth.[5]

Also Proculus, a first Century A.D Jurist is said to be the last Roman Jurist whose works had lots of influence on the later development of Groundwater law.[6] He stated that:

> when somebody carries out work legally on his own property, even if he has made an undertaking to his neighbour against anticipated injury, nonetheless, he is not bound by this stipulation; for example, if you have buildings next to buildings of mine and you increase their height in accordance with your rights or if you divert my water supply by means of a canal, open or closed, on a field of yours, even though in the latter case you deprive me of my water and in the former case you block my light, nonetheless, no action is available to me under this stipulation; the grounds for this are that a person who prevents somebody from enjoying an advantage which he has hitherto enjoyed should not be held to be causing injury, there being a great difference between the causing of injury and the prevention of enjoyment of an advantage previously enjoyed.[7]

Applying the above principle to the theory of wells interference today, means that there will be no liability against landowners whose development of ground water causes another landowner's well to become dry. This is the essence of the rule of capture as it is applied to oil and gas today. Thus, Dylan summed up the excerpts of these eminent Jurists when he stated that no action will lie against a landowner:

> for rightful, non-defective work done on his land even if it resulted in the loss of stream flow, loss of a well, or other damages to a neighbour's property especially in instances where the damage was anticipated and the damaged neighbour did nothing to protect against it.[8]

In the middle of the thirteenth century, this Roman water law as stated by the Justinian was incorporated expressly by the Courts in England, into the common law of England.[9]

---

4. Pomponius was a first century A.D. Roman Jurist who along with Ulpian, was said to be one of the principal writers on water law that appeared in the Digest. See Ware, 'Roman Water Law: Translated from the Pandects of Justinian 23', (1905) cited in Dylan et al., *supra* at 23 at n. 118.
5. DIG. 39.3.21 (Pomponius, Quintas Mucius 32) (as translated in 3 The Digest of Justinian, P. 402) cited in Dylan et al., *supra* at 27. It was on the basis of this pronouncement that the Texas Supreme Court held in the case of *Texas Co. v. Burkett* (1927) 117 Tex. 16, 28-29. 296 S.W. 273, 278 that ground water belongs to the landowner on whose land it emerged.
6. Watson & El Fadl, 'Fox Hunting, Pheasant Shooting, and Comparative Law', (2000) AM.J.COM-P.L.I, 48: 21 cited in Dylan, et al., at 25 at n. 146.
7. DIG. 39.2.26 (Ulpian, Ad Edict 81) cited in Dylan et al., *supra* at 28.
8. Dylan et al., 'The Rule of Capture in Texas-Still So Misunderstood After All These Years', at 29.
9. Encyclopedia Britanica 1969 (911th ed. 1910).

Thus, the first English case to address the question of percolating water, relied on the Marcellus' writings as contained in the Digest that 'no action can be brought against a person who while digging on his land, diverts his neighbour's water supply.'[10]

Three years later, another water law case came up before the English court. The case of *Acton v. Blundell*[11] represents the first case where the modern rule of capture was declared. In this case, a coal mining company dug coal pits to such depth as to deprive the neighbouring cotton mill owner of his supply of well water. The issue before the court was whether the same rules of law governing watercourse flowing on the surface also governs underground spring. The court held that the case does not fall under the rule pertaining to surface streams and neither is it to be governed by analogy therewith. The court concluded that:

> the case was not to be governed by the law which applies to rivers and flowing streams, but that it rather falls within that principle, which gives to the owner of the soil all that lies beneath his surface; that the land immediately below is his property, whether it is solid rock, or porous ground, or venous earth, or part soil, part water; that the person who owns the surface may dig therein, and apply all that is there found to his own purposes at his free will and pleasure; and that if, in the exercise of such right, he intercepts or drains off the water collected from underground springs in his neighbour's well, this inconvenience to his neighbour falls within the description of *damnum absque injuria*,[12] which cannot become the ground of an action.'[13]

One thing that is notable in the case is that the attempt made by the Acton's counsel to rely on cases on surface streams as well as Marcellus' writing in the Digest was rejected by the court as Marcellus' writing was against his case. Marcellus' writing was interpreted to mean that *'if a man digs a well in his own field and thereby drains his neighbour's, he may do so, unless he does it maliciously'*.

The court refused to apply the law governing surface water but applied rules relating to subterranean water because it is impossible to see or understand the characteristics of subterranean waters and as such no one could have sufficiently defined interests in them to justify the prevention of another person from exercising their land ownership rights in a way that might affect the waters.[14] This shows that the Rule has been employed to allocate resource entitlements between the parties in a way that subordinated exercise of real property rights of one landowner to the other.

The opinion expressed by the judge is also important as it is a pronouncement to the effect that there is a limitation on the application of the rule of capture. It shows that there is malicious injury restrictions imposed on the rule of capture. This can be regarded as one of the ways to tame the rule of capture. Where there is a malicious intent on the part of the drainer, the rule of capture will not protect him and therefore,

10. DIG.39.3.1.12 (Ulpian, Ad, Edict 53. See *Hammond v. Hall* (1840) 59 Eng Rep. 729.
11. (1843) 152 Eng. Rep. 1223. Several English cases also followed the decisions of the court in Acton's case e.g., *Chasemore v. Richards* (1859) 7 H.L. Cas 349, 11 E.R. 140 and *Bradford Borough v. Pickles* (1895) 1 A.C. 587 (HL).
12. Meaning 'an injury without a remedy'.
13. *Acton v. Bludell* (*supra*), at 1235.
14. *Ibid.*, at 1234.

will be liable for the injury inflicted on his neighbour. Mucius must have been right when he declared that:

> the construction of ditches to drain fields counts as something done for the purpose of cultivating the property, but that ditches should not be constructed for the purpose of causing water to flow in one stream since one must only improve one's field in such a way as not to reduce the quality of one's neighbour's field.[15]

This had introduced liability for an intentional harm caused by one property owner to his neighbour in the course of lawful use of his property. The rule of capture is therefore, not an absolute property right rule when applied to subterranean water cases. But when the court analogised water law cases in solving oil and gas drainage disputes, malicious or intentional drainage was never exempted in applying the rule of capture.[16] Therefore, in oil and gas cases, the rule of capture was applied as absolute property rule.

However, to prove malicious intent will be a herculean task. To establish this, the plaintiff must show that there was no other possible explanation as to why the defendant was draining the plaintiff's property other than malicious spite. In oil and gas drainage, it may not be difficult to prove malice especially if the drainer employed horizontal drilling or hydraulic fracturing to drain the resources from the plaintiff's lease area. The same thing should hold for vertical drilling where the drainer, after becoming aware of the straddling resources, he proceeded to unilateral development and production from the common pool without notifying the adjacent lessee and the Regulator.

The analysis above has briefly shown the origin of the rule of capture and how it was applied in water law cases. The follow up sections in this chapter will show how it was applied to oil and gas cases in the United States.

3. UNITED STATES

The oil boom witnessed by the United States in the latter part of the nineteenth century was not without its own legal problem. The race to produce oil in order to take the benefit of the oil boom also triggered disputes concerning ownership of in situ oil and gas especially in States where private ownership of land was the norm. The courts were confronted with upsurge of litigations on this issue and therefore, had no alternative than to devise property rules that will solve the ownership problems. The court felt that the existing rules of real property rights were not adequate to address the problem and therefore, found convenient rules in the law relating to subterranean waters and wild animals. The court analogised them and applied their rules to oil and gas which, as we shall see further in this book, did not fit squarely into the peculiar nature of oil and gas.

---

15. DIG. 39.3.1.12 (Ulpian Ad Edict 53 (as translated in 3 The Digest of Justinian, P. 395).
16. See the cases of *Hague v. Wheeler* 157 Pa. 324, 27 A, 714 (1893); *Tyner v. People's Gas Company* 131 Ind. 408, 31 N.E. 59 (1892) *Acheson v. Stevenson* (1892) 145 Pa. 228; *Bernard v. Monoghahela* 216 Pa. 362, 365, 65 A. 801, 802 (1907).

In addressing the ownership of oil and gas conflicts, ownership concepts were fashioned around the rule of capture by the courts to govern resource appropriation in order to avoid allocation problems. The Judges also concentrated more on ownership concepts at the expense of property rights. This has further plunged the industry into more serious problems that continued till today. From Chapter 2, we have seen that at common law the concept of ownership has insignificant meaning as regards land as there are other fragmented bundles of rights called interests, for example, fee simple, leasehold; *profit a prendre,* easement and rent which the court appeared to have ignored while deciding drainage (ownership) disputes between two competing users.

It is to be noted that there are various ownership theories in the US - Non-ownership theory and Ownership in place theory. The third which is more like Non-ownership theory is termed 'Qualified ownership' theory.[17]

3.1 Non-ownership Theory

In States where Non-ownership theory was adopted, the courts placed emphasis on the fugacious character of oil and gas and compared them with subterranean waters and wild animals *(ferae naturae).* The settled principles of the law relating to subterranean waters was applied because, oil and gas, like subterranean waters, was regarded as incapable of stabilising under a single tract of land for any definite period, but constantly wandering at the subsurface and because of this, it can flow from one tract of land to another, thus rendering it capable of capture from beneath the surrounding land. In their belief, oil and gas in the underground behave like a free flowing underground river without regards to surface boundaries and cannot be quantified or allocated among surface owners.[18]

This attitude stems from improper judicial understanding of the nature of reservoir structure. As shown in Chapter 4, it has been established geologically, that petroleum deposits usually occur in porous rocks confined by traps. Therefore, oil in reservoirs is capable of bounds and as such can be quantified and appropriated to surface owners even while still in underground. Unless there is an intervention, it will remain confined to the reservoir. Therefore, where a well is drilled to any part of the reservoir formation, a lower pressure is created thus, causing the oil to move from its natural state to the state created by man, i.e. the well bored.

Wild animal analogy was also made as it was thought that oil and gas was fugitive in nature and capable of escaping from the land in one locality and passing on to another like a wild animal.[19] As a result of the aforesaid analogies, it was thought that ownership of oil and gas *in situ* could not be ascribed to the surface owner of the land. The right the owner of the land is seized of is the exclusive right to search, drill and

17. See Chapter 3 pp. 76-79 where the three ownership theories were used to explain the nature of the Landowner's interest in the underground oil and gas in the US.
18. *Hail v. Reed,* 54 Ky. 383 (15 B. Mon. 479) (1854).
19. See *Medina Oil Development Co. v. Murphy,* 233 S. W. 333 Tex. Civ. App. (1921). The court declared that '*because of their fugitive nature, since they are supposed to percolate restlessly about under the surface of the earth, even as the birds fly from field to field and the beast roam from forest to forest. ...*'

recover or capture the oil and gas. Title only vests in him when he reduced it to possession[20] but that the State has the power to out-law or regulate the capture just as in the case of wild animals.[21] In cases where the underground water analogy was applied, the court had held that the land owner could drain oil and gas from his neighbour's land through a well bore on his land, since such right was given to a landowner in the case of underground waters.[22]

The analogy made to subterranean water has been regarded as inappropriate because 'a landowner has no right to collect subterranean water for the purpose of merchandise, if by so doing, he seriously damage his neighbour's use of such waters while the whole purpose of oil and gas production is to secure the minerals for the purpose of selling them'.[23]

Also the weakness of the analogy to wild animal has been exemplified by the Court's decision in the case of *Ohio Oil Co. v. Indiana*[24] which though adopted the non-ownership theory because of the fugacious character of oil and gas, held that unlike the privilege of taking wild animal which vests in the public (i.e. State), the right to take oil and gas from the earth is vested exclusively in the owner of the surface, so long as it shall remain within the soil. This is so because title to wild animals is in the public and that the landowner has no property interest in them even when they are on his land. Also, while the public may completely prohibit an individual from hunting all or any of the wild animals on his premises, the right of an individual to take oil and gas underneath his land, though may be regulated, cannot be completely prohibited. In other words, the landowner's interest in oil and gas is materially different from his interest in wild animals on his premises.

3.2 Ownership in Place Theory

In States adopting ownership in place theory, the court adopted the principle of absolute ownership which has been well established in solid minerals like coal and iron and also in subterranean waters. In solid minerals however, absolute ownership principle was however qualified by the legal maxim *'sic utere tuo ut alienum non laedas'* so that one may not use his own land so as to injure his neighbour. As a result, it is settled law that the owner of land has an easement of lateral support in the land of his neighbour.[25]

20. John S. Sawyer, 'Interests Created by Oil and Gas Leases in Pennsylvania', (1937-1938) U. Pitt. L. Rev. 4: 274. See also Robert J. Blake, 'The Oil and Gas Lease', (1939-1940) S. Cal L. Rev. 13: 305, at p. 305.
21. *Westmoreland & Cambria Natural Gas Co. v. De Witt*, 130 Pa. 235, 18, Atl. 724 (1889).
22. Williams & Meyers, 'Oil and Gas Laws', vol. 1 (2004), Chapter 2, p. 33 referring to the case of *Acton v. Blundell* (1843) Exch. 12 M. & W. 324.
23. Farnham, 'Waters and Water Rights', 938; 53 L. R. A. (N. S.) 369.
24. (1899)177 U.S. 190, 209.
25. W. L. Summers, 'Property in Oil and Gas', (1919-1920) Yale L.J.: 175 at 178 referring to Tiffany, 'Modern Law of Real Property', (1903), s. 19.

However, the court in oil and gas cases, did not apply the absolute principle exactly the way it was applied to solid minerals and subterranean waters.[26] This is because in applying the absolute ownership principle to oil and gas, qualifications and exceptions (e.g., Rule of capture) were made to weakened absolute ownership principle rather than strengthened it. The court's aim was to make the principle fit into the peculiar nature of oil and gas. The reason given was that the wandering and fugitive nature of oil and gas could not lend it to the application of the same principles with solid minerals. The failure of the court to apply the principle of absolute ownership to oil and gas as applied to solid minerals consequently resulted into rules of property believed to be 'unsound in theory and unjust in application.'[27] This has produced an awkward situation because the landowner is given an absolute ownership of oil and gas in place with right to take oil and gas beneath his land even if in doing so his neighbour's. Substances are drained. On the other hand, the same principle of absolute ownership was not recognised in enforcing or protecting the ownership of one whose oil or gas is drained. The principle does not also recognise the remedy available to the landowner if his oil or gas is drained by his neighbour. This means that the law did not protect him from drainage even though he is proclaimed to be the absolute owner of oil and gas in place. In a nutshell, the principle allows A to take the property of B but refused to give remedy to B because B is denied absolute ownership over his property. The absolute ownership principle therefore, suffers from internal inconsistency which it dogmatically took from its analogy to law relating to solid minerals, subterranean water and animal *ferae naturae.* This had led it to a state of self-contradiction and destruction. Thus, the inconsistency arose from the mixture of these separate and distinct principles of law.

3.3 Qualified Ownership Theory

In States adopting qualified ownership theory, property right to oil and gas in place is recognised but that such property right may be lost if the oil or gas migrates from the land to an adjoining tract. The theory introduced the correlative right doctrine to protect property interest in the oil and gas in place prior to actual possession. In practical terms, qualified ownership is the same with non-ownership but conceptually, they are different. Qualified ownership recognises property right in oil and gas in place and may be ready to protect same prior to actual possession while Non-ownership denies such property right and allowed the rule of capture without qualifying ownership concepts. Qualified ownership will protect property right in oil and gas in place against injury to the producing formation and unreasonable use of the substances such as wastes but will not protect it against drainage. Therefore, qualified ownership

26. In Texas for instance, the court is of the opinion that the owner of the land is a fee simple owner of the oil and gas in place but that it is a defeasible fee. This means that the owner is liable to lose his oil if someone draws it away, but until that happens his ownership is absolute. This means that while carrying out lawful activities on your land you could affect the rights of your neighbour without incurring any liability. But the principle of absolute ownership as applied to solid minerals says you cannot do that without incurring some liabilities.

27. *Ibid.*, at 178.

recognises absolute ownership when it said that 'oil and gas belongs to the owner of the land, and are part of it' but however qualifies it by introducing the rule of capture to the effect that 'when they escape and go into other land, or come under another's control, the title of the former owner is gone.'[28] This had imported the rule of capture which made the new owner not liable and thereby permitting him to produce without accounting to the former owner.

In Oklahoma State, qualified ownership theory was adopted. Thus in the case of *Rich v. Doneghey*,[29] the court rejected the ownership in place theory and declared that:

> But with respect to such oil and gas, they had certain rights designated by the same courts as a *qualified ownership thereof*, but which may be more accurately stated as exclusive right, subject to legislative control against waste and the like, to erect structures on the surface of their land, and explore therefore by drilling wells through the underlying strata, and to take therefrom and reduce to possession, and thus acquire title as personal property to such as might be found and obtained thereby. This right is the proper subject of sale, and may be granted or reserved ... The right so granted or reserved, and held separate and apart from the possession of the land itself, is an incorporeal hereditament; or more specifically, as designated in the ancient French, a profit a prendre, analogous to a profit to hunt and fish on the land of another.... Considered with respect to duration, if the grant be to one and his heirs and assigns forever, it is of an interest in fee.... An interest of less duration may be granted, and that for a term of years has been denominated by this court a chattel real.[30]

From the above, it suffices to say that absolute title to oil and gas in place is not recognised going by this theory but a qualified title.

Qualified ownership theory was meant to mitigate the difficulties or the negative effects of the absolute ownership theory as stated above (i.e., the internal inconsistency of the theory). Thus, in reliance on the analogy between oil and gas and animals '*ferae naturae*', the Pennsylvania Supreme Court in the case of *Westmoreland Natural Gas Company v. DeWitt* (*supra*) declared that:

> oil and gas belong to the owner of the land so long as they are in it or on it, but when they escape, and go into other land, or come under another's control, the title of the former owner is gone.

In Indiana State, the case of *Ohio Oil company v. Indiana*[31] disagreed with the analogy drawn to animals *ferae naturae* by the *Westmoreland Natural Gas Company's case* (*supra*) and declared that the landowner has no property interest in the oil and gas in place and can acquire no title to them until he reduces them to possession and that in doing so, he can reduce to possession all or every part, if possible, of the deposits without violating the rights of other surface owners. The court said that:

28. See *Westmoreland & Cambria Natural Gas Co. v. De Witt* (*supra*).
29. 71 Okla. 204, 177 P. 86, 3 A.L.R 352 (1918).
30. *Ibid.*, at pp. 206-207, 177 P. at 89 see also Williams and Meyers, Oil and Gas Laws at 42.
31. 177 U. S. 190 (1899).

> There is no limit on the extent to which he may exercise his right to take oil and gas, except perhaps, he can be restrained from *unreasonable waste of the minerals* … .[32]

The court went further and introduced the correlative right doctrine to oil and gas dispute when it declared that:

> As to gas and oil, the surface proprietors within the gas field all have the right to reduce to possession the gas and oil beneath. They could not be absolutely deprived of the right which belongs to them without a taking of private property. But there is a co-equal right in them (surface proprietors) to take from a common source of supply, the two substances … the use by one of his power to seek to convert a part of the common fund to actual possession may result in an undue proportion being attributed to one of the possessors of the right, to the detriment of the others, or by waste by one or more, to the annihilation of the rights of the remainder. Hence it is that the legislative power … can be manifested for the purpose of protecting all the collective owners, by securing a just distribution, to arise from the enjoyment by them, of their privilege to reduce to possession, and to reach the like end by preventing waste …

The decision in this case was in realisation of the fact that the public has a great interest in the natural resources and that some measures need to be taken to conserve and prevent waste of this resources. Consequently in this case, the Indiana court while departing from the earlier decision of the court[33] held a statute enacted to prevent the waste of gas constitutional and that it does not constitute an interference with property rights.[34]

The Supreme Court refused to follow the theory of absolute ownership as enunciated by the Pennsylvanian courts and produced a new one. The court, while disagreeing with the lower court's analogy to animals '*ferae naturae*' as adopted by the non-ownership State pointed out that, although there may be an analogy between oil and gas and animals '*ferae naturae*' but there is no identity between them.

Therefore, the Supreme Court neither adopted the absolute ownership theory nor the Non-ownership theory before upholding the constitutionality of the Indiana statutes regulating waste. From this case it is clear that the court has provided the platform upon which the State can regulate the waste of this natural resources without violating the property rights of the land owner but since the land owner has been denied property rights in oil and gas under his land, his neighbour cannot be held liable for draining his oil and gas. His property right is not protected from violation by his neighbour.

The only difference between the absolute ownership theory as propounded by Pennsylvanian courts and the qualified ownership propounded by the Indiana courts is

32. Professor James W. Simonton, 'The Nature of the Interest of the Grantee under an Oil and Gas Lease', (1917-1918) W. Va. L. Q. 25: 295 at 299.
33. *People's gas Co. v. Tyner* (*supra*) the court in this case employed the analogy to subterranean water which the Pennsylvania court adopted to produce the absolute ownership. The court held that an owner of a gas well might shoot it with nitro-glycerine to increase its flow regardless of an injury to his neighbour's well.
34. See also the earlier case of *Townsend v. State* (1896) 147 Ind. 624,47, N. E. 19.

that, while the absolute ownership defines property right, but fails to protect it, the qualified ownership denies any right of property in one whose oil or gas is taken.[35] It is submitted that what is common to both theories, is the existence of the rule of capture as both of them allow its operation albeit, in different manners.

In 1905, the Indiana court again was confronted with a case in which a life tenant contended, in an action against him for waste, that since the remainder-man had no property in the oil and gas, his own act of mining the oil and gas was not waste. Here the court having realised the problem his earlier decisions of no ownership in oil and gas will cause, quickly qualified it by ruling that the landowner has exclusive right to mine oil and gas underneath his land and that in itself is a property right.[36]

However, in the *Manufacturer's Gas and Oil Co. v. Indiana and Natural Gas & Oil Co*[37] the court adopted the reasoning of the Supreme Court in the case of *Ohio v. Indiana* (*supra*) and rejected both the absolute ownership doctrine as applied to percolating water and the animal '*ferae naturae*' analogy which says that landowner has no property right in oil and gas in place. The question for determination by the court in this case was whether an owner of oil and gas land could prevent his neighbour from using artificial means to increase the flow of gas wells to the alleged injury of the plaintiff's well. The court declared that the owners of oil and gas lands are *common owners of the oil and gas beneath* and that in the exercise of the right to take from the common source, neither of the owners could destroy the common source. Furthermore, the court declared that either of the owners could bring an action to enjoin the acts of the other that would materially injure or destroy the common property source.

This case appeared to have departed from the extreme position taken by the court in the case of *Ohio Oil Co. v. Indiana* (*supra*) which held that the landowner has no property right in oil and gas in situ. This case is to the effect that the land owner has exclusive right to take oil and gas underneath his land but that the right must be exercised in such a way as not to injure his neighbour who also has a right to take oil and gas from the common fields. However, it has not completely ruled out the application of the rule of capture in that a landowner who also takes as much oil and gas from the common reservoir in excess of the quantity underlying his own surface land will not be liable to his neighbour as long as his action does not constitute unreasonable use or cause an injury to the producing formation. The court however, stressed the correlative rights in each producer because the reservoir was physically connected and as such 'any diminution, waste, destruction, or injury anywhere within the structure will affect all other overlying owners.'

Some Kentucky cases[38] have jettisoned the earlier position held by the State and have followed the Indiana cases that were built on the theory of qualified ownership.

35. W.L. Summers, 'Property in Oil and Gas', (1919-1920) Yale L.J.: 175, at p. 183.
36. *Richmond National Gas Co. v. Davenport* (1905) 37 Ind. App. 25, 76 N.E. 525; *Manufacturer's Gas Co. v. Indiana & Natural Gas & oil Co.*(1900) 155 Ind.451, 57 N.E. 912.
37. 155 Ind. 461, 57 N.E 912 (1900).
38. *Louisville Gas Co. v. Kentucky Heating Co.* (1903) 117 Ky. 71 at 78; *Commonwealth v. Trent* (1903) 117 Ky. 451, 104 S. W. 259; *Louisville Gas Co. v. Kentucky Heating Co.* (1909) 132 Ky. 435 III S. W. 374. In the *Louisville Gas Co. case*, the plaintiff, in order to force the defendant out of competition, employed the use of a sham carbon black factory to draw gas out of the same

These cases established the rights of the surface owners to take oil and gas from the common reservoir as a right in common but that in doing so it must be taken for a lawful purpose and in a reasonable manner. Since the surface owners can be regarded as a *tenant in common*, the right to take the substances from the straddling reservoir is regarded as a right in common and that property in the substances vest only when they are taken. Thus the court declared in the case of *Louisville Gas Company's case* (1903) (*supra*) that:

> .... in the case before us the plaintiff and the defendant have each the right to take gas from the common source of supply, but neither may by waste, destroy the rights of the other; and, as in the case of other like wrongs, the action for redress may be brought in the name of the real party in interest.

Similarly in *Louisville Gas Company's case* (1909) (*supra*), the court declared that:

> Each tenant in common is restricted to a reasonable use of this right, and each is entitled to the natural flow of the gas from the subjacent fields, and any unlawful exercise of this right, by any tenant in common, which results in injury to the natural right of any other tenant or surface owner, is an actionable wrong.

Even though the declarations of the courts in the above Kentucky cases appeared to have rescinded their earlier opinion of absolute ownership doctrine, the rule of capture has not been completely overruled because the courts in these cases are still of the view that:

> [T]here is no property in the gas until it is taken. Before it is taken it is fugitive in its nature, and belongs in common to the owners of the surface. The right of the owners to take it is without stint; the only limitation being that it must be taken for a lawful purpose and in a reasonable manner.

The court appeared to have equated the term 'property' with 'ownership'. The two concepts are different from one and another under the common law of property. Ownership is more restrictive while property is wider, covering wide range of interests that do not amount to ownership. Such interests are protectable property under the common law.

It must be noted that the qualified ownership principle as enunciated by the Indiana and Kentucky cases stated above merely introduced the correlative right concepts to oil and gas especially in relation to cases in which a remedy is sought against waste or a malicious sapping of the gas contained in a reservoir. It has not been applied to cases where the landowner has both innocently or wilfully drained oil and gas from his neighbour's land by a well bored on his land.

---

common reservoir from which the defendant took its own gas. This was a deliberate attempt to destroy the common reservoir and the defendant's heating gas supply. The action of the defendant also reduced the reservoir gas pressure tremendously within six months. The court held that even though, natural gas is not subject to absolute ownership, the owner of the soil must use his own property with due regards to the rights of his neighbour and cannot deliberately waste the gas to the injury of his neighbour. He is only allowed to make a 'reasonable use of those natural supplies which are for the common benefit of all'. See p. 369.

Furthermore, the analogy made by the qualified ownership theory to the theory of reasonable use as applied to percolating water has also been faulted. The theory of reasonable use as applied to water is to the effect that any use of water for the purpose of the enjoyment or improvement of the land particularly when they are used for agricultural purposes is reasonable but taking the water for merchandise or wasting it is unreasonable if it injures the neighbouring owner. The objection had been that the nature of the subterranean water is different from the oil and gas underground and as such the same theory cannot be applied to them. While water is generally recognised as necessary for the use, enjoyment and improvement of land, e.g., for agricultural purposes, that is not so for oil and gas. The purpose of oil and gas production is only for sale and manufacture which of necessity must be removed and carried away from the land.

However Professor Summers[39] has contended that since both of these substances are things of value, the fact that the tests of reasonableness of use of these different classes of property are not the same, is not a sound reason for objecting to the application of the same theory of property to both of them. He contended further that the doctrine of correlative rights is the proper rule of property that should govern them owing to their fugitive and wandering nature under the ground 'in liquid or gaseous form so that any taking by one may have some effects on the presence of these things under the land of another.' It is submitted that geologically, oil and gas has been proved not to wander restlessly in the underground like water. They have stable existence in their habitat unlike subterranean water. Whether the analogy made to the doctrine of reasonable use as applied to percolating water is the correct approach or not, the qualified ownership principle says that the adjoining landowners have property rights to the oil and gas in the common reservoir – in that they respectively have exclusive right to take them – and that in exercising this right, either of them must so act as not to unreasonably injure the other. However, the property right created by the theory of correlative right can still be defeated by the application of the rule of capture in that there will be no liability for drainage.

American Oil Industry has been facing this problem for over a century and the courts have been replete with enormous cases bordering on these issues. There had been conflicting decisions of the courts and opinions on these issues among eminent jurists are divided and also difficult to reconcile.

From the above, there appeared to be some confusion or inconsistencies in the three ownership theories. Conceptually, the three Ownership theories which are separate and distinct from one another were formed around the rule of capture. The Rule of capture is also a separate and distinct principle from Ownership concepts. Yet, the Rule was applied to the three ownership concepts. Therefore, the importation of the rule of capture into all the ownership theories accounted for the confusion and the irreconcilable Ownership cases.[40] If the decisions of the courts had been based on

39. W.L. Summers, 'Property in Oil and Gas', at 186.
40. Pierce, Coordinated Reservoir Development – 'An Alternative to the Rule of Capture for the Ownership and Development of Oil and Gas', at 23 and 26.

ownership theories only without applying the rule of capture, the conflicting decisions might perhaps be reconcilable.

4. CLASSICAL RULE OF CAPTURE CASES

It should also be noted that drainage of oil or gas as between adjoining lessors or licensees was not directly in issue in the earlier cases in which analogy was made to the principles of the Rule as established in water law and law relating to wild animals.[41] The issue in contention was as to who has the legal possession or ownership of oil and gas in situ as between the lessor and his lessee. The first oil and gas case in which allusion was made to the Rule was the case of *Wood County Petroleum Co. v. Virginia Transportation Co.*[42] In this case, the lessee was granted a lease to excavate rock or carbon oil in consideration of payment of royalty to the lessor. The lessee in the process of mining for oil also struck gas which he appropriated to himself without accounting for the proceeds to the lessor, claiming that the lease did not cover gas. The lessor on the other hand argued that the gas forms part of the land and as such belongs to him so that the appropriation of the gas by the lessee was unlawful. The court held that the lease gave the lessee legal right to enter upon the property and as such could use or appropriate anything un-owned such as animals *ferae naturae* or percolating waters even if by so doing another person having an equal right is deprived of power to do so. The court opined further that animals *ferae naturae* or percolating waters are not subjects of absolute property but qualified ownership only and as such the first appropriator becomes the owner. The court regarded oil and gas as belonging to the same class with those un-owned things mentioned above because it possesses similar character with them unlike things capable of absolute property. Consequently the court awarded ownership of the gas to the lessee. Though the court ruled that subterranean water, oil and gas are incapable of absolute ownership, the right of the first person that appropriated them for his use was regarded as absolute even if in doing so adjoining wells are drained. Another case with similar facts with the above case is *Westmoreland Natural Gas Company v. De Witt.*[43] In this case, the land owner granted an oil and gas lease to the Plaintiff, Company. A second lease was granted by the land owner to the defendants in the belief that the plaintiff's lease has been forfeited because of failure to make certain payments at the appropriate time as provided by the lease. There was an obligation on the plaintiff under the lease to drill a gas well which he did. The plaintiff however did not produce the gas. The lease also provided for a fixed rental for gas wells which was payable whether the wells were producing or not. The plaintiff took an action in the court to restrain the defendants from drilling a gas well covered by the lease. The defendants objected to the suit contending that injunction is not available to the plaintiff as he was not in possession of the premises and rights granted in the lease. The lower court agreed with the defendants and held that gas being mineral is part of

41. Terrence Daintith, 'Finders Keepers? How the Law of Capture Shaped the World Oil Industry' (Washington, D.C., London: RFF Press, 2010), at 21-25.
42. (1886) 28 W Va. 210.
43. (1889) 130 Pa. 235, 18 Alt. 724.

the land while in place and that possession of the land must be possession of the gas. The Supreme Court however disagreed with the lower court and held that what was relevant in this case was the possession of the gas or oil contained in the land and that the plaintiff was clearly in possession. The court declared that:

> Tested by these principles, there is not the slightest doubt that the possession of the gas, as well as the right to it under this lease, was in the complainants when the bill was filed. They had put down a well, which had tapped the gas bearing strata, and it was the only one on the land. They had it in their control, for they had only to turn a valve to have it flow into their pipe, ready for use ... Brown [owner of the land] had no possession of the gas at all. His possession of the soil for purposes of tillage, etc. gave him no actual possession of the gas; and he had no legal possession, for his lease had conveyed that to another.[44]

Thus, in reliance on the analogy between oil and gas and animals '*ferae naturae*', the Pennsylvania Supreme Court in the case declared that:

> They [oil and gas] belong to the owner of the land so long as they are in it or on it, and are subject to his control; but when they escape, and go into other land, or come under another's control, the title of the former owner is gone. If an adjoining or even a distant owner, drills on his own land, and takes your gas so that it comes into his well and under his control, it is no longer yours but his. And equally so as between lessor and the lessee in the present case, the one who controls the gas, has it in his grasp so to speak, is the one who has possession in the legal as well as in the ordinary sense of the word.

Two conflicting sets of facts could be deduced from the reasoning of the court to wit: First, it signifies that a lessee has title to gas or oil in the reservoir which he struck by drilling a well underneath his land even though the oil or gas has not been produced. This is because a grant of oil and gas lease invariably puts the lessee in legal possession of the oil and gas in place especially where he has drilled a well and discovered oil or gas even if they had not been produced.

Second, such title may however be lost if the oil or gas escape into an adjoining land. The first interpretation which is more relevant to the facts of the case is preferable as it is in accord with the principle enunciated by the court to resolve the issue as to who has the rights, as between the lessor and lessee, to the gas in place. This explained why in spite of the above apparent ambiguity, some cases however, appeared to have interpreted the principle enunciated in this case to mean that the owner of the land or lessee has title to discovered oil and gas reservoir under his land not yet tapped by any well.[45]

The second interpretation is totally not relevant to the facts of the case as drainage was not an issue in the case. This was why professor Daintith commented that:

> one is struck by the almost offhand manner in which the crucial sentence – 'If an adjoining or even a distant owner, drills on his own land, and takes your gas so

44. *Westmoreland Natural Gas Co. v. DeWitt* (*supra*) at 725.
45. *Brown v. Spillman*, 155 U.S. 665 (1895).

> that it comes into his well and under his control, it is no longer yours but his' – was introduced.

This he regarded as not the conclusion of the argument but a mere reason towards it. It is therefore not the *ratione decidendi* of the case. But unfortunately, subsequent cases clung to this second interpretation and applied it to cases where drainage was directly in issue in disputes between lessors or lessees to deny lessee or lessor who suffered drainage, taken.[46] The combined effects of these principles as has been shown in Chapter 4, is antithetical to sound investments decisions as it portends strong danger to security of title of licensee to oil and gas while in place. The cases of *Acheson v. Stevenson*[47] and *Tyner v. People's Gas Company*[48] followed the *Westmorland's case* by upholding the principles of the rule of capture but granted injunction to restraint further production from the common pool in order to preserve the value of the residential property or on the ground that comfortable enjoyment of property will be impaired. However, subsequent cases in Pennsylvania State did not rely on the above case. For example in 1893, the issue of capture was presented before the Supreme Court of Pennsylvania in the case of *Hague v. Wheeler*.[49] The issue was whether the defendants could be restrained from draining the gas from the underneath of the

46. Daintith, 'Finders Keepers? …', at 25.
47. (1892) 145 Pa. 228. In this case, the plaintiff, as part of his town development scheme, divided his land into building lots. He sold one plot to one Mrs Effie Schmitz and in the conveyance, prohibited both parties from drilling or mining for petroleum or other mineral substances on the plot sold to her. Mrs Schmitz however allowed the defendant to drill a well on her plot and oil was discovered. The plaintiff also granted an oil and gas lease in respect of his land near Mrs Schmitz plot though outside of his town development scheme. The lessees also struck substantial oil. The plaintiff took an action in court to restrain the defendants from drilling and for damages for the oil unlawfully taken through drainage from his other land. The court held that '… Oil is a mineral *ferae naturae*, and is part of the land and belongs to its owner only so long as it is in the land and under his control; and as soon as the oil left the land of the plaintiff and flowed on or into the lot of Mrs Schmitz, it belonged to her, unless some contract or covenant existed between the plaintiff and her by which this rule of property in oil in situ was inoperative … .' The court found that there was no such agreement and therefore concluded that the plaintiff is not entitled to damages for the oil drained by the defendant through his well or any part of it. As per the injunction sought by the plaintiff, the court held that he is entitled to the injunction in order to preserve the residential value of the town lot.
48. 131 Ind. 408, 31 N.E. 59 (1892). The defendant enlarged his well by the explosion of Nitro-glycerine at the foot of the wellbore in order to increase the flow of petroleum into his well. The plaintiff alleged that such action had caused underground fractures through which gas under his property has flowed into the defendant's well. The plaintiff's property is a residential house located across the street from the site of the well. Relying on the authority of Westmoreland's case, the Indiana court held that the defendant is entitled to use such method in order to increase the flow of gas into his well on the basis of the principle of the Rule of capture. However, an injunction was granted in favour of the plaintiff on the ground of private nuisance in that it interferes with the comfortable enjoyment of life or property.
49. 157 Pa. 324, 27 A, 714 (1893) contrast with *Jones v. Forster Oil Co* (1900) 194 Pa. St. 379 at 383 where in 1900, the issue presented before the court was whether the owner of an oil well has the right to produce oil from his well regardless of injury to his neighbour. The court, realising the inapplicability of the absolute ownership doctrine in the sense of absolute right to take, held that 'possession of the land is not necessarily possession of the oil and gas' and that 'the property of the owner of the lands in oil and gas is not absolute until it is actually within his grasp and brought to the surface.' In another twist the court in *Hamilton v. Forster* (1922) 272 Pa. 95, 116 A. 50 held that just like other minerals under the ground, oil and gas is capable of ownership even while in place and can be made a subject of separate grant.

plaintiffs' lease through a well bored by the defendant on his lease area, even though the gas is been wasted by the defendant. The court followed the absolute ownership doctrine and refused to apply the legal maxim '*sic utere tuo ut alienum non laedas*' by holding that the owner has an absolute dominion over the oil and gas just like the solid minerals. The Court did not cite its own opinion in the Westmorland's case. The court refused to restrain the defendants from draining the plaintiff's lease through an open gas well on their own land even though they are wasting the gas by allowing it to escape into the air. In a similar fashion, the case of *Kelley v. Ohio oil company*,[50] where the defendant had placed a well 25 feet. from the boundary of the adjoining lands and drained oil from there, the court upheld the drainage and declared that:

> whatever gets into a well belongs to the owner of the well, no matter where it came from ... The right to drill and produce oil on one's own land is absolute, and cannot be supervised by a court or an adjoining landowner.

Although the above cases are the traditional rule of capture cases, the recent cases of *Coastal Oil and Gas Corp. v. Garza Energy Trust* (2008) and *Butler v. Charles Powers Estate* [2011] brought to the court based on the Rule showed that the Rule is still controversial most especially in the domanial regimes and with the advent of shale gas extraction revolution. These cases are discussed in section 8.3 below.

5. EFFECTS OF THE RULE OF CAPTURE

5.1 Negative Effects

The above cases have shown that the Rule was upheld not only in cases of ordinary drilling but also in cases of 'illegality, wastage of oil and use of harmful method of oil recovery' (i.e., high explosives).[51] Adjoining lessee has no other remedy than to do likewise.[52] In addressing the legal challenge, several problems were further created. In this era of globalisation, the problem goes beyond the earlier problems of reservoir management, and physical and economic wastes, to include investments and human rights problems.

5.1.1 *Competitive Drilling*

With the rule of capture, coupled with multiple firms holding production leases to common-reservoirs, competitive drilling became prevalent. The race to produce also creates a race to waste important resources. As a result of the fluidity of the oil and gas while in the reservoir, it is able to move from place of high pressure to low pressure and as such, a well bottomed anywhere in the reservoir would be able to capture the resource. Excessive capital expenditures were incurred on drilling more wells that were technically unnecessary in order to drain as much oil as possible from adjacent

50. 57 Ohio C.C.R. 511 (1897).
51. Daintith, 'Finders Keepers? ...', at 28-29.
52. *Barnard v. Monogahela Natural Gas Co.* (*supra*); *Brown v. Humble Oil & Ref Co.* (*supra*).

leaseholders. Consequently, building unnecessary surface storage facilities to store the oil was on the increase while little reservoir rents and royalties were recorded because markets were over flooded with oil produced without regards to market forces and price. The firms recorded high cost of production by engaging in production profile that ran against maximum value for the resources. Reservoir energy was quickly dissipated leading to loss of total recovery. This eventually had an increasing effect on production costs and the ultimate consumer had to suffer the price increase. The irony of it is that in the short run prices will be low because market will be over flooded with the commodity while at the long run prices will increase due to the investor holding back their investment as a result of low returns on investment. As a result of low prices, wastage occurs as consumers will put the resource into inferior uses.[53]

5.1.2 *Physical and Economic Wastes*

Sound conservation practices were also affected by the application of the rule. This is because the Rule had modified the existing ownership principles and created a property system that encouraged the race to produce oil and gas without regard to reservoir pressure that would have enhanced oil recovery. It therefore, discourages producers to embark upon unitised development and provides 'element of chance for additional reward' as individual tries to maximise his gain through drainage.[54]

The physical and economic wastes emanating from competitive drilling and the ensuing reduction in total recovery and reservoirs rent were colossal.[55] The quantum of economic wastes as shown empirically, in the US ranged well above 50% in terms of lost production potentials. In 1910, up to 11% of California's annual production was lost due to fire while in surface storage and in 1914 the Director of the Bureau of Mines estimated that the cost of excessive wells equalled about a quarter of the value of annual US oil production.[56] The problem in the US was caused partly because there were no clear property rights to subsurface oil and gas deposits as it was thought that property rights to petroleum can only be acquired upon extraction and partly because at the early petroleum extraction there was lack of adequate knowledge of reservoir mechanics that could have propelled solution to the problems. As a result of the magnitude of the quantity of oil lost during recovery operations, research were thus,

53. For a detailed economic analysis of this long, intermediate and short run price effects, see Stephen L. McDonald, 'Petroleum Conservation in the United States: An Economic Analysis' (Baltimore and London: Resources for the Future, Inc. by The John Hopkins Press, 1971), at 96-105. He is of the view that the price of crude oil is more stable under unitisation than under the rule of capture.
54. Pierce, 'Coordinated Reservoir Development – An Alternative to the Rule of Capture for the Ownership and Development of Oil and Gas', at 31.
55. J. L Weaver, 'Unitisation of Oil and Gas Fields in Texas, A Study of Legislative, Administrative, and Judicial Policies', (1986) at 27. He noted that Economists have analysed the effects of the rule of capture on the price of oil. The short-term effect of the rush to produce and avoid drainage is that the price of oil falls below that which would obtain were the field unitised and produced at the socially efficient rate.
56. Gary D. Libecap & James L. Smith 'The Economic Evolution of Petroleum Property Rights in the United States' paper prepared for the conference on the Evolution of Property rights, Northwestern University School of Law, 20-22 April 2001 at p. 7.

stimulated into the nature of reservoirs mechanics and efficient oil recovery. The result of the research revealed amongst other things, that drilling too many wells in particular parts of the reservoir could 'cause reservoir water or gas to break through the producing column of oil, thus trapping significant volumes of unrecoverable oil in lost pockets within the pool'.[57] The rule of capture has shown that where the law fails to protect investments, there will be increased efforts by individuals to protect their investments through self-help and this could result into over-investments and excessive wastes. This is counter-productive as investment expectations will be negatively affected.

5.1.3 *Enhanced Oil Recovery*

The Rule discourages secondary and other enhanced recovery operations. For example, in carrying out water flooding operations, water is pumped into one end of the field in order to push oil to producing wells at the other end. A single operator will disallow secondary recovery operations like water flooding and gas injection for pressure maintenance especially where it will affect his underlie reservoir. He may also benefit from such recovery operations if the well on his property is strategically positioned to drain oil from the property of the person carrying out secondary recovery operation. The party who intends to carry out the operation will be discouraged as the other party draining will not suspend capture activities owing to the rule of capture. Moreover, if individuals attempt to flood fields unilaterally, subsurface trespass may be committed because of water invasion.

5.1.4 *Common Property Regime*

The Rule subjected property in oil and gas while in the reservoir to common property regime. Consequently, individual owners of the land overlying the reservoirs had attempted to maximise their individual gain to the detriment of the common resource and ultimately to the rest landowners whose properties overlie the reservoir. From Chapter 4 of this book, we have seen that where there is no distinct property right to a particular resource, there would be an individual race to capture the resource as much as possible to the detriment of all. Common property (open access regime) arises where a resource 'is owned by no one but is equally available to everyone.'[58] Becker argued that where a thing is held in common but owned by no one, a valid appropriation by one person without the consent of the others can take place.[59] This is exactly what the rule of capture has done and that is, to validate appropriation of oil from straddling oil

57. *Ibid.*, at p. 9. Contemporary estimates from the early part of the twentieth century places the average recovery of oil at only 10-20% of the total resource in place, but in many cases it would have been much less than this overall average. Joseph E. Pogue, 'Economics of Petroleum' (New York: John Wiley and Sons, 1921), 343-344.
58. Becker, 'Property Rights: Philosophic Foundations', at 25 citing Samuel Pufendorf, 'De Jure Naturae et Gentium, translation of 1688 edition by C.H. and W.A. Oldfather' (Oxford: Claredon Press, 1934), bk IV, iv, 2-6.
59. *Ibid.*

and gas reservoir by one licensee or lessee. But as has been seen, oil and gas in the reservoir are not things un-owned. The application of the rule of capture is therefore, misnomer.

The application of the rule of capture has led to an imperfection in the definition of property rights to oil and gas in the reservoir. As suggested by the Economic theory of transaction cost, where private property right to a resource has not been properly defined and enforced, there will be increased efforts to capture the value of such resource especially as the potential value of the resource increases.[60] Thus, because the nature of the rights of licensee over oil and gas reservoir has not been properly defined or identified in our legal jurisprudence, there had been successful capture of this resource. This has led to increased efforts, such as offset well drilling, by individuals to protect such property from capture thus, culminating in competitive drilling and wastes. The resultant effect is over investment of capitals which are eventually counter-productive. The risk of capturing this oil and gas reservoir reduces the ability of the adjoining licensee to appropriate the value of the resource. This situation could also be likened to the 'tragedy of the commons' syndrome espoused by Hardin[61] in which he gave example of grazing land. Marine fishery is also a classic example of property that had been hitherto, subjected to open access regime. Tragedy of the common has therefore been created by the application of the rule of capture to oil and gas.[62]

5.1.5 *Destroyer of Title to Reservoir Oil and Gas*

The Rule destroys title (i.e., 'the bundle of rights' – right to possess, the right to use, the right to manage, the right to the income of the thing, the right to the capital) of the lessee to oil and gas in situ. From Chapters 2 and 3, we have seen that an oil and gas lease or licence is a property right. Since reservoir oil is an important or valuable attributes of the licence, we have seen in Chapter 4 that a licensee's interest in the reservoir oil is equally proprietary. This finding is reinforced by interpretation of the licence granting clauses, the modern conception of property under the Hohfeld-Honore theory and International Investment and Human rights laws. Since the rule permits one person to take the property of another without compensation and which is subsequently sanctioned by the State's Regulatory organs, it may incur a breach of the international obligations of the State under Investment treaties and probably, also tantamount to 'indirect taking' as it will be shown in Chapter 7 of this book. It erodes the security of oil and gas title of the licensee both when it is under the ground and when it has been produced. The security of expectation in the use and enjoyment of the

60. Guilherme Fowler de Avilla Monteiro, 'Property Rights Strategy: Market Structure and Competition in Brazilian Soybean Seed Industry', at p. 5.
61. See Chapter 4 at p. 171.
62. The effect of this tragedy of the common as applied to oil and gas would now be fully felt as the price of crude oil has increased to over $100 per barrel. Other tragedies are uncontrolled competitive drilling, loss of reservoir energy, loss of total recovery, loss of oil through surface storage, increased gas flaring because there were no immediate markets, drilling of unnecessary wells with the attendant costs.

resources and also against interfering forces in society at large are negatively impacted by the Rule. This has a wider implication on investment in the industry at the long run as part of what investors consider before investing in a particular country is the extent to which their petroleum laws and regulations encapsulates the law of capture.

5.1.6 *Violates Fundamental Rights of the Investor*

Under the human rights laws as discussed in Chapters 2 and 7, oil and gas licence and hence reservoir oil qualifies as property rights or 'possession'. Possession has autonomous definition and has been defined broadly for instance, by the ECtHR so that an interference with the property of one person by the State or even by another private person is against the fundamental rights of the person.[63]

5.2 Positive Effects

In spite of the negative implications of the Rule as adumbrated above, it also has some positive implications. It must be noted that the Judges adopted the Rule as a rule of necessity[64] owing to their inadequate knowledge of reservoirs mechanics.[65] It was simply convenient for the Judges to use the rule to solve difficult ownership problems. As the rule were being applied, those with financial muscles and technical know-how were racing against one another to produce oil. There was an incentive to produce as fast as possible. It is therefore, a rewarder of those that diligently seek the oil and produces it. Commenting on the general lack of knowledge with regards to the mechanics of oil and gas reservoir, Professor Kuntz, an ardent supporter of the Rule, was of the view that even though the Rule was adopted in time of limited scientific knowledge, subsequent advances in scientific knowledge do not necessarily lead to another rule.[66] It is submitted that where subsequent scientific knowledge has shown that the rule had worked some incurable injustices, the rule ought to be jettisoned. The law is an instrument of social change and as such should keep the same pace with scientific advances.

The Labour theory and the theory of first possession discussed in Chapter 4 of this book, appeared to have supported the Rule.[67] The essence of Locke's theory is the idea that since one's body is one's property (i.e., self-ownership) and the produce, i.e. labour is also one's property, it follows from there that the labour's product will also be

63. See Article 1 Protocol 1 of ECtHR.
64. As noted above, false analogies were made to subterranean waters, animal *ferae naturae* and solid minerals while failing to adopt the rules relating to them in totality.
65. In the case of *Barnard v. Monongahela Natural Gas Co.*, 216 Pa. 362, 365, 65 A. 801, 802 (1907), the Pennsylvania Supreme Court declared that 'Exact Knowledge on this subject is not at present obtainable ... This may not be the best rule; but neither the Legislature nor our highest court has given us any better. No doubt many thousands of dollars have been expended "in protecting lines" in oil and gas territory that would not have been expended if some rule had existed by which it could have been avoided.'
66. Kuntz, 'The Law of Capture', (1957) Okla. L. Rev. 10: 406, at 406-407.
67. See Locke's labour theory discussed in Chapter 4.

one's property. This stem from the value addition of labour to what labour produces which Locke gave as ratio 9/10 or 99/100 in favour of labour. This proposition may be correct with respect to the difference in the value of oil when under the ground as compared to when it is brought to the surface. Considering the enormous resources in terms of the capital, technical, man hours work and even the risk that are undertaken on its development and production from reservoir, it may be justified to give property in oil and gas to whoever produces it regardless of where it comes from. But as it has been shown in Chapter 4, the question has been raised as to why the labourer should be entitled to both the thing and the value added. Some writers have suggested that, he should only be entitled to the value added and not both of them. Others have argued that since it may not be possible to separate the thing and the improvements made on it, perhaps the labourer should be entitled to both.[68] With regards to oil and gas, the labour added is the expenditure incurred and the technical resources deployed in the development and production of the resources which have already been mixed with the substances the moment of their production. Separating the two after production would be difficult. In this light, property rights of capture might be justifiable. However, the problem is the Locke's proviso which restricted acts of appropriation. A drainer who captures about 75% of the total gas underneath adjoining premises or maliciously wastes the gas of his neighbor cannot be said to have left 'enough and as good ...in common for others'.

Since the game of capture is to reward those who diligently capture other's petroleum, there was an incentive to explore, discover new horizons and promptly produce oil and gas.

6. ALTERNATIVES TO THE RULE

Edward Pierce commented that the simplicity of the rule must be taken into consideration when alternatives to the rule are being considered. He said that ownership in place was rejected on the ground that it will be difficult to trace the migration of specific molecules of the substance. Again, 'Fair share' principle was also rejected because of the difficulty in determining what would be a 'fair share' for each landowner over a common reservoir.[69]

Professor Daintith considered some alternatives to the rule such as Accounting in equity, Lateral support and First appropriation and concluded that the alternatives to capture had not been brought forcefully before the judges in these capture cases.

Accounting in equity was suggested by Justice Woodward in the case of *Kier v. Peterson*[70] to enable a party who suffers drainage to claim the market value of the oil less cost of production and separation. This means that where the act of drilling on one's land is lawful but its result is to produce oil which is the property of someone

68. See Chapter 4 at pp. 155-156.
69. Pierce, 'Coordinated Reservoir Development – An Alternative to the Rule of Capture for the Ownership and Development of Oil and Gas', at 29 referring to Professor Kuntz 'The Law of Capture', at 407-408.
70. (1862).

else, he must account to his neighbour for the value of the oil produced that originated from the neighbour's land. This in effects necessitates an evidence of 'how much oil produced from a particular well might have been drained from under other properties'[71] which as stated by Professor Kuntz, is a futile exercise.[72] This alternative will however be feasible only in States where oil is regarded as forming part of the land like Pennsylvania and Texas.

Withdrawal of lateral support was raised by the plaintiff's counsel in the case of *Kelley v. Ohio oil Co. (supra)*. The counsel contended that the defendant by drilling close to the plaintiff's property lines, had deprived the plaintiff's oil of lateral support to which he was entitled. The withdrawal of the lateral support had caused him to lose some oil from his land to the defendant's land. This he claimed was an actionable wrong. Although Lateral support had been well established in cases of mineral rights and it is to the effect that owner of mineral rights should not deprive the surface of support when using his land for mining activities, the court was of the opinion that in the case at hand, the surface of the neighbouring land was unharmed and that 'lateral support cannot be claimed purely for subsurface mineral deposit.' There was no authority to support as well that it applies to subterranean water. The lower court dismissed the case for disclosing no cause of action which was confirmed by the Supreme Court.

First appropriation is to the effect that the first appropriator of the petroleum under the ground should be protected by law. In other words, the person who discovers oil first should be protected from the 'activities on the neighbouring land that have the effect of diminishing the flow obtained.'[73] This is also a principle that has been firmly rooted in both English and American surface water laws. But in water law, first appropriation rule was later changed to the notion of 'shared natural rights of riparian owners to reasonable water use.'[74] The problem with this alternative is that it is a form

71. Daintith, 'Finders Keepers? ...' at pp. 42-43.
72. However, see Chapter 4 above where we argued that scientific advances in Reservoir Engineering makes it now possible to estimate with certain degree of precision, the amount of oil which underlies a particular lease. The courts in the US have required certain evidence to prove that drainage had occurred - (see *Breaux v. Pan American Petroleum Corp* 163 So.2d 404 (La. Ct. App. 1964) and *Renner v. Monsanto Chemical Co.* 354 P.2d 326, 329 (Kan. 1960)). The party alleging drainage must show that the well causing drainage is in proximity to his boundary line and that the well produces large amount of petroleum. He may prove this by maps, records, ordinary witness, and expert opinion or by a well belatedly drilled upon the lease that there is substantial petroleum under his lease to be drained (see Howard R. Williams & Charles J. Meyers, 'Oil and Gas Law' (1991) at 823.1). Seismic data could also be used through expert, to prove existence of petroleum under the lease but the sufficiency or otherwise of such data is left for the regulatory authority to decide. (See *Moncrief v. Wyoming Oil & Gas Conservation Commission* 981 P.2d 913 (Wyo.1999); Eugene Kuntz, 'Recent Natural Resources Cases', (1965) Nat. Resources J. 5: at 213, citing the case of *Vogel v. Corporation Commission* 399 P.2d 474 (Okla. 1965).) Similarly in Nigeria, to show that oil exists in a reservoir that straddles the party must prove this by both seismic surveys and well drilling - (see Article 2.3 (a) (i) (ii) of the Year 2008 Guidelines for Unitisation). Also in Netherlands, the court held in the *Unocal v. Conoco Netherlands B.V. (supra)* that the party alleging drainage must show that his prospect is economically recoverable. This means that he will not only show that oil exists in his side but that it is of commercial quantity.
73. Daintith, 'Finders Keepers? ...', at pp. 48-49.
74. *Ibid.*

of capture itself. However, it will be succour for the first to capture in that his right will be preserved against subsequent drilling on neighbouring land.[75] Professor Daintith concluded that Justice Woodward's opinion of Accounting in equity were neglected, the right of lateral support canvassed in Kelley's case were not convincing and first appropriation had not also been recognised for the possible means of settling oil and gas property claims.[76] As has been shown in Chapter 4, it is submitted that property rights in petroleum reservoir would be an appropriate response to the rule of capture and which is akin to the doctrine of accounting in equity alternative suggested by Justice Woodward.

7. RESPONSES TO THE ADVERSE EFFECTS OF THE RULE OF CAPTURE

7.1 Enactment of Conservation Laws

In the United States (US), Conservation laws were adopted by some States to address the problem of wastes and competitive drilling. Production conservation involves a geo-scientific study of the nature of the reservoir. During the study, the physical characteristics of the reservoir, its mechanics and the behaviour of the oil and gas contained therein would be identified before and after the starts of production.

The aim of conservation practices therefore, is to make efficient use of natural oil and gas reservoir energy. They were initially designed to curb production excesses and wastes so as to stabilise oil prices. This could have promoted the economic welfare of the oil operators and thus stimulate further investments in the upstream oil and gas industry but because the conservation laws also preserve the rule of capture as the ultimate principle controlling property in oil and gas in situ, this aim was never achieved. Conservation laws therefore, only addressed the side effects of the rule of capture but failed to address the root cause of the problem which is the rule itself, hence enormous wastes of the resources continued.[77] Conservation practices established through legislations were Production limitations (Markets demand estimates, Prorationing and Allowables), Well Spacing, Pooling and Unitisation.

7.1.1 *Production Limitations (Market Demand Estimates, Prorationing and Allowables)*

Production limitation is pursued through market demand approach. This involves a system whereby, the total national oil needs are forecasted by the US Federal Conservation Board[78] and the estimates demand are divided among the producing States. Through the Prorationing rules established by each State, the established State-wide production limitation is then allocated among State's oil and gas fields by

75. *Ibid.*
76. *Ibid.*, at 50.
77. See generally Piece, 'Coordinated Reservoir Development – An Alternative to the Rule of Capture for the Ownership and Development of Oil and Gas', at 62.
78. *Ibid.*, at 64.

the State's Conservation Commission. Production allocated to each field (technically called Allowables) is then divided among each well in that field. Each well is given maximum amount of oil and gas it could produce (also known as production quotas).[79] No State is allowed to exceed its share of the forecasted national needs. This however caused a reduction in the production capacity of each well because each well, in keeping within its quotas, often produced less than its flow capacity. Although, price level may be stabilised, this is contrary to reservoir conservation methods. A determination of the optimal rate of production of a well depends on its reservoir characteristics as evidenced by Geo-physical study of the field's production potentials and not economic factors such as market forecasts. This presents a case in which economic factors were allowed to overshadow reservoir engineering considerations in the determination of wells production capacity.[80]

Under the Prorationing rule, production was restricted and thus, placing constraints on competitive drilling and production of oil resource. However, in some States like Texas, the small (high cost) producers were granted quota concessions as a result of their political influence. They were given minimum allowable which varies according to the depth of the well and its production capacity. They thus, have incentives to drill more wells than are technically necessary to recover oil from a reservoir, which eventually led to a great number of violations of prorationing regulations.[81] The statutes also made it unlawful to curtail the production of small producers below the minimum Allowables.

As a result of the above, unlike the small producers, large (low cost) producers were more restricted by the conservation regulations. Because the small producers are allocated their minimum allowables first from the State's permitted allocation before sharing the rest with the large producers, small producers reduces the Allowables for the large producers that could have produced with low lifting costs. Moreover, it does not make economic sense to keep small wells producing while restricting the more efficient wells as this will increase the costs of production.

79. *Ibid.*
80. See the case of *Champlin Refining Co. v. Corporation Commission* 286 U.S. 210 (1932) where the production capacity of the plaintiff's oil well were limited by 6% in spite of the fact that he has markets for its full production capacity. The US Supreme Court upheld this restriction noting that if plaintiff is allowed to produce at full capacity, other operators will in an attempt to prevent drainage and protect their correlative rights, also do likewise which will in turn lead to earthen pit storage and other forms of wastes. Contrast however with the case of *Thompson v. Consolidated Gas utilities corp.* 300 U.S. 55 (1937) where the Texas Railroad commission's proration order was annulled on the ground that the proration order had the effect of taking the plaintiff's property for the benefit of other private's Operator's in the field.
81. These small producers are also called marginal wells owners. In Texas the worst case allowable is 10 barrels a day while the Kansas statutes allows a minimum of 25 barrels minimum per well allowable a day. See Pierce, 'Coordinated Reservoir Development – An Alternative to the Rule of Capture for the Ownership and Development of Oil and Gas', at pp. 68-70. The aim of minimum well allowable is to prevent situation whereby low producing wells are prematurely abandoned as a result of loss from recoverable oil. But, in reality, because the firms raced to meet their allowables, significant oil is lost as a result of unnecessary well drilling because reservoir energy is easily dissipated. Production costs will also increase meaning that there will be less capital for exploration activities and thus resulting into high prices of crude oil.

Small tracts producers had the tendency to drain adjoining lands when given large Allowables[82] while it becomes uneconomical for them to drill and produce when given Allowable commensurate with the oil and gas underneath their lands. Consequently, wells on adjoining large tracts could drain their oil and gas. To regulate the relationship between the small producers and the large producers in this sense became a serious challenge for the Commission. Prorationing, as a conservation technique for regulating competitive production, was soon defeated as a result of pressure on the regulatory commission to allow greater overall production.[83] In addressing this challenge of drainage, the court's quest to provide a way to deal fairly with large and small tracts owners, as the rule of capture could not help owing to the ownership in place principles enshrined especially in the State of Texas, resulted into conflicting decisions.[84]

Moreover, offset drilling which could have been used to protect drainage is limited by Rule 37.[85] However, the case of *Halbourty v. Railroad Commission*[86] introduced the fair share doctrine to give substance to the absolute ownership of oil and gas in place theory. This fair share principle sees the rule of capture in a different fashion. It sees ownership in place as a limitation on rule of capture instead of rule of capture being a limitation on ownership.[87] In other words, the rule of capture has been regarded as a rule of non-liability for drainage instead of a licence for drainage.[88] 'The land owner is entitled to an opportunity to obtain his fair share of the minerals under his land, not his share, and enough of his neighbour's to enable him drill and turn a profit'[89] In trying to adjust and protect private rights under the existing conservation laws, the Texas's court has held that the proration order of the conservation commission must give to the several property owners a fair opportunity to produce the

82. See the case of *Railroad Commission v. Rowan & Nichols Oil Co* 311 U.S 573 at 579-580 (1940) where as a result of the quota restrictions on the large producer (the defendant) in favour of a small adjacent producer, its oil was drained by the latter. The defendant contended that its property was confiscated as a result of the proration order. The court while restating the constitutionality of proration order, ruled that it was a question of administrative and not judicial judgement. In another case involving the same parties with similar facts, the Court again upheld the commission's proration order. See *Railroad Commission v. Rowan & Nichols Oil Co* 311 U.S 570 (1941).
83. Pierce, 'Coordinated Reservoir Development …', at 70.
84. *Railroad Commission v. Humble oil & Ref Co* 193 S.W.2d 824 (1946) contrast *Ryan Consol. Petroleum Corp v. Pickens* 175 Tex. 221, 285 S.W.2d 201 (1955).
85. 'Pierce Coordinated Reservoir Development …', at 16.
86. 163 Tex. 417, 357 S.W.2d 364 (1962).
87. Pierce, 'Coordinated Reservoir Development - An Alternative to the Rule of Capture for the Ownership and Development of Oil and Gas', at 20.
88. *Ibid.* He quoted the court's dictum on p. 375 as holding that 'To infer that the rule of capture gives to the landowner the legally protected right to capture the oil and gas underlying his neighbour's tract is entirely inconsistent with the ownership theory. To harmonise both rules, the rule of capture can means little more than that due to their fugitive nature, the hydrocarbons when captured belong to the owner of the well to which they flowed, irrespective of where they may have been in place originally, without liability to his neighbour for drainage. That is to say that since the gas in a continuous reservoir will flow to a point of low pressure the landowners is not restricted to the particular gas that may underlie his property originally but is the owner of all that which he may legally recover.'
89. *Ibid.*

recoverable oil underlying their lands or its equivalent.[90] Subsequent cases[91] however substituted the words 'fair opportunity' with the words 'fair share' and held that the prorationing formula adopted by the commission must allow ratable production and give opportunity to each owners to produce his 'fair share' of the oil and gas from the reservoir. Therefore, where from a common reservoir, one tract owner produces oil and gas that is more than the quantity underlying his tract, he has denied the other owner of the reservoir a fair opportunity to recover oil and gas underlying his tract. As a matter of public policy therefore, the regulatory agency has the duty and power to regulate the flow of oil from a common reservoir to protect correlative rights.

In all, prorationing as a conservative technique produces serious problems. It encourages unnecessary well drilling and increases well drainage. In fact it 'substitutes competitive drilling for competitive drainage.'[92] It does not take into consideration whether a well should produce having regards to its geological characteristics but only determines how much it can produce under the applicable allocation formula. Rational economic judgments are not exercised in its practice in terms of the best way to develop a reservoir and it also increases costs of production by restricting the more efficient wells to unrealistic levels. This in turn leads to inflation or price increases as the production is restricted to forecasted market demand. It fails to eliminate rule of capture and encourages competitive drilling thereby making secondary recovery programmes difficult to achieve.

7.1.2 *Well Spacing*

In Texas, regulations were made by the Texas Railroad Commission to set the minimum distances for oil and gas wells in order to prevent wastes and to preserve ownership of oil and gas.[93] Spacing, though reduced drilling which would have taken place under the rule of capture, did not eliminate unnecessary well drilling.

However, because compulsory pooling was not adopted in Texas, spacing rules could not be enforced against small tracts owners whose tracts are not large enough to be combined to form a drilling unit so as to be granted drilling permit.[94] Even though, minimum spacing rules were introduced to curtail excessive drilling of wells, exceptions were occasionally granted to small firms where it is necessary to prevent wastes

90. *Railroad Commission v. Humble Oil & Refining Co.* 193 S.W.2d 824 (Tex. Civ. App.).
91. *Atlantic Ref. Co v. Railroad Commission* 162 Tex. 274, 346 S.W.2d 801 (1961) and *Halbouty v. Railroad Commission* 163 Tex. 417 S.W.2d 364 (1961).
92. Pierce, 'Coordinated Reservoir Development - An Alternative to the Rule of Capture for the Ownership and Development of Oil and Gas', at 68 citing Marshall & Meyers, 'Legal Planning of petroleum Production', 41 Yale L.J. 33, 49-51 (1931) at 58.
93. *Ibid.*, at 15. This rule is usually referred to as 'Rule 37'. See Tex. ADMIN. CODE tit. 16, s. 3.37 (1980). This Rule allows one well per twenty acre tract which was later increased to one well per forty-acre tract. Rule 37 also provides that no well shall be drilled nearer than 467 feet to any property line, lease line, or sub division line. Exceptions may however be granted in order to prevent wastes or to prevent the confiscation of property.
94. *Ibid.*, at 16. Even though Mineral Interests Pooling Act was made in 1965 in Texas, to require tracts of land to be consolidated for development in certain circumstances, exceptions can still be secured in several situations. For example application requesting force pooling must be made by one of the owners before the Commission can order force pooling.

or to protect the property from drainage. The same small tracts with spacing exception could however drill his tracts and drain oil and gas from adjoining lands. This was legitimate under Texas law which permits ownership of oil and gas in place. They are therefore, entitled to not only the oil and gas underneath their tracts but also those drained from adjoining tracts. Many small producers obtained exceptions to drill wells on tracts less than an acre in size. Also, because the small producers have the advantage of minimum allowable, they could produce same quantity of oil as their adjoining large tracts owner. Therefore, they could receive more than their just share of the oil under their tracts at the expense of their adjoining large tracts owners. It did not consider whether it is even necessary to drill any well at all on the approved drilling unit. It therefore, failed to take into consideration well location pattern from geological and reservoir engineering angles that will ostensibly guarantee optimum production. In a prorationing conservation regime, spacing might be desirable so as to guarantee marginal wells production allowables.[95]

7.1.3 *Pooling*

Pooling is the process of combining separately owned, small tracts of land into drilling units or spacing units, for example 40 acres for an oil well or 640 acres for a gas well. In the United States, pooling is done to avoid unnecessary well drilling during the primary recovery phase of production.

In Louisiana State however, conservation laws empowered the regulatory agency to enforce compulsory pooling of interests into a single unit where voluntary pooling has failed among Mineral interest owners.[96] In Texas, pooling is made voluntary. Therefore, if parties failed to pool their tracts, the regulatory authority cannot compel them. It is evident that in the US, the Regulatory regime that governs common pool resources during primary production except State lands and Federal Lands, is the various conservation laws such as pooling, prorationing and well spacing which though, prevents physical wastes of petroleum and guarantees interest owners fair share of production, offered less benefits to the interest owners than when reservoirs-wide unit formation is achieved under complete Unitisation.[97]

7.1.4 *Unitisation*

As a result of the obvious problems created by the rule of capture and the less beneficial conservation laws, Unitisation scheme was developed to mitigate these problems. Unitisation is a scheme employed to develop straddling petroleum reservoir between

95. *Ibid.*, at 76.
96. It is to be noted that Louisiana operates Non-ownership in place system having been influenced by the United States' Supreme Court decision in *Ohio Oil Co v. Indiana* (*supra*). See also the Louisiana's Supreme Court case of *Rives v. Gulf Ref. Co* 133 La. 178, 62 So. 623 (1913).
97. David Asmus & Jacqueling Wearver, 'Unitizing Oil and Gas Fields around the World: A Comparative Analysis of National Laws and Private Contracts', at 6 n. 2. Available at http://www.ssrn.com.

two or more adjoining licensees as a single unit under a single operator and common production facilities. Thus, a single unit is created over the straddling reservoirs. A single operator is also appointed from the tracts owners to manage and operate the reservoir as a single Unit. It is a regime for exploitation of a single geological structure straddling two or more concessions boundaries which preserves the rights of all the parties. This takes place in absolute disregard of artificial boundaries created by men and the legal concept of capture.

Unitisation can be distinguished from pooling though the terms are sometimes used interchangeably. Unitisation 'is a process of combining separately owned portions of a common producing reservoirs or field into a large field-wide unit. Pooling by contrast is the process of combining separately owned, small tracts of land into drilling units or spacing units, for example 40 acres for an oil well or 640 acres for a gas well'. In the United States, while Unitisation is done to implement secondary recovery of oil (except onshore federal lands), pooling is done to avoid unnecessary well drilling during the primary recovery phase of production.[98]

Unitisation provides opportunity, during secondary recovery operations, for enhanced oil recovery technique to be used to pump more oil into the surface. This is achieved by injecting the well with gas, water or other fluids in order to increase reservoir pressure. This was as a result of the gradual declining of oil recovery in late 1940s based on subsurface natural pressure existent in primary recovery operations.

Therefore, with a complete Unitisation among the licensees, a single licence holder is appointed as the unit operator to develop the reservoir while the other licence holders share in the Unit profits and production costs according to agreed ratios usually in proportion of individual's interests in the productive land encompassed by the unit. In Unitisation, the lease loses its production importance because the Unit operator is vested with authority to locate appropriately production and injection wells in order to maximise unitised reservoir's output. The Unit operator also determines whether to shut in a particular well or to drill additional well or even to convert production well to an injection well within the unit. With this scheme, significant gains from capital savings and production increases would be achieved. This is because production costs would be reduced; reservoir energy would be utilised thereby increasing ultimate recovery at both primary and secondary recovery operations. It has been argued that overall production can increase from two to five time's unregulated output.[99] Unitisation could be voluntary or compulsory depending on what the legislation of a particular country provides. Unitisation offers a viable alternative to spacing and prorationing conservation methods as it can eliminate wasteful drilling. This is because it takes into consideration geological factors in determining how a field should be developed and produced. In this context, natural boundaries as opposed to man-made boundaries are used as the determinant of course of development.

98. *Ibid.*
99. Garry D. Libecap & James L. Smith, 'The Self-Enforcing Provisions of Oil and Gas Unit Operating Agreements: Theory and Evidence', at 4 (Cambridge, MA: National Bureau of Economic Research, 1999). They stated that '[F]or instance, Libecap and Wiggins (1985) reported that as late as 1975, only 38 percent of Oklahoma production and 20 percent of Texas production came from reservoir-wide units.'

To date, it has been identified as the most effective mechanism by which the disastrous effects of the Rule can be eliminated as it provides parties with unequal opportunities to obtain production from a common reservoir.[100] Although, unitisation laws were designed in a way to serve the goals of conservation in terms of good oil field development practices, it did not address ownership or property rights to oil and gas while still in the reservoir and hence could not completely eliminate the rule of capture.

The benefits derived from Unitisation were expected to be a motivation for licence holders to unitise common-pool resources. In US, empirical evidence has shown that this is however, far from the case.[101] The reasons for this were attributed to difficulty in reaching agreement on a unit contract among licence holders. Contract Agreements often drag for too many years of negotiations before completion and by which time many efficiency losses would have already occurred. Again, from empirical evidence in a US study, it has been shown that an average time for negotiating Unit Agreement takes between four to ten years.[102] Example of Unitisation negotiation that took such a long time before consummation was the Prudhoe Bay Field in Alaska, US. It has been noted for its complexities and cumbersome process culminating in about 1,000 pages.

Among the difficult issues that often lead to long contracting process includes – Tract participation (TP) defined as the percentage unit interest of each of the licence holders in the Unit, definition of the phases of production as primary and secondary (Multi-phase units) and the minimum requirements for the change from one phase to the other, dual participation areas (oil rims and gas cap) and the sharing formula that is, cost and production sharing options, etc. Reaching agreement on these issues is often contentious and can delay Unitisation for years or even where there is one eventually, it leads to incomplete Unitisation agreements as incentives of parties are not completely aligned or harmonised.

Moreover, unitisation agreements are entered into after the discovery of petroleum and especially in the US, after the primary production phase. It is therefore, possible that substantial drainage would have occurred before parties commence or conclude unitisation discussions and processes. Besides, drainage could still occur to or from a unitised reservoir even though the potential for capture is eliminated within a unitised area.

In addition, where unitisation laws did not provide for compulsory unitisation, its formation is left at the whims and caprices of competitors and the regulatory authority will be incapacitated in forcing them to carry out unitise development. Its role will only be limited to a mere mandate to persuade and 'encourage' unit formation.[103] Some

100. David Asmus & Jacqueling Wearver, 'Unitizing oil and Gas Fields Around the World: A Comparative Analysis of National Laws and Private Contracts', (2006) at 11-48. Available at http://www.ssrn.com.
101. See Garry D. Libecap & James L. Smith, 'The Self-Enforcing Provisions of Oil and Gas Unit Operating Agreements: Theory and Evidence', at 4 (3 December 1998).
102. Weaver, Asmus, Walde, Marmud, Ifesi, Bastida, Ross in 'AIPN International Unitisation of oil and gas fields: the legal framework for analysis of international law, national laws and private contracts', at p. 11.
103. Cecilia A. Low, 'The Rule of Capture: Its Current Status and Some Issues to Consider', (2008-2009) Alta. L. Rev. 46: 799 at 821 citing Alberta Conservation Act, s. 79 (1).

States in US had merely provided that majority of the unit interest owners must agree on unitisation before the remaining minority can be forced into Unitisation. The refusal of the majority to undertake unit development means a denial of unitisation benefits to the minority. The resultant effect is that many straddling fields are developed without unitisation in place to day in the US and thus, causing wastage of oil and gas resources.

As a result of the aforesaid obstacles, pooling or unitisation has not been able to prevent all times drainages.

7.1.5 *Correlative Right*

The Correlative rights doctrine is a devise of both the courts and the legislatures to modify or restrain the disastrous consequences of the rule of capture. However, the common law courts have defined and applied the doctrine broadly than the statutes. The result of such difference is that common law correlative rights provide more protection than the statutory correlative rights. The court has by the 'Qualified ownership theory' demonstrated the inapplicability of the absolute ownership doctrine, as applied to solid minerals, to oil and gas and introduced the correlative rights doctrine into the settlement of disputes emanating from capture of petroleum from straddling reservoirs. The doctrine is to the effect that each of the owners of the tracts of land overlying a producing formation has correlative rights and duties in respect of the oil and gas contained therein. Each of the tract owners has a right to produce and may take as much oil and gas from the common-pool through a well bore on his tract even though the oil and gas might have come from the land of his neighbour. There is however a corresponding duty not to waste the oil and gas or to damage the producing formation in the course of such production. The only limitation he has is that if such production will result into waste or damaging the producing formation in a way that reduces ultimate recovery, the adjoining land owner may be able to bring an injunctive claim against him.[104] The question that one may ask here is that on what basis would such an action be founded if the land owner has no property in the oil and gas in place? The supposed right granted to the landowner by correlative doctrine is not a protectable right if the landowner can still lose the oil to drainage from the adjoining landowner. This shows that qualified ownership principle which introduced the correlative rights doctrine has also been expressed in terms of the possibility of the land owner's title to oil and gas in place to be defeated by the operation of the rule of capture.

However, the design of the correlative right doctrine by court is actually meant to protect both the oil and gas in the reservoir and also the natural reservoir pressure so as to ensure efficient production of the resources.[105] It has also been able to protect both private and public rights in the sense that a landowner is protected from improper development of the common reservoir by his neighbouring landowner and the public

104. *Richmond National Gas Co. v. Davenport* (1905) 37 Ind. App. 25, 76 N.E. 525; *Manufacturer's Gas Co. Indiana Gas Co.* (1900) 155 Ind.451, 57 N.E. 912.
105. Pierce, 'Coordinated Reservoir Development – An Alternative to the Rule of Capture for the Ownership and Development of Oil and Gas', at 50.

is also protected from activities causing waste of the reservoir pressure that may have negative impact on the total oil and gas recovery.[106]

In the same vein, where one party through negligent operation of a well causes a blow out and which wastefully drained oil from an adjoining property into his property, the court awarded damages in favour of the injured party. The court rejected a defence fathomed on the rule of capture and declared that the negligent destruction of the common producing structure has denied the plaintiff opportunity to produce his fair share of the recoverable oil and gas under his land.[107]

To sum up, correlative rights doctrine connotes:[108]

(1) due care and attention should be exhibited by the producers in order not to waste or injure the common producing reservoir;
(2) right of each producer in a common reservoir, to an opportunity to produce his fair share of the recoverable oil lying under his tract;
(3) right of each producer against malicious sapping of the common reservoir;
(4) right to conduct operations to enhance recovery from the common source.

In spite of the above correlative rights, judicial recognition of new rights is apposite. As Edward pierce had correctly pointed out scientific advances in petroleum reservoir engineering may prove an allocation formula to be improper even though it was proper under information available when it was made. Therefore the formula may prove unjust as knowledge advances.[109] The courts therefore need to dissociate from the rule of convenience and recognise more rights that will produce just results when applied between adjoining landowners with common reservoir.

8. IMPACTS OF TECHNOLOGICAL ADVANCES IN WELLS DRILLING ON RULE OF CAPTURE

8.1 Horizontal Well

Horizontal well drilling, also known as directional or slant hole drilling, occurs where a Company drills a vertical hole and gradually changes the direction of the drilling bit in a horizontal fashion before the hole reaches the target formation. The aim is to have the horizontal portion of the hole in the target formation. More contact with the producing formation can be achieved in horizontal well than in vertical well. This means that production flow rates in horizontal well can be greater than the vertical

106. See the cases of *Manufacturer's Gas & Oil v. Indiana and Natural Gas & Oil Co* (*supra*) and *Louisville Gas Co. v. Kentucky Heating Co.* (1903) (*supra*).
107. *Elliff v. Texon Drilling Co.* v146 Tex. 575, 210 S.W.2d 558 (1948).
108. Eugne Kuntz, 'A Treatise on the Law of Oil and Gas' (1987 1st ed.) at 120.
109. Pierce, 'Coordinated Reservoir Development – An Alternative to the Rule of Capture for the Ownership and Development of Oil and Gas', at 55.

well.[110] It has also been argued that greater ultimate recovery can be achieved through horizontal wells.[111] In addition, greater drainage area can be achieved than vertical well, meaning that fewer wells will be needed to develop a field. This will significantly reduce costs of permitting, production, site preparation and restoration. It will also have less impact on the environment as less surface area is utilised.[112] Moreover, certain reservoirs can be more economically developed by horizontal well technique than vertical well, for example, reservoirs characterised by thin, large area, low permeability, vertical fractures and reservoirs that have been damaged by high flow rates.[113] However, the cost of drilling a horizontal well is higher than that of a vertical well.[114]

All the above shows that the industry will witness upsurge in the number of horizontal wells that will be drilled in the future.[115] This will invariably lead to controversy as to the equitable entitlement to petroleum not only between competing working interest owners but also between adjacent concession holders. This is because horizontal well bore could cross subsurface property lines and thus, leading to increase in incidence of capture of petroleum not only from straddling reservoirs but also from non-straddling ones.[116] The law has recognised that when this happens, the driller will be liable for subsurface trespass[117] and conversion if petroleum is taken from the formation.[118]

110. R.E. Pelzer et al., 'Horizontal Drilling: Regulatory and Contractual Implications', (1991) Alta. L. Rev. 30: 272 at 274, citing Alberta Department of Energy, Horizontal Well Royalty Backgrounder, 2 April 1991. The Department had said that productivity for horizontal wells can be five times greater than the average productivity for vertical wells in the same pool.
111. *Ibid.*, citing P.C. Crouse, 'A Review of the Reservoir Considerations for Horizontal Wells in the Bakken Formation' presented at the 1990 Calgary Horizontal Drilling Conference, August 1990. He stated that 'up to 35 billion barrels of additional oil equivalent could be recovered with horizontal technology in the United States', while Canada's recoverable oil could increase by 50%. See C. Donville, 'Making Hole Sideways Gives Oil Patch New Lease', The Globe and Mail Report on Business, 29 March 1991.
112. *Ibid.*, at 275.
113. *Ibid.*
114. *Ibid.*, citing J. Burtner, 'Horizontal Well Completion Technology,' presented at the 1990 Calgary Horizontal Drilling Conference, August 1990. He stated that with advances in technology, it may gradually reduce as have been witnessed in Texas where the cost of drilling has reduced from between USD 600 and USD 1,200 per lateral foot in the first well drilled to USD 300 per lateral foot.
115. For example, the number of horizontal wells drilled in Alberta, Canada increased from 12 in 1987 to 29 in 1990 while that of Saskatchewan increased from 1 to 77 over the same years period as Alberta. In Texas, US the number of horizontal wells drilled in 1990 were 127 which was estimated to have increased to 1,000 in 1992. See Horizontal Drilling Report, 1991 Canadian Discovery Digest Ltd, cited by R.E. Pelzer et al., 'Horizontal Drilling: Regulatory and Contractual Implications', at 276.
116. Even where well spacing conservation regime is in place, horizontal well has capacity to traverse spacing unit boundaries. The regulated size of a spacing unit in Canada and US is 160 acres for an oil well and 640 acres for a gas well. For example see sections 4.020 (1) and (3) of the Regulations to the Oil and Gas Conservation Act (Alberta). In the North Sea, it is on record that horizontal well had been drilled 'with horizontal displacements exceeding 5,000 feet. See R.E. Pelzer et al., Horizontal Drilling: Regulatory and Contractual implications', at 281.
117. See *Bocardo SA v. Star Energy UK Onshore Ltd* [2008] EWHC 1756 (ch).
118. The term subsurface trespass has been defined as 'acts which although occurring on the surface of land overlying the mineral rights in question, nevertheless have their purpose the piercing of

It has been recognised that during drilling, a well could unintentionally deviate from the vertical (known as 'crooked wells') or be purposely deviated from it. The degree and direction of deviation could also be detected by subsurface surveys. In both instances the court is faced with difficult tasks of determining the rights and remedies of the parties whose interests are affected by the subsurface trespass. However where a well is aimed directly below the surface and its deviation is at a small angle, it is still regarded as vertical well since almost all wells deviate from the vertical plane to some degree.[119] In essence therefore, the difference between a crooked well and straight well depends on the degree of deviation. The degree of deviation in the former is substantial while in the latter it is insignificant.[120] With the improved technology today, since well precision drilling can be achieved, a significant deviation from vertical plane could either be intentional or as a result of negligence.[121] It will therefore, be difficult to establish unintentional trespass where there is horizontal well that is bottomed under someone else land. Such drilling will likely be considered as an intentional trespass.[122] Therefore, the law as it stands today is that all horizontal wells whether crooked or intentional may attract trespass and conversion liabilities if they cross property lines. They are regarded as trespass in bad faith and the trespasser is liable for the market value of the oil at the surface without compensation for drilling and operating costs.

But where the trespasser is considered to have entered under a honest and reasonable belief that he has a claim right to enter, the trespass is in good faith and, though the trespasser is liable for the market value of the oil at the surface, he might be able to 'offset against the value of the products converted, the reasonable costs of drilling, completing, operating and producing.' The credit for costs will, however, not exceed the extent to which a benefit has been conferred upon the owner of the land overlying the subsurface area trespassed.[123] Where benefits have not been conferred on the owner of the property (e.g., adding value to it) only lifting and production costs are credited to the trespasser.[124]

In the case of *Edwards v. Lachman*,[125] the defendants had drilled a well that was completed to two separate structural formations before becoming aware seven months after through survey that the wells had bottomed under plaintiff's land. The defendant however concealed this from the plaintiff. The plaintiff subsequently drilled a well at the shallow portion of the defendant's wells that were already producing. The plaintiff, on becoming aware of this trespass sued for accounting. The court held that the

possible petroleum reservoirs'. See Richard W. Hemingway, 'The Law of Oil and Gas', 3rd edn (West Publishing Co., 1991), at175.

119. John D. McKinnis, 'Directional Drilling, Subsurface Trespass, and Conversion', (1988-89) J. Min. L. & Policy 4: 235 at 238 citing C. Gatlin, 'Petroleum Engineering', at 142 (1960).
120. *Ibid.*, see pp. 238-239 for examples of crooked wells. It is on record that well of about 5,100 feet depth had wandered about 2,470 feet horizontally. Such a well is regarded as a crooked well.
121. *Ibid.*, at 241.
122. See *Bocardo SA v. Star Energy UK Onshore Ltd* (*supra*).
123. Williams & Meyers, 'Oil and Gas Law', vol. 1 (1990) at 227. He is of the view that injunction can also be granted to restrain oil production from the well. See also Hemingway, 'The Law of Oil and Gas', at 178 at n. 44 & 45.
124. Hemingway, 'The Law of Oil and Gas', at 178 citing the case of *Carter Oil Company v. McCasland C.A* 10th, 207 F.2d 728.
125. 534 P.2d 670 (Okla. 1874).

defendant was a good faith trespasser up to the time he became aware of the trespassing wells through the directional survey but that thereafter, he becomes a bad faith trespasser as a result of his silence and that he can only deduct his expenses if the expenditures benefited the plaintiff. The court held further that since the defendant had drilled a well and would presumably drain the formation in which its wells had struck, the defendant was not entitled to costs attributable to that production. But for the deeper zone in which the plaintiff's well did not reach, the defendant was allowed to offset his costs of drilling, completion and equipping the well to the extent that the defendant's well conferred benefit upon the plaintiff prior to the time of the directional survey. This was upheld on appeal.

However, in the case of *A.E. Bell Corp v. Bell View Oil Synd.*,[126] the defendant drilled two horizontal wells which were bottomed under the plaintiff land. The defendant claimed that an owner of the land overlying a reservoir has, in common with all other property owners overlying the reservoir, the right to drill and extract from the common reservoir if the well extends beyond the vertical boundary of that owner's tract. The defendant further argued that since California is a non-ownership State where title to oil and gas is not acquired until produced, each lessee has the right to bottom its wells as it deemed fit in the reservoir in order to withdraw its proportionate part of the oil. Furthermore, it was argued that each lessee was entitled to a prorate portion of the oil in the reservoir without regard to where a well was positioned. The court rejected these arguments and declared that:

> [N]o one has a right by reason of the ownership of a surface location lying above an oil zone, to extend his oil wells without the boundaries of his own surface location, vertically, extended downward so as to trespass upon the premises of adjoining owners ... .[127]

This means that the defendant was entitled only to that portion of the oil that it could withdraw from wells bottomed on his own lands. The court found the defendant to be a wilful or bad-faith trespasser and was not allowed to recoup his costs.

This case has shown that the vertical boundary of a lease area or tract can be known at the subsurface. By this, the extent to which a reservoir extends beyond a lease boundary into an adjacent lease can be ascertained. This will make it possible to estimate the quantity of oil removed from a reservoir at any given time. It also means that, if a vertical well is drilled and bottomed in the portion of the common reservoir lying under the person's land, there is no trespass and conversion even though part of the oil withdrawn from the reservoir comes from the other portion lying outside his land. However, if the vertical well deviates horizontally and continued downwards to bottom at the portion of a common reservoir outside the person's land or lease area, there will be liability for trespass and conversion if oil is withdrawn from the reservoir. In fact, the trespasser will be liable for all petroleum wrongfully withdrawn and commingled with other petroleum owned by the trespasser. If the petroleum had been

126. 76 P.2d 167 (Cal. Dist. Ct. App. 198), aff'd on rehearing, 116 P.2d 786 (Cal. Dist. Ct. App. 194).
127. *Ibid.*, at 176. See also *Accord Edwards v. Lachman* 534 P.2d 670, 676 (Okla. 1974).

sold, he 'will be liable for the value of all the petroleum produced and sold from both wells.'[128]

The question to be asked is that why should this kind of liability be limited only to a situation of horizontal well that is bottomed at the portion of the common reservoir outside the trespasser's lease area? Why should it not be extended to vertical well that is bottomed at the portion of the common reservoir lying within the lease area of the driller? To address this question the common law rule as regards trespass to chattels will be examined.

8.2 Trespass to Chattels

Trespass to chattels arises from any act of direct physical interference with chattels in the possession of another person without lawful justification.[129] Therefore, since he has severed the oil and gas from the realty and caused a withdrawal of same from the possession of the adjacent lessee, the oil and gas becomes chattels and therefore, he may be liable in trespass to chattels. For the offence of trespass to chattels to hold, a mere act of interference is sufficient and special damage need not be proved. It is not also necessary to prove a denial of title.[130] The requirement of physical interference or contact is satisfied at the moment the oil from adjoining lands cross property lines and enters the well bored by the licensee. Moreover, the tort may be committed without entry into the premises where the chattel is kept. For example, where a person wilfully frightens a horse so that it runs a way, or drives cattle out of a field in which they lawfully are,[131] or kills a dog by giving it a poisoned meat, the tort is committed. In addition to trespass to chattels, the licensee may be liable to conversion. Conversion is defined as 'an act (or complex series of acts) of wilful interference with the right of another, whereby that other is deprived of the use and possession of it'[132] The tort consists of dealing with a chattel in manner that is inconsistent with the right of the person entitled to it and an intention to deny the person's right to it.[133] It is to be noted that since the tort does not apply to real estate; the tort of conversion is committed against mineral at the point of severance from the earth. By the severance, the mineral is converted from realty to personal property.[134] Therefore, a vertical well drilled and bottomed at the portion of a common reservoir would cause oil or gas to move from the other portion into the well bore and would thus, capture the oil. Oil is being converted at the point of severance and entry into the well bore.

From the above analysis, it has been seen that in determining entitlement to oil and gas where a directional well is drilled and bottomed at another person's land, the

128. Hemingway, 'The Law of Oil and Gas', at 181 referring to the case of *Gibben v. Carpenter*, 323 Pa. 243, 185 A. 712.
129. R.F.V. Heuston, 'Salmond on the Law of Torts', 16th edn (London: Sweet & Maxwell, 1973), at 92.
130. *Ibid.*
131. *Ibid.*, citing *R v. Riley* (1853)22 L.J.M.C. 48.
132. *Ibid.*, at 97.
133. *Ibid.*
134. McKinnis, 'Directional Drilling, Subsurface Trespass, and Conversion', at 276.

rule of capture and ownership theories are not considered. This means that in appropriate circumstances, the rule can be suspended to dispense justice between the two competing claimants. In this circumstance, the wrongful party is regarded as a bad-faith trespasser and held liable for trespass to sub-surface land and conversion if petroleum is produced therefrom. It is submitted that where vertical well is drilled and is bottomed at the driller's portion of the common reservoir, the rule of capture should be suspended so that the driller can be regarded as good-faith trespasser, and held liable for trespass to chattels and conversion if petroleum is severed and moved into the well bore. This is premised on the point that the severance is caused by human interference or intervention as opposed to natural causes for example, like 'when a wild animal strays across a boundary or escapes and is caught by another person or when water runs freely from one tract to another.'[135]

8.3 Hydraulic Fracturing

Hydraulic fracturing, otherwise known as 'fracing' or 'fraking', is a technique used to extract gas from 'tight reservoirs formations with low permeability, through which the gas will not flow naturally to the well head.'[136] Fracing involves pumping of fluid like water and ceramic beads into a well at high pressure so that it is forced down into the structural formation. As a result of the pressure created, fractures developed along the fault lines in an elongated pattern in opposite directions from the well. Gas or oil will flow through the fractures to the well bore.[137] While the operators might be able to control the length of the fractures, they may not be able to determine the directions. Fracing technique has been used in the US to develop shale gas in Pennsylvania, New York and Texas States. Economically, it is important to develop the gas considering the abundance of the resource in these States. This resource which lies in about two miles beneath the earth can only be recovered through fracing or hydraulic fracturing. The technique when used could extend several thousand feet laterally crossing several property boundaries. This raises issues like trespass and conversion of the gas between property owners.

135. See Bryan Clark, 'Migratory Things on Land: Property Rights and a Law of Capture', (2002) EJCL 6.3: at 13. He explained that Roman law through the doctrine of *occupatio* permits a person to acquired ownership of anything capable of private ownership by taking possession of the thing. However, the thing must have been previously un-owned or ceased to be owned. Therefore, appropriation of things that are currently the property of another is not permitted under Roman law. Under Scots law which had adopted Roman law, where migratory things is owned in situ, another party cannot claim ownership rights on it on ground of *occupatio* except where the ownership of the thing has been lost by the original owner (e.g., wild animal). He argued further that *occupatio* will not vest ownership in the capturing party where ownership of the original party is lost due to the act of the capturing party. Therefore, oil and gas that migrates as a result of the drilling activities of one party is different from the one that migrates as result of natural causes beneath the land of another.
136. Daintith, 'Finders Keepers ...', at 299.
137. Billie Ann Maxwell, 'Texas Tug of War: A Survey of Urban Drilling and the Issues an Operator Will Face' (2008-2009) Tex. J. Oil, Gas & Energy L. 4: 337 at 340. See also *Coastal Oil and Gas Corp. v. Garza Energy Trust* (2008) 268 S.W.3d 1.

In both the cases of *Delhi-Taylor Oil Corp v. Gregg*[138] and *Holmes v. Delhi-Taylor Oil Corp*,[139] the plaintiffs sought an injunction to restrain the defendants from using fracturing techniques on their nearby gas wells which were just within 40 feet of the plaintiffs' lease lines. The cases went to the Texas Supreme Court and the question raised in that court turned out to be on Jurisdiction. The issue was as to which organ has primary jurisdiction, as between the Railroad commission and the District court, to entertain cases bordering on trespass. In resolving the issue in favour of the District court, the Supreme Court declared in Gregg's case that:

> We think the allegations are sufficient to raise an issue as to whether there is a trespass. The invasion is direct and the action taken is intentional. Gregg's well would be, for practical purposes, extended to and partially completed in Delhi-Taylor's land. The pleadings alleged a physical entrance into Delhi-Taylor's leasehold. While the drilling bit of Gregg's well is not alleged to have extended into Delhi-Taylor's land, the same result is reached if in fact the cracks or veins extend into its land and gas is produced therefrom by Gregg. To constitute a trespass, 'entry upon another's land need not be in person, but may be made by causing or permitting a thing to cross the boundary of the premises.

Thus, Texas Supreme Court held that such technique is an invasion of property when the fluid moves across property lines and as such constitutes subsurface trespass.[140] In the Appeal of the other case, the Supreme Court affirmed the temporary injunction granted by the trial court against proposed fracturing to maintain the status quo pending a trial on the merits of the issue of trespass. However, the law reports contained no further record about the progress on the trespass issue.[141]

The court had another opportunity to decide on the issue of trespass again in the case of *Geo-Viking Inc. v. Tex-Lee Operating Co.*[142] In this case, the plaintiff (Tex-Lee) hired the defendant (Geo-Viking) to fracture a well to a propped half-length of 1000 feet but the defendant only did it to 600 feet. The plaintiff sued for breach of contract and the jury awarded $300,000 damages. The measure of damages took into account the amount of oil not recovered by the plaintiff because of the poor fracing work. The jury did not limit the damages to the oil which would have been recovered within the boundaries of the plaintiff lease but included those that were outside it. In reliance on the rule of capture, this measure of damages was upheld on appeal. Subsequently, a motion was brought for rehearing of the case again at the Court of Appeal. On rehearing, the issue of trespass came up because the defendant's counsel contended that damages should be limited to the loss of oil the plaintiff could have obtained by legal methods. Because fracing would constitute trespass, the measure of damages should have been limited to the amount of oil lost within the plaintiff's lease

138. 337 S.W. 2d 216, 13 O. &G.R 58 (Tex. Civ. App. 1960), aff'd 344 S.W. 2d 411, 14 O. & G.R. 106 (Tex. 1961).
139. 337 S.W. 2d 479, 13 O. &G.R 80 (Tex. Civ. App. 1960) rev'd 344 S.W. 2d 420, 14 O. & G.R. 103 (Tex 1961).
140. *Gregg v. Delhi-Taylor Oil Corp.*, 344 S.W. 2d 411, 14 O. & G.R. 106 (Tex. 1961).
141. Jacqueline Lang Weaver, 'Unitisation Revisited' in Carol J. Holgren the 'Proceedings of 45th Annual Institute On Oil and Gas Law and Taxation' (Dallas, Houston: Southwestern Legal Foundation, 1994).
142. 839 S.W.2d 897 (Tex. App. 1992).

boundaries. The majority of the Judges rejected this contention and upheld the trial court's decision. In their view, the issue of trespass should be sorted out between the plaintiff and the adjoining land owner. A dissenting judge agreed with the submission of the defendant.

The defendant filed a writ of error at the Texas Supreme Court which was granted. The court reversed the Appeal's court decision and held that fracing under the surface of another's land constitutes a subsurface trespass and that the rule of capture would not apply to capture by trespass. Therefore, damages should have been limited to the oil that could be legally recovered. With this opinion, the court ought to have awarded the appropriate damages and then close the case but they never did and instead remanded the case for a new trial on damages.

The case came to the Supreme Court six months after. This time, the Justices retracted their earlier opinion on the issue on the ground that it was 'improvidently granted'. The court added that in doing this, they should not be understood as approving or disapproving the opinions of the court of appeals analysing the rule of capture or trespass as they apply to hydraulic fracturing.

It should be noted that the case came up twice at the Court of Appeal and the court did not rule or determine the issue of trespass but rather upheld the trial court's decision on measure of damages. In their view, the issue of trespass should be settled between the plaintiff and the adjoining land owner. But since drainage has not actually occurred no action could be brought by the adjoining land owner. Therefore, this case cannot be said to have authoritatively concluded the issue as to whether fracing constitutes subsurface trespass or not.

Another opportunity came for the Texas Supreme Court to decide on the issue again in 2006. Thus, in the case of *Coastal Oil and Gas Corp. v. Garza Energy Trust* (2008) (*supra*), the Garza family leased the minerals under their tract of land to the Appellant. The Appellant also owned an adjacent tract of land to the one leased to them by the Garza family. The Appellant employed hydraulic fracturing on the well on their own land which crossed the lease lines and drained oil and gas from the land leased to them by Garza family. This case presented serious emotive profile among the regulators, the royalty holders and the oil companies resulting in amicus curiae briefs filed in support of the Appellant to emphasise the effects of a wrong decision by the court on production, employment, tax revenues and exploration in Texas.[143] After hearing oral evidence in 2006 and in which the jury awarded USD 10 million punitive damage for trespass, the Supreme Court waited for two years to deliver its judgment. The Judges were divided in their judgment; five were in support while three dissented. The majority held that the rule of capture precluded the plaintiff from recovering damages for drainage caused by hydraulic fracturing. The court was of the opinion that though the Garzas family could maintain an action for trespass on the basis of actual injury to their residual non-possessory interest (royalty interest) since their alleged injury was based on the loss of gas, they cannot recover because of the rule of capture. The dissenting judges were of the view that fracing constitutes subsurface trespass and that

143. Daintith, 'Finders Keepers ...', at 301.

the rule of capture cannot apply since it only protects lawful drainage. The minority opinion accepted the argument put forward by the Garza's lawyers that there is no difference between fracing which causes drainage through sub-surface cracks and horizontal well that is bottomed on the neighbour's property and through which drainage occurred. However, the majority were of the view that the notion of trespass should be adjusted to the circumstances of this case in the public interest and that causing cracks by the injection of fluids and ceramic beads two miles down the earth should not be simply taken as trespass.

This case cannot represent good authority in other jurisdictions for the following reasons. First, it shows that the majority places public interest over and above private interest. Eliminating trespass in hydraulic fracturing may be in the public interests in view of the resources that will be quickly produced but the resources could still have been produced through unitised development[144] and by that, both private and public interests would have been served. Even though there is nothing wrong in putting public interest over and above private interest in appropriate circumstances, there are instances where the court has held that an individual should not be made to bear the burden of the whole public.

This is a clear case in which private interest has been sacrificed on the altar of public interest. Second, the case stands in great contradistinction to the earlier opinions of the courts on the issue[145] and also runs contrary to the cases decided consistently in respect of horizontal well that is bottomed on adjoining land and in which the court had held constitutes trespass. Third, the majority opinion confirmed the reasons why capture is still been retained till to day in US in spite of several criticisms - These are that 'people had been doing it for years, intervening will upset established relationships, evidence was difficult to obtain and that a self-help solution was available.'[146] This is why professor Daintith comments that:

> Coastal demonstrates the extraordinary difficulty of eradicating, or even modifying, a common-law rule of property in a country that gives constitutional protection to property rights. It reflects ... the paradox that the rule of capture has actually been strengthened by the creation of the massive regulatory apparatus it

144. By recognising the property rights of landowners to resources under their lands and forcing them to pool or unitise their interests for coordinated development or fracing. As we have pointed out above, conversion would follow trespass to chattels. Conversion can arise even where there is no trespass to subsurface land but the moment mineral is severed from the subsurface and taken, trespass to chattels and conversion can be validly invoked. Therefore, even if the court regards the act of fracing and its attendant fissures as not constituting trespass, the moment the oil or gas flows through the fissures and enters the operator's well, trespass to chattels has arisen and conversion may follow. See Weaver, 'Unitisation Revisited', in Carol J. Holgren the 'Proceedings of 45th Annual Institute on Oil and Gas Law and Taxation', at pp. 7-23. The professor is of the view that even if fracing is protected against trespass liability, the fracing operator is not protected against damage suits brought for conversion, nuisance or negligence. Actual damages can still be recovered even though it may be difficult to prove but that it is not impossible. Therefore, injunction and punitive damages (which are normally remedies for trespass) may not lie against the operator; actual damages may follow from conversion.
145. The twin cases of *Delhi-Taylor Oil Corp* (*supra*).
146. Daintith, 'Finders Keepers ...', at 302.

engendered, because that regulation had been constructed on a property right foundation of which capture forms part.

This is a truism because Conservation laws were only enacted with the aim of tempering the operation and evil consequences of the rule of capture but not to eliminate it totally. Contrary to the Supreme Court's opinion, conservation laws were meant to reduce the strength of the rule of capture and not to strengthen it. If the rule is abolished, conservation law would have been unnecessary and that would mean its demise. But justice and equity would have been served among the landowners and their lessees and the whole society would have been saved from its disastrous consequences. Therefore, the minority opinion in the Coastal's case appears to be preferable on the strength of the reasons given above.

Recently in the Pennsylvania State, the Superior Court has an opportunity to decide in the case of *Butler v. Charles Powers Estate*[147] whether shale gas is a 'mineral' in that it contains unconventional gas reservoirs that cannot be separated from the shale they inhabit except through a process called 'fracking.' If it is regarded as a mineral, the landowner who owns the shale will be regarded as the owner of the gas because the shale will be regarded as part of the realty. The implication is that drainage caused by hydraulic fracturing will attract payment of damages as the rule of capture will not apply. The Superior court did not answer this question but however reversed the lower court's decision that had classified shale gas as conventional natural gas. The Superior court subsequently remanded the case to the lower court for expert evidence to be taken for proper classification of shale gas.

This shows that another stage has been set for the conflicting decisions of the court in the US to arise again as regards the applicability of the rule of capture in resolving ownership disputes. If the Pennsylvania courts eventually decide that Marcellus shale gas is analogous to 'Minerals', the resultant effect is that the rule of capture will be excluded and this will be inconsistent with the Texas Supreme Court's decision in *Coastal Oil and Gas Corp. v. Garza Energy Trust* (*supra*).

9. CONCLUSION

The jurisprudence of the three ownership doctrines consists of irreconcilable differences. The adoption of this varied ownership theories laced by rule of capture, resulted into significant conflicting decisions despite the fact that the issues are the same (drainage) and that it concerned the same privately owned land and in the same country. This stemmed from lack of standardised rule that would have served as a basis for all the courts to reach reconcilable decisions and ensured consistency and predictability.

From the above, we have seen that what is common to all the States in the US is the application of the rule of capture. The Rule is used as a matter of convenience to solve entitlements allocation problems. It is used when it is convenient to do so but dropped when it is not. This has aggravated the conflicts. When it is used, it destroys

147. [2011] WL 3906897 (Pa. Super.).

property rights of landowner or lessee to the oil and gas underlying his land or lease. The Rule proceeds from false analogies and failed to apply the reasoning established in those rules that it analogised. The Rule also failed to realise that if both adjoining landowners have property rights to the oil and gas underlying their respective land, rational development of the common pool will take place as neither of them can undertake unilateral development without accounting to the other, either in form of compensation or damages for drainage.

We have also seen that the court tried to introduce a rule that will ensure fairness between the parties but in effect did not abolish the rule of capture. This has negated the correlative rights doctrine and reduced its effectiveness to a case where there is malicious damage to the producing formation. There is a persistent recurrence of ownership been gained only upon production despite the fact that the surface owners are regarded as either tenant in common or common owners or that each have exclusive right to mine oil and gas beneath their respective land. This means that common pool oil and gas is still being regarded or operated on the basis of an open access regime since act of appropriation is complete and ownership gained only when oil and gas comes to the surface.

Paradoxically, ownership in place theory professes landowner's ownership of underlying minerals but failed to protect it with property rules by granting exemption from trespass and conversion liability in fracing activities. Paradoxically too, non-ownership theory states that landowner has no ownership of underlying minerals but protects the minerals from trespass and conversion by an adjoining operator who employs horizontal drilling to bottom a well under his land and remove oil or gas. These two paradoxes follow the application of the Rule and have created so many inconsistencies in the oil and gas jurisprudence.

The above analysis has helped us in understanding that recognition and protection of property rights in oil and gas in place is the superior method of ensuring compulsory pooling or unitisation, prevention of wastes and protection of correlative rights of the owners of the oil and gas in straddling petroleum reservoirs. This will also guarantee consistent and predictable decisions of the court.

CHAPTER 6
The Regime of Unilateral Capture II – Domanial Jurisdictions

1. INTRODUCTION

Some countries adopted domanial ownership of petroleum regime as the governing path for their oil and gas development by providing in their constitutions or legislations that ownership of petroleum *'in situ'* belongs to the State.[1] They have also by regulations provided for compulsory unitisation of straddling reservoirs with powers invested on the Minister to compel parties to unitise so as to inhibit unilateral withdrawal of petroleum from the reservoirs. One of the reasons why these countries adopted this system is attributed to their desire to avoid the extractive anarchy that pervaded the US oil and gas Industry. The assumption of these countries was that it was the uncontrolled exercise of private property rights in oil and gas that made the rule of capture to operate in US with severe consequences. It was thought that eliminating private property rights will either eliminate the rule of capture or fit it into a 'broader regime of production control.'[2]

It is against this backdrop that this chapter is aimed at analysing the licensing granting clauses and the unitisation laws and regulations of these countries to see whether or not they have capacities to prevent unilateral capture of petroleum from straddling reservoirs and to examine Judicial and administrative policies on unilateral capture.

1. Examples are Nigeria, United Kingdom, Australia, Netherlands, etc.
2. Daintith, 'Finders Keepers? ...' at pp. 12-13 & 359. See also N. Ely, 'The Conservation of Oil', (1938) Harvard Law Review 51: 1209, 1218, 1219.

2. UNITED KINGDOM

We have seen in Chapter 3 that property in all petroleum existing in its natural condition in strata in Great Britain is vested in the Crown. In the offshore, the Crown exercises sovereign rights over the natural resources of the United Kingdom Continental Shelf. Under the 1998 Act, the Crown exercises power to grant oil and gas licences to companies within the onshore, territorial sea and the United Kingdom Continental Shelf (UKCS).[3] Also, Compulsory unitisation is provided in the law and it applies to both onshore and offshore operations.

The question is that, given the above regulatory framework, does the rule of capture forms part of the UK oil and gas licensing regime? It is necessary to examine the granting clause of the licence and the unitisation clause. The Licence granting clause provides that:

> ... the Minister, in exercise of the powers conferred upon him by the Act hereby *grants to the Licensee exclusive licence and liberty during the continuance of this licence and subject to the provisions hereof* ***to search and bore for, and get, Petroleum in the sea bed and subsoil under the seaward area more particularly described in Schedule 1 to this licence being the area comprising Block(s) [blocks] on the reference map*** *deposited at the principal office of [the Department for Business, Enterprise and Regulatory Reform] ...* [4]

The test for the interpretation of the above provision suggested by Professor Daintith is as follows:

> [A] granting clause that made it clear that the title holder could produce only the petroleum that, at the time of grant, lay beneath the area of land or sea referred to in the grant would effectively displace the rule of capture. Conversely, a clause that, following the principle of article 552 of the French Civil Code, stipulated that the grantee would obtain ownership of any petroleum it might recover within the area of its title, without making reference to the original location of that petroleum, might be taken to indicate that the rule would apply, at least if there were indications that the rule formed part of the general property law of the country relating to underground fluids like water.[5]

In his view, the granting clause of the petroleum licence in the UK should be interpreted in accordance with the second leg of the test stated above. This means that a statutory rule of capture has emerged so that drainage that occurred by lawful operations on an adjacent block is legitimate.[6] He interpreted similar granting clause contained in the leases granted by the US Federal government in the Outer continental shelf (OCS), in

3. Section 3 (1).
4. Clause 2, Schedule 4 of the Petroleum Licensing (Exploration and Production) (Seaward and Landward Areas) Regulations 2004. (SI 2004/352) as amended by the Petroleum Licensing (Exploration and Production) (Seaward and Landward Areas) (Amendment) Regulations 2006 (SI 2006/784); an identical provision is contained in the Petroleum Licensing (Production) (Seaward Areas) Regulations 2008, Schedule, clause 2. The model clauses for PEDL can be found in Schedule 6 of the aforesaid Regulations. The licence granting clauses for Seaward (offshore) licences contained identical provisions with Landward (onshore) Licences.
5. Daintith, 'Finders Keepers? ...', at 359.
6. *Ibid.*, at 360.

the same fashion. However, it must be noted that unlike the UK, the preamble of the OCS unitisation regulations, expressly provides that 'the lease does not grant the lessee ownership of the mineral in place and that the law of capture applies to the development and production of the OCS minerals.'[7] Thus, it is very clear that the intention of the regulators is to allow the rule of capture to govern exploitation of OCS minerals. Such intention is however not made clear either in the unitisation laws or licence granting clauses in the UK.

The substance of Professor Daintith's argument is that a licensee can directly restrain an unlicensed drilling or other exploratory activity taking place in his licensed area and also an unlicensed or unlawful activity taking place outside of it that is having effect of diminishing the value of his interest, e.g., drainage of oil from his common reservoir. But drainage that took place outside the 125 meters[8] regulated boundary and in accordance with the relevant development consent is lawful and therefore, cannot be restrained. This is because the licence, even though is proprietary in character, did not convey property in any specific parcel or volume of petroleum such as that existing under his licensed area at the time of the award.[9] On the contrary, the licence only confers a right, within a defined area to search, bore for, and gets whatever petroleum that may be present there for the time being.

It follows from Professor Daintith's argument above that a holder of production licence has no protection from drainage by virtue of the licence. The protection he may get could only come from an ordered unitisation scheme.[10] Therefore, where unitisation is not ordered by the Minister and the parties could not reach voluntary unitisation agreement, unilateral drainage could occur and the affected party would not be able to claim redress in spite of the proprietary character of his licence.

With profound respect to the erudite professor, there are compelling reasons why the granting clause should be interpreted differently. The clause grants exclusive liberty and right to 'search, bore for, and get petroleum' ... *under the Seaward area defined in the map annexed to the licence.* The boundary of the licence is well defined. At the surface, the boundary does not extend to the adjoining area that has been granted to another licensee. The right granted is confined to that area and cannot be interpreted to encompass area outside the area as already defined. This is the area defined and granted to the licensee when the licence was signed and at that time, it cannot be contemplated to encompass any other area thereafter. When a document, be it contract or statute is not ambiguous, the courts will give the words expressed therein its plain meaning. In fact the Latin phrases *'expressio unis est exclusio alterius'*[11] is usually applied in those circumstances. Therefore, the contention that the rights conferred on the licensee is not in respect of petroleum existing under his licence at the time of the grant but that it is in respect of the petroleum at any given time is contrary

7. *Ibid.*, at 359.
8. See clause 20 in Schedule to Petroleum Licensing (Production) (Seaward Areas) Regulations 2008.
9. Daintith, 'Finders Keepers? ...', at 359.
10. *Ibid.*
11. Means 'the expression of one person or thing implies the exclusion of other persons or things of the same class but which are not mentioned.'

to what is expressly stated in the granting clause – 'to search and bore for, and get, Petroleum in the sea bed and subsoil under the seaward area more particularly described in Schedule 1 to this licence being the area comprising Block(s) [blocks] on the reference map' – Petroleum at any given time would include petroleum coming from the adjoining lease after the grant or even during exploitation. Any petroleum that can be proved to have come from adjoining licence during exploitation cannot be said to have formed part of the petroleum existing under his defined licence area at the time of the grant of the licence.

Second, the idea that man-made surface boundary cannot possibly correspond with the nature's boundary at the subsurface may have become anachronistic with technological advances in the fields of petroleum geology and reservoir engineering. With these advances, the boundary of a concession at both the surface and subsurface can be known through modern 3-D or 4-D seismic survey or exploratory drilling. The precise location of petroleum reservoir can now be known by geological surveys.[12] Therefore, surface boundary is expected to translate or coincide vertically to subsurface boundary. As a result, the surface concession boundary delineated at the time of grant translates to the same boundary delineation at the sub-surface. It does not change as the surface boundary is what is predominantly considered in the determination of the extent to which a reservoir in one concession area extends to another at the sub-surface.

Even though it may not be possible to ascertain a given quantity of petroleum lying under a concession boundary at the time of its grant, it has been scientifically demonstrated that proven reserves within a concession can be known before development and exploitation[13] and so if the reservoir extends beyond the concession, it will accordingly affect the proven reserves. With all these facts, it cannot be the intention of the drafter of the licensing clause that the rights conferred by the licence at the time of the grant is in respect of petroleum that he finds in the reservoir at any given time but rather it is confined to the quantity of oil lying under his concession at the time of the grant. He is expected to unitise development where such reservoir extends to adjacent concession. In light of the forgoing, it may be argued that there is no statutory codification of the rule of capture in the UK as the licence granting clause does not encompass the rule of capture. This interpretation is more in line with the legal character of the licence and the proprietary interests it confers on the licensee.

However, because of the operation of the common law rule of capture the property right of the licensee in the oil and gas underlying his lease area may be lost if the petroleum migrates to adjoining lease during extraction of petroleum from that lease. In the UK, a direct judicial decision on the rule of capture is yet to be seen but there are judicial authorities that applied the rule to underground water.[14] In all these

12. Alisa Newman Hood, 'We Shale Overcome? A U.S. Court Issues an Unsettling Decision on Marcellus Property Rights' (March 2012) JWEL&B 5(1): 78 at 80.
13. Stoneley, 'Introduction to Petroleum Exploration for Non-geologists', at 81-95. See also Chapter 4 at pp. 140-141 of this book for a discussion on reserves evaluation methods and classification into proven, probable and possible.
14. See the cases of *Acton v. Blundell* (*supra*); *Bradford Corporation v. Pickles* (*supra*); *Chasemore v. Richards* (*supra*).

water law cases, the courts held that the owner of the land overlying underground percolating water has the right to divert or appropriate such water within his own land even if by such diversion or appropriation his neighbour is deprived of the water. But the water cases did not border on problem of water which was already in someone's land that was abstracted by the owner of the adjoining land and yet was applied to ownership of oil and gas cases.[15]

Therefore, as it has been shown in Chapter 5 of this book; underground water may not be a good analogy for oil and gas cases that borders on drainage. Confirming this assertion is the judgment of the judicial committee of the Privy Council in the case of the *Trinidad Asphalt Co. v. Ambard & Another.*[16] The plaintiff was granted a concession to mine for Asphalt in the Great Pitch Lake in Trinidad by the government in 1888 for forty-two years. The defendant, in search of a mineral known as Pitch,[17] carried out some excavations on his land up to the boundary line between him and the plaintiff's land. As a result, some of the boundary posts fell in and Pitch began to ooze out of the plaintiff's land into the portion excavated by the defendants. There was subsidence of plaintiff's land and as a result of which his building or sheds of insignificant value caved in and damaged. In the process, the defendant converted a total of 200 to 300 tons of pitch that had come from the plaintiff's land. The plaintiff claimed for injunction from the court to restrain the defendant from further act of digging on its land as it would deprive their land of lateral support. The court granted the injunction and awarded damages to the value of the Pitch withdrawn from the plaintiff's land by the defendant. The defendants relied on the rule of capture and analogised pitch to subterranean water because of its semi-fluid nature, to argue that the pitch does not become plaintiff's property until they had reduced it to possession. They also argued that there was no right, in English law, to support from underground water. The court ruled that Pitch is mineral and not water. The damages awarded in effect, means that the rule of capture was denied in respect to pitch. This is because the measure of the damages awarded by the court did not flow from the loss suffered by the plaintiff as a result of the subsidence of the land but rather from the value of the plaintiff's Pitch that was scooped by the defendants. This mode of valuation as pointed out by Daintith, suggests that the 'lateral support' attaches to the pitch as much as to the surface of the land. Applying this to oil and gas, if the concept that oil and gas in the reservoir is relatively stable and has bounds had been accepted by the court, then a claim that lateral support attaches to oil and gas would have succeeded in the case of *Kelley v. Ohio Oil Co (supra).*[18] But the *Trinidad Asphalt Co's* case appeared to have accepted that concept and also the concept of absolute ownership of petroleum before it is reduced to possession.

Realising however, the obvious consequences that this judgment might have in the exploitation of Pitch (i.e., stifling rapid exploitation of pitch in that it will prevent

15. J.M. MacIntyre, 'The Development of Oil and Gas Ownership Theory in Canada', (1969) U. Brit. Colum. L. Rev. 4: 251, at 251.
16. (1899) A.C 594 (P.C).
17. Both the physical and chemical composition of Pitch (Asphalt) is similar to oil as it has tendency to flow as well.
18. Daintith, 'Finders Keepers? ...', at 138-139.

an owner of a land containing pitch to excavate the pitch where it will affect his neighbour's rights), the Court was of the opinion that legislative intervention or some sorts of agreement among adjoining Pitch owners for the exploitation of Pitch will be necessary.[19]

But what is very clear in the judgment was that the rule of capture was overruled in that analogy to subterranean water was rejected, pitch was held as a mineral forming part of the land and that the adjoining landowners had reciprocal rights to lateral support which precluded individual production resulting in migration.[20]

Subsequently, about thirty years later, the Privy Council had opportunity to consider the question about ownership of petroleum before it is reduced to possession in the case of *U Po Naing v. Burma Oil Company Limited.*[21] The plaintiff in this case had leased his rights in some Government 'oil sites' to the defendant. Even though he was not entitled to royalty on gas, he claimed that he is entitled to compensation on gas produced from the 'oil sites' by the defendant. The court held that he was not entitled as there was no authority to show that the gas was his property before it was reduced to possession by the defendant. Here the court analogised subterranean waters to gas to deny the plaintiff the compensation claimed. It is very obvious that there is a conflict between the two Privy Council cases. In the latter case, the court in effect held that it is not possible to own gas while in place before it is reduced to possession while in the former case it is possible to own flowing Asphalt while in place before it is reduced to possession. Yet, both substances shared similar characteristics physically and chemically. (They are both minerals)

About twenty-three years later, another ownership of petroleum in situ dispute came from Canada before the Privy Council. *Borys v. Canadian Pacific and imperial Oil Limited.*[22] The defendant (CPR) conveyed a land in fee simple to the Plaintiff (Boris). CPR reserved to itself coal, petroleum and valuable stone under the land. This arrangement is referred to as a split title lands. CPR then leased to Imperial Oil Ltd. (Company) the petroleum under the same land. The Company made a discovery of reservoir containing three (3) layers of substances – Natural gas, oil and water under the land. The oil layer also contained gas in solution (Solution gas). The Company, in producing the oil will have to penetrate through the Gas cap and which means that drainage of the natural gas from the cap will occur as well as solution gas. On the surface, phase changing takes place which resulted in the solution gas changing back to natural gas. The questions that arose were:

19. *Ibid.*, at 129 referring to Lord Macnaghten's pronouncement at p. 603 that 'if the inhabitants of La Brea cannot dig their own pitch without invading their neighbours' rights, it is quite possible that the hope of reciprocal advantage and the apprehension of mutual liability may lead to some arrangement for their common benefit, or the difficulties of the case may induce the Legislature to step in and regulate the digging of pitch and the management of the pitch lands.'
20. Michael Crommelin, 'The U.S. Rule of Capture: Its Place in Australia', (1986) AMPLA Yearbook at 272.
21. (1929)56 LR (IND APP) 140.
22. (1953) 2 D.L.R. 65 (P.C.); (1952) 7 W. W. R. (N.S.) 546.

(1) Whether Borys was entitled to the Natural gas and the solution gas produced by the Company as the solution gas had changed to natural gas at the surface?
(2) Whether in exercising its right to explore and exploit the petroleum, the Company had any right to interfere with the right of Borys in the natural gas and to what extent.

The court was of the view that Borys has a right to the natural gas *in situ* but not to the Solution gas because the reservation of 'petroleum' includes the 'Solution gas.'

With regard to the second issue, the court held that the Company was entitled to the petroleum produced even though in doing so the natural gas and the solution gas were produced along with it which might belong to the owner of residuary interests in the estate. Borys was neither entitled to injunction nor damages against the Company. Thus, the decision of the court has denied right of Borys to the Natural gas produced by the company despite the holding of the court that Borys owns the Natural Gas *in situ*. In delivering the judgment, Lord Porter declared that if any oil or gas lying in the landowner's property filters from it to the surrounding lands, then the former owner has no remedy. He went further however, that for the purpose of its decision the board was 'prepared to assume that the gas whilst in situ is the property of the Appellant even though it has not been reduced into possession.'[23] From this decision, it is clear that landowners' ownership right to oil and gas in place is proclaimed but that it could be defeated by the rule of capture.

The three English Court's decisions (though arose from Trinidad, India and Canada respectively) above appeared to be irreconcilable in the sense that *Trinidad's* case proclaimed absolute ownership of the mineral in place; *U Po Naing* case denied ownership of the gas in place completely while *Borys* case accepted defeasible absolute ownership in place. While unilateral capture was completely ruled out in the first case, it was allowed in the last two cases. The first case also borders on disputes between adjoining property owners while the last two cases concerned situations of vertical title split between oil and gas on the same tract.

Another opportunity came for an English court to determine dispute concerning unilateral drainage of oil and gas in 2008 but this time, it was between a fee simple owner of land and a holder of a production licence. However, because property in petroleum in situ vests in the Crown, the case turned essentially on the issue of sub-surface trespass. Thus, in *Bocardo SA v. Star Energy UK Onshore Ltd*[24] the plaintiff was the freehold owner of a developed property (Oxted Estate). The defendant was a holder of petroleum production licence granted under the Petroleum Act, 1934. The defendant discovered oil field known as Palmers Wood oil field (oilfield) in his licensed area but part of the oil field extended beneath the defendant's estate. The defendant drilled three horizontal wells which were bottomed at the plaintiff's estate. Two of the wells were used to extract more than one million barrels of petroleum from beneath the Estate. The plaintiff's claims were for damages for subsurface trespass to the tune of 12.5% of extracted petroleum from his estate and an injunction to restrain the

23. *Ibid.*, at 559.
24. [2008] EWHC 1756 (ch).

defendant from further extraction of the petroleum beneath his estate. His claims were anchored on the failure of the defendant to negotiate for a way-leave payment with him as provided by statutes. The plaintiff admitted that he has no claim to the oil itself as same is vested in the Crown. The court held that the defendant committed trespass *before and after the severance* of the petroleum from the plaintiff's land having failed to negotiate access for the removal of those substances. The plaintiff was awarded 9% of the past total income received by the defendant from the sale of the petroleum drained and also damages assessed at 9% of future income from the un-extracted oil and gas.

The award of 9% of the income received from the past oil captured from beneath the plaintiff's property through directional drilling as well 9% of the un-extracted oil as compensation to the plaintiff appeared to have suggested the proprietary nature of the plaintiff's interest in the petroleum resource beneath his land despite the fact that ownership of petroleum in situ belongs to the Crown. This is important because for there to be recovery of economic losses, there must be a link to a proprietary interest in the damaged thing.[25] It also suggests that if the plaintiff had been a holder of a production licence, the court would have probably reached a conclusion that the oil drained from underneath his land constitutes expropriation or conversion of his proprietary interest. However, the court made it clear that what were expropriated were the plaintiff's way-leave right and not the appropriated oil and as such the compensation awarded is in respect of way-leave right of the plaintiff.

The question as to what extent the minister is under a duty to compel unitisation of straddling reservoirs can be considered by analysing the unitisation clause. As it has been stated in Chapter 5, the gains from unitisation are expected to incentive the operators to unitise straddling fields but from US experience, unitisation has achieved minimal success in taming the rule of capture or eliminating all together, its disastrous consequences especially in privately held lands. An examination of the unitisation clauses in the laws and regulations of Domanial countries would also reveal that compulsory unitisation will not in all cases, be able to do the magic. For instance the UK law on unitisation provides that:[26]

> If at any time at which this licence is in force the Minister shall be satisfied that the strata in the Licensed Area or any part thereof form part of a single geological Petroleum structure or Petroleum field (hereinafter referred to as "an Oil Field") in respect of other parts of which licences granted in pursuance of the Acts are then in force and the Minister shall consider that it is in the national interest in order to secure the maximum ultimate recovery of Petroleum and in order to avoid unnecessary competitive drilling that the Oil Field should be worked and developed as a unit in co-operation by all persons including the Licensee whose licences extend to or include any part thereof the following provisions of this clause shall apply … .

25. Barnes, 'Property Rights and Natural Resources' at 371.
26. For the offshore, see the Petroleum Licensing (Exploration and Production) (Seaward and Landward Areas) Regulations 2004/352, Schedule 4, Cl. 23 of the Model clauses for standard Production Licences. For the onshore, see Cl. 23, Schedule 6 Model clauses for Petroleum Exploration and Development Licences (PEDLS).

The above provisions may appear to have given the Minister discretion as to when to compel unitisation because exercise of his power is made conditional upon national interests, maximum ultimate recovery of petroleum and avoidance of unnecessary competitive drilling so that where these conditions are not satisfied the Minister will not order compulsory unitisation.[27] Professor Daintith gave example of how this could happen. He opined that where a small portion of a reservoir in one licence extends to another licence area, because of the high cost of producing such a small extension alone especially in the difficult terrain such as North Sea, it becomes uneconomical to drill a well. The licensee with the larger portion could appropriately place a well in his licence area to drain the oil and gas in both his portion and the small extension. This presents an excellent scenario in which Unitisation agreement would be very difficult to reach between the parties as there will likely be 'hold outs' and 'strategic bargaining' problem. Besides this, competitive drilling is not likely to occur as it is uneconomic to drill by the owner of the small extension and since the pool can be effectively drained from the larger portion, unitisation will not increase ultimate recovery. The conditions for the exercise of power of compulsory unitisation of the minister will be absent and therefore, the minister is incapacitated. Arguing further, he contended that the licensee in the small extension will not be able to restrain drainage by the other licensee except where it can be shown that the well was placed within the 125 metres of the boundary line between them or that the rule of capture did not form part of the licensing regime of UK. Furthermore, that the power of the minister to withhold development consent or to refuse to grant approval for well drilling even though unqualified, will not also protect the owner of the small extension as the minister cannot lawfully exercise such power to defeat the right of capture granted by the licensing clause.[28]

It is submitted that while the scenario given by Daintith could happen, the example however also ignores the fact that the owner of the small extension may want to drill a well and produce if he can appropriately place a well on his own side of the reservoir to drain oil from the whole reservoir since the license clause encapsulates the rule of capture as interpreted by Professor Daintith. Once this happens, there will be competitive drilling which will lead to reduction in overall production of both parties and thereby affecting national interests. Therefore, even where there is a small extension of a reservoir into adjoining land; unitisation can still increase overall production of both parties. One important question posed by John Keen on this issue was 'would not all unitisations lead to more effective recovery of petroleum from common pool?'[29] The answer would definitely be in the positive considering the enormous benefits derivable from unitisation. Consequently, it is difficult to conceive a situation where the conditions stated in the unitisation clause will not be present whenever there is straddling petroleum reservoir. The minister is expected to order unitisation in all circumstances of straddling petroleum reservoir by the above clause.

27. Daintith, 'Finders Keepers? ...', at 349.
28. *Ibid.*, at 350.
29. John P. Keen, 'Commonwealth Draft Guidelines for Trans-boundary Unitisations and the Rule of Capture', (1998) AMPLA Yearbook: 440, at 448.

Our interpretation in this book that the granting clause does not encapsulate the rule of capture appeared to have been justified by this unitisation clause. This is because if the licence clause is interpreted not to encapsulate the rule of capture then whenever there is a small extension the conditions in the unitisation clause are triggered. It will now be in the interest of the State to have the fields developed so as to generate revenues. In this wise, the minister will be expected to order unitisation because neither of them will be able to produce without unitisation. The owner of the larger portion will be eager to develop while the owner of the smaller portion will also want to develop because it is now economical with unitisation. The presence of reciprocal advantage and apprehension of mutual liability will be incentives for them to negotiate and conclude unitisation agreement without any 'strategic hold out.' Therefore, the fact that unitisation clause made enforcement of unitisation subject to certain conditions does not abdicate the Minister from enforcing it because those conditions are what unitisation is meant to achieve and they will always be present whenever there is straddling reservoirs. There is no conceivable instance when unitisation will not be in the interest of the State as it will enhance ultimate recovery.

ii) The above provisions have shown that the State is more concerned about national interest and also about securing maximum recovery of petroleum than issues of equity and fairness between groups of licensees. This attitude was brought to bear when DTI in 1997 reversed its official position of no rule of capture in UK.[30] Its current position is reminiscent of its policy statement which pointed to the fact that the rule of capture will be allowed to operate between licensees rather than delaying field development. Paragraph 2.5.1 (a) of the DTI Oil and Gas Directorate - Regulation Guidance Notes, provides that:

> [T] he Secretary of State will not necessarily refuse to grant development consent to a particular group of Licensees who have not concluded an agreement with the Licensees of an adjacent block on the basis that they have not concluded a unitisation agreement. The Department does not consider that powers to require unitisation extend to issues of fairness and equity between groups of licensees. The Department's position is that proprietary rights do not exist in un-extracted hydrocarbons under the UKCS and ownership of hydrocarbon arises only once they have been extracted under appropriate regulatory consent.[31]

This shows that power given to the minister under the law to compel unitisation is insufficient to deal with all instances where unitisation will be suitable or necessary. The interest of the licensee ought to be considered in exercising power to compel unitisation.

It also ignores the huge amount of resources expended by licensee to discover petroleum reservoir which straddles adjacent concession. To deny him remedy, if petroleum is captured from the reservoir by an adjoining licensee before he did, will not be fair and equitable. The above stance of the Regulator will give incentive for one

30. See the DTI Oil and Gas Directorate - Regulation Guidance Notes of 1997.
31. David Asmus & Jacqueling Wearver, 'Unitizing Oil and Gas Fields around the World: A Comparative Analysis of National Laws and Private Contracts', (2006) at 47–48. Available at http://www.ssrn.com.

licensee to quickly capture petroleum as much as possible, from straddling reservoir without waiting for Unitisation agreement to be reached with an adjoining licensee. In addition, this position also contravenes the Minister's obligation to compel unitisation under the law. If the rule of capture is allowed to operate, obviously there will be competitive drilling, ultimate recovery will be affected, and that will not be in the interests of the public as well as the licensees.

3. NIGERIA

In Chapter 3 of this book, we have shown that ownership of petroleum in both onshore and offshore vests in the Federal Government of Nigeria. The Petroleum Act of 1969 provides for a three stage rights system in respect of upstream petroleum operations. First, Oil exploration licence, second, Oil prospecting licence, and third, Oil mining lease. The Act provides that the Minister may grant a lease, to be known as an oil mining lease:

> 'to search for, win, work, carry away and disposes of petroleum.' It further provides that an OML may be granted only to the holder of an oil prospecting licence who has—(a) satisfied all the conditions imposed on the licence or otherwise imposed on him by this Act, and (b) discovered oil in commercial quantities.

The Form of the lease is provided in the schedule to the Petroleum (Drilling & Production) Regulations of 1969 as 'Form D'. It provides that:

> This Oil Mining Lease is granted to ... of... for a term of ...years commencing on the...day of... to search for, win, work, carry away and dispose of all petroleum in, under or throughout the lands described in the schedule hereto and delineated in red in the plan attached.

In Chapter 3 we have found that this type of granting clause operates as a conveyance of the oil and gas discovered in the reservoir by the lessee at the time of grant and that this is more than a *Profit a prendre*.[32] The licensing regime in Nigeria with respect to an oil mining lease cannot be said to encapsulate the rule of capture. Arguments in support of this position had already been canvassed in Chapter 3 and therefore, need not be repeated here but needless to add that the discovered petroleum while still under the ground qualifies as a real interest as it is connected to land.[33] Thus, from the wordings of the granting clause, a full ownership interests can be said to have been granted to the holder of an OML and such interest is an interest in land.

32. Defined as 'an incorporeal interest in land authorising entry upon a tract of land and severance and removal of a part of the corpus of the land.' See Williams & Meyers, 'Oil and Gas Laws', at 17-18; see also Megarry & Wade, 'The Law of Real Property', at 729.
33. Roderick Paisley, 'Aspects of Land Law Relative to the Transportation of Oil and Gas in Scotland', in Greg Gordon et al., 'Oil and Gas Law: Current Practice and Emerging Trends' (Dundee University Press, 2007), above at 412. He listed the three most suitable real rights in Scotland and most legal systems as (a) ownership (b) lease and (c) Praedial Sevitude.

The Marginal fields development regime in Nigeria is a good example with which to demonstrate the real interest nature of the holder of an OML. Paragraph 17 of the first schedule to the Petroleum Act, 1969 (as amended in 1996) provides that the holder of an OML may on its own volition farm-out a marginal field existing in his lease area to a third party subject however, to the consent of the President of the Federal Republic of Nigeria. The grounds upon which the President could give his consent to a farm out are (i) if it is in the public interest, (ii) if the marginal field is non-producing and have been left unattended for a period not less than ten years, and (iii) if the parties to the farm out are acceptable to the President.[34] The President on his own volition can cause a farm out of a Marginal field (whether producing or non-producing) that has been left unattended for a period of ten years from the date of discovery.

The recognition of the proprietary or real interest nature of the holder of OML lies in the implementation and practice of the above legislation. In practice, DPR would normally forward letters to the OML holders requesting submission of a list of marginal fields in their Portfolio before the exercise of the powers of Mr President under the law. After completing the process of the award which is either by discretionary or auction, successful companies are mandated to enter into a farm out agreement with the holder of the OML.[35] The Marginal field operator is also expected to pay overridden royalty or tariff to the holder of the OML.[36]

This is negotiated by the parties with due regard to equity and fairness. The matters that are taken into consideration when negotiating the amount or percentage of the overridden royalty or tariff include the status of the field (whether it is in appraisal or development stage), its value (reserves) and the associated risks.

While the whole gamut of the marginal field regime in Nigeria is outside the scope of this research, it is pertinent to point out that it is on the basis of the proprietary nature of the interest of the holder of an OML in the underlying petroleum that informed the Government's approach to the implementation of the Marginal field law in this fashion. Even though, the President can cause a farm out of a marginal field, the power is not absolute and the exercise of his consent to marginal field farmed out by the OML holder is also not absolute. The fields are not taken arbitrarily or with impunity (not expropriated). It is subject to agreement between the leaseholder and the marginal field operator. In other words, the OML holder receives adequate compensation for allowing a third party to take over such fields. The OML granting clause in Nigeria cannot therefore, be read to encapsulate the rule of capture.

34. Paragraph 17 (3) (a) (b) of the 1st schedule to the Petroleum Act, 1969.
35. Guidelines for Farm-out and Operation of Marginal Fields in Nigeria, paras 17-18. Para. 17.2 provides that: '[T]he leaseholder and selected parties shall promptly enter into negotiations regarding the terms and conditions of the Farm-out Agreement. The parties shall endeavour to reach an agreement within 150 days from the days of award. However, in the event that the parties fail to reach an agreement with respect to any of the terms and conditions within the 150 days, either party may notify DPR. Under such a situation, the Minister shall adjudicate in respect of the relevant terms and conditions within 30 days and the decision of the Minister shall be final.'
36. *Ibid.*, para. 18 (1) (2)-(1).

3.1 Unitisation Practice in Nigeria

The unitisation clauses in Nigeria and UK are identical. They are identical in the sense that the conditions stipulated for the exercise of the powers of the Minister are the same except that the Nigerian clause added the interests of the licensees to those conditions. The Nigerian Petroleum regulations provide for compulsory unitisation called 'joint development schemes' in cases where there is straddling reservoirs and cases where the reservoirs may not be straddling but are contiguous so that a scheme of joint development would be the appropriate method.[37] Section 48 - (Joint Development Schemes) provides that:

> (1) if at any time during the term of a licence or lease–
>
> (a) the Minister, after consultation with the licensee or lessee (referred to in this regulation as "the grantee"), is satisfied that the relevant area or any part thereof forms part of a single geological petroleum reservoir (referred to in this regulation as "the oilfield") in respect of other parts of which any other licence or lease is in force, and that the oilfield is susceptible of being developed as a unit in accordance with good oilfield practice; and ...

The above provision either by design or careless drafting places the duty of initiating unitisation process on the Minister and not on the Licensee. This arises from the opening sentence which provides that the Minister will first have to consult with licensee or lessee and be satisfied before compelling unitisation. Could this mean that the minister would have to get the licensee to agree with him that the field straddles before he compels unitisation? Such consultation is really unnecessary because licensees are expected to forward field development plan for approval before commencing any development.[38] At that point, the minister should have known and should be able to satisfy himself that the fields straddle. Moreover, a licensee is expected to shoot seismic across licence border line into his neighbour's licence area so that straddling can be detected and copies of such survey and all other data acquired subsequently on the field are to be deposited with the Minister.[39] In this paragraph, it appears that the compulsory unitisation power of the minister has been made conditional upon prior consultation with the licensee. Second, compulsory unitisation is also made conditional upon the fields been susceptible of being developed as a single unit taking into consideration good oil field practice. The other conditions can be found in paragraph 48 (1) (b) which are[40] – that the unit development must be in the interest

37. Section 48 Petroleum (Drilling and production) Regulations, 1969 LFN, 2004.
38. *Ibid.*, s. 38 – It provides that the field development programme must be submitted to DPR for approval prior to commencement of actual development. The programme must contain details of the estimated size and physical parameters of the pool, the intended drilling and production pattern and anticipated drive mechanism of the pool.
39. See para. 1.1 of the '2000 DPR Procedural Guideline for Establishing Joint Development/ Unitisation of Offset Structures/Fields in Nigeria'. It mandated operating companies to shoot across the concession boundary into the adjacent concession to a distance of about two kilometres. Data acquired should be processed and interpreted.
40. 'The Minister considers that it is in the interests of Nigeria, the grantee and the licensees or lessees of any other part of the oilfield (those licensees or lessees being referred to in this

of Nigeria and all the parties to the proposed unit agreement (grantees and other parties), and must be to 'secure maximum ultimate recovery' of hydrocarbons.

The example given by Professor Daintith of an oil field that has a small extension to an adjacent concession is only relevant in this instance because one of the conditions for the exercise of the Minister's power is that unitised development must also be in the interests of the licensee. Where the estimated oil underlying such extension area is so insignificant that it becomes uneconomical for the owner of the extension to consider participating in the whole trouble of unitisation expenses (costs of unitisation agreement and development), compelling unitisation will not be in his interest. The licensee with small extension cannot also embark on unilateral development because the right conferred by the lease does not encapsulate the rule of capture. It will not be in the interest of Nigeria too and maximum ultimate recovery will not also be secured by unitisation. Other options like buy out will be preferable in this circumstance assuming transaction costs is less than the benefits to be derived by parties from such arrangement. By the mere fact that this option is chosen is a demonstration that neither the parties can undertake unilateral development until an arrangement that will take into account the interests of both parties and that will promote ultimate recovery has been reached. Where the transaction costs are more than the benefits, then the State will have to come in by objectively determining the price to be paid by the licensee with the larger portion. This according to the Economist is an instance where entitlements protected by property rule can change to entitlement protected by liability rule.[41]

The wordings of section 48 (2) suggests that the licensee is also not expected to unitise unless he is required to do so by the minister in a notice served on him. The paragraph provides that 'the grantee shall, *upon being so required by the Minister by a notice in writing* specifying the other parties, co-operate with the other parties in the preparation of a scheme (referred to in this regulation as "the development scheme")....'

However, it is submitted that where the minister fails to serve written notice, the licensee would still be required to unitise based on its licence granting clause that does not permit or encapsulate unilateral capture. Where the Minister served one belatedly after unilateral drainage had already occurred, the question as to when unitisation takes effect will arise. This perhaps explains the occurrence of numerous cases of drainages and competitive drillings witnessed at present in Nigeria. Nigeria may not be alone in this regulatory failure as any country with similarly worded unitisation clause would likely face this problem. For example in Netherlands, unilateral capture has also slipped the minister as shown below in this book, which had already resulted into litigation among the affected licence holders, because of the way the unitisation clause is drafted. This presupposes that until the minister make a request that the field should be unitised; there is no obligation on the licensees to unitise.

---

regulation as "the other parties") in order to secure the maximum ultimate recovery of petroleum that the oilfield should be worked and developed as a unit in cooperation by all those who hold a lease or licence over any part thereof, paragraphs (2), (3) and (4) of this regulation shall apply ... .'

41. Calabresi & Melamed, 'Property Rules, Liability Rules, and Inalienability Rules: One View of the Cathedral', at 1089.

Section 48 (4) is to the effect that where the parties failed to submit a joint development scheme after the notice has been served on them or that the one submitted is not approved by the Minister, the Minister can prepare one that is fair and equitable to the parties. There had been no instance of where the Minister had exercised this power in spite of the numerous straddling fields that are on production either competitively or unilaterally as shown in Tables 3-6 below.

3.2 Capture Problem in Nigeria

In Nigeria the problem of unilateral capture arose from failure of the Regulatory Agency, The Department of Petroleum Resources to enforce compulsory unitisation at the appropriate time where licence holders could not agree on unitisation terms. This has resulted to a situation where one licence holder developed and produced from a reservoir that straddles a field operated by another licence holder for over thirty (30) years without unitisation agreement.

This problem occurred with respect to several petroleum fields[42] in which either unilateral capture has occurred (Brown – Green fields, see Tables 6.1 and 6.2) or both licensees have engaged in competitive drilling and production (Brown – Brown fields, see Tables 6.3 and 6.4). Typical example of this situation is the Opugbene field in OML 36 and Tebidaba field in OML 63 operated by both Shell Petroleum Development Company (SPDC) and Nigeria Agip Oil Company (NAOC) respectively. The facts of the matter can be put succinctly as follows:

In 1972, NAOC drilled 14 wells in Tebidaba field and started production from 12 of the wells that penetrated oil and gas pools, in 1975. In February 1990 SPDC drilled an exploration/appraisal well in Opugbene field which proved that the reservoir straddles Tebidada field. The well also penetrated oil bearing sand in the straddling reservoir. Following this development, both Companies jointly acquired a Three Dimensional (3D) seismic survey across both concession between 1992 and 1996. In 1999, SPDC notified NAOC of its intention to unitise the field and a copy of the letter was sent to the Regulatory Authority. In response to SPDC's request, a Pre-unitisation meeting was held in 1999 which was deadlocked over technical clarifications regarding sharing of data that could have propelled them to progress discussions on unitisation. Due to the Regulator's intervention, the data was eventually shared between the companies in 2000. SPDC further conducted technical study of the straddling reservoirs identifying the scope for joint development. The study was shared with NAOC who undertook to give SPDC feedback on the issue. NAOC never did but chose to drill two additional sidetrack wells and employed Electric Submersible Pumps to drain the reservoirs without Unitisation, claiming that there was no spare capacity in its flow station to accommodate production from the SPDC's side. NAOC also refused to

42. About 138 petroleum fields require unitisation in Nigeria, out of which 44 fields had engaged in unilateral capture, while 36 fields engaged in competitive production and 54 fields are yet to be unitised or produced. The terms Brown fields and Green fields denote producing and non-producing fields respectively. Tables 6.1-6.4, are some petroleum fields that are either engaging in competitive production or in unilateral production.

divulge information as to the current production level at which the field was being depleted. The Regulatory Authority only intervened on 8 February 2008 to stop NAOC's aggressive drilling and production conduct without unitisation of the straddling reservoirs after much protest from SPDC. As at September 2008 the cumulative oil production by NAOC from the common reservoir was 123,162,453 Mbbls out of total recoverable oil of 137.19 Mbbls. The remaining oil reserve was 13.99 MMstb as at September 2008. The total recoverable gas in the common reservoir was 329.56 BSCF as at January 2008. NAOC has produced 203.49 BSCF leaving a balance of 126.07 BSCF as at September 2008.

In another straddling reservoirs operated by SPDC and NAOC (Afuo field / Ogbainbiri field), in which the reservoir was unitised in 1991, there had been unilateral production by NAOC from the straddling reservoirs. When the reservoirs were unitised, the tract participation was 75% for NAOC while 25% was for SPDC. NAOC was recorded to have drained about 37 MMstb of oil from SPDC side. It was determined that crude pay back to

SPDC should be satisfied by taken 10% from the 75% of NAOC's tract participation in future production from the straddling fields.

Table 6.1 Fields Involving Unilateral Capture in Nigeria (Brown–Green Cases) 1

S/N	*Company*	*OML/OPL*	*Fields*	*Remarks*
1	SPDC / NAOC	39/60	Okwuibome / okapi	
2	SPDC / Chevron	40/49	OML 40 / Igbokoda	
3	SPDC / Chevron	40/49	40 / Ojumole	
4	SPDC / Chevron	18/23/25	OMLs18 / 23 / 25	
5	SPDC / Chevron	41/49	Sapele North / OML49	
6	SPDC / Chevron	18/23/55	OMLs 18, 23 / Jokka	
7	SPDC / Chevron	43/49	Benin Estuary / Kito	
8	SPDC / Chevron	40/49	Tsekelewu / Opukeba	
9	SPDC / NPDC	1/110	Oki / Oziengbe south	
10	SPDC / Pan ocean	4/98	Oben / Owe	
11	Elf/Mobil	102/67	Asasa-West / Asasa	

Source: The Department of Petroleum Resources.

Table 6.2 Fields Involving Unilateral Capture in Nigeria (Brown–Green Cases) 2

S/N	*Company*	*OML/OPL*	*Fields*	*Remarks*
12	NAOC / SPDC	22 / 61	Oshi / Ubie	
13	NAOC / SPDC	63 / 36	Tebidaba / Opugbene	
14	NAOC / SPDC	63 / 46	Clough Creek / Kanbo	
15	Shell / Elf	21 / 58	Ahia / Sombreiro	

S/N	Company	OML/OPL	Fields	Remarks
16	Shell / Chevron	43 / 90	Afremo / Meji	
17	Shell / Chevron	41 / 49	Sapele / Abigborodo	
18	Chevron / Shell	49 / 42	Abiteye / Nana Creek	
19	Chevron / Shell	49 / 40	Gbokoda / Gbokoda/North	
20	Moni Pulo Brass / Shell	114 / 14	Efiat/Abana	
21	Chevron / NPDC	49 / 64	Abiteye / 64	
22	Famfa / Chevron	216 / 217	Ekoli / Agbami	

Source: The Department of Petroleum Resources.

Table 6.3 Fields Involving Competitive Drilling in Nigeria (Brown–Brown Cases) 1

S/N	Company	OML/OPL	Fields	Remarks
1	SPDC / NAOC	35 / 63	Afuo / Ogbainbiri	
2	SPDC / NAOC	20 / 60	Akri / Oguta	
3	SPDC / NAOC	35 / 62	Okpokunmo / Tuomo West	
4	SPDC / NAOC	61 / 27	Samabri / Samabri E./Biseni	
5	SPDC / Chevron	40 / 49	Tsekelewu / opuekeba	
6	Shell / Chevron	25 / 55	Belema / Belema North	
7	Shell / Chevron		Sapele / Abigborodo	
8	Shell / Chevron	11 / 51	Yorla / Yorla North	
9	Shell / Chevron	42 / 49	Jones-creek / Utonana	
10	Shell / Chevron	24 / 55	Ekulama / Robertkiri	
11	Shell / Pan Ocean	98 / 4	Oben / Owe	

Source: The Department of Petroleum Resources.

Table 6.4 Fields Involving Competitive Drilling in Nigeria (Brown–Brown Cases) 2

S/N	Company	OML/OPL	Fields	Remarks
12	Chevron / shell	41 / 42	Utonana / Jones Creek	
13	Chevron / Consolidated oil	95 / 113	West-Isan / Bella	
14	NAOC / SPDC		Idu / Adibawa NE	
15	NAOC / SPDC		Pirigbene / Diebu Creek	
16	Elf / Mobil	99 / 70	Amenam / Kpono	
17	Addax / Chevron	118 / 53	Izombe / Jisike	
18	Atlas Pet / Chevron	109 / 90	Ejulebe / Mefa	

Source: The Department of Petroleum Resources.

3.3 The Approach of the Regulatory Agency (DPR)

The oil and gas industry in Nigeria is replete with these sorts of problems and since the issue is yet to come before the court even though it has attracted so much dusts within the oil and gas industry practitioners, it now behoves on the Regulatory Authority to find solution to the problem. The approach adopted by DPR in addressing the problem was that in 2000, DPR made provisional policy guidelines for the establishment of joint development or unitisation of offset structures/fields (hereinafter called 'Year 2000 guidelines'). The Year 2000 guidelines were meant to cover the procedures for carrying out Joint development schemes but as the DPR was being confronted with numerous problems arising from unilateral capture and competitive drilling, it was soon discovered that Year 2000 guidelines were not robust enough to supplement the provisions of the Petroleum (Drilling and Production) Regulations on Joint development schemes. Consequently, the DPR in 2007 set up a committee comprising representatives of the private oil companies, the State oil company and the Regulatory agency (DPR) to review the Year 2000 guidelines. The committee submitted its report and from which the DPR issued in 2008, a new Policy Guidelines called 'Guidelines for Unitisation in Nigeria.' (Hereinafter called 'Year 2008 guidelines')

It is expedient to examine some of the provisions of these guidelines in order to assess whether it has adequately addressed the issue of unilateral capture from straddling reservoirs. It will be examined in respect of straddling between Non-producing reservoirs (Green–Green), straddling between Producing reservoirs and Non-producing reservoirs (Brown–Green reservoirs), and straddling between Producing reservoirs (Brown–Brown).

3.3.1 *Non-producing Reservoirs (Green–Green)*

These are straddling reservoirs from which neither of the parties has produced petroleum and as such captures cases are absent. The guidelines laid down the procedure for initiating unitisation where there is straddling reservoirs in the future. The relevant provisions of the guidelines are Articles 2 and 4. Article 2 governs notification of discovery of straddling reservoirs[43] while Article 4 deals with the development of such reservoirs. It should be noted that both Articles imposed on the licensee the duty to initiate joint development of straddling reservoirs unlike section 48 of the Petroleum (Drilling and Production) Regulations of 1969 (1969 Regulations) which imposed such duty on the Minister. This is a feature of a compulsory unitisation regime in which the licensee is mandated by law to unitise once a reservoir is known to have straddles adjacent concession whether consulted by the minister or not.

Article 2 provides that once straddling reservoir has been discovered, the licensee must suspend work and shall report such discovery to the DPR within two months of

43. It provides that once reservoirs have been confirmed as straddling by a Licensee, he shall immediately inform the DPR of such discovery.

suspension of work.[44] The DPR shall within one month of the receipt of the report, inform the other concession holder(s) to commence exploratory activities in the affected part of the concession to confirm the straddling.[45] The other concession holder must within two months submit to the DPR a statement of willingness to confirm the existence of petroleum in the straddling reservoir.[46] Thereafter, he shall within three months either informs the DPR of his intention to conduct an acceptable exploration work in the affected part or submits a rebuttal of straddling which he must also serve on the Licensee that discovered the straddling reservoirs.[47] DPR will intervene and resolve issues that arose in the reservations, failure of which will now compel unitisation. Unitisation will be deemed to have commenced on the date DPR directs all the parties to unitise.[48]

3.3.2 *Producing Reservoirs and Non-producing Reservoirs (Brown–Green Reservoirs)*

This provision is aimed at addressing the existing problem of unilateral production from straddling reservoirs. Where one of the parties have commenced production in his part of the straddling reservoir, the DPR would on confirmation of such straddling, direct all the parties to take appropriate steps to develop the reservoir as a unit.[49] Once this is done by the DPR, no well shall be drilled into the reservoir except as agreed by both parties.[50]

The problem here is that in most cases unilateral production would have taken place before the DPR issue the directives. The question is – when would such directive take effect? Would it take effect on the date of the directive or on the date the party commenced production? In addressing this problem, the 2008 Guidelines provides that the directive will take effect on the date that the non-producing party established straddling through seismic data, drilling and discovery.[51] This means that where the non-producing party had not done any work to establish straddling, oil and gas drained from the straddling reservoirs belongs to the producing party even though part of it might have come from the non-producing party's concession. Thus, the rule of capture applies in this circumstance. This implicitly violates the provisions of the granting clause of an OML. Where the non-producing party is a holder of an oil mining lease, it

44. Article 2.1, 2008 Guidelines.
45. *Ibid.*, Article 2.2 (a) (1).
46. *Ibid.*, Article 2.2 (a) (2).
47. *Ibid.*, Article 2.2 (a) (2) (i) (ii).
48. *Ibid.*, Article 4.1.(a) (b).
49. *Ibid.*, Article 2.2 (b).
50. *Ibid.*, Article 4.2 (a).
51. *Ibid.*, Article 4.2 (d) it provides that '[T]he Reference Date shall be the date that DPR states in writing to be the time at which the non-producing Party established straddling through seismic data, drilling and discovery. If there is evidence of possible straddling shown by seismic or well data; and a statement of possible straddling was not communicated to DPR by the producing Party, the Reference Date shall be the date the producing Party commenced production in the field, provided however that there is no evidence that the non-producing Party had knowledge of the straddling.'

will definitely violate his property right 'to search for, win, work, carry away and dispose of all petroleum in, under or throughout his concession.' This section provides further that where the producing party concealed straddling by failing to communicate it to the DPR, the directive will take effect from the date the producing party commenced production. There is a proviso to this – 'provided however, there is no evidence that the non-producing party had knowledge of the straddling.' In effect, even if the producing party conceals straddling, he will be allowed to keep substances drained from adjacent lease where the adjacent leaseholder had knowledge of the straddling but did nothing to take action. It is not clear from the 2008 Guidelines the kind of action the non-producing party is expected to take in this circumstance. Probably, he is expected to confirm straddling and report same to the DPR or to simply protect himself from drainage by drilling an offset well. The example given above between SPDC and NAOC shows that there had been a situation in which the non-producing party is aware, confirmed straddling through drilling and pressed for unitisation but the producing party was uncooperative and continued drainage. There are other times where the producing party informed the DPR of the straddling, and DPR did nothing to halt production for the unitisation of the reservoirs. Therefore, the above provision will work out injustice to the non-producing party unless the directive of the DPR is made to commence from the date the producing party started production.

3.3.3 *Producing Reservoirs (Brown–Brown)*

Article 4 (3) applies in situation where both parties have engaged in competitive drilling and have produced from the common reservoirs. In this type of situation one party might have drained more than his share of the common reservoir while the other received less.[52] Either of the party can initiate unitisation by communicating such intention to both the DPR and the other party. Once this notification has been done, neither of the parties can drill a well into the said reservoir except as agreed by both parties.[53] The crucial question is when would unitisation take place if eventually the reservoir is unitised? How will past costs and production be re-adjusted where both parties have been producing unilaterally for appreciable length of time or where one party has produced more than the quantity of oil underlying his lease area?

Article 4.3 (d) is to the effect that unitisation will be deemed to have commenced when the second party established straddling through seismic, drilling and discovery. What happens to the production had by the first party before the other party could

52. This has happened between SPDC and NAOC in the Oshi field (OML 61) and Ubieh field (OML 22) straddling structure. Both companies started production competitively in 1973 without unitisation. The DPR has fixed March 2009 as the reference date for commencement of unitisation. This has called for production and cost readjustment between the parties. It was found that NAOC has lifted more than SPDC in the common reservoir.
53. *Ibid.*, Article 4.3 (a) (b).

establish straddling? This means that the rule of capture will apply to that ones.[54] The issue of re-adjustment of production and costs will also arise and it is the responsibility of the DPR to fix the Reference date.[55]

The limiting date would probably be when unitisation is deemed to have commenced which has been stated to be when the second party established straddling.

One striking feature of these guidelines is the stipulation of the period of time in which licensee must report straddling to the DPR. It places time limitation on every participant in the unitisation process. Thus, if this time stipulation is enforced, the efficacy of unitisation regime will no doubt be achieved.

Moreover, the various conditions that must be satisfied before unitisation can be ordered appeared to have given so much discretion to the minister as to when to compel unitisation. Those conditions cannot be strictly called conditions as they will always be the reasons why unitisation is necessary. In other words, those conditions were the same goals of unitisation so that the minister is under a duty to compel unitisation whenever there is a straddling reservoir. Where the minister fails to exercise this duty to order unitisation where straddling reservoir is proved to exist and drainage arises, he will be taken to have violated the duty imposed on him as the law gave him no discretion in the strict sense of the clause.

From the above analysis, it can be seen that the attitude of the regulating authority is to allow the rule of capture to govern the development of the oil and gas in certain circumstances which as we have pointed out is contrary to the granting clause of the OML. From what has happened in Nigeria, the licensees have latched on the Minister's failure and have proceeded on unilateral drainage. Given the nature of the rights granted to the lessee by the lease granting clause under the Petroleum Act of Nigeria which we have interpreted as not encapsulating the rule of capture, the unitisation clause and the Year 2008 guidelines should not be interpreted to have entitled the licensee to proceed on unilateral development and production from straddling fields without unitisation. There appears to be conflict between the Lease granting clause as specified under the Petroleum Act, the Unitisation clause under the Petroleum (Drilling and Production) Regulations and the Year 2008 Guidelines. The provision of the Petroleum Act will in this circumstance prevails over the Regulations and Guidelines.

54. *Ibid.*, Article 4.3 (d) provides that 'the Reference Date shall be the date the second party established straddling through seismic data, drilling and Discovery. DPR shall state in writing to the parties the date unitisation shall be deemed to have commenced, for the purpose of sharing past production and costs.'

55. The purpose of the 'Reference date' is stated in Article 4.4 of the 2008 Guidelines. It is 'to determine the date when unitisation is deemed to have commenced and to establish when the re-adjustment of past costs and production shall take effect in respect of the straddling between producing and non-producing fields (Green / Brown) and straddling between producing fields (Brown / Brown)'.

4. CANADA AND AUSTRALIA

4.1 Canada

In *Canada*, there is a three stage petroleum licensing regime in the offshore provided under the Canada-Nova Scotia Offshore Accord Implementation Act of 1988 and the Canada-Newfoundland Offshore Accord Implementation Act of 1987[56] (Accord Implementation Acts). These are exploration licences, significant discovery licences and production licences.[57] We shall however limit our analysis to the granting clause of a production licence since the wordings are the same with the granting clauses of exploration and significant discovery licences.

The Canada-Nova Scotia Offshore Accord Implementation Act of 1988 provides that:

> 'the Board, on application made in the form and manner and containing such information as may be prescribed,
>
> (a) shall issue a production licence to one interest owner, in respect of any one commercial discovery area or portion thereof that is subject to an exploration licence or a significant discovery licence held by that interest owner; and …'[58]

Section 83 (1) provides that:

> a 'production licence confers, with respect to the portions of the offshore area to which the licence applies,
>
> (a) the right to explore for, and the exclusive right to drill and test for, petroleum;
> (b) the exclusive right to develop those portions of the offshore area in order to produce petroleum;
> (c) the exclusive right to produce petroleum from those portions of the offshore area; and
> (d) title to the petroleum so produced.'

Rights conferred on a production licensee are identical to those conferred on the holders of exploration and significant discovery licences except that the production licence confers title to the petroleum produced, on the holder of the licence.

The question now is whether the granting clause of the production licence and the rights it confers on its holder encapsulate the rule of capture. Analysis of this issue is reserved till when we consider the licence granting clause of Australia as they are similar.

4.2 Australia

The relevant provisions of the law in Australia are Sections 52 (a) and 127 (a) (b) of the repealed Petroleum (submerged lands) Act 1967. These sections are reproduced by

56. See Chapter 3 of this book.
57. Section 68 Canada-Nova Scotia Offshore Accord Implementation Act of 1988.
58. Section 84.

sections 161 and 285 of the current Offshore Petroleum and Green House Gas Storage Act of 2006. The sections also provide for a three stage licence regimes - Petroleum exploration permit, Petroleum retention lease and Petroleum production licence. These sections have also raised the issue as to whether the common law rule of capture has been given statutory teeth in Australia.

Sections 52 (a) provides that:

> A licence, while it remains in force, authorises the licensee, subject to this Act and the regulations and in accordance with the conditions to which the licence is subject:
>
> a) to recover petroleum in the licence area and to recover petroleum from the licence area in another area to which he has lawful access for that purpose;
> b) to explore for petroleum in the licence area; and
> c) to carry on such operations and execute such works in the licence areas as are necessary for those purposes.

Section 127 (Property in petroleum) provides that:

> Subject to this Act, if petroleum is recovered by a permittee, lessee or licensee in the permit area, lease area or licence area:
>
> (a) the petroleum becomes the property of the permittee, lessee or licensee; and
> (b) it is not subject to any rights of other persons (other than any person to whom the permittee, lessee or licensee transfers, assigns or otherwise disposes of the petroleum or an interest in the petroleum).

The licence granting clauses from the two jurisdictions are similar. In Canada, a production licence is granted in respect of any portion of the offshore area in which a commercial discovery has been made and it entitles the holder, within the portions of the offshore areas, exclusive right to explore for, to drill and test for petroleum, to develop and to produce petroleum from that portion. With respect to Australia, a production licence authorises the licensee to recover petroleum both 'in the licence area' and 'from the licence area in another area.' This latter right concerns the situation of horizontal well drilled from one licence area to another held by the same person.[59] It could also concern the situation where a licensee has authority to go onto neighbouring licence area to extract petroleum from his own title by horizontal drilling.[60] In both countries, title or property to petroleum vests in the holder of the licence when produced or recovered in the licence area.

From Chapter 3 of this book, we have seen that in both Canada and Australia, the notion of Crown sovereign rights to petroleum resources in the sea bed and subsoil of the Continental shelf was emplaced by judicial pronouncement in Canada[61] and by

59. Crommelin, 'The U.S. Rule of Capture: Its Place in Australia', at 280 citing Explanatory Memorandum on the Petroleum (Submerged Lands) Amendment Bill 1980 clause 8, 20.
60. Keen, 'Commonwealth Draft Guidelines for Trans-boundary Unitisations and the Rule of Capture', at 440.
61. See *Reference Re: The seabed and subsoil of the Continental Shelf Offshore Newfoundland (Hibernia Reference), supra.*

legislation in Australia.[62] This may account for the policy behind the above statutory provisions as the other States we have studied in this book made no such provision in their petroleum legislations as to when title passes to the licensee. This may be because they wanted to avoid the common law rule of capture, or as Daintith pointed out, it could be an oversight on the part of the law makers not to have designed the law in a way that eliminate the problem of capture.[63]

Again opinions of legal experts are divided on whether the granting clause of the production licence in Australia and the rights it conferred on its holder encapsulate the rule of capture. Professor Daintith has argued that there is a statutory codification of the rule of capture in Australia. He opined that 'whether by accident or design, the PSLA produces a position in which production by the title holder cannot be sterilised by an adjoining title-holder who does not want to produce, that is the Act applies the so-called 'rule of capture ...'[64] He based this proposition on the interpretation of sections 39, 52 (a) and 127 of the PSLA. He argued that the combined effects of these sections are that 'rights and prohibitions under the Act are defined by reference to geographically circumscribed activities (to recover petroleum in the licence area) and not geographically delimited deposits.'[65] Elsewhere, he had also argued that the granting clause in the Australian legislation should be read in the same manner as the US OCS lease clause and that the clause if read in conjunction with other provisions on well spacing requirement, competitive drilling prevention and unitisation, drainage from an adjacent lands through operations that are in compliance with all relevant laws are legal.[66] In support of his view is John Keen, who argued that 'petroleum in the licence area' may well include 'petroleum that finds its way into the licence area by migration resulting from drilling'. He argued further that if the phrase 'petroleum in the licence area' is interpreted to mean the petroleum there at the time the formation was breached, then the rule of capture will be excluded.[67] He concluded that section 127 has removed the possible rights of adjoining title holder in that it constitutes a statutory equivalent of the common law rule of capture. Also, Keen ruled out the application of the common law rule of capture in Australia.[68] Miller has argued that the impacts of the common law rule of capture on both private and public interests have been whittled down considerably by the offset rules, correlative rights doctrine and the various anti-wastes conservations measures. As a result, a discussion of whether it applies to Australia as a common law rule has become a moot point. He therefore, concludes that it is of very little consequence in Australia except in issues relating to 'Gas banking' owing to the fact that the existing legislations do not seems to cover gas that is not the

62. Section 11 of Seas and Submerged Lands Act of 1973 (Commonwealth).
63. Daintith, 'Finders Keepers? ...', at 361.
64. Terrence Daintith, 'A Critical Evaluation of the Petroleum (Submerged Lands) Act as a Regulatory Regime', APMLA YEARBOOK 2000 at 104.
65. *Ibid.*
66. Daintith, 'Finders Keepers? ...', at 360.
67. John P. Keen, 'Commonwealth, Draft Guidelines for Trans-boundary Unitisations and the Rule of Capture', (1998) AMPLA Yearbook, at 440.
68. *Ibid.*, at 451.

property of the Crown. As a result, the rule of capture will be applicable to gas stored in underground which migrated to an adjoining property.[69]

Professor Crommelin on the other hand, is of the view that:

> [S]ection 127 of the PSLA merely serves to indicate when full property in petroleum passes to the holder of a permit or licence. There is no necessary inference that the licensee has no proprietary right to petroleum, or in the common reservoir, prior to production.[70]

If the word 'title' or 'property' used in both the Canadian and Australian legislations respectively, is construed as meaning 'ownership', then the interpretation given by Crommelin would be preferable as there is a difference between 'ownership' and 'property interest'. A licensee would have property interests in petroleum while in place and obtain ownership thereof when produced and reduced to possession.[71]

In addition, Crommelin's position above would appear to have supported our interpretation of the UK licensing clause. Since the licence granting clauses in UK, Canada and Australia produced identical results, we adopt our argument in support of the view we had expressed to the effect that once the licence granting clause professes to have authorised the licensee to produce or recover petroleum in or under a geographically defined licence area, it cannot be construed to have given the licensee the right to produce or recover petroleum that he can find at any given time but rather the petroleum that is within his licence area at the time of grant. Title to petroleum produced from his licence area is restricted to those that came exclusively from beneath his licence. The petroleum he captured from adjacent land if proved, cannot be included. With the advances in technology in the field of petroleum geology, geo-sciences and engineering, proving the quantity of oil and gas in a particular reservoir presents no difficulty. Therefore, the act of recovering petroleum in the geographically defined licence area should be confined to geographically delimited deposits. Section 127 cannot be read as having codified the common law rule of capture.

Having established that there is no statutory codification of the rule of capture in Australia, a conclusion which also applies to Canada, the next question is to determine whether the common law rule of capture applies in both countries. There is no direct judicial authority on the rule of capture in Australia. Therefore, reliance will be placed on the Canadian and United States cases given that they all have common legal heritage. The Privy Council cases will also have direct influence on the Australian jurisprudence on this issue. However, it is doubtful if the Privy Council cases will be followed in view of the apparent conflicting decisions of the court.

Gerlach has argued very strongly that the common law rule of capture will apply in Australia because, the rule as applied in the US is not based on any American theory of petroleum ownership in place but rather on question of ownership of petroleum

69. R.I. Milliner, 'Comment on the U.S. Rule of Capture: Its place in Australia', (1986) AMPLA Year Book at 299.
70. Crommelin, 'The U.S. Rule of Capture: Its Place in Australia', at 279.
71. A.W. Walker Jr., 'The Nature of the Property Interests Created by an Oil and Gas Lease in Texas', (1928) Texas Law Review 7: 1, at p. 2 (n. 2).

once extracted and the conduct which is permitted in the process of extraction.[72] Relying on the English water cases and the fact that the rule of capture was derived from those cases by the American courts, he argued further that Australian court will also by analogy apply such cases when confronted with issues bordering on the rule of capture. But it is to be noted that there had been strong criticisms against the analogy drawn from those water cases as they are not suitable for the issue of drainage of oil and gas cases.[73]

Therefore, Gerlach's proposition on this may produce an unjust result in Australia if accepted. Moreover, those Privy Council cases of Trinidad, Du Po Naing and Borys have produced conflicting decisions which may present problem to any court as to which one to follow. Gerlach's view that there is nothing in the Australian legislation that is inconsistent with the existence of the common law rule of capture though very persuasive, failed to mention specifically whether section 127 of the PSLA constitutes statutory rule of capture. According to him, provisions in the States petroleum legislation in Australia requiring consent of the minister before a well is drilled within 325 feet of the licence boundaries and those relating to the powers of the minister to prevent wastes and to order unitisation are pointer to the fact that the States accept rather than deny the existence of the rule of capture and that it may cause difficulties and therefore, seek to curb these difficulties.[74] This is reminiscent of the practice in the US in which conservation laws were made not to abolish the rule of capture but to moderate it in order to prevent waste. He concluded that unless there is a legislation (either State's or commonwealths') overruling the effects of the rule of capture, the offset rules and the correlative doctrine, the Rule would apply but would have its effects regulated by legislation.[75] These are in the areas of some controls exercised over well positioning and petroleum production throughout all phases of recovery operations. Therefore, problems that could warrant the court to apply the rule may never arise in practice because the Regulatory authorities in Australia would have invoked their statutory powers such as pooling and unitisation to resolve the matter.[76] However, we have seen such problems of the rule of capture arising in Nigeria and Netherlands. Nigerian petroleum laws and regulations provided for similar controls like prohibition of well drilling within 400 feet of licence boundaries, prior approval of field development programme and compulsory unitisation and yet the problems of rule of capture have arisen. In addition, the circumstances in which the problems will arise may not be limited to petroleum ownership disputes between two or more adjoining

72. S. Gerlach, 'Comment on the U.S. Rule of Capture: Its Place in Australia', (1996) AMPLA Yearbook at 283.
73. Crommelin, 'The U.S Rule of Capture: Its Place in Australia', at 267. Crommelin's view is that such analogies - water, solid minerals and animal *ferae naturae* - constitute a distortion of the physical characteristics of petroleum.
74. *Ibid.*, at 285 referring to s. 80 (a) (c) of the Petroleum Act of South Australia and equivalent provisions in other States and Northern Territory. See also s. 6 (A), 59, 97, 100 of the Petroleum (Submerged Lands) Act (Cth) 1967 for the offshore.
75. *Ibid.*, at 287. He noted that the effects of the rule has in practice, been whittled down if not completely nullified by the application of the petroleum Act of all the States in Australia as well as the PSLA (both commonwealth and the States).
76. *Ibid.*, at 288.

landowners in which all those control measures in the legislations would have been able to address if applied at the right time. The problem could arise in situations not even envisaged or provided by the legislations for example, disputes between two interests owners in one land (i.e., split title lands) as have been seen in Canada and India. In this circumstance, the reservoir did not cross licence boundaries. We have also seen that because of the manner in which unitisation clauses are couched, the minister could have misconstrued it as given him discretion in compelling unitisation. He may decide not to compel unitisation because the supposed conditions triggering the excise of the power have not been present. In addition, because of the difficulties associated with voluntary unitisation processes, an operator who stands a better chance to drain or who gets there first would not exercise restraint in producing from the shared reservoirs unless the licence clause is construed as not encapsulating unilateral capture. Therefore, the problem of the common law rule of capture can still arise in Australia in spite of all those regulatory controls because if unilateral capture eluded the Minister, the questions will turn out to be whether common law rule of capture applies or not. There is no judicial decision on this in Australia and as such we would refer to Canadian Judicial approach to this issue.

The problem has arisen in Canada in split title situations in which an analogy was drawn from the common law rules on percolating or underground water. In Canada the set of facts in which the rule of capture was applied were not exactly the same factual situations in which it was applied in the US. In spite of this, there is general acceptability among the courts, the legislators and academic writers that the common law rule of capture applies to oil and gas extraction in Canada.[77]

The first case in which the rule of capture was raised in Canada was *Boris V. C.P.R. (supra)*. As the facts have been stated above, we need not repeat it here. Although the rule of capture was not necessary for the court's decision, however, the stage for the subsequent application of the rule was set by the dictum of Lord Porter.[78] After reviewing the cases bordering on right to support, rights to interfere with ground water, and implied right to work and win in grants or reservations of mines and minerals, the Alberta Court of Appeal declared that:

> the reservations of the petroleum in the grant enables the appellants to use all reasonable means to extract the petroleum from the earth; that gas in the earth

77. Cecilia A. Low, 'The Rule of Capture: Its Current Status and Some Issues to Consider', (2008-2009) Alta. L. Rev. 46: 799 at 806, nn. 40-42.
78. At pp. 67-68 His Lordship declared that 'The petroleum, in so far as is material to the present case, is found in a bed of porous rock underlying the plaintiff's land and the surrounding property, which contains at the bottom water, then the petroleum and on top a layer gas ... The substances are fugacious and are not stable within the container although they cannot escape from it. If any of the three substances is withdrawn from a portion of the property which does not belong to the appellant but lies within the same container and any oil or gas situated in his property thereby filters from it to the surrounding lands, admittedly he has no remedy. So, also, if any substance is withdrawn from his property, thereby causing any fugacious matter to enter his land, the surrounding owners have no remedy against him. The only safeguard is to be the first to get to work, in which case, those who make the recovery become owners of the material which they withdraw from any well which is situated on their property or from which they have the authority to draw.'

> may be likened to subterranean waters and they are subject to like principles of law.[79]

Consequently the court held that the defendants were entitled to extract all the petroleum from the earth even if by so doing there is interference or wastage of the plaintiff's gas, so long as the defendants used modern method reasonably, and observed provisions of relevant statute and regulations. At the Court of Appeal level, what was considered mainly was the appropriate analogy to be used, whether the case law dealing with withdrawal of support or those that were dealing with groundwater. The court however adopted the latter analogy which invariably denied the plaintiff right to maintain the gas in place or right to compensation (or to secure his just and equitable share of the production of the gas), holding further that subterranean water analogy applies to both cases where the competing interests were in split title lands and adjacent lands. This decision was upheld by the Privy Council. Thus, Borys' case implicitly endorsed the application of the rule of capture to oil and gas in Canada having analogised subterranean water cases.

Also in the case of *Imperial Oil Ltd. V. Placid Oil*,[80] where a statute provides that 1.88% of recoverable oil in every producing reservoir shall be deemed to be within, upon or under road allowances and shall be the property of the Crown,[81] a question arose as to whether the lessee of a private land should pay royalty to the lessor on all the oil produced from the leased lands or the 1.88% deemed to be the property of the crown should be subtracted. The Supreme Court of Canada held that the effect of the statute is that 1.88% of all the oil produced from the lands regardless of where it originated, belonged to the crown and as such the defendant did not have to pay royalty on that oil. Here a strict application of the rule of capture would have vests in the producer ownership of all petroleum recovered from the reservoir. The court's decision has however, slightly modified the rule of capture. The holding of the court suggests that the rule of capture can be modified by statutes and that statutes may attach property interests to petroleum no matter where it is located in the reservoir or where or by whom it is produced and that the property remained attached to the petroleum when it is produced.[82] The Supreme Court referred to Borys' case as an authority establishing the law on the rule of capture in Canada but that statute could modify or rendered it inoperative. This case is important in one more respect. It shows that a portion of the 'recoverable oil in the reservoir' can qualify as a property interest and

79. *Ibid.*, at 237.
80. (1963) S.C.R 333.
81. Section 3 of The Road Allowances Crown Oil Act S.S 1959, c. 3.
82. The court declared in p. 338 that 'Lord Porter has here summarised the legal position of a land owner from within whose lands oil has migrated to the land of an adjoining landowner by reason of the operation of a well upon that land. Such, in the absence of section 3 of the Act, would have been the legal position of the crown in respect of oil which migrated from beneath a road allowance because of the operation of a well on adjoining land. Section 3 however, declares a property interest in the Crown of 1.88 per cent of all the recoverable oil within the whole of a producing reservoir. This a property interest, not in relation to oil situated beneath the surface of specific lands, but in respect of a portion of all the oil in the whole of a reservoir. The result is that, no matter to where the oil migrates, the Crown's interest remains in it and, on production, the property interest still remains.'

that the property interest attaches to the oil even after production. Ownership of the property interest does not change even if produced by person other than the owner of it when in the reservoir.

The case of Foralta Resources, also known as *Lickacz v. Magna Petroleums Ltd.*[83] also shows that statutes can modify the rule of capture. Here four adjoining tracts of lands were pooled together for the purpose of establishing a single drilling unit. The four tracts overlie a single reservoir but the producing well was located on one of the tracts so that all the petroleum produced was from that well. The plaintiff, who was the owner of the tract, claimed royalty on all gas produced from a well located on his tracts on the basis that the rule of capture had trumped the pooling agreements. The defendant company wanted the royalties calculated in such a way that the gas it produced could be taken to have been produced equally from all the pooled tracts. The effect of the plaintiff's claim would prevent the defendant from being able to pay royalty due to the remaining three tracts owners. The court held that the production and associated royalties should be allocated among all the pooled lands. The trial judge adopted the doctrine of equitable pooling as developed in the US because it ensures the allocation of production and sharing of royalties among all the pooled lands in the same spacing unit overlying the pool. The Judge preferred in effect, to use apportionment rule rather than capture rule.

In addition, the judge was of the opinion that it would be unjust enrichment for the plaintiff to be entitled to royalty based on the 100% of the production since the well was capturing reserves underlying the other three properties. The Judge relied on the Judicature Act[84] which required the Court to take judicial notice of equitable principles. Keen had examined this alternative remedies postulated by the Judge and asserted that 'even if a permittee has no title or property interest in petroleum until it is recovered under a production licence, the fact that he has a statutory right to be issued a licence which will then give the permittee title to any petroleum recovered means that the petroleum underlying a permit is *a benefit, resource, asset or other form of wealth or potential wealth* which would be protected by the laws of unjust enrichment'[85]

According to Keen, unjust enrichment can form an independent cause of action in the United Kingdom and Canada but not in Australia as it can only be claimed in an action for other restitutional remedies such as mistake, duress or illegality.[86]

Another Canadian case that not only endorsed the judicial reasoning in Borys' case but also extended its principles is the case of *Alberta Energy Co. v. Goodwell Corp Ltd.* It is a case of split title in lands. Both the plaintiff and the defendant had different Crown leases over the same land. The defendant was given rights in the lease to

83. [1994] 162 AR 180; [1993] 160 A.R 193 (QB).
84. R.S.A. 1980, c j-1, s. 17(4).
85. Keen, Commonwealth Draft Guidelines for Trans-boundary Unitisations and the Rule of Capture', at 446.
86. *Ibid.*, Deane J. described the principle of unjust enrichment as 'A unifying legal concept which explains why the law recognises, in a variety of distinct categories of cases, an obligation on the part of a defendant to make fair and just restitution for a benefit derived at the expense of a plaintiff and which assists in the determination by ordinary processes of legal reasoning, of the question of whether the law should, in justice, recognise such an obligation in a new or developing category of case.' See *Pavey and Mathews Pty Ltd v. Paul* (1987) 162 CLR 221.

produce natural gas while the plaintiff's right in the lease was in respect of bitumen. The plaintiff had drilled bitumen wells while the defendant had not taken any step to exercise its right to produce the natural gas. On the application of the defendant, the Regulatory authority, Energy and Utilities Board, shut in the bitumen wells drilled by the plaintiff. The Regulator took this action for conservation reason and on the grounds that the plaintiff had no right to produce gas cap gas. The court found that the plaintiff had taken adequate conservation measures and therefore, found no basis for the shut in order. In reliance on Borys case, the court held that the plaintiff was entitled to produce the gas cap gas as it is incidental to petroleum recovery. The defendant's attempt to distinguish this case from the Borys case was rejected by the court. The Court of Appeal extended Borys case and declared that when two parties have sought, paid for and received the right to work and recover different hydrocarbons from the same land, they do not need the agreement of the other party prior to exercising their rights.[87] The court however was very careful in the interpretation of the respective granting instruments so as not to diminish the value of either lessee's interest. The court recognised that both parties had their respective expectation of profiting from their investment and the references to Good-well's compensation are pointer to this. This is unlike the earlier rule of capture cases in which the issue of compensation is never considered as there is no actionable loss arising from capture.[88]

In the case of *Anderson v. Amoco Canada Oil and Gas,* the Supreme Court of Canada considered a dispute that arose from split title lands - between petroleum owner and non-petroleum owner. The issue in the case turned out to be ownership of various reservoir substances especially where the substances undergo phase changes in the course of production from the reservoir. It was argued that gas in solution in the reservoir which belonged to the petroleum owner should become the property of the natural gas owner when it changed phase and evolved to natural gas in the wellbore. In effect, this argument will mean that the rule of capture has been modified or extended because by the Rule, who ever produces first owns the substances. The court upheld this argument and declined to apply the rule of capture. The court was further of the view that the Rule cannot be applied to alter the division of interests in petroleum and non-petroleum substances which the parties had originally agreed to.[89]

From the above cases, it is clear that in split title situation, each of the parties has different grants to different resource over the same tract of land. Therefore, exercise of the rights by one will definitely affect the other. The approach of the court had been the application of the rule of capture to address the two competing rights. As one writer has rightly pointed out, the court has however, not been very clear as to whether the party who in the exercise of his rights unavoidably captures the other's resource becomes the owner of the captured resource or that he is simply not liable.[90] According to her, in the former situation, he can deal with the resource as he pleases without further recourse to the other party but in the latter, he will be liable to account as a trustee of the other

87. *Ibid.*, at 80.
88. Low, 'The Rule of Capture: Its Current Status and Some Issues to Consider', at 814.
89. *Ibid.*
90. *Ibid.*, at 815.

party.[91] From the split title cases above, the party whose resource was captured goes home without compensation or any other form of redress. In Canada, unitisation laws did not make provision for this type of situation. It is therefore, left for the parties to agree on methods of mutual development of the fields. This is comparable to the US where the field to be unitised consists of dual substances – oil rims and gas cap. In this instance, one lessee holds title to oil and the other to gas. But as has happened in the US, this is one of the situation in which it is difficult to reach unitisation agreement. For instance, parties may not agree on timing for development. Party with a relatively large interest in gas might favour early extraction even though the gas might be very useful if left in place to maintain reservoir pressure and enhance oil recovery. The oil rim owner would prefer to delay production of gas until after substantial oil has been recovered from the reservoir. Intervention of the State in the form of compulsory unitisation built on the recognition of property rights of the parties to their respective substance while in place will be very necessary. This will eliminate heavy transaction costs arising from holdouts and strategic bargaining that usually militate against consensus.[92] In other words, it will encourage parties to reach agreement quickly as neither of them can embark on unilateral development. A judicial move to this direction has already been seen in the cases of *Placid oil*[93] (*supra*) and *Lickacz* (*supra*) where the court had modified the rule of capture and that legislation can completely eliminate it. From the cases, this can be done through legislation in several ways – by placing limitation on the quantities of fugacious substance a landowner can withdraw from under his lands. A violation of such limits would attract liability to his neighbour for any injury occasioned. Second, Conservation legislation can modify or topple the rule of capture, and lastly, legislation can establish ownership in oil and gas regardless of their origin within the reservoir.

Having examined the licence granting clauses in both Canadian and Australian legislations and also the common law rule of capture, we shall now analyse their unitisation laws in order to determine the extent to which a Regulator is under a duty to compel unitisation.

Enactment of compulsory unitisation laws in Australia dates back to 1938 in response to the promotion by the commonwealth government, petroleum exploration and production in the administered territories of Papua and New Guinea. The need for compulsory unitisation was further reinforced by the submissions made by the oil companies to the government who feared that drilling on their permits boundaries by rival operators might happen when exploration showed prospects.[94] Consequently, identical ordinances were made, each for Papua and New Guinea called Petroleum

91. *Ibid.*
92. Gary D. Libecap et al., 'The Economic Evolution of Petroleum Property Rights in the United States', at 31. He opined that even though unitisation along with buyouts offered the most complete solution to common pool extraction, disputes over share formula to assign property rights to reservoir revenues and costs made negotiation long and contentious. Where both oil and gas are present in the reservoir in large quantities, agreement is even made more difficult because of 'volatile prices, disparate expectations and the owner's need to manage financial risk as well as reservoir behaviour'.
93. (1963) S.C.R 333.
94. Daintith, 'Finders Keepers? …', at 352-353 at nn. 47 & 48.

(Prospecting and Mining) Ordinances, 1938. These ordinances provided for compulsory unitisation in a similar fashion like the one provided under the Petroleum (production) Regulations 1935 of the U.K. The clause empowers the minister to demand unitisation agreement in appropriate circumstances and to impose one if parties failed to unitise. However, exercise of the minister's power is made conditional in that he can only order unitisation 'for the purpose of securing economy and efficiency and of avoiding wasteful and harmful development practices ...'[95] Issues of equity or interests of the licensees are not mentioned as condition for imposition of unitisation. Other Provinces in Australia subsequently followed the regulations above and enacted uniform unitisation clauses although at different times between 1939 and 1967. However, in 1967 the PSLA was made and the unitisation clause provided therein modified the criterion for compulsory unitisation. Section 59 (3) of the Act provides that:

> [T] he Joint Authority, of its own motion or on application made to the Joint Authority in writing by:
>
> (a) a licensee in whose licence area there is a part of a particular petroleum pool; or
> (b) a person who is lawfully entitled to carry on operations for the recovery of petroleum in an area outside the adjacent area that includes part of a particular petroleum pool that extends into the adjacent area;
>
> may, *for the purpose of securing the more effective recovery of petroleum from the petroleum pool,* direct any licensee whose licence area includes part of the petroleum pool, by instrument in writing served on the licensee, to enter into an agreement in writing, within the period specified in the instrument, for or in relation to the unit development of the petroleum pool and to lodge an application in accordance with section 81 for approval of any dealing to which the agreement relates.

In this clause, compulsory unitisation is made conditional upon been able to '*secure the more effective recovery of petroleum from the petroleum pool.*' It is our view that even though the unitisation clause appeared to have given the minister discretion as to when to compel unitisation, he has no choice other than to order unitisation whenever there is straddling reservoir as the overall goal of unitisation is to secure more effective recovery of petroleum.

It is to be noted that the issues of fairness or equity among adjoining licensees are not addressed in the Unitisation clause above. Therefore, where the Joint Authority refused to order unitisation on the delusion that he is exercising the discretion given in the unitisation clause, drainage may occur if parties could not voluntarily agree to unitise. This clause was incorporated almost in verbatim into the current laws on unitisation (the Offshore Petroleum and Green House Gas Storage Act of 2006). It is to be noted that the power to order unitisation applies only when reservoirs is shared between two holders of production licences, or such a holder and person who is lawfully entitled to recover petroleum outside the offshore area. This provision has

95. *Ibid.*

effectively shut out a holder of exploration permit. A permit holder also enjoys right to recover petroleum in the permit area on appraisal basis, and to carry out operations and execute such works as are necessary for that purposes. Therefore, where he has not obtained production licence, he cannot request compulsory unitisation even if his oil is being drained by a holder of production licence.[96]

In Canada, there is provision for both voluntary and compulsory unitisation in the offshore. For example, voluntary unitisation is provided under section 177 (1) of the Canada-Nova Scotia Accords Implementation Act. It provides that:

> any one or more working interest owners in a pool or part thereof ... together with the royalty owners, may enter into a unit agreement and operate their interests pursuant to the terms of the unit agreement or any amendment thereto ... .

A copy of such agreement or amendment thereof must however be filed with chief Conservation officer.

Section 178 provides for compulsory unitisation. Exercise of the power appeared however, to have been subjected to the discretion of the chief Conservation officer and the Committee. The Conservation officer can only apply to the Committee for an order to compel unitisation, if in his opinion unit operation of a pool will prevent wastes. As we have pointed out one cannot imagine any circumstance in which unitisation will not prevent physical and economic wastes where reservoirs straddles. Therefore we are of the view that the minister has no choice other than to order unitisation once there is straddling reservoir as the necessity to prevent waste automatically presents itself.

Hearing is conducted by the Committee at which all interested persons will be given an opportunity to be heard.[97] The parties must conclude Unit agreement and Unit operating agreement (jointly referred hereafter as 'Unitisation agreements') within the time stipulated (not less than six months) of the making of the order otherwise drilling and production operations will cease until the unitisation agreements are approved by the Committee and the parties have filed them with the Conservation officer.[98] The Committee may however permit the parties to continue operations after the expiration of the six months if in his opinion parties had made progress on reaching unitisation agreements.[99]

Another form of compulsory unitisation is provided under section 179 of the Act. It provides that one or more working interest owners who are parties to unitisation agreements and owned in the aggregate 65% or more of the working interests in the unit area may apply for a unitisation order with respect to the agreements. Hearing is conducted by the committee to determine amongst other things, that 'the unitisation order applied for would accomplish the *more efficient or more economical production of*

96. *Ibid.*, at 355.
97. Section 178 (3) provides that 'if, after the hearing referred to in subsection (2), the Committee is of the opinion that unit operation of a pool or part thereof would prevent waste, the Committee may by order require the working interest owners in the pool or part thereof to enter into a unit agreement and a unit operating agreement in respect of the pool or part thereof.'
98. Section 178 (4) of the Canada-Nova Scotia Accords Implementation Act (*supra*).
99. *Ibid.*, section 178(5).

petroleum from the unitised zone'.[100] The only condition that effectively limits the power of minister to approve request for unitisation is when 65% of the working interests and royalty interests owners have not agreed to the proposed unitisation. The other condition – *'efficient or more economical production of petroleum from the unitised zone'* – will most likely be satisfied once there are straddling reservoirs.

Section 182 provides that unitisation order becomes effective on the day that the Committee determines in the order, but that day shall be not less than thirty days after the day on which the order is made.

Section 186 prohibits further activities within the unit area for the purpose of drilling for or producing petroleum from the unitised zone after the date on which a unitisation order comes into effect except in accordance with the provisions of the unit agreement and the unit operating agreement.

The Act also contains identical provision for voluntary pooling. Where parties do not pool voluntarily, compulsory pooling order is made on the application of one or more working interest owners in a spacing unit. The order directs the working interest owner and royalty owners within the spacing unit to pool their interests in the spacing unit for the purpose of drilling for and producing, or producing, petroleum from the Spacing unit. The effect of the order is that where it is made, all parties to the unit are deemed to have entered into a pooling agreement as set out in the pooling order and it constitutes a binding contract between the parties. Unlike unitisation, the applicant for compulsory pooling order does not have to own 65% of the total working interest in the unit and the unit agreement is not required to be executed by one or more person who owns 65% of the total working interests in the unit. There is prohibition on production of petroleum within a spacing unit in which there are two or more leases or two or more separately owned working interests unless a pooling agreement has been entered into. However, production of petroleum for testing in any quantities approved by the Chief Conservation Officer is exempted.

From the above, we have seen that there appears to be an absolute duty imposed on the Chief conservation officer and the Committee to order compulsory unitisation even though expressed in the law as if they have discretion in the matter. The 'conditions' specified in the law are not strictly 'conditions' as once there is straddling reservoirs the conditions crystalises to 'compulsion.' Once this happens, the minister has no choice other than to enjoin unitisation.

The other form of compulsory unitisation places a limit on the power of the committee to order unitisation in that the applicants must own 65% of the total working interests in the Unit and must have signed the unitisation agreements. The other conditions will in most cases be satisfied because unitisation will accomplish

100. *Ibid.*, section 181. It provides that the committee after conducting hearing on the application, if he found that (a) the unitisation agreements have been executed by one or more working interest owners who own in the aggregate 65% or more of the total working interests in the unit area, and the unit agreement has been executed by one or more royalty owners who own in the aggregate 65% or more of the total royalty interests in the unit area, and (*b*) the unitisation order applied for would accomplish the *more efficient or more economical production of petroleum from the unitised zone,* the Committee may order that the various agreements are valid contract enuring to the benefits of the parties.

more efficient or more economical production of petroleum from the unitised zone. Therefore, this compulsory unitisation provisions cannot prevent all times drainage in certain circumstances (that is where 65 % of working interest owners have not agreed) However, if the Chief Conservation officer and the Committee exercise the mandatory power to compel unitisation in the first form that we stated above, agreement of 65 % will not be necessary as all parties will be mandated to comply with the order.

In the onshore, conservation laws were made by all the oil and gas producing provinces in Canada. Alberta was the first province to enact conservation laws as a direct response to the disastrous consequences of the application of the rule of capture especially as witnessed in the US[101] Among the conservation measures adopted were well spacing, production limitation, drilling targets and minimum setbacks. By well spacing, a number of drainage locations necessary to maximise the recovery of oil and gas were established. It therefore, provides equitable protection for the mineral rights owners and maximises the conservation of the resource. By this, well spacing could protect property rights and mitigate the rule of capture.[102] For example in Saskatchewan province, horizontal well drilling is very common because most of the oil produced is heavy oil. The minimum set-back requirement was set at 100 metres from lease boundary by the Saskatchewan Oil and Gas conservation Regulations. This is to provide some protection from capture. Enough buffer zones were expected to be proposed by applicants for well spacing exemption so that there will be enough spacing between their proposed well and the unit area.[103] Other conservation measures include, Production orders and ratable take orders, Common carrier, Common purchaser, and common processor orders, Pooling and unitisation, and the doctrine of correlative rights. All these measures were introduced to tame the rule of capture but as we have pointed out herein before, they lack capacities to completely eliminate capture. For instance, unitisation agreements are entered into after oil discovery and at secondary recovery operation especially in the US. Most times drainage would have occurred before it is concluded. Moreover, even if drainage is eliminated within a unitised area, it is still possible for drainage to the unitised area or from the unitised area to occur.

5. NETHERLANDS

Netherlands is a civil law country that has experienced the problem of unilateral drainage in oil and gas industry. In Chapter 3, we have shown that in Netherlands, the

101. See Alberta Oil and Gas Conservation Act R.S.A.2000; Oil and Gas Act, R.S.Y. 2002, C.162 (Yukon Oil and Gas Act); Petroleum and Natural Gas Act, R.S.B.C. 1996, C.361 (B.C. Petroleum and Natural Gas Act); Oil and Gas Conservation Act R.S.S. 1978, C.0-2 (Saskatchewan Conservation Act); Canada Oil and Gas Act operations Act, R.S.C 1985, c. 0-7 (COGOA); Oil and Gas Act S.M. 1993, c. 4, CCSM. c. 034 (Manitoba Oil and Gas Act); Gas and Salt Resources Act, R.S.O. 1990, c. P.12 (Ontario Resources Act).
102. Pow, 'The Rule of Capture: Its Current Status and Some Issues to Consider', at 818 citing Rowland Harrison, 'Regulation of Well Spacing in Oil and Gas Production', (1970) Alta. L. Rev. 8: 357 at 363.
103. *Ibid.*, at 819 n. 103.

Mining Act of 1810 and Article 626 of the Dutch Civil Code of 1838 did not make very clear provisions on ownership of mines or minerals.

However, Article 5 of the Mining Act of 1810 provides that 'mines may be exploited only by virtue of a deed of concession'. This includes a landowner who discovers minerals on his own land. Thus, the grants of the concession transferred ownership of the mines to the concessionaire.[104] Perpetual ownership of the minerals is conferred on the concessionaire when a deed of concession is executed in his favour and he has a right of occupation if it is necessary for exploitation. The grant of concession creates a new property in the mineral underneath the land[105] and that the ownership of the mine is separate from the ownership of the surface. Moreover, the ownership would also be regarded as a 'new' ownership for a landowner who acquires a concession over the mine. This will entitle the landowner to payment of compensation.[106] Like in the offshore, three different licences are required for onshore petroleum operations – Reconnaissance work, exploration drilling, and exploration of the minerals (production licence).[107]

In the offshore, the Continental Shelf Act of 1965 provides in Article 22 that 'the minerals present in or on the Continental shelf are the property of the State. Article 23 of the same Act provides that 'the ownership of the minerals produced under a production licence shall pass to the licence holder through the fact of being produced'

An important question is whether the rule of capture has been incorporated by this licensing arrangement. This question is addressed in the case of *Unocal Netherlands B.V & Other v. Continental Netherlands Oil Co. & Others (Conoco)*.[108]

In 2003, a new Mining Act was made by the Dutch Government to replace the 1810 Mining Act, which now vests ownership of minerals in the State.[109] This Act applies to both onshore and offshore petroleum as well as geothermal energy activities.[110] By Article 2 (2), this Act applies to minerals situated at a depth of more than 100 metres below the surface of the earth. Therefore, State ownership is limited to minerals located beyond this depth. Ownership rights of landowners are preserved in respect of

104. Articles 7 and 44.
105. Article 19 of the Mining Act of 1810.
106. Martha Roggenkamp, 'Oil and Gas: Netherlands Law and Practice' (Chancery Law Publishing, 1991), at 25, referring to the Supreme Court case of Weekblad van het Recht, No. 8606 of 25 October 1907.
107. *Ibid.*, at p. 200. Martha Roggenkamp recalled that before the Mining Act of 1903 was enacted to empower the crown to revoke a concession and to make regulations regarding safety matters, the grant of concession meant that the crown has relinquished all control over mining activities. The Mineral exploration Act of 1967 was enacted to enable exploration licence to be granted for onshore exploration activities especially drilling. This system replaced the system whereby the landowner's consent is paramount before a concessionaire can enter upon his land for exploration activities.
108. Case C04/127HR, 14 October 2005, Hoge Raad (Ruling of the Supreme Court of Netherlands) Reported also in http://www.kernkamp.nl/case-law/2009/10/unocal-v-conoco/.
109. Article 3 (1) of the Act provides that 'Minerals are the property of the State.
110. The Act also applies to mining activities such as salt, production of marl and supervision of pitholes. Geothermal energy is the subsoil heat that has its source from natural causes located in 500 metres or more beneath the earth surface.

minerals located above 100 metres.[111] This Act has resolved the lingering problems of ownership of minerals before the grant of a concession as the 1810 Mining Act did not expressly provide for such. Article 3 of the 2003 Mining Act also provides that 'ownership of the petroleum produced under a production licence is transferred to the licence-holder by the production of the said minerals' A very important chapter is the transitional provisions contained in Article 143 (2) (4) which provides that the owner of the previously held onshore concessions shall now hold it as a production licence and shall continue to own the mines underlying its licence area for the duration of the licence.

Article 6 of the Act provides that 'without permission from our minister, it is prohibited (a) to explore for minerals; and (b) to produce minerals. Article 7 confers exclusive rights on the holder of both licences. Under Article 10, a production licence is granted to the holder of exploration licence who has demonstrated the presence of minerals. The licence will be granted for those minerals in the area to which the exploration licence applies. Where the area of the exploration licence has not been delineated, the production licence will only be granted for that part that has been demonstrated contained minerals.

Article 11 (3) provides that:

> [A] licence will specify for which area it is applicable. For the delineation of this area, the limits on the surface are indicated. Unless the licence specifies otherwise, the area shall consist of the surface area indicated and its subsoil.

The necessary question here is whether the above provisions can be interpreted to encapsulate the rule of capture or not. The first leg of the test for determining such question as given by Daintith obviously applies here. The provision of section 11(3) is very clear on this. The production licence is granted over an economically recoverable mineral and its delineated surface area is meant to coincide with the subsurface area – this interpretation is based on the phrase of the licence granting clause – '... *Unless the licence specifies otherwise, the area shall consist of the surface area indicated and its subsoil.*' To this extent, the licensee can only lawfully withdraw the recoverable oil underlying its licence area at the time of grant of the licence. If he withdraws part of the oil coming from adjoining licence area and it can be proved, he may be liable to account to the holder of the licence of that adjoining licence area.

5.1 Unitisation Practice / Capture Problem in Netherlands

The Dutch Royal Decree of 1967 provides in section 28 that:

> [I]f, in the licence area, an economically exploitable quantity of oil or natural gas is demonstrated in a deposit which, at the discretion of the minister is deemed to go beyond the boundary of the licence area, the licensee, *in accordance with a request thereto by the minister, is required to cooperate in reaching an agreement*

111. See Martha Roggenkamp, 'A New Mining Act for the Netherlands – The End of a 200 – Year Debate', [2003] I.E.L.T.R. at pp. 185-186. See also Land Clearing Act of 1996 (as amended). The normal accession rule of the Civil Code applies. Minerals accede to the ownership of the land.

> *between the licensee and the party entitled to produce oil or gas in the adjoining area,* in pursuance of which the production will be carried out in mutual consultation.

The necessary question that follows the above provision is as to whether a holder of a production licence has a duty to exercise restraint in draining petroleum from a straddling field without unitisation. This was one of the issues that came up in the case of *Unocal Netherlands B.V. v. Continental Netherlands Oil Co.* (*supra*). The plaintiff (Unocal) held a production licence in respect of block Q1 while the defendant (Conoco) also held a production licence in adjacent block L16a. Unocal had not yet operated a well in the block. Both blocks form part of the Logger Field, an oilfield in the Continental shelf in North Sea. Before 1985, Conoco drilled some wells in its block. In 1984 and 1985, the parties exchanged information and on that basis agreed that the reservoir in the Logger field extends to adjacent block, Q1. In 1985, Conoco started production from two wells and one of the wells had been drilled within 125 meters from the border between the blocks contrary to the Government licensing regulations. By virtue of section 28 of the Royal Dutch Decree of 1967, where there is straddling reservoir, a licensee is expected to cooperate, upon request by the minister, with the adjoining licensee in reaching agreement as to how production will be carried out in mutual consultation.[112]

However, neither of the parties reported the straddling to the Minister until December 1992 when Unocal filed in its report on the straddling and requested the minister to order unitisation. The minister initially accepted Unocal's request but later reversed the decision in 1994 when Conoco objected on the ground that there were no longer economically recoverable oil in Unocal's block as it has all been produced by Conoco. As a result of the exhausted status of the oilfield, the minister was of the opinion that there exists no legal ground to force the parties to enter into unitisation agreement as the law did not contain regulations regarding unitisation of historical revenues. Therefore, any disputes concerning rights to past oil produced would have to be addressed by the civil courts. In 1998, Unocal took the matter to court claiming that Conoco acted or were acting unlawfully or at least enriched themselves unjustly at the expense of Unocal and also the sum of USD 97,524,713 as damages. Unocal based the above claim on the premise that Conoco had violated the exclusive subjective right of Unocal to produce oil found in its licence area and that Conoco has acted in conflict with what is befitting in a social and economic sense by not informing Unocal that block Q 1 overflows to block L 16a. Conoco in its defence, argued that even if they had extracted any oil from block Q 1 – which they had disputed – they were entitled to do

112. Daintith, 'Finders Keepers? ...', at 363. The criterion for ordered unitisation by the minister is that there must be present economically exploitable quantity of oil or natural gas in the deposit. The court has interpreted this provision to the effect that the extension must contain economically exploitable quantity of oil before unitisation can be ordered. Daintith had argued correctly that the criterion is satisfied if exploitation is economic by way of recovery via a well or wells placed in the block covering the main area of the field. Our view in this book is that the criterion will also be satisfied even if economically exploitable quantity of oil exists in only one of the blocks covering the area of the field. Economically exploitable quantity of oil does not have to exist at both sides of the divide by virtue of the wordings of the regulation.

so based on the rule of capture which according to her, forms part of Dutch law. The District Court rejected Unocal's claim on 1 April 1998 on the ground that the rule of capture applies. Unocal appealed to the Appellate Court in The Hague. Conoco argued in the appeal that they did not know and still do not know whether block L16a was a field that straddles block Q1 and that Unocal did not demonstrate such straddling.

Two interlocutory rulings were delivered by the appellate court – The first one was delivered on 19 October 2000. The Court ruled that:

> 1 A production licence gives the licence holder the exclusive right to produce petroleum (among other things) in the licence area. The exclusive right is a proprietary right, the value of which is determined by the quantity of minerals that can be produced from or in that area and the extent to which this production, in view of the costs it will involve, is economically feasible.'
> 2 With regards to the rule of capture, the court ruled that in Public law, the regulation on straddling fields though it is important, but it is not decisive. This is because it is written in the public interests, which the Government would have to promote, and not so much in the interests of the licensee in the adjacent licence area. Therefore, 'the extraction of petroleum from an adjacent licence area, for which another party holds a production licence, is an infringement on the subjective right of that other party because this affects the petroleum deposit in that area and with the value of the other party's exclusive right to produce petroleum.'
> 3 From social and economic point of view, a licence holder must observe due care when producing from a field that straddles adjacent licence area. The due care implies that he must inform the other licensee as he ought to reasonably assume that he was producing or has produced in its licence area an economically extractable, more than negligible, quantity of oil originating in the licence area of another party. If he wishes to continue the production he ought to open negotiations about unitisation agreement.
> 4 From the circumstances of this case, the court assumed that, except there is evidence to the contrary, there was an overflowing oil field and that reasonably, Conoco ought to have known that they had produced an economically extractable quantity of oil from the production of which Unocal was entitled as the licence holder of block Q 1. This is a rebuttable presumption and as such, the court further ruled that Conoco will have to give counter-evidence in support of the argument that they *'could reasonably have expected that the field overflowed to such an extent that, from an economic point of view production was negligible for Q 1 licence holders.'*
> 5 The mere fact that Unocal was aware that there was possible overflow of its field into Conoco's field and nevertheless did not undertake production (but sat idly by), is not enough to create an assumption that Unocal had relinquished its right to utilise its production licence in respect of oil which was found in block Q 1 or of its right to compensation of damages. Although the late claim of Unocal would make it difficult for Conoco to furnish evidence to rebut the presumption mentioned above, this difficulty created by Unocal is not unreasonable considering the circumstances of this case, including Conoco's attitude of concealing the facts of straddling.

On 18 December 2003, the appellate court gave a second interlocutory ruling. The ruling explained the manner of conduct expected of a production licensee in a social and economic sense when he produces from straddling fields, thus:

(1) A production 'licence holder who extracts petroleum from straddling fields in which another party is a production licence holder, infringes unlawfully on the subjective right of that other party to the exclusive production of petroleum from that adjacent area if it must reasonably assume that it has extracted or is extracting oil from the licence area of the other party in such quantities that from the point of view of the other licence holder, this is an economically extractable quantity, and it does not inform the other party and does not open negotiations with that other party about the conclusion of a unification agreement.'

(2) 'The proprietary right of the holder of the production licence does not consist in ownership of the oil found in the licence area, but in the exclusive right to produce this oil, and the value of that right is determined (not so much by the quantity of oil located in that area) by the quantity of oil that can be produced from that area and the extent to which this production is economically feasible. The mere extraction of oil from the adjacent area therefore, does not necessarily mean an infringement on the value of the exclusive right of the neighbouring licence holder.'

(3) For there to be an infringement, there must be an 'economic extractable quantity of oil that has been or is being extracted from the adjacent licence area. Whether it is ultimately indeed produced by the person extracting it is not important. What is important is whether the extracted oil would have been economically extractable in any way for the licence holder of the block from which it was extracted.'

(4) The court specified that economic extractability must be judged by using an Objective standard. The court posited that 'The question whether the party extracting the oil should reasonably have assumed that – from the point of view of the other licence holder – it involved a quantity of oil that was economically extractable must be judged according to objective standards. The point of departure is what a skilled licence holder with the knowledge and the State of the art which was available at the time ought to have understood.'

(5) 'In determining the quantity of oil that is economically extractable from the point of view of other licence holder, one must look at the economic extractability of oil which is/was located in the part of the field flowing over into the licence area of the other party. The extra costs that would be entailed in the production of this oil must be weighed against the yield to be expected from that oil. An estimate of these costs must be based on the most attractive manner of production in an economic sense, so perhaps also – if necessary after a unification agreement has been concluded – production from a well in the licence area of the party extracting that oil.'

(6) 'The court agreed with both parties that if the posited circumstances occur, the operator of the field informs the licence holder of the adjacent licence area and opens negotiations about a unification agreement, but not that it ceases production.'

(7) The court concluded that based on the testimony and other details, Conoco had provided sufficient evidence to rebut the presumption that he ought reasonably to have known he was extracting an economically extractable quantity of oil from the adjacent licence area. Consequently, the court ruled that Conoco was not obliged to inform Unocal at any time before 1992 and also need not approach Unocal for unification agreement. Unocal is not entitled to damages as he was not involved from the outset or during the exploitation of the straddling fields.

Subsequently, the court considered whether the action of Conoco could be regarded as an unlawful extraction of oil from block Q 1. Conoco had calculated that the quantity of the oil in place in block Q 1 was 910,000 barrels out which they extracted some 500,000 barrels via block L 16a. (From the investigation carried out in Netherlands, we gathered that the total quantity of production from the L 16a block was 30 million barrels out of which 330,000 barrels originated from block Q 1). According to Conoco these are not quantities that would be economically extractable from the point of view of Unocal.[113] Unocal disputed these figures and argued that the circumstance that Conoco extracted the oil and subsequently made profit on it together with the other oil which it produced in that field, implies that the quantity of oil removed from block Q 1 was an economically extractable quantity.

Arising from the above, apart from the obligation to inform Unocal during the course of exploitation after 1992, the extraction of oil from Q 1 by Conoco is an infringement of the personal exclusive right of Unocal to produce oil from block Q1 provided, the oil would have been economically extractable by Unocal in some other way. The damages suffered by Unocal can be measured by determining the yield from the oil to be produced less the costs that Unocal would have had to incur in order to produce the oil, whether or not this production will take place via an existing well in block L16a - after concluding an agreement to that end with Conoco. The appellate court noted that it would require expert testimony to determine how many barrels of oil were removed by Conoco from Q 1, how many barrels could Unocal produce out of the removed oil (whether or not via block L16a after an agreement with Conoco) and what profit Unocal could have made on that.

The appellate court concluded that assuming that it has been established that Conoco extracted a given quantity of oil from Block Q 1; it could be required of Conoco to provide detail facts to substantiate their defence that from the point of view of Unocal, this quantity was not economically extractable.

Dissatisfied with the above ruling, Unocal lodged an appeal at the Supreme Court against both Interlocutory rulings while Conoco also cross-appealed. The Supreme

113. Conoco has argued that based on the extensive reservoir/production field modeling, a total of 330,000 barrels of oil was produced from block Q 1 out of a total production of 30 million barrels (up to the time the filed was sold) and as such the amount of oil would not have covered unitisation cost of Unocal. Conoco therefore argued that Unocal has yet to prove that he has suffered any economic loss as a result of the development of Block L 16a (Logger field).

Court, after assessing all the grounds of both appeals, rejected them and confirmed the two interlocutory ruling of the appellate court.

At the Supreme Court, Unocal amongst other things, argued that the appellate court erroneously ruled or gave insufficient grounds for having ruled that Conoco was only obliged to inform Unocal and to open negotiation for the conclusion of unitisation agreement from the time when Conoco should reasonably have assumed that they were removing a quantity of oil that, from the point of view of Unocal, was economically extractable. Unocal argued further that Conoco was acting unlawfully as soon as he suspects that there is such a big chance that, by removing oil, they are infringing on the subjective right of Unocal or conducting themselves contrary to what is befitting in a social and economic sense, that they should have refrained from this conduct and should either have informed Unocal and held negotiations with them, or have stopped.

In assessing this argument, the Supreme Court considered the ruling of the appellate court on the issue. The appellate court was of the view that on the basis of what is deemed to be fitting in a social and economic sense, Conoco is obliged to inform Unocal as soon as they had to take into account the fact that their field might flow over into Unocal's field. The Court then went further to consider the point at which Conoco was obliged to inform Unocal. The appellate court ruled that it is at the point where Conoco reasonably had to assume that they were removing oil, or would remove oil, from block Q 1 in a quantity that was economically extractable for Unocal. After extensive investigation, the appellate court ruled that it had not been established that Conoco should reasonably have assumed at any moment that they were removing from the block Q1, a quantity of oil that was extractable from the point of view of Unocal and that for this reason it cannot be concluded that Conoco were obliged to inform Unocal at any time before 1992. The Supreme Court ruled that the Appellate court's ruling above is not incomprehensible and that sufficient reasons had been given for it. The court also ruled that the requirement of due care does not imply that Conoco should stop production.

Investigation at Conoco office in Netherlands reveals that parties have not yet commenced implementation of the judgment since the case is not yet closed as it is yet to be established whether Unocal has been successful in proving damages. The parties have however appointed an independent expert who will construct an economic model that would mimic a situation that Unocal would have come into the field and unitised in 1994. The model however is still a big 'what if' scenario. All the inputs parameters such as the equity split have still not been agreed by both parties.

The reasoning of the court, it is submitted, represents a modern way of viewing a production licence. It was treated as a property in that it constitutes a legal right that is directly enforceable against third parties by the holder of the licence. Therefore, drainage of oil from a production licence area was regarded as a violation of that right as it affects the quantity of oil in that area and consequent diminution in the value of the party's exclusive right to produce oil.[114] The ruling of the court also reflects the basic principles underlying unitisation scheme, i.e., entitlement of each of the parties

114. *Ibid.*, at 362.

to the oil reserves underneath his licence area. Hence, the learned Justices at the Court of Appeal relied on the explanatory memorandum to section III: 28 of the Royal Decree of 1967 which provides that in unitisation agreement, as a rule, parties will first determine to which reserves each of the parties is entitled.[115]

One other point to note in this case is that it borders on production licence in the Continental shelf where the statute has expressly vested ownership of the oil in place in the State while title to oil produced, is vested in the licence holder that produces it.[116] Notwithstanding this provision, the court overruled the rule of capture and allowed the apportionment rule to prevail. The economic extractability criterion prescribed by the court only goes to the root of damages/compensation assessment or whether or not Unocal is entitled to compensation in the circumstance. All these depends on proof which Unocal according to the court, has not been able to establish, that is, Conoco reasonably ought to have known that they were extracting volume of oil that was economically extractable in some way by Unocal (whether or not via block L16a after an agreement with Conoco). That was why the court held that Unocal cannot be compensated for oil withdrawn by Conoco before 1992 because that was the date that both parties reported the straddling to the Regulator. However, this does not defeat the holding of the court that the unilateral extraction by Conoco was an infringement of the production rights of Unocal.

It is to be noted that the unitisation provisions under the 1967 Royal Decree has been slightly modified in sections 42 (2) and 23(1) (2) of the 2003 Mining Act. Section 42 (2) provides that:

> if a licence for the production of minerals or terrestrial heat applies to an area in which a deposit is present which can reasonably be expected to extend beyond the boundary of the licence area, the licence holder is obliged to cooperate in reaching an agreement between the licence holder and the party entitled to produce minerals or terrestrial heat in the adjacent area, unless Our minister grants an exception from this obligation. The agreement shall be aimed at production in mutual agreement.

Section 23 (1) provides that a licensee shall not proceed with production from straddling reservoirs without unitisation agreement or cooperative exploitation except the Minister grants an exemption with respect to obligation to conclude agreement. Section 23 (2) makes the obligation to continue even during or after production had taken place. The combined effect of the above provisions is that there is a positive obligation on licensees to unitise where there is straddling reservoirs unless the minister grants an exception. The ground upon which the minister may grant exception is not specified. It may probably be at his discretion. Where he does not grant an exception, it becomes mandatory for licensees to unitise and as such the provision will have the effect of eliminating capture completely. However, where the Minister grants such an exception that has the implication of allowing drainage, capture issue may still

115. *Ibid.* He is however of the view that the memorandum referred to above carried no implication as to the pre-existing rights of the parties.
116. Sections 22 and 23 of the Continental Shelf Mining Act 1967.

be relevant. Therefore, the party whose acreage is drained can still invoke the Unocal's case.[117]

6. CONCLUSION

The petroleum laws and regulations of some countries are silent on whether or not the rule of Capture will govern petroleum extraction (UK and Nigeria). To determine this, the relevant Petroleum licence granting clauses will have to be interpreted to see whether or not the Rule will apply. In the UK, one school of thought has interpreted the licence granting clause as encapsulating the rule of capture because the clause granted to the licensee exclusive rights 'to search, bore for and get petroleum' that is not restricted to the petroleum underlying his lease at the time of the grant, but that it covers any petroleum that he gets therein at any time. Therefore, if petroleum from adjoining lease migrates to the lease of the licensee at the time of extraction, the petroleum belongs to him when it enters his well. We have argued that the said clause should be interpreted to mean that the rights conferred by the licence is restricted to the petroleum underlying the lease area at the time of the grant and does not cover petroleum migrating from adjoining lease during exploitation. It is also noted that there is no statutory rule of capture as it is not an incident of the rights granted by the licence. The unitisation clauses of some of the countries that we referred to herein appeared to have given the Minister discretion to compel unitisation and that a licensee is only under a duty to unitise when directed to do so by the Minister. However, in spite of this, we have argued that the supposed 'discretion' given to the Minister would crystalise to 'compulsion' the moment there is a straddling reservoir. This is because the conditions that must happen before the Minister can compel unitisation have self-enforcement capacity as they become real the moment there is a straddling reservoir. For example, unitisation will promote ultimate recovery; it will also eliminate competitive drilling and therefore, will promote national interests and the interests of both licensees. There is therefore, no room for the exercise of ministerial discretion once there is straddling reservoir. Where the interest of one licensee (i.e., licensee with small extension) will not be served by unitisation, the solution lies in 'buy-out' and not in unilateral development as this will violate the licence conditions. In addition, the fact that the licence granting clause does not encapsulate the rule of capture means that the minister is expected to order unitisation at all times. This also translates to the duty of the licensee such that where the Minister failed to order unitisation, a licensee will still be under an obligation to unitise. Therefore, where the Minister neglected or failed to enjoin unitisation in reliance on the discretion in the unitisation clause and drainage occurs, the Minister may be in violation of the laws.

The petroleum legislations of some other countries however, provided that 'property' or 'title' or 'ownership' of petroleum vests in the licensee by virtue of been produced (Australia, Canada and Netherlands). For these countries, it may by implication means that the rule of capture will govern petroleum extraction. However, in

117. Daintith, 'Finders Keeper? ...', above at 367.

practice the court of one of the countries (Netherlands) has ruled otherwise. Netherlands' approach represents an effective way of tackling the problems of unilateral capture. This is illuminating considering that the notion of property has been given a restrictive definition in that country. A production licence is regarded as not property but contractual rights. Yet the court has equated this right to property and thus, gave it a legal force that binds third party. If the word 'title' or 'property' used in both the Canadian and Australian legislations respectively, is construed as meaning 'ownership', it is submitted that since there is a difference between 'ownership' and 'property interest', a licensee would have property interests in petroleum while in place and obtain ownership thereof when produced and reduced to possession.[118]

The above reasoning is in line with our analytical framework in Chapter 2, the analysis of legal nature of petroleum lease and the interests created in the licensee in Chapter 3 and our conclusion in Chapter 4, where we have seen that there is commonality among the countries we have studied that the 'property' concepts encompasses varieties of interests and rights that are proprietary in nature even though they do not rise to the status of 'ownership.' For instance a Petroleum production licence/lease is one of such proprietary rights which we have said encompasses the underlie assets (Reservoir oil). In other words, Reservoir oil constitutes a fundamental strand in the sticks that make up the proprietary rights of the licensee in the licence.

However, contrary to our view of the law above, the approach adopted by the Regulators in practice have shown that:

(i) the Regulators in some of the countries (Nigeria, Netherlands and UK) that we have examined have either neglected to enforce unitisation or have evinced an intention by policy, not to enforce unitisation whenever there is straddling reservoirs.

(ii) the Regulators are more concerned with national interest than issue of equity and fairness between groups of licensees. This is because mineral oil resource belongs to the State. The State only assigned its rights in the resources to the companies through Licensing for consideration of production shares, taxes, royalties and rents or other benefits from the licence area. The Host State's interest lies in speedy production of hydrocarbons and as such the State is not adversely affected in the short run where there is drainage of oil resources by one licensee from reservoir that straddles adjoining licence area. Where the petroleum contractual regime is based on concessionary or licensing model, State's revenue stream lies only in taxes and royalty. In such cases, if the drainage is from a lower royalty and tax field to a higher royalty and tax field, the drainage is more beneficial to the State. Where the contractual regime is founded upon Production Sharing Contract (PSC) in which the National Oil Company (NOC) is the Concessionaire, whichever side the drainage falls, the State will not lose especially if the State's profit oil split is the same on each side of the divide or if the profit oil

118. A.W. Walker Jr., 'The Nature of the Property Interests Created by an Oil and Gas Lease in Texas', (1928) Texas Law Review 7: 1, at p. 2 (n. 2).

split is larger in the field that is draining oil. Moreover, in typical PSC regime, the State oil company is the Concessionaire and as such where the field is operated on PSC is draining a field operated on a sole risk or Joint venture basis, the State benefits more and consequently, the Regulator may not order unitisation and where drainage had occurred before the State Regulatory organs compel unitisation, the order is not made effective from the date of first production. There are regulations empowering the Regulatory Authority to force Unitisation by imposing a field development plan on the licensees where they could not reach agreement. However, such power is either exercised belatedly or not at all because of the reasons stated herein.

(iii) Regulators themselves may have been captured by the oil Operators. This may happen where the Regulator does not have access to an independent source of information or data on a particular field. The Regulators have no other alternative than to rely solely on the information supplied by the Operators. We have seen in several cases in Chapter 5 where the Operators concealed from the Regulators, straddling reservoirs and deviated vertical wells. In Nigeria and Netherlands, most of the cases of unilateral drainage and competitive drilling were as a result of concealment on the part of the Operators. It is either inadequate data were supplied to the Regulator or field development plan submitted to the Regulator concealed straddling. There is therefore information asymmetry between the Regulator and the Operators leading to the capture of the former. However, there were some cases of straddling that were reported to the Regulator that it also failed to compel unitisation at the appropriate time.

(iv) Unitisation clauses are not appropriately worded. The ‘conditions’ attached to the exercise of the Minister’s power cannot be regarded as ‘conditions’ in the strict sense of the word and as such, the duty to order unitisation is mandatory on the Regulator. However, because they did not realise this, they had allowed unilateral capture to take place rather than withholding development licences and then referred the innocent party to seek remedies in the law court. The courts in the common law countries that we have examined would, following the precedent in the United States, likely apply the common law rule of capture in spite of the compulsory unitisation laws.

(v) Licensees have latched on to these defects and the delusion of the Regulators as to the correct application of the clause, to violate their licence obligations by carrying out unilateral development and production from straddling reservoirs.

From the decisions of the courts in one of the common law countries (Canada), we have also discovered that where it favours the Government in order to fulfil tax purposes, the rule of capture has been modified so that property interests will attach to petroleum no matter where it is located in the reservoir or by whom it is produced and that the property remained attached to the petroleum when it is produced. But this same principle was denied a licensee. However, this shows that it is plausible to attach proprietary interest to reservoir oil.

Moreover, the case has shown that in appropriate circumstances, the court is enjoined to take judicial notice of equitable principles as provided in the Judicature Act. This means that compulsory unitisation, built on the recognition of property rights of the parties to their respective oil and gas while in place, is very necessary for equitable reasons.

Drawing together our findings and observations above, the facts remained that the property rights of a holder of production licence in the oil and gas while still in the reservoir has not been adequately protected as it may be lost through drainage by an adjoining licensee and as a result of the approach adopted by the Regulators to unitisation which has shown that they embraced the application of the common law rule of capture. The necessary implication of this is that there is no protection for the property right of the licensee in the oil and gas while still in the reservoir in all the countries that we examined except Netherlands. The property right, though recognised by the municipal legislations, is not protected due to the operation of the common law rule of capture. Therefore, the next chapter is aimed at investigating whether, having regard to the findings regarding the Regulators' failure to enforce unitisation as provided in the laws, the State can be held to have violated its international obligations especially where a foreign investor has been adversely affected due to unilateral drainage. The chapter will also examine the extent to which this property right of an investor could be protected under the Investment treaty and International human rights instruments.

CHAPTER 7

Protecting Property Right in Discovered Petroleum Reservoir

1. INTRODUCTION

In the domanial regimes, petroleum laws and regulations were enacted to provide for compulsory unitisation of straddling oil and gas reservoirs with the hope that it will permanently annihilate the rule of capture. This assumption was wrong because as shown in Chapter 6, the Regulators are more often than not, failing to compel unitisation at the appropriate time. In addition, unitisation agreements are difficult to reach among licensees.[1] For instance, in Nigeria where over 138 fields are begging to be unitised, only three unitisation agreements (Amenam / Kpono fields, Samabri/Biseni fields and Jisike/Izombe fields) have been successfully concluded since oil was discovered in 1956.[2] Consequently, an Operator may become impatient and pursue unilateral development option.

As a result, once drainage occurs, issues of property rights protection will arise. Ancillary issues that may also arise are how to prove drainage[3] and apportionment of past costs and production. Moreover, in Chapters 3, 4 and 6 it has been shown that Petroleum production licence is a property and that it grants proprietary interest to the licensee in respect of the underlie oil and gas resources. Reservoir oil is therefore, one of the species of property rights at play in upstream oil and gas projects. In the US and Canada, we have seen that, even though there is both judicial and legislative

1. See pp. 214-215 for the reasons.
2. See Olufemi A. Ajayi et al., 'Current Challenges in Unitisation – The Nigerian Experience', A paper presented at the 34th Annual SPE International Conference and Exhibition held in Tinapa-Calabar, Nigeria, 31 July-7 August 2010, published in SPE International (SPE 140614) at p. 2. The Samabri / Biseni fields – were finally unitised in 2011 after eighteen years of protracted negotiation – see M. Oriafor, 'Unitisation & Joint Development in Nigeria' (Unpublished paper) presented at the Department of Petroleum Resources on the 12 December 2012.
3. Evidence to prove drainage includes expert opinion, seismic data and drilling of wells to show that oil exists.

recognition of the correlative rights of landowners in the oil and gas in the common reservoir, this specie of property right has not been given protection at common law as a result of the operation of the rule of capture.

From the manner in which the unitisation clauses are couched, coupled with the policy Statements made by UK Department of Trade and Industry (DTI) in its Guidance notes and the 2008 Guidelines for unitisation in Nigeria, it can be discerned that there is no protection of this property right even though this specie of property right exists in the domestic laws of these common law countries. It is only in Netherlands, a civil law country that the property right has been given some level of protection by its Supreme Court.

One of the most serious problems posed by unilateral capture is therefore, its potential of destroying property rights to unexploited oil and gas resources. Efforts by the lessee or lessor to vindicate this specie of property right were only confined to seeking contractual or private law remedies through the domestic courts in the US and hence, minimal success was achieved. No effort has been made to vindicate this right at the international tribunals or courts where the State has through its regulatory Agency mediated in the disagreement between the two licensees in this context, and has rendered one form of decision or the other, that makes either of the parties unsatisfied or where the State itself is guilty of some misconducts, an alternative avenue for protecting the rights of the dissatisfied party may be possible through the International investment treaties[4] and international human rights norms regarding property protection.

Therefore, this chapter examines the legal issues of retroactivity of costs and production and the implication of failure by the Regulators to compel unitisation or to make unitisation order effective from date of first production, on the States' obligations under investment treaties and Human rights instruments. It also explored the plausibility of protection for the rights under modern Investment treaty and International human rights laws under A1P1 of ECHR.

2. RETROACTIVITY OF UNITISATION ORDER, COSTS AND PRODUCTION

2.1 Accession Regimes

In the United States, the issue of retroactive production and costs is tied to the question of whether the spacing or pooling order of the regulatory authority should have retroactive effects or not. The issue has not been very simple to resolve as it has generated conflicting decisions of the courts. Before we consider this issue in the domanial ownership of petroleum regimes, it will be necessary to consider the jurisprudence on the issue in the US in order to understand the policies and interests considered by the courts in determining whether spacing or pooling order is effective retroactively.

4. Michael Polkinghorne, 'Unitisation and Redetermination: Right or Obligation', (2007) J. Energy Nat. Resources L. 25(3): at 319.

For the purpose of this research, five States will only be considered. These are Texas, Louisiana, Oklahoma, North Dakota and Nebraska.[5] The common issue of unilateral drainage and retroactivity among these States is whether or not the spacing or pooling order of the Regulatory Authority should be effective from the date the order was made or from the date of the first production or from the date of application for spacing or pooling.

2.1.1 *Texas*

Texas is an ownership in place State but also applies the rule of capture so that such ownership may be lost to the neighbour through legitimate drainage.[6] In response to the negative effects of the rule of capture, conservation laws were made so that the Regulator (Rail Road Commission) can compel pooling of interests. This power cannot be exercised however, unless the Regulator receives petition from one party to that effect.[7] Where the Regulator receives petition and issue a unit order, the question that arises is whether such order can have retroactive effect. In the case of *Buttes Resources Co. v. Railroad Commission of Texas*,[8] Sixty days after hearing an application for pooling, the Regulator issued an order pooling the applicant's interests with part of an existing unit operated by the plaintiff. The Regulator made the order effective from the date of hearing the application. The Texas appellate court upheld the order for pooling but refused to make it retroactive on the ground that it will interfere with the producing owner's vested property right to do as to what he pleases with his property as guaranteed by the Texas constitution.[9]

2.1.2 *Louisiana*

Louisiana is non-ownership in place State and has by its Mineral Code, adopted the rule of capture to straddling oil and gas extraction.[10] In spite of this however, the code recognises the correlative rights and duties the owners of land overlying the producing formation have to each other in the development and production of oil and gas from the

5. Even though the Mineral codes of these States differ in wordings, they have similar effects as to the issue of unilateral drainage and retroactivity.
6. *Elliff v. Texon Drilling Co.* (1948) Tex. 575, 210 S.W.2d 558 at 561, the court declared that 'In Texas and in other jurisdiction, a different rule exists as to ownership. In our State the landowner is regarded as having absolute title in severalty to the oil and gas in place beneath his land. The only qualification of that rule of ownership is that it must be considered in connection with the rule of capture ... .'
7. The party seeking pooling will have to first make a fair and reasonable offer of voluntary pooling to the producing party. If such offer is not accepted, he will forward a petition to the Regulator. See The Minerals Pooling Act, Tex. Natural Resources Code Ann. Section 102.001-112 (Vernon 1978) cited by Stephen S. Williams, 'Can A Louisiana Unit Order be effective retroactively' (1988-1989) 49 La. L. Rev. 1119 at 1125.
8. 732 S.W.2d 675 (Tex. Ct. App. 1978).
9. *Ibid.*, this case has been criticised by Stephen Williams as dubious and could not be persuasive enough because of the imprecise nature of the court's reasoning.
10. *Ibid.*, this case has been criticised by Stephen Williams as dubious and could not be persuasive enough because of the imprecise nature of the court's reasoning.

common reservoir.[11] In response to the rule of capture, the conservation law also provides for compulsory pooling of minerals interests into drilling units when the owners failed to pool voluntarily.[12] Once a unit is established, none of the parties can explore or develop their respective tracts for oil and gas.[13]

The issue of retroactivity of the order of the Regulator came up in the case of *Desormeaux v. Inexco Oil Co.*[14] The defendant drilled and produced oil and gas on the 20 September 1970 from the land leased from the plaintiff. The Regulator established a spacing unit that comprised both the land leased by the defendant and the one owned by the plaintiff which he had not leased out. The unit order was made effective from 30 June 1971. The defendant had paid royalty on the leased land to the plaintiff prior to the effective date of the spacing order. With respect to the un-leased land, the plaintiff claimed that the spacing unit order should be made retroactive to 20 September 1970 when the defendant began production so that he can be entitled to the net production attributable to the un-leased land. Alternatively, the plaintiff claimed production attributable to the un-leased land from the effective date of the spacing order but without any deduction of costs of drilling and completion of the well.[15] The trial court refused to make the spacing order retroactive on the ground that Louisiana is a non-ownership State and as such, the rule of capture applies to production had before the spacing unit was established. The plaintiff's alternative claim was upheld because the court felt that the well has paid out prior to the effective date of the spacing and therefore, the costs of drilling the well and its completion cannot be charged against the production share of the plaintiff. This is to disallow the defendant from obtaining double recovery, one from the production prior to the date of spacing, and another from production thereafter. This means that production was allocated to the plaintiff from the date of spacing order but the costs of well drilling and completion was not charged against his production share.

There are other cases that followed the above case in Louisiana and they are to the effect that a unit order cannot be made retroactive to the date of first production and that the adjacent owners cannot share in production until a unit is created.[16]

2.1.3 *Oklahoma*

Oklahoma is a non-ownership State that also applies the rule of capture. Its unitisation law is similar to that of Louisiana. The issue of retroactivity has also resonated in the jurisprudence of the State.

---

11. Louisiana Minerals Code, La. R.S. (1989) Articles 1-215 cited by Williams, 'Can A Louisiana Unit Order be effective retroactively'.
12. *Ibid.*, Article 9.
13. *Ibid.*, Article 31:10 (A) (1).
14. *Ibid.*, Articles 9 & 10.
15. 298 So.2d 897 9La. App. 3d Cir.
16. *Pierce v. Goldking* 396 So. 2d 528 (La. App. 3d Cir.) and *Burley v. Sunbelt Royalty Inc.* 543 So. 2d 101 (La. App. 3d Cir. 1988).

In the case of *Wood Oil Co. v. Corporation Commission,*[17] the plaintiff began production on 21 December 1946. Spacing unit was established by the Regulator on 1 April 1947 followed by a compulsory pooling order in July 1947 after voluntary pooling had failed. The Regulator made the pooling order to take effect from 21 December 1946 when the first production began which also has the effect of allocating production from that date. The Oklahoma Supreme Court held that the Regulator's pooling order can only be made retroactive to the date that spacing unit was established. Therefore, allocation of production can only take effect from that date and not from the date of first production.

The court based its judgment on the fact that Oklahoma is a non-ownership State and that the rule of capture applies though, subject to the power of the Regulator to prevent waste. The estoppel argument of the plaintiff to the effect that the defendant delayed in asserting his right to share in the production was however rejected by the court on the ground that the plaintiff suffered no prejudice by the delay. With regards to the cost of well drilling, completion and maintenance, the court held that the defendant was liable to pay his proportionate share notwithstanding that he did not share in the production before the spacing unit was established.

The case of *L.O Ward v. Corporation Commission*[18] followed the above reasoning and held that Regulator's order can only be made retroactive to the date that spacing unit was established because that was the date that the defendant's right to drill a well was denied. Therefore, the defendant can share in production from that date. The plaintiff's contention that the sharing of production by the defendant should take effect from the date of pooling order (which came after the date of spacing order) was rejected by the court.

The above position has been slightly modified based on the wordings of the Oklahoma statute which prohibited drilling once an application for spacing is filed.[19] Therefore, in the case of *C.H. Kuykendall v. Helmerich & Payne Inc.*,[20] the Oklahoma Supreme Court held that a pooling order should be made retroactive to the date the application is filed and not when the spacing unit or pooling unit was established. The right to share in the production from that unit is retroactive to that date as well.

However, as regards the drilling costs, the non-drilling party may be charged with a share of the drilling costs even though he did not receive share from production had before the application for spacing order. This was in agreement with the court's decision in *Wood Oil Co case.*

17. (1950) OK 207, 205 OKla. 537,239.P.2d 1023, see also *Cowling v. Board of oil, Gas and Mining* (1991) 830 P. 2d 220. The court held that Conservation Act might have modified the rule of capture but it has not wholly displaced it and that before a spacing order is entered, the statutory correlative rights was nothing more than a 'a right to an undifferentiated and unquantifiable interest in an oil or gas pool beneath one's land'. That it was wrong to make pooling order retroactive to a time before the spacing order was made because this 'would give adjoining interest owners correlative rights before those rights are definable' see also Daintith, 'Finders Keeper? ...', at 296.
18. 01 P.2d 503 (Okla. 1972).
19. 52 O.S. 1981, s. 87. 1(e).
20. 741 P. 2d 869 (Okla. 1987).

2.1.4 *North Dakota*

The issue of retroactive pooling orders could also arise in situation in which the two parties hold an undivided interest in a piece of land. According to Professor Owen L Anderson, the issue is well settled in North Dakota and in many jurisdictions as the decisions were based on the principles of co-tenancy law.[21] The court's decisions are to the effect that allocation of production and costs is retroactive to the date of first production. The parties are regarded as co-tenants and as such each has present vested interest in the property. They are therefore, accountable to each other at the inception of production.[22] Although, pooling is not always necessary in case of an undivided interest in a well spacing unit, it may become helpful in addressing disputes concerning accounting for costs and production between the parties.

The principle of co-tenancy is well stated by the court in the case of *Schank v. North AM. Royalties, Inc.*[23] as follows:

> ...the owners of undivided portions of oil and gas rights in and under the same land are tenants in common and each co-tenant may enter the premises for the purpose of exploring for oil and gas and may drill and develop such premises. Each cotenant may exercise the same right and privilege with reference to the common property. Each owner in co-tenancy acts for himself, and no one is the agent for the other nor has any authority to bind the other merely because of the relationship, unless authorized to do so. Upon discovery of oil and gas upon the premises, the producing cotenant must account to the non-consenting or nonproducing cotenant for his pro rata share of the net profits apportioned according to the fractional interest of said cotenant. Each cotenant may lease his undivided interest in the common property without the consent of the other cotenants and such lease is effective as to his interest in the property but ineffective as to the interest belonging to his cotenant.

In undivided interests in underlying oil and gas, opinion is divided as to the ability of one cotenant to develop the resources without the consent of the other cotenant. The majority's view is that the development of the resource by one cotenant does not constitute a waste to the other. Therefore, a denial of the right of a cotenant to remove minerals means a denial of his beneficial enjoyment of his interests in the land.[24] The minority's view on the other hand, is that development of minerals by one cotenant constitutes waste to the other cotenant. This means that all cotenants must give consent to minerals development. Otherwise, non-consenting cotenant may bring action against the developing cotenant for penalty for waste. To solve this problem, it

21. Owen L. Anderson, 'Compulsory Pooling in North Dakota: Should Production Income and Expenses Be Divided from Date of Pooling, Spacing, or "First Runs"?', (1982) N.D. L. Rev. 58: 537 at 539.
22. *Ibid.*, at 539.
23. 201 N.W. 2d 419 (N.D.1972).
24. Anderson, 'Compulsory Pooling in North Dakota: Should Production Income and Expenses Be Divided from Date of Pooling, Spacing, or "First Runs"?', at 539.

has been suggested hat compulsory pooling statutes will be necessary so that parties' respective rights can be determined in order to facilitate mineral development.[25]

2.1.5 *Nebraska*

The issue of retroactivity of pooling order also came up in Nebraska State. The Supreme Court in the case of *Application of Farmers Irrigation District v. Schumacher*[26] upheld the order of Nebraska Oil and Gas Commission which made pooling retroactive to the commencement of first production. According to the Court this is:

> to permit an adjoining owner to obtain, recover, and receive his just and equitable share' and that 'unless the order may be made effective retroactively, it may on occasion verge on the confiscatory.

In this case, production had commenced on the 15 October 1964. The plaintiff filed its application for pooling on the 16 January 1967 although it had notified the defendant that it claimed an interest in the well on 22 December 1964. The plaintiff had requested that pooling order be made retroactive to the date of first production. The Commission accepted. The Supreme Court was of the view that production and costs should also be made retroactive to the date of first production. The Supreme Court upheld the commission's order so as to protect correlative rights of all interest owners. The court however added a qualification to this holding when it declared that pooling need not be retroactive where it is inequitable to do so. For example where the other party:

> sits back to await the successful outcome of drilling operations without asking for a pooling agreement, it would place the entire risk and the entire expense upon the party drilling in the event of an unsuccessful operation. This would ordinarily be inequitable and will not justify retroactive order.[27]

In this case however, since the plaintiff had notified the defendant of its claim shortly after the well's completion, the court held that it was just and equitable to grant a retroactive order.[28]

In a similar case again, the court followed the principles established in the case above and upheld a retroactive pooling order to the date of first production. However, the court expressed doubt in the equity of retroactive order but nevertheless upheld the principles.[29]

---

25. *Ibid.*, at 541. He stated that the measure of damages is the value of the oil and gas at the 'well head', meaning that the developing co-tenant is not allowed to deduct drilling and lifting costs from the proportionate share of the non-consenting cotenant.
26. 187 Neb. 825, 194 N.W.2d 788, 42 O. & G.R. 600 (1972), See also Williams & Meyers, 'Oil and Gas Laws', vol. 6 (2004), pp. 821-822-3, Chapter 9.
27. Williams & Meyers, 'Oil and Gas Laws', vol. 6 (2004), Chapter 9, at 832.
28. It should be noted that three of the judges dissented from the opinion of the majority. They were of the view that pooling order should be made retroactive to spacing order. They were however prepared to make it retroactive to the date of filling application for spacing unit and not as far back as the date of first production. In their thinking, the rule of capture should apply to production had before that date.
29. *Ohmart v. Dennis* 188 Neb. 260, 196 N.W.2d 181 (1972).

The above cases have shown that the Nebraska Supreme Court have taken a position that pooling order, production and costs should be made retroactive to the date of first production.

From the above, it is clear that there are varying policies and interests that have influenced the decisions of the courts on the issue of retroactivity. These are: application of the rule of capture, conservation laws which also differ from State to State (the conservation laws are similar but they are not identical), constitutional provisions on takings and issue of equity among licensees. These varied interests accounted for the conflicting decisions.

For instance, Texas which is an ownership State that one expected to have adopted retroactivity, completely ruled otherwise because of the rule of capture. Louisiana and Oklahoma where non-ownership principles are enshrined, allowed retroactivity to some extent, i.e. to the date of spacing order (Louisiana) or the date of filling application for spacing unit (Oklahoma). The reasons given by the courts of both States were constitutional provisions against taking of property. The lessee is prevented from drilling any well once he files application for spacing order or when the order for spacing is declared by the Regulator. So the courts thought that if retroactivity is not allowed up to that dates, that may amount to taking of property rights under the constitution. This is an important lesson because it helps in understanding that the court can on constitutional ground allow retroactivity of unit order and thus, moderating the effects of the rule of capture. In Nebraska, retroactivity is allowed to the date of first production where it is equitable to do so. Equity will be in favour of the party seeking retroactivity where he has not delayed or behaved unreasonably in asserting his right. The court allowed retroactivity so as to avoid confiscation of property. In North Dakota, there is no court decision on retroactivity with respect to divided interests in spacing unit like the other States discussed above. However, in cases where the parties have undivided interests in land, retroactivity is allowed to the date of first production because the parties are regarded as co-tenants. Each party has beneficial vested property interests or rights in the underlying assets. This is important because in a straddling reservoir, each party has been regarded as tenant in common when correlative doctrine was applied. The only difference is that the rule of capture was allowed to operate so that neither of the party is accountable to the other for any oil taken from the common reservoir unlike in co-tenancy principles. The position that allows retroactivity is in tandem with the goals of conservation laws which is to moderate the disastrous effects of the rule of capture. Therefore, a position that disallows retroactivity represents an extreme case and may run afoul of the constitutional provision on takings.

2.2 Domanial Regimes

Analysis of retroactivity in domanial regimes will be done using Nigeria as an example because the issue has arisen because the Regulator has either taken or failed to take a decision at the appropriate time leading to drainage of oil between licensees.

2.2.1 *Nigeria*

As stated in Chapter 6, the problem of unilateral capture emanates from failure of the Regulatory Agency (DPR)[30] to initiate unitisation as provided by law or to enforce it at the appropriate time where licence holders could not agree on unitisation terms. This has resulted to a situation where one licence holder exploited and produced from a reservoir that straddles a field operated by another licence holder for over thirty (30) years without Unitisation agreement.

A good illustration of the problem is between SPDC and NAOC.[31] NAOC unilaterally commenced production in 1975 from a straddling reservoir up to 2008 when the DPR stopped further drilling and production from the field and ordered both parties to commence unitisation process. SPDC had proposed 16 February 1990 as the Reference date for commencement of unitisation because that was the date SPDC drilled a well on its side and established straddling. NAOC proposed 8 February 2008 since that was the date DPR wrote to her to commence unitisation process with SPDC. The DPR however, fixed the Reference date as 2006. This means that the unitisation would be deemed to have commenced in 2006 for the purpose of apportioning past costs and production despite the fact that SPDC established straddling through well drilling in 1990 and notified NAOC and the DPR of its intention to unitise the field in 1996. The implications of the decision of the DPR can be summarised as follows: first, it failed to enforce compulsory unitisation law between the parties at the appropriate time. Second, it failed to order retroactive unitisation to either the date NAOC commenced production or the date when SPDC established straddling through well drilling or the date SPDC served a notice on NAOC of its intention to unitise. Third, it applied the rule of capture to production obtained between 1975 and 2006.

The legal issues that have arisen from the above decision can also be stated as thus: was the order of the regulatory authority directing unitisation to commence in 2006 rather than the start of production in 1975 or 1990 when SPDC discovered oil by well drilling lawful? Can the failure of the Regulatory authority to enforce unitisation retroactively to 1975 or 1990 constitute a breach of the State's obligations under the relevant investment treaty and human rights instruments (e.g., AIPI and ECHR)? Is a Licensee under a duty to exercise restraint in extracting petroleum from a straddling reservoir without Unitisation?[32] Is the Regulatory Authority under a duty to enjoin unitisation when there is straddling reservoirs?[33] Does a licence holder has property rights in the oil and gas discovered but yet to be produced (oil field or reservoirs)?[34]

As regards the first question, i.e. whether unitisation order should be made retroactive to the date of first production or to the date of the unit order, which ever position that one may take borders on both legal and policy issues. From the legal

30. Note that DPR represents the Minister of petroleum resources and exercises power delegated to it by the Minister as provided in section 12 of the Petroleum Act 1969. Where DPR is mentioned here it is assumed it is exercising the power of the Minister.
31. See Chapter 6 of this book at p. 250.
32. This question has been addressed extensively in Chapter 6.
33. This question has been addressed in Chapter 6.
34. This question has been addressed extensively in Chapter 4.

perspective, one must examine the licence granting clauses and other provisions of the petroleum laws and regulations. From the policy angle, we will have to examine other soft law instruments to discover the policy reasons behind the position that the Regulatory authority had taken.

As shown in Chapters 3 and 6, the licence granting clause of the oil mining lease in the Petroleum Act of 1969 (Nigeria), conveys the underlie petroleum to the licensee which we have interpreted is restricted to the petroleum discovered in the defined area of the lease at the time of the grant. The licensing regime in Nigeria with respect to an oil mining lease cannot be said to encapsulate the rule of capture. The discovered petroleum while still under the ground qualifies as a real interest as it is connected to land. Thus, from the wordings of the granting clause, a full ownership interests can be said to have been granted to the holder of an OML and such interest is an interest in land. Therefore, failure to order unitisation retroactively to the date of first production would contravene the provisions of the Petroleum Act.

The unitisation clause contained in the Petroleum (Drilling and Production) Regulations 1969 imposes on the Minister the obligation to initiate unitisation between the licensees. Exercise of Ministerial power to compel unitisation is also made conditional upon: (1) the fields been susceptible of being developed as a single unit taking into consideration good oil field practice, (2) the unit development must be in the interest of Nigeria and all the parties to the proposed unit agreement (grantees and other parties), and (3) must be to 'secure maximum ultimate recovery' of hydrocarbons. We have argued in Chapter 6 that the aforesaid 'conditions' possess the propensity to crystalise to 'compulsion' once there is a straddling reservoir. Therefore, where the minister fails to compel the licensee to unitise or impose an FDP where parties failed to reach unitisation agreement, the minister will be in breach of the regulation. If on account of this failure, the licensee unilaterally proceeds to development and production, the licensee may also be in violation of the unitisation clause. This is because the licence granting clause in the Petroleum Act only conveys to the licensee petroleum lying under his lease area at the time of the grant. Similarly, failure by the Regulator to make unitisation order effective retroactively may be in violation of the petroleum Act. However, because of the operation of the common law rule of capture, the licensee may not be liable for drainage and to compensate the other party. Therefore, at the municipal level, there is no adequate protection for the property rights to reservoir oil in spite of the statutory recognition of the proprietary rights of the licensee to it.

By virtue of sections 4.2 (d) and 4.4 (b) of the 2008 Unitisation Guidelines,[35] unitisation will take effect from the date the non- producing party (i.e., party alleging drainage) established straddling by seismic data, well drilling and discovery. If the DPR specifies a contrary date as commencement of unitisation, it will be acting contrary to

35. Section 4.2 (d) provides that the 'Reference date shall be the date that DPR states in writing to be the time at which the non-producing party established straddling through seismic data, drilling and Discovery … .'

Section 4.4 (b) provides that the Reference date shall serve the purpose of determining the date when unitisation is deemed to have commenced, and to establish when the re-adjustment of past costs and production shall take effect.

its own policy guidelines. This is because where the DPR has confirmed straddling and notified the parties involved, drilling of further well is prohibited by virtue of section 4.2 (a) of the guidelines. Therefore, if the party producing is not restrained from further drilling and production while the non- producing party abstained from drilling and production as a result of this prohibition, unitisation order that fails to take effect retroactively to the date of first production (Brown - Green fields) or the date that the DPR notifies the parties of the straddling (Green - Green fields) will be unlawful.[36] In the case between SPDC and NAOC stated above, it is on record that SPDC established straddling in 1990 but notified NAOC and DPR of its intention to unitise the fields in 1996. NAOC commenced unilateral production in 1975 up till 2008 when DPR ordered her to stop further production.

From the licence granting clause in the petroleum Act and the Regulations, unitisation ought to be made retroactive to 1975 when the first production was made by NAOC or 1990 when SPDC made discovery. However, from the Year 2008 Unitisation Guidelines, unitisation ought to be made retroactive to either 1990 when SPDC confirms straddling or 1996 when it notified both NAOC and DPR of its intention to unitise.[37] The 2006 date fixed by the DPR is contrary to the aforesaid laws and guidelines.

We have seen from the Louisiana and Oklahoma cases that retroactivity is allowed to some extent, that is, to the date of spacing order (Louisiana) or the date of filing application for spacing unit (Oklahoma) because of the constitutional provisions against taking of property. The lessee is prevented from drilling any well once he files application for spacing order or when the order for spacing is declared by the Regulator.[38] Nebraska and North Dakota however, applied pooling order retroactively to the date of first production. North Dakota regards the parties as co-tenants when undivided interests are involved in a spacing unit. There is no reason why the same principle (co-tenancy) should not be applicable to situation of straddling reservoirs. In fact the court was close to this principle when it adopted the correlative rights doctrine in the cases of *Ohio Oil Co. v. Indiana (supra) and Manufacturer Gas Co. v. Indiana & Natural Gas & Oil Co (supra)*. The courts in these cases regarded them as common owners or common tenants. In the Kentucky cases of *Louisville Gas Co. v. Kentucky Heating Co. (1903) (supra)*, *Commonwealth v. Trent (supra)* and *Louisville Gas Co. v. Kentucky Heating Co. (1909) (supra)*, the courts regarded them as Tenants in common. The only difference between the Co-tenancy principles enunciated by the North Dakota case and the Tenants in common principle postulated by the Indiana and Kentucky

36. The only danger here is where the Regulator fails to notify the party at the appropriate time as the regulator may neglect to send the notice on time. However, the 2008 Unitisation guidelines provide in section 2.2 (a) (1) that DPR shall within one month of the receipt of notification of straddling inform the other party to commence work in the 'affected part of the concession to confirm existence of petroleum in the geological trap which appears to have straddles a concession boundary'.
37. The provision of the Guidelines on this issue when applied has the potential of running contrary to the Petroleum Act and the Petroleum (Drilling and Production) Regulations.
38. See *L.O Ward v. Corporation Commission (supra) C.H. Kuykendall v. Helmerich & Payne Inc (supra)* (Oklahoma cases) and *Desormeaux v. Inexco Oil Co (supra)* (Louisiana case).

cases above is that the rule of capture was not allowed at all in the former case while it was allowed in the latter cases.

Therefore, in domanial regimes especially in Nigeria, unitisation ought to be made retroactive to the date of first production or the date the non-producing party establishes straddling through seismic data or well drilling and discovery. The non-producing party needs to prove that oil exists under his lease by seismic and well drilling in order to prove straddling or drainage. This view is consistent with the licensing granting clause, the goals of unitisation – to prevent waste, to prevent drilling of unnecessary wells, to increase ultimate recovery, to promote national interests, and to protect fully correlative rights.

The only exception to the above view is where the party alleging drainage is guilty of bad faith or unreasonableness. In this case, retroactive unitisation order to date of first production may not be just and equitable.[39] Thus, where one party is aware of the straddling but failed to notify the Regulator and the other party of his intention to unitise and production continues to his knowledge for a considerable length of time, he will be guilty of bad faith if he subsequently showed up for unitisation. It will amount to compensating the other party for doing nothing or investing nothing. In the same vein, where the producing party concealed straddling from the Regulators in spite of the evidence available through seismic or well data, he will be guilty of bad faith and unitisation will be retroactive to date of commencement of production.[40]

2.3 Policy Analysis

The decision of the Regulator in the case between SPDC and NAOC above could only be rationalised on policy grounds. Where unilateral production has taken place for considerable length of time (e.g., thirty years), making unitisation order to commence retroactively to the date of first production may present serious problem both on the State and the company that committed drainage. For example, in Nigeria most of the fields affected by unilateral drainage are operated on Joint Venture arrangements in which the State has equity participation interest of 55% while the company has 45%. Since retroactive unitisation order has potential impact on past costs and production pay back, it means that the State would have to pay back production received from drainage. Where the fields' life span contained insufficient hydrocarbons to meet the pay back, production in cash might be the alternative remedy. But because production received by the State has been sold and money realised commingled with the State's treasury or federation account, it becomes impossible for the State to pay back in cash.

To pay back oil or cash would require the approval of the National oil company, the National Parliament, the Revenue Mobilisation and Fiscal Commission and the Federal Inland Revenue Service (FIRS). This approval process is a herculean task to be accomplished that could be abandoned in view of the costs that will be involved. This problem might also be applicable to the other Joint Venture partner, though as a private

39. See the *Farmers Irrigation Dist. v. Schumacher* (*supra*).
40. See section 4.2 (d) of the 2008 Unitisation Guidelines.

company, the problem might be easier to overcome than the State partner. It is as a result of this complex problem that the Regulator would be reluctant to make a sweeping retroactive unitisation order. The potential impacts on the State where it is holding an interest is weighed by the Regulator before arriving at a decision.

In addition, the major policy goal of the State is to rapidly develop oil and gas resources in order to receive quick revenues for meeting other developmental needs of a modern society. Without the rule of capture, adjacent landowners could sterilise production from straddling reservoirs by his neighbour. Therefore, Unilateral capture if allowed will increase the race to develop and exploit oil and gas resources as neighbouring leaseholder would not be able to claim title to the oil produced even though part of it might have come from beneath his lease area.[41]

Whether the underlying policy goal is sufficient to justify the measures taken by the Regulator is another question which would be considered when addressing State's obligations under the investment treaty and human rights below.[42]

3. TRIGGERS FOR PROPERTY RIGHTS IN DISCOVERED PETROLEUM RESERVOIR

In Chapter 4, we have in reliance on Labour theory, argued that a licensee who has expended heavy capital investments (both human, technical and financial) to acquire acreage, worked on same and discovered petroleum reservoir has a legitimate expectation in the results of his labour and that property rights ought to be ascribed to the result of his labour. Also in Chapter 4, we have shown that petroleum discovery is made after exploration survey stage of the petroleum development phases. At the Exploratory and Appraisal wells drilling stage, prospect evaluation is carried out to determine whether there is petroleum accumulation or not.[43] If the result is positive, the discovery[44] is further evaluated to determine the volume of the petroleum in place. Under modern PSC or PSA regime (hereinafter jointly referred to as IPA), the IOC or

41. Alisa Newman Hood, 'We Shale Overcome? A US Court Issue an Unsettling Decision on Marcellus Property Rights', (March 2012) Journal of World Energy Law & Business 5(1): 78, at 80.
42. It may be argued that the refusal to make unitisation order retroactive to the date of first production in this instance is in the public interests. However, the jurisprudence of the ECHR analysed below has shown that taking of property for public interests requires payment of compensation. This has also found support from some theories which are to the effect that compensation should be paid so that there is equal sharing of public burdens. The Utilitarian perspective on this principle is that compensation should be paid where property is taking for public interests because there is the need to ensure security and stability of property regimes so as to encourage private individuals for fruitful investments. See Coban, 'Protecting Property Rights within the European Convention on Human Rights', at 192 citing Franc I. Michelman, 'Property, Utility, and Fairness: Comments on the Ethical Foundations of "Just Compensation Law"', (1967) Harvard Law Review 80: 116-1258.
43. Five requirements are considered in prospect evaluation. These are Source rocks, Migration Paths, Reservoir, Trap and Cap Rock/Seal. The existence or otherwise of these elements will determine whether there is 'Prospect' (i.e., Petroleum Accumulation).
44. Discovery arises where an operator struck a petroleum-bearing Geological structure that is worthy of further evaluation by appraisal drilling- see the definition of Discovery in the year 2007 Model Nigerian PSC.

Contractor is expected determine the commerciality of the discovery.[45] This involves economic or profitability analysis that considers the recoverable reserves, production, pipelines and terminal facilities required, estimated crude oil prices and other technical and economic factors.[46] Within the exploration phase, if Petroleum discovery is made and notice of it is given to the Host State, the IOC is expected to carry out appraisal drilling under an approved work programme.[47] Where the discovery is found to be commercial, the IOC is expected to make a declaration of commerciality but where it is otherwise, the IOC is not expected to make declaration of commerciality and hence, will be required to relinquish or surrender the discovery usually but not necessarily at the end of the exploration.[48] Most IPAs allow the IOC to decide whether the discovery is commercial or not while in some other jurisdictions, an objective criteria such as minimum production level from a well (Egypt) or field (Nigeria) is specified.[49] Once a discovery has been declared commercial and the operator has considered it worthy of development, detailed FDP is submitted to the Regulators for approval. Once approved, the IOC is granted exploitation or production licence to develop and mine the petroleum discovered. In a PSC regime therefore, the trigger points for Property rights to discovered petroleum reservoir are as follows: Petroleum discovery, Appraisal of the discovery, Evaluation of the discovery, Declaration of commerciality, Submission of FDP and grants of Production licence, Lease or Authorisation.

In the Licensing regime, some countries provide for new separate licence for each of the petroleum development phases.[50] This means that new right is granted for each of the phases of petroleum development. However, a Production licence is granted at the end of the exploration phase when licensee discovers a given quantity of petroleum that is commercial, submits an FDP and relinquishes the portion of the acreage that is outside the FDP. This may serve as an equivalent position in the PSC regime where

45. See the Nigerian and Peruvian Model PSC. The Nigerian PSC provides that 'Upon the Discovery of Commercial Quantity, CONTRACTOR shall recommend to the CORPORATION conversion of the OPL to OML. Such recommendation shall include delineation of the proposed OML area. The CORPORATION shall review CONTRACTOR's recommendation and if satisfied apply for the conversion of the OPL to OML. The Peruvian PSC provides in Article 5(1) that 'the exploration period shall commence on the day following the declaration of a commercial discovery. The exploitation starts with Development.' See Duval et al., 'International Petroleum Exploration and Exploitation Agreements: Legal, Economic & Policy Aspects', at 138.
46. Duval et al., 'International Petroleum Exploration and Exploitation Agreements: Legal, Economic & Policy Aspects', at 137.
47. *Ibid.*, at 135. The Mozambican PSC provides that 'Contractor shall advise the Host State immediately when petroleum is discovered in a well ... .' The Contractor thereafter submits an appraisal programme of such discovery for approval before proceeding on the appraisal works.
48. *Ibid.*, at 139.
49. In Nigeria, by the Petroleum Act, a field is considered commercial if 10,000 bbls (Onshore) or 25,000 bbls (Offshore) can be produced per day, while in Egypt, by the IPA, a well is commercial if it can produce 2,000 bbls per day.
50. For examples in Canada, Exploration licence, Significant discovery licence and Production licence are granted in succession as the work progresses from one phase to the other. In the same vein, Petroleum exploration permits, Petroleum retention lease and Petroleum production licence are granted in the Offshore in Australia. In Nigeria, three stage rights are also granted in succession i.e. Oil exploration licence, Oil prospecting licence and Oil mining lease. In Netherlands, two stage rights are granted – Exploration licence and Production licence.

Production licence is granted after the contractor or IOC makes declaration of commerciality.

However, other country such as UK grants Standard Production Licence (Seaward licence) to cover the various phases of Petroleum development. In the landward areas, Petroleum Exploration and Development Licence (PEDL) is granted in the like manner. These licences are granted as a result of an initial work programme commitments proposed to the Minister at the time of the application for a licence. If such work programme commitments are accepted by the Minister, the licensee is issued the licence.[51] After awarding a standard production licence on the strength of the initial work programme commitments, the licence is divided into three distinct terms, namely:

(1) Initial term of four years[52] – the Contractual parties (through Joint Operating Agreement) focuses on exploration works set out in the initial work programme that they have bided. These include seismic survey of a given quantity and type and exploration well drilling to a specified depth.[53] One of the Contractual parties is designated as the Operator and is vested with power to conduct the joint operations on behalf of the non-operators however, under the supervision and control of the Operating Committee (OPCOM). The Venturers are required to surrender or relinquish 50% of the acreage at the end of the initial term and by that time, petroleum discovery might have been made.
(2) Second term of four years – This term focuses on appraisal well drilling. The OPCOM which comprises representatives of each of the Venturers prepares the work programme which is subsequently passed to the Operator to carry out. At this stage, the Operator appraises the discovery and determines how to exploit petroleum discovered in the initial term. Unlike the initial term, the Operator is not required by any regulation to surrender any part of the acreage but he must give at least three months' notice to the Minister of his intention to move to the next stage. He is allowed to continue to the next stage however, only in respect of the 'producing part'.[54] The determination of the producing

51. Greg Gordon, 'Petroleum Licensing', in Greg Gordon et al., 'Oil and Gas Law – Current Practice and Emerging Trends', (Dundee University Press, 2007), at 51-52.
52. *Ibid.*, at 54. Under the 2008 Model clauses, the initial term is no longer fixed by statutory instrument at four years. This is now to be determined by the Department of Energy and Climate Change (DECC) and it is included in Schedule 5 to the Licence by virtue of Model clause 6 (3) of the Petroleum Licensing (Production) (Seaward Areas) Regulations 2008, SI 2008/225. Under Model Clause 7 of the 2008 Model Clauses, the Minister has the power to extend the initial term for a period and subject to such terms and conditions as he shall deem fit. However, the PEDL is divided into an initial term of 6 years, a second term of 5 years and a production period (third term) of 20 years (see Model Cl. 1 of the Petroleum Licensing (Exploration and production) (Seaward and Landward Areas) Regulations 2004 as amended in 2006. See also Dr. Mohammad Alramahi, 'Oil and Gas Law in the UK' (Bloomsbury Professional Ltd, 2013) at 50. See generally T. Daintith, Willoughby & Hill, 'United Kingdom Oil and Gas Law', 3rd edn (Sweet & Maxwell, September 2013), Release 72, Chapters 6 and 7 and para. 1-645 at p. 1156.
53. *Ibid.*, at 54. See Model Cl. 4(5).
54. *Ibid.*, at 55. See Model Cl. 5(1).

part is at the sole discretion of the Operator. The Minister has no role to play in this decision making by the Operator. The Operator submits the FDP on behalf of the other Venturers in respect of the 'Producing part' and relinquishes the non-producing part to avoid payment of high rentals on acreage that is not being utilised. In the Licensing regime, the determination of the 'producing part' by the Operator and relinquishment of 'non- producing part' that is outside the approved FDP could be regarded as the equivalent position of 'commerciality declaration' by the Contractor under the PSC regime. The Minister recognises that commerciality has been achieved at this point. If it is shown in the FDP submitted that the reservoir extends beyond the Venturers' acreage into an acreage owned by another licence group, the Minister is expected to order compulsory unitisation as discussed in Chapter 6 of this book. The Venturers are expected to enter into Unitisation and Unit Operating Agreements with the adjacent Licence group in respect of the straddle reservoirs before proceeding to the next term of the licence. At the end of the second term, the licence will continue in respect of 'Producing part' as provided in Model Clause 8 (1) of the 2008 Model Clauses. Also by virtue of Model Clause 7, the term may be extended by the Minister as he shall deem fit.

(3) Third term of eighteen years – focuses on development and production period. The production period allows the licensee to develop, mine and carry away petroleum discovered in the earlier stages of the licence. The duration may be extended at the discretion of the Minister where the field is still producing. However, the operator must apply for extension not less than three months before the expiration of the Field's life span by virtue of Model clause 9 of the 2008 Model Clauses. The JOA usually provides that each licensee has the right to take in kind and separately dispose of its share of petroleum won. This is in line with the legal nature of a JOA in which the relationship between the parties is that of Joint Venture and not Partnership. Each Licensee has an obligation to lift its separate share of petroleum. Failure to lift may lead to reduction of production or complete shut in if the storage capacity becomes full. This implies that each participant is liable only to its pro-rata percentage interests in the Venture and equally receives benefits according to its pro-rata percentage interests. The liability of the Venturers is several and not joint or collective and they are not jointly liable for the gross costs of any particular operation since each Venturer prepares budgets for its net percentage share of the Venture's obligations. The JOA also spells out arrangements regarding offtake of petroleum produced which may be tailored towards matching production with individual requirements for oil and gas so as to ensure optimum use of installed capacity and to promote equity among the participants.

From the above, it is clear that at the end of each phase of the standard production licence or PEDL, certain works or expenses must have been carried out. Notices by the Operator to the Minister and subsequent movement from the initial term to the second and third terms are evidence that licensee has carried out some works and that certain expenditure has been incurred. In the Licensing regime, where production licence is granted based on work programme commitments at the time of the application for award of acreage, the determination of the 'producing part', relinquishment of 'non-producing part' and obtaining an approved FDP by the Operator could be regarded as the equivalent position of 'commerciality declaration' by the Contractor under the PSC regime.

4. PROTECTING PROPERTY RIGHTS IN DISCOVERED PETROLEUM RESERVOIR: APPLICABILITY OF INVESTMENT TREATIES AND INTERNATIONAL HUMAN RIGHTS LAWS

4.1 Investment Treaties (BITs/MITs)

As noted above, where the State has through its Regulatory Agency mediated in the disagreement between the two licensees in this context and have rendered one form of decision or the other that makes either of the parties unsatisfied or where the State itself is guilty of some misconduct, an alternative avenue for protecting the rights of the dissatisfied party may be possible through the International investment treaties[55] and international human rights norms regarding property rights protection. In this regard, the first port of call is for the investor to seek a claim through any relevant BIT or MIT that provides him direct recourse against the Host State and also protects his rights to the enjoyment of his investment.

In analysing this issue in the context of unilateral capture, we shall divide it into two parts namely; (1) where the Regulator, due to its action or inaction, fails to enjoin unitisation to prevent unilateral drainage from straddling petroleum reservoir and (2) where the Regulator did not make its unitisation order retroactive to the date of first production or the date straddling was established as has been shown in Chapter 6. It is trite that under the doctrine of State responsibility, a State will be held responsible for the actions of its organs.[56] Therefore, in this book, the actions or inactions of the Regulatory Agency will be assumed to have been attributed to the Host State.

4.1.1 *Failure to Enjoin Unitisation to Prevent Unilateral Drainage*

The issue that may arise in International investment treaty law is whether the Host State's failure to order unitisation at the appropriate time could constitute failure to provide full protection and security to the investment or property of a foreign licensee

55. Michael Polkinghorne, 'Unitisation and Redetermination: Right or Obligation', (2007) J. Energy Nat. Resources L. 25(3): at 319.
56. See Art. 4 of the International Law Convention on State Responsibility which provides that (1) 'the conduct of any State organ shall be considered an act of that State under international law, whether the organ exercises legislative, executive, judicial or any other functions, whatever position it holds in the organisation of the State, and whatever its character as an organ of the central government or of a territorial unit of the State.' (2) 'An organ includes any person or entity which has that status in accordance with the internal law of the State.'

whose petroleum was captured by either the State oil company or another foreign licensee or a domestic licensee.[57]

It must be noted that the protective mechanism of the investment treaty is triggered only after it has been shown that the in rem rights is recognised by the domestic law.[58]

Moreover the notion of protected property comprising an investment has been given an expansive definition in national investment laws, BITs and MITs.[59] Licences, leases, permits, concessions, production sharing agreements, joint venture agreements, service contracts, etc. which can be categorised as administrative rights,[60] are the vehicle of foreign investment and have been variously described as proprietary, *'profit a prendre'* or contractual rights.[61] In Chapters 4 and 7, we have seen that Reservoir oil and gas is a property right and that where a foreign investor has in consequence of the production licence granted to him expended both capital and human resources to discover petroleum reservoir, it qualifies as an 'investment' given our analysis of the notion of an 'investment' in Chapter 2. Some treaties have expressly recognised these property rights as protected property in investment laws.[62] Because of their value, withdrawal of them by the Host State or its agency will render the investment of the investor useless. As a result, the treaty has technically removed the discretionary powers of the Host State to interfere with these intangible rights throughout the duration of the treaty.[63]

Consequently, rights acquired under the domestic law by the foreign investor could be converted to rights protected by international law through the BIT. This protective mechanism is safeguarded by the insertion of a clause in the treaty providing

57. It could also raise the question of whether the Host State might be in breach of minimum standard of protection under International law or the applicable BIT. It is also assumed here that the licensee suffering drainage is a foreign investor and that the drainage was committed by either a State oil company or an indigenous company or another foreign investor.
58. See a discussion on this in Chapter 2 at p. 43 of this book.
59. See Chapter 2 at pp. 43-52 of this book for a discussion of what constitutes an 'investment'.
60. Sornarajah argued that administrative rights though, as a grant of the State that can be technically withdrawn by the State, can be lifted from the province of the State through treaty so that a withdrawal of the rights by the State can attract State responsibility. Administrative rights however must comply with the conditions stipulated for its grant otherwise treaty violations cannot be successfully invoked. See Sornarajah, 'The International Law on Foreign Investments', at 16.
61. See Chapter 3 above for detailed analysis of the legal nature of these administrative rights.
62. See the model UK BIT and the U.S. BIT quoted in Chapter 2. See also Sornarajah, 'The International Law on Foreign Investments', at 191 n. 73 for the Australia – Vietnam treaty which includes contractual rights in the list of protected property – '... rights to search for, extract or exploit natural resources ...' See also the BIT between Nigeria and Netherlands which provides that the term '"investments" shall comprise every kind of asset and more particularly, though not exclusively ... rights granted under public law, including rights to prospect, explore and extract natural resources.'
63. For the legal implication of including these public law rights granted by Host States in the international treaty, see Sornarajah, 'The International on Foreign Investments', at 192-193.

'full protection and security' for the foreign investment. For example the BIT between Nigeria and Netherlands[64] provides in Article 3 (2) that:

> [E]ach Contracting Party shall accord to such investments full physical security and protection which in any case shall not be less than that accorded either to investments of its own nationals or to investments of nationals of any third State, whichever is more favourable to the national concerned.

The 'full protection and security' standard clause has its root in the early BIT of friendship, commerce and navigation.[65] It is also a principle used under customary international law rules relating to the protection of the property of aliens through the invocation of diplomatic protection. This often attracts claims based on State responsibility under customary international law. Cases decided on this issue by the Iran-US Claims Tribunal are many and they were decided based on customary international law. In the modern BITs, it is usually combined with the principle of Fair and Equitable Treatment (FET). Some treaty tribunals have equated the standard with the FET,[66] while others have applied them separately.[67]

From the wordings of the above treaty clause, the State is under an obligation to take active measures to protect the investment of a foreign investor from adverse effects. This protection standard unlike FET, covers situations of failures by the State to protect investor's property from actual damage caused by the action of either State officials or third parties and in which the State has failed to exercise due diligence.[68] This could also arise in situations where the State omits to provide protection to alien's investment.[69] In both *AMT v. Zaire case* (*supra*) and *Wena Hotels v. Egypt*, (*supra*), the tribunals held that the States were liable for failure to provide full protection and security because they were aware of the seizures of and acts of violence against the investors' property by miscreants but failed to prevent damage to them or to compensate them.

However, there are authorities to the effect that this obligation may not be limited to protection against physical violence or invasion of the investor's premises alone but

64. Agreement on encouragement and reciprocal protection of investments between the Kingdom of the Netherlands and the Federal Republic of Nigeria of 2 November 1992 available at www.minbuza.nl/en/key-topics/treaties/search-the.../005112.html.
65. See Campbell McLachlan QC et al., 'International Investment Arbitration: Substantive Principles' (Oxford University Press, 2007), at 214 referring to the 'United States-Paraguay Treaty of Friendship Commerce and Navigation' 1859 Article IX at n. 69.
66. *Wena Hotels Ltd v. Arab Republic of Egypt*, (Award, 8 December 2000) 6 ICSID Rep 89 at paras 84-95; *Occidental Exploration and production v. Ecuador*, (Award 1 July 2004), 12 ICSID Reports 59, at para. 187.
67. *Azurix Corp. v. The Argentine Republic*, (Award, 14 July 2006), at para. 407.
68. McLachlan QC, et al., 'International Investment Arbitration: Substantive Principles', at 247. See also R. Dolzer & C. Schreuer, 'Principles of International Investment Law' (Oxford), at 149 See also the case of *Toto Construzoni General S.P.A. v. Republic of Lebanon*, Award, ICSID Case No. ARB (07/12) at para. 210, where the tribunal opined that the Host State's alleged failure to prevent owners and occupants from obstructing the works (Road construction) could, if proven, constitute a failure to protect the investment of the investor under the applicable treaty.
69. See *AAPL v. Sri Lanka*, (Award) 4 ICSID Rep. 245 (ICSID, 1990), *American Manufacturing and Trading Inc. v. Republic of Zaire*, (Award) 5 ICSID Rep. 11 (ICSID, 1997), *Wena Hotels Ltd v. Arab Republic of Egypt*, (Award) 6 ICSID Rep 67 upheld on annulment 6 ICSID Rep 129.

could extend to 'guarantees against violation of the investor's right by the operation of laws and regulations of the Host State.'[70] For example, in *Azurix Corp. v. The Argentine Republic*,[71] the tribunal declared that the standard is breached even where there is no physical violence or damage. The tribunal held that 'The cases referred to above showed that full protection and security was understood to go beyond protection and security ensured by the police. It is not only a matter of physical security; the stability afforded by a secure investment environment is as important from an investor's point of view. ... [W]hen the term 'protection and security are qualified by "full" and no other adjective or explanation; they extend, in their ordinary meaning, the content of this standard beyond physical security.'[72]

The treaty tribunal has also held that because the definition of investment in BIT applies also to intangible assets, the obligation of the State to provide full protection and security goes beyond physical security and extends to legal protection as it is difficult to see how physical security of intangible asset could be achieved.[73] In *CME Czech Rebublic BV (The Netherlands) v. The Czech Republic*,[74] where the regulatory authority had created a legal situation that enabled the local partner of the investor to terminate the contract on which the investment is depended, the tribunal declared that 'the Host State is obligated to ensure that neither by amendment of its laws nor by actions of its administrative bodies is the agreed and approved security and protection of the foreign investor's investment withdrawn or devalued.' Also where investor suffers loss due to the failure of the State to take court action to protect an investment, State responsibility is engaged.[75]

However, in the case of *Lauder v. Czech Republic*,[76] the tribunal was of the view that the duty of the Host State under the 'protection and security' clause had been to grant investor access to its judicial system. The tribunal therefore, held that there was no violation of the standard even though the facts are similar to the CME case. In *Saluka v. Czech Republic*, the tribunal was of the view that the standard concerned diminution of the physical security of the investment and that it goes beyond physical violence and requires legal protection of the investor.[77]

70. Dolzer & Schreuer, Principles of International Investments Law', at 149.
71. Award, 14 July 2006.
72. *Ibid.*, at para. 408.
73. *Siemens v. Argentina* (Award 6 February 2007).
74. Partial Award, 13 September 2001, 9 ICSID Reports 121, para. 613.
75. See Case concerning *Elettronica Sikula, SPA (ELSI) (United States v. Italy)* Judgment of 20 July 1989, (1989) ICJ Reports 15. Also the Arbitral tribunal has recognised that a State could be held responsible for problems in its administration of justice and has accordingly regarded the actions of a State-imposed expert to be the actions of a judicial authority of the State, the proper conduct of whom can give rise to State responsibility – see *Loewen Group, Inc and Raymond L Loewen v. United States of America*, (ICSID Case No. ARB (AF)/98/3, Award of 26 June 2003) 7 ICSID Reports.
76. Award, 3 September 2001, 9 ICSID Reports 66, para. 314.
77. *Saluka Investments BV (The Netherlands) v. The Czech Republic*, Partial Award, 17 March 2006, para. 483, 484.

It has been however, agreed that this obligation of the State is not one of absolute or strict liability to prevent physical or legal violations.[78] The obligation is satisfied so long as the Host State exercised due diligence and took such measures that are reasonable in the circumstance to protect the property of the investor. In the case of *Toto Construzoni General S. P A. v. Republic of Lebanon (supra)*, the tribunal found that the temporary obstructions by some persons whose property had been expropriated to allow for road construction by the claimant did not amount to an impairment affecting the physical integrity of the investment and that since the claimant did not demonstrate that Lebanon could have taken preventive or remedial action that it failed to take or that it acted negligently in relation to the property owners' obstructions to the road construction, Lebanon has not acted in breach of Article 4.1 of the Treaty. It is to be noted that if the violation is caused by acts of the State organs or that they contributed significantly to such action; issues of attribution or due diligence will not arise because the State will be held directly responsible.[79]

Thus, the recent awards above have shown that the standard has been given a new meaning that promotes stability of the investment, a meaning that reflects the new interpretation given to FET standard. Therefore, any interference with the legal and economic stability of the investment will amount to a violation of the standard.[80] Even if there is no damage to the asset but the investment stability is destroyed, the standard will be breached.[81] State's measures that caused significant depreciation in the value of the investment either wilfully or negligently will attract State responsibility under the full protection and security clause. Therefore, in the context of unilateral capture, where a licensee engages in unilateral withdrawal of petroleum from straddling fields on the basis of the State's failure to compel unitisation as required by its own law and a foreign investor suffers substantial diminution in the value of his investment, the arbitral tribunal may hold the State responsible under the relevant BIT or MIT.

4.1.2 *Failure to Make Unitisation Order Effective from Date of First Production or the Date the Innocent Party Established Straddling Reservoir*

In Chapter 6 we have stated that the petroleum laws and regulations of the countries in which domanial petroleum regime is adopted cannot possibly encapsulate the common law rule of capture and that this will necessitate the regulator making its unitisation order to take effect retroactively. This construction will raise the issue of whether failure by the regulator to make unitisation order retroactive to first production amounts to indirect taking of property of the party suffering drainage. Therefore, the

78. See *Toto Construzoni General S.P.A. v. Republic of Lebanon* (*supra*), n. 953 above where the ICSID tribunal referred to the ICJ case of *Electtronica Sicula S.P.A. (ELSI) (United States of America v. Italy* which found that the provision in a treaty for 'constant protection and security' cannot be construed as the giving of a warranty that property shall never in any circumstances be 'occupied or disturbed'.
79. Dolzer & Schreuer, 'Principles of International Investment Law', at 150.
80. Sornarajah, 'The International Law on Foreign Investments', at 360.
81. *Azurix v. Argentina* (*supra*) and *Occidental v. Ecuador* (*supra*).

important factors are the substance of the action taken by the Regulator and whether or not a petroleum regime encapsulates the common law rule of capture. Where the regime does not encapsulate the rule, failure by the Regulator to make unitisation order effective retroactively may amount to indirect taking of property (i.e., the State imposing an unjust decision that allows an investor to appropriate the property of another investor). This means that within the context of investment laws, the rule of capture may, under certain circumstances, be regarded as an expropriator rule as it legitimise the taking of the property of one investor for the benefit of another investor[82] with no remedy or compensation to the party whose property right has been violated. This scenario may appropriately qualify as indirect expropriation under customary international law and the investment treaties clauses on 'indirect taking.' Therefore, an attempt by the Regulator to apply the common law rule of capture in defiance of legislative provisions will trigger the question as to whether indirect expropriation claims can be made or not.

Since a licensee has property rights to un-extracted petroleum, any substantial withdrawal of oil from the un-extracted pool will affect the economic value of the proprietary rights of the licensee in the petroleum pool. Where the State fails to prevent such withdrawal or to order unitisation retroactively to the date of first production, State responsibility may be engaged under both customary international law and international investment laws.

It is settled that property that may be expropriated by the State either directly or indirectly, comprises both tangible and intangible properties.[83] Several judicial and arbitral practices especially under ICSID Convention, NAFTA, Iran-US Claims Tribunal

82. This is because unilateral drainage, even though leaves the title to the entire lease area untouched may under certain circumstances (e.g., when a substantial part of adjoining reservoir is drained) constitutes substantial diminution in value of the lease and thus, tantamount to taking. 'Indirect expropriation leaves the investor's title untouched but deprives him of the possibility to utilize the investment in a meaningful way.' See Dolzer & Schreuer, 'Principles of International Investment Law', at 92. Moreover, customary international law and treaty law not only covers direct expropriation but also provides for indirect expropriation. For example, the 1967 OECD Draft Convention on the Protection of Foreign Property provides in Article 3 that 'no Party shall take any measures depriving, directly or indirectly, of his property a national of another Party ...' Also The Draft United Nations Code of Conduct on Transnational Corporations referred to 'any such taking of property whether direct or indirect ...' and Article 10. III of the Harvard Draft Convention on the International Responsibility of States for Injuries to Aliens by Professors Baxter and Sohn, reprinted in 55 AJIL 545 (1961) ("Harvard Draft"). states: "A "taking of property" includes not only an outright taking of property, but also any such unreasonable interference with the use, enjoyment, or disposal of property as to justify an inference that the owner thereof will not be able to use, enjoy, or dispose of the property within a reasonable period of time after the inception of such interference." The BIT between Netherlands and Nigeria provides that 'Neither Contracting Party shall take any measures, depriving directly or indirectly, nationals of other Contracting Party of their investments unless the following conditions are complied with.. .' Also all MITs prohibit expropriation or measures tantamount to expropriation. Article 1110 of NAFTA provides that 'No party may directly or indirectly nationalise or expropriate an investment of an investor of another Party in its territory or take a measure tantamount to nationalization or expropriation of such an investment ("expropriation") except ...' See also Article 13 of the 1994 Energy Charter Treaty for similar provision.

83. August Reinisch, 'Expropriation', in Peter Muchlinski et al., 'The Oxford Handbook of International Investment Law' (2008) at 410.

and judgments of the ICJ, including its predecessor PCIJ support this assertion.[84] The tribunals in NAFTA cases have held that '... in legal theory, rights other than property rights may be expropriated'[85] The UNCITRAL Tribunal cases have shown that intangible rights could be expropriated. Therefore, contractual rights of an investor in an investment were held as a potential object of indirect expropriation through various acts and omissions of governmental authorities.[86] This is undisputed under international law.'[87]

Answer to the question as to whether failure by the Regulator to compel unitisation or to make unitisation order effective retroactively could amount to indirect taking of property demands an examination of what State measures would constitute an indirect expropriation. It is a settled law that certain types of measures affecting foreign investor's property will be regarded as compensable expropriation even though the investor retains formal title to the property. The contentious issue had been how to draw a distinction between non-compensable regulatory and other governmental activity and measures amounting to indirect, compensable expropriation.[88] As shown by the decisions of the investment tribunals, cases on international law and the 2004 Canada and US (now 2012) Model BITs, a case-by-case fact-finding inquiry is crucial in the determination of whether an action or series of an action by a State constitutes expropriation.

Indirect expropriation has been held by the Arbitral tribunals to have occurred when measures short of an actual taking 'result in the effective loss of management,

84. *Norwegian ship builder's case. (Norway v. USA)*, Permanent Court of Arbitration, Award of 13 October 1922, 1 RIAA 307; *Oscar Chin case (UK v. Belgium)*, Judgment, 12 December 1934, PCIJ Ser A/B, No. 63 (1934); *Chorzor Factory case (German Interests in Polish Upper Silesia) (Germany v. Ploand)*, Judgment 25 May 1926, PCIJ Ser A, No. 7 (1926). For the Iran-US Claims tribunal cases, see *Starret Housing Corp v. Government of the Republic of Iran* (*supra*); *Amoco International Finance Corp v. Iran* (*supra*) and *Philips Petroleum Co v. Iran* (*supra*). In Philips case the tribunal found a compensable expropriation when it declared that 'whether the expropriation is formal or de facto and whether the property is tangible, such as real estate or a factory, or intangible, such as the contractual rights involved in the present case'. For the ICSID tribunal cases see *SPP v. Egypt* (Pyramids case) Award, 20 May 1992, 3 ICSID Reports (1995) 189 at 228 paras 164-167; *Wena Hotels v. Egypt*, Award, 8 December 2000, 41 ILM (2002) 896, para. 98.
85. *SD Meyers, Inc v. Government of Canada* (Partial Award of 13 November 2000), 40 ILM 1408 (2001) para. 281. See also *Methanex Corporation v. United States of America*, NAFTA Arbitral Tribunal, Final Award on Jurisdiction and Merits, 3 August 2005 and *Pope & Talbot, Inc. v. Government of Canada*, Interim Award of 26 June 2000 (here the tribunal found that investor's access to the US market is a property interest worthy of protection under Article 1110 of NAFTA. However, the tribunal found that the State's regulatory measures did not constitute interference with investment business activities substantial enough to be characterised as expropriation under international law).
86. *Biloune and Marine Drive Complex Ltd v. Ghana Investments Centre and the Government of Ghana*, UNCITRAL Ad Hoc Tribunal, Award on Jurisdiction and Liability of 27 October 1989, 95 ILR 183. See also *CME Czech Republic BV v. The Czech Republic* UNCITRAL Arbitral Tribunal (Partial Award of 13 September 2001), 9 ICSID Reports 121, where Tribunal held that the contractual rights of the investor have been expropriated by the interference of a regulatory body of the Host State.
87. *Ibid.*, at paras 591 & 604.
88. Dolzer & Schreuer, 'Principles of International Investment Law', at 93.

use or control, or a significant depreciation of the value of the assets of the foreign investor.'[89]

Arbitral tribunals have also held the view that the concept of 'indirect expropriation' encompasses several other terms such as 'De facto', 'Creeping' expropriation, or measures 'tantamount to ' or 'equivalent to' expropriation.[90] These are forms of indirect expropriation which going by the arbitral decisions, cannot readily be differentiated as their scope can be regarded as 'functionally equivalent.'[91] Creeping expropriation occurs where a measure or series of measures taken by the State gradually and by small steps lead to expropriation of the foreign property.[92] In *Siemens v. Argentina*,[93] where the State took series of measures, including postponement and suspensions of the investor's profitable activities, fruitless renegotiations and ultimately the cancellation of the project, the tribunal found that these measures amounted to creeping expropriation.

The phrase, measures 'tantamount to' or 'equivalent to' expropriation, were also used in some MITs and BITs. The NAFTA tribunal in *Pope & Talbot v. Canada (supra)* considered the phrase together and declared that '... the Tribunal does not believe that the phrase "measure tantamount to nationalisation or expropriation in Article 1110 broadens the ordinary concept of expropriation under international law to require compensation for measures affecting property interests without regard to the magnitude or severity of that effect" ... "Tantamount" means nothing more than equivalent. Something that is equivalent to something else cannot logically encompass more'[94]

Therefore, the phrase requires that the substance of what has occurred and not the form should be the focus. The real interests involved and the purpose and effect of

89. *Ibid.*, at 421 citing UNCTAD, 'Taking of Property, Series on Issues in International Investment Agreements' (New York and Geneva: United Nations, 2000), at 2.
90. See *Tecmed SA v. Mexico* (*supra*) and *Feldman v. Mexico* (*supra*) where NAFTA Tribunal held that creeping expropriation is a form of indirect expropriation, and may accordingly constitute measures 'tantamount to expropriation'.
91. Mclachlan QC et al., 'International Investment Arbitration: Substantive Principles', at 295, para. 8.83 relying on *Feldman v. United Mexican States* (*supra*).
92. See *Compania del Desarollo de Santa Elena, SA v. Republic of Costa Rica*, (Award) 5 ICSID Rep 153, 172 (2000) and the case of *Generation of Ukraine Inc. v. Ukraine*, (Award) ICSID Case ARB/00/9 (2003) where the ICSID tribunal described 'creeping expropriation' as follows '... It is clear however, that a measure or series of measures can still eventually amount to a taking, though the individual steps in the process do not formally purport to amount to a taking or to a transfer of title. What has to be identified is the extent to which the measures taken have deprived the owner of the normal control of his property' where the tribunal also described Creeping expropriation as a form of 'indirect expropriation with a distinctive temporal quality in the sense that it encapsulates the situation whereby a series of acts attributable to the State over a period of time culminate in the expropriatory taking of such property. See also *Pope & Talbot Inc. v. Government of Canada* (Interim Award) 7 ICSID Rep. 69, 82; *Philips Petroleum Co Iran v. Islamic Republic of Iran & the National Iranian oil company* (1989) 21-USCTR 79, 116. Here there was no outright seizure of the claimant's property by the State but the tribunal held that he was deprived of his property through series of concrete actions attributable to the Government of Iran. In *Tradex v. Albania*, (Award, 29 April 1999), 14 ICSID Review-FILJ (1999) 197, the tribunal explained the need to have regard to the cumulative effect of the measures taken by the State. If a single event does not constitute expropriation, it is still possible that all the events when considered together can qualify as amounting to expropriation.
93. Award, 6 February 2007.
94. *Pope & Talbot v. Canada* (*supra*), at 85-87.

the Government measures must be considered by the tribunal.[95] Therefore, measures which substantially interfere with the investor's business activities may be considered by the tribunal to be tantamount to an expropriation. If the measure has the effect of depriving the investor of the use and benefit of his investment, even though he retains title to his investment, such measures are regarded as 'creeping' or 'indirect' expropriation or as measures the effect of which is 'tantamount to expropriation.'[96] The legal consequences of such 'indirect' 'creeping' or 'de facto' expropriation are the same as formal expropriation.

It is to be noted that what is paramount is the effects of the measure on the business of the investor and not its form. The effect on the economic benefit and value as well as upon the control over the investment is the uppermost consideration. In this regard, a positive act of the State may not be necessary as it makes no difference whether the deprivation was caused by actions or inactions.[97] Even though the sole effect doctrine is controversial, it is generally agreed that a significant interference by the State with the economic use and enjoyment and associated benefits or income of investment will amount to indirect expropriation.[98] Therefore, even if the investor still retains legal title to its investment, there could be a finding of expropriation if the rights to go with the legal title have been rendered useless. For example, where the Host State increases tax to the extent that the investor can no longer have effective control over use and operation of his properties, expropriation claim can be sustained by the investor even though he is still in possession of the mining lease and the plant and other facilities.[99] This means that the tribunals placed more emphasis on economic considerations in arriving at their decisions on what measure or measures constitute an indirect expropriation. Accordingly, State measure that affects significantly economic value of an investment would most likely constitute an indirect expropriation.[100]

95. *SD Meyers v. Canada* (*supra*) approving the reasoning in *Pope & Talbot* case.
96. *Middle East Cement Shipping and Handling Co SA v. Arab Republic of Egypt*, (Award) ICSID Case ARB/99/6 (2002).
97. *CME Czech Republic BV v. Czech Republic* (Partial Award) 9 ICSID Rep. 121, 236 (UNCITRAL 2001).
98. *Metalclad v. Mexico* (*supra*). The tribunal declared that 'expropriation under NAFTA includes not only open, deliberate and acknowledged takings of property, such as outright seizure or formal or obligatory transfer of title in favour of the Host State, but also covert or incidental interference with the use of property which has the effect of depriving the owner, in whole or in significant part, of the use or reasonably-to-be expected economic benefit of property even if not necessarily to the obvious benefit of the Host State.' See also *Tecmed v. Mexico* (*supra*) and *Feldman v. Mexico* (*supra*). In the *Glamis' case* (*supra*), the tribunal considered whether the Government's action was sufficient to potentially constitute a 'taking'. In addressing this issue, the tribunal referred to Tecmed case and opined that the claimant must demonstrate that it was 'radically deprived of the economical use and enjoyment of its investments' in order to succeed. The tribunal further indicated that the claimant would have to prove that its property rights were rendered essentially 'useless' and not restricted. This represents a very high standard with regards to what constitute expropriation.
99. *Revere Copper & Brass Inc v. Overseas Private Investment Corp* (1980) 56 ILR 258. See also *Strarret Housing Corp v. Islamic Republic of Iran* (*supra*); *Tippets &others v. TAMS-AFFA Consulting Engineering of Iran* (1984) 6 Iran-USCTR 219, 225.
100. See *Occidental Exploration and production Company v. Republic of Iran* (*supra*).

From the discussion above, it is clear that certain legal rules have been developed by Arbitral tribunals to help in determining whether measures taken by the government is expropriatory or is a legitimate exercise of regulatory authority. These are:

(a) Substantiality of interference: This goes to the degree at which the property rights of an investor has been interfered with. The test accepted among the tribunals is that there must have been 'substantial loss of control or value'[101] or 'severe economic impact.' In *Pope & Talbot v. Government of Canada* (*supra*), even though the tribunal was of the view that the investment's access to the U.S. market is a property interest subject to protection under Article 1110, it does not believe that the regulatory measures taken by the State constitute an interference with the Investment's business activities substantial enough to be characterised as an expropriation under international law. According to the tribunal 'the test is whether the interference is sufficiently restrictive to support the conclusion that the property has been "taken" from the owner.'[102]

The Harvard Draft Convention on the International Responsibility of States for Injuries to Aliens also supports the above assertion when it refers to interference that would justify an inference that the owner … will not be able to use, enjoy, or dispose of the property …'.[103] The Restatement (Third) Foreign Relations of the United States however, talked about 'action that is confiscatory, or that prevents, unreasonably interferes with, or unduly delays, effective enjoyment of an alien's property.'

The extent to which the State's interference has affected the investment is also considered. In *Occidental case,* the ICSID tribunal held that the various governmental measures did not constitute an indirect expropriation and as they did not amount to such a 'substantial deprivation.' In the tribunal's view, 'the investor is in control of the investment; the government does not manage the day-to-day operations of the company; and the investor has full ownership and control of the investment.[104] Similarly, in *Feldman case,* substantiality of the government interfering measure on the investor's rights was considered by the tribunal before rejecting the applicant's expropriation claim. Applicant was denied tax refund and as a result, he lost effective ability to export cigarettes and derived profits from cigarette export. In spite

101. Reinisch, 'Expropriation', in Peter Muchlinski et al., 'The Oxford Handbook of International Investment Law', at 438-439 citing UNCTAD 'Taking of Property' (*supra*) at 41.
102. *Pope & Talbot v. Government of Canada* (*supra*) at 87.
103. (1961) 55 AJIL 545, 553. See Article 10 (3) (a) Article 10 (3) (a).
104. See also *CMS Gas Transmission Company v. The Argentine Republic,* ICSID Case No. ARB/01/8, Award of 12 May 2005 at para. 263. In *SD Meyers case,* the tribunal alluded to this substantiality of interference when it held that 'An expropriation usually amounts to a lasting removal of the ability of an owner to make use of its economic rights although it may be that, in some contexts and circumstances, it would be appropriate to view a deprivation as amounting to an expropriation, even if it were partial or Temporary.' See para. 283. However, a temporary export ban on certain hazardous wastes was not considered as amounting to expropriation.

of this finding however, the tribunal believed that there was no expropriation. The reason was that the enforcement of the Mexican law has not deprived the claimant of control of the investment, interfered directly in the internal operations or displaced him as the controlling shareholder.

This was the reason the arbitral tribunals have held that the intention of the State in taking the measure is less important than the impact of the measure on the investment.

Although, the intention or motivation of the State in taking the measure may be taken into account by the tribunals in reaching their decision, where the effects on the investment weighs more heavily in the balance than the motivation, the tribunal will more likely find an expropriation. In *Tippetts & others v. Iran (supra)* the tribunal declared that 'The intent of the government is less important than the effects of the measures on the owner, and the form of the measures of control or interference is less important than the reality of their impact.'[105] Also in *Biloune & other v. Ghana Investment Centre & other (supra)*, the tribunal was of the view that 'the motivations for the actions and omissions of Ghanaian governmental authorities are not clear. But the Tribunal need not establish those motivations to come to a conclusion in the case....'[106] Similarly in *Santa Elena case*, the tribunal also emphasised the importance of the effect of governmental measures when it declared that '... a property has been expropriated when the effect of the measure taken by the State has been to deprive the owner of title, possession, or access to the benefit and economic use of his property.'[107]

(b) Legitimate expectation of Investor: In indirect taking claims, investor's legitimate expectation may be an issue. This is evident in cases where the State took some regulatory measures or the State entity exercised some administrative powers. In this instance, the State's right to set its own rules of property (which the investor accepted at the time of investment) and the protection of the investor's legitimate expectation in an investment would have to be reconciled by the arbitral tribunal. In reconciling this, the question as to whether the foreign investor could have reasonably expected that the economic value of its property would be lost in whole or significant part by the regulatory or administrative measures taken by the State must be considered. In the *Metalclad award*, the tribunal considered the reasonably

105. At p. 225. See also *Ebrahimi v. Islamic Republic of Iran* (1994) 30 Iran-US CTR 170 at 190 where the tribunal declared that '... the tribunal precedent make it clear that the key issue is the objective impact of measures affecting shareholder interests, not the subjective intention behind those measures. ... The Respondent's reasons and concerns for taking control of the company cannot relieve it from responsibility to compensate the Claimant for the taking ... . Moreover, a Government cannot avoid liability for compensation by showing that its actions were taken legitimately pursuant to its on laws.' In *Philips Petroleum Company Iran v. Islamic Republic of Iran & another (supra)*, the tribunal declared that '... a Government's liability to compensate for expropriation of alien property does not depend on proof that the expropriation was intentional ... .'
106. *Biloune's case (supra)* at 209.
107. *Santa Elena's case (supra)* at para. 77.

to be expected economic benefit of property as one of the important factors in assessing the validity of an expropriation claims.[108] The tribunal in the case found that the claimant had relied on the representations of the Mexican Federal Government of its exclusive authority to issue permits for hazardous waste disposal facilities. A finding of expropriation may be made where the State had disappointed the legitimate expectation of the investor.[109] Thus, legitimate expectation arises where a State's conduct creates reasonable and justifiable expectations on the part of an investor to act in reliance on such conduct, such that failure by the State to honour those expectations could cause the investor to suffer damages.[110] However, investor's expectation may be regarded as less legitimate where he was not specially made to believe in certain State assurances[111] or where he was entering a particular high risk markets.[112] Even in these exceptional circumstances, other investment standards such as the fair and equitable treatment can still be invoked by the investor.[113] The 2004 Canadian and 2012 U.S Model BITs respectively, also codified the notion of investor's legitimate expectation when it states that 'the extent to which the measures or series of measures interfere with distinct, reasonable investment-backed expectations ...'

From the above, it is clear that the question of what State measures constitute indirect expropriation is based on the circumstances of each case. Even though the arbitral tribunals have fashioned out some principles to determine this, there are still no hard and fast rules.

The failure by the regulatory authority to enforce compulsory unitisation of straddling oil and gas fields also raises the issue of whether omission alone may amount to an expropriation in international investment laws. In *Amco Asia Corporation v. Republic of Indonesia*,[114] the ICSID tribunal declared that 'expropriation in

108. It is to be noted that the Supreme Court of British Colombia had set aside the award partially but the expropriation finding in the award was not affected. The tribunal had declared that 'These measures, taken together with the representations of the Mexican Federal Government, on which Metalclad relied, and the absence of a timely, orderly or substantive basis for the denial by the Municipality of the local construction permit, amount to an indirect expropriation.'
109. *Texaco Overseas Co. & others v. Government of Libyan Arab Republic*, (Award) Ad Hoc Arbitration 1977, 53 ILR 389.
110. *International Thunderbird Corp v. Mexico*, (Award) (*supra*) (NAFTA/UNCITRAL 2006).
111. See *Methanex Corporation v. United States of America* (*supra*), where the NAFTA tribunal rejected a claim that the State's ban on certain gasoline additives produced and marketed by the claimant constituted an indirect expropriation on the ground that the investor did not enter the US market because of any special representations made to it.
112. See *Generation of Ukraine, Inc. v. Ukraine* (*supra*), where the Tribunal considered the vicissitudes of the economy of the Host State in determining the reasonableness of the investor's legitimate expectations.

    Because the investment was made in high risk environment with potential of above-average return, the tribunal held that there was no indirect expropriation when the investor encountered various forms of frustration and delay.
113. *MTD Equity Sdn Bhd and MTD Chile SA v. Republic of Chile*, Case No. ARB/01/7, Final Award of 25 May 2004, 44 ILM 91 (2005).
114. ICSID Case No. ARB/81/1, Award, 20 November 1984, 1 ICSID Reports 413, 455 (1993).

international law also exists merely by the State withdrawing the protection of its courts from the owner expropriated, and tacitly allowing a de facto possessor to remain in possession of the thing seized, as did the Roman praetor in allowing *longi temporis praescripto.'* Also in *Eureko case*, the tribunal held that 'the right of an investor can be violated as much by failure of a contracting State to act as by its actions.'[115] The tribunal rejected the argument that a provision in the BIT protecting against expropriatory measures was meant to exclude omissions from the purview of the treaty. The above decisions can be contrasted with the ICSID case of *Olguine v. Paraguay* where the tribunal in rejecting an argument that expropriation may take place through omission, said that 'expropriation therefore, requires a teleological driven action for it to occur; omissions, however egregious they may be, are not sufficient for it to take place'.[116]

From our policy analysis above,[117] the measure of the Host State could be seen as being taken in order to protect public interest. It could be argued that the purpose of such administrative measure is legitimate and as such not expropriatory. In international law, certain types of State measures have been identified as legitimate. Professor Brownlie has opined that:

> State measures, prima facie a lawful exercise of powers of government, may affect foreign interests considerably without amounting to expropriation. Thus, foreign assets and their use may be subjected to taxation, trade restrictions involving licenses and quotas, or measures of devaluation. While special facts may alter cases, in principle such measures are not unlawful and do not constitute expropriation.[118]

Identification of the borderline between indirect expropriation and regulatory measures that are taken for legitimate purposes is very difficult. Some arbitral tribunals have acknowledged that the test to be applied in determining legitimate purposes of regulatory measures has not been provided by international law. For example, the UNCIRAL tribunal in the case of *Saluka (supra)* opined that '... International law has yet to draw a bright and easily distinguishable line between non-compensable regulations ... and measures that have the effect of depriving foreign investors of their investments ...'[119]

It has been asserted that too far-reaching protection against expropriation should not serve as de facto substitutes for investment insurance. It has at the same time been asserted that any substantial deprivation of value regardless of its purposes should be considered expropriatory.[120]

---

115. *Eureko BV v. Poland (supra)*, at para. 186.
116. *Eurodro A Olguin v. Republic of Paraguay*, ICSID Case No. ARB/98/5, Award, 26 July 2001, 6 ICSID Reports 164 (2004) para. 84.
117. See pp. 306-307.
118. I. Brownlie, 'Principles of Public International Law', 6th edn (Oxford: Oxford University Press, 2003), at 509.
119. *Saluka v. Czech Republic* UNCITRAL Partial Award, 17 March 2006, para. 263.
120. Reinich, 'Expropriation', in Peter Muchlinski et al., 'The Oxford Handbook of International Investment Law', at 433.

In *Sedco Inc v. National Iranian Oil Co.* (*supra*), the US-Iran Claims tribunal opined that a State is not liable for economic injury which is a consequence of a bonafide 'regulation within the accepted police power of States'. Also in *SD Meyers case,* the NAFTA tribunal opined that 'the general body of precedent usually does not treat regulatory action as amounting to expropriation.'[121] The OECD, Ministerial Statement on the Multilateral Agreements on Investment (MAI) also supports this view when it states that 'the MAI would establish mutually beneficial international rules which would not inhibit the normal non-discriminatory powers by governments and such exercise of regulatory powers would not amount to expropriation'[122] In *Saluka case,* the investment tribunal declared that 'it is now established in international law that States are not liable to pay compensation to a foreign investor when, in the normal exercise of their regulatory powers, they adopt in a non-discriminatory manner bona fide regulations that are aimed at the general welfare.'[123]

Therefore, in international laws, 'bona fide general taxation, regulation, forfeiture for crime, or other actions of the kind that is commonly accepted as within the police power of States'[124] may be considered legitimate State measures that are not expropriatory.

Moreover, welfare objectives, such as public health, safety, and environment have been regarded as legitimate State regulatory measures in the US-Singapore Free Trade Agreements.[125] Investment Arbitral tribunals have also regarded taxation, environmental concerns and protection of cultural property as basis for legitimate regulatory measures by the State.[126]

However, if the taxation measures are implemented over a period of time, they could be regarded as 'creeping' or indirect expropriation or tantamount to expropriation.[127] This view is supported by the case of *Occidental Exploration and Production Co. v. Republic of Ecuador* (*supra*) where the tribunal declared that expropriation need not involve transfer of title to a given property and that it may affect the economic value of an agreement. The tribunal added that taxes can result in expropriation as can other types of regulatory measures. With regards to environmental measures of the State, some tribunals have disregarded the intention of the legislators and have focused on the effects of the measure on the investments of the foreign investor. In *Santa Elena case*, the tribunal opined that 'where property is expropriated, even for environmental

121. *SD Meyers* (*supra*) at para. 281, 40 ILM 1408 (2001).
122. MAI, Paris, 27-28 April 1998 para. 5, available at http://www.oecd.org/media/release/nw98-5oa.htm.
123. *Saluka v. Czech Republic*, (*supra*) at para. 255.
124. Restatement (Third) of the Foreign Relations Law of the United States, s. 712 comment (1986) at 201.
125. Cited in August Renisch, 'Expropriation', in Peter Muchlinski et al., 'The Oxford Handbook of International Investment Law', at 435 n. 163.
126. See *Feldman v. Mexico* (*supra*) and *SPP v. Egypt* (the Pyramids case) (*supra*) where the tribunal was of the opinion that the decision of the State to cancel a tourist development project situated on its territory for the purpose of protecting antiquities constituted a lawful exercise of the right of eminent domain. However, the cancellation of the contract for the construction was regarded as expropriation.
127. See *Feldman case* (*supra*).

purposes, whether domestic or international, the State's obligation to pay compensation remains.'[128] The ICSID tribunal in the *Tecmed case* was also of the opinion that regulatory administrative actions such as environmental protection, even if they benefit the society as a whole, may be regarded as compensable taking 'if the negative economic impact of such actions on the financial positions of the investor is sufficient to neutralise in full the value, or economic or commercial use of its investment.[129]

On the other hand, a NAFTA tribunal has excluded non-discriminatory regulatory measures from the scope of indirect expropriation. It declared that such a non-discriminatory regulation for a public purpose which is enacted in accordance with due process and which affects a foreign investor is not expropriatory unless the regulating government had given specific commitments to the putative investor contemplating investment that it will refrain from such regulation.[130] Following this approach, is the tribunal in the *Saluka's case*, which opined that when the State adopts general regulations that are commonly accepted as within the police power of the State, the State is not liable to pay compensation as it does not constitute expropriation.

The propriety or otherwise of using public purpose as the sole criterion to remove Host State action from the scope of indirect expropriation has been an issue of concern to some investments tribunals. In *Azurix case* for instance, the ICSID tribunal declared that 'the issue was not so much whether the measure concerned is legitimate and serves a public purpose, but whether it is a measure that, being legitimate and serves a public purpose, should give rise to a compensation claim.' According to this case the public purpose criterion should be supplemented with other criteria such as proportionality and non-discrimination in order to determine whether regulatory actions would be expropriatory and give rise to compensation.[131]

4.1.3 *Fair and Equitable Treatment*

In investment treaty adjudication, the concept of FET has been the most widely used standard for challenging Host State's action that has detrimental effect on the investor's business or property. Most modern BITs contained provision on FET. For example the BIT between Nigeria and Netherlands provides in Article 3 (1) that:

> [E]ach Contracting Party shall ensure fair and equitable treatment of the investments of nationals of the other Contracting Party and shall not impair by

128. *Santa Elena v. Republic of Costa Rica* (*supra*) at 192.
129. See *Tecmed case* (*supra*) at para. 121.
130. *Methanex case* (*supra*), at IV D, para. 7. See also *Glamis Gold Ltd v. United States of America* (*supra*) where the State proposed series of legislation targeting at the claimant in order to stop its mineral extraction project, the tribunal after recognising the difficulty in 'ascertaining the legislative intent', declared that the law 'appears to apply to potentially several mines, if not yet at present, then in the future ... . In addition, it applies for the broad goal of preventing the imminent destruction of important Native American sacred sites threatened by proposed strip mining and ... ensuring these mining activities are adequately mitigated through implementation of new State reclamation requirements at the earliest opportunity'. See Allan Ingelson et al., 'NAFTA takings update the Glamis decision' (March 2012) JWEL&B 5(1): 27, at 40.
131. *Azurix v. Argentina* (*supra*) at paras 310-312.

unreasonable or discriminatory measures, the operation, management, maintenance, use, enjoyment or disposal thereof by those nationals.[132]

Where specific rules are unsuitable to address some governmental actions that affect investment, FET could help to address such issues with successful outcome. It is reminiscent of the civil law traditions in which specific rules is complemented with a general clause of good faith in order to serve as overarching principle that fills the gaps and aids understanding of specific clauses.[133] However, there is a caution that in view of the heterogeneity of the clause's language in most treaties, each of the clauses must be interpreted 'in accordance with Article 31 of the Vienna Convention on the law of treaties, taking into consideration its context, and as appropriate, its history.' Its meaning will depend on the circumstances of each case as the standard is a broad and flexible one that can be adapted to specific cases.[134]

The FET, as a rule of international law, is not to be determined in accordance with the Host State's law and it is independent of the national treatment standard. Therefore, the standard may be breached even though the Host State accords the foreign investor the same treatment given to those investors that are its national. So also, the foreign investor does not have to show that other nationalities received better treatment in order to prove that he has been unfairly or inequitably treated.[135]

The FET standard is not also 'frozen in time' but it keeps on evolving and therefore the high threshold laid down in the 1926 Neer case[136] has been departed from by some treaty tribunals. Some treaty tribunals have instead embraced the less stringent standard laid down in the case of *ELSI (United State v. Italy)*.[137]

The tribunals have applied the FET in two broad factual situations.[138] The first situation concerned with the treatment of the investors by the Host State's courts while

132. Other treaty provisions include the French Model Treaty which provides that 'Either Contracting Party shall extend fair and equitable treatment in accordance with the principles of International Law to investments made by nationals and companies of the other Contracting Party on its territory … .' Multilateral treaty also contains provision on FET. NAFTA provides in Article 1105 (1) that 'each party shall accord to investments of investors of another Party treatment in accordance with international law, including fair and equitable treatment and full protection and security'.
133. Dolzer & Schreuer, 'Principles of International Investment Law', at 122.
134. *Ibid.*, at 121.
135. *Mondev v. The United States*, Award 11 October 2002, 42 ILM (2003) 85, para. 118; *Waste Management v. Mexico*, Final Award, 30 April 2004, 43 ILM (2004) 967, para. 93.
136. Dolzer & Schreuer, 'Principles of International Investment Law', at 123.
137. *L F H Neer v. Mexico, Opinion, US-Mexico General Claims Commission*, 15 October, 1926 21 AJIL (1927) 555. One US citizen was murdered in Mexico and it was alleged that Mexican authorities did not exercise diligence in investigating and prosecuting the crime. The commission declared that the treatment meted on the alien must have amounted to an 'outrage, to bad faith, to wilful neglect of duty, or to an insufficiency of governmental action so far short of international standards that every reasonable impartial man would readily recognise its insufficiency' in order to constitutes an international delinquency'.
138. ICJ Reports 1989, 15. See also the case of *ADF Group v. United States*, Award, 9 July 2003, 18 ICSID Review – FILJ (2003, 195, 6 ICSI Reports 470. But see the decision of the ICSID tribunal in the NAFTA case of *Glamis Gold Ltd v. United States of America*, (*supra*) cited by Allan Ingelson et al. (*supra*), p. 27 at 34-39. In this case the applicant had applied for permits to mine Gold and had expended the sum of USD 15 million in pursuance of the mineral development before the State passed series of legislations specifically designed to stop the mineral extraction

the second situation deals with administrative decision making.[139] However, of relevant to our research is the second situation and so we shall limit our analysis to the cases decided by the tribunals in which FET was applied to such factual situation. Among other criteria, two principles are involved in the application of FET by the tribunals in reviewing administrative decision that has adverse effects on the investor. These are the principles of legitimate expectation and due process.

The principle of legitimate expectation is to the effect that any decision that will affect the investor's business should be traceable to the legal and business framework existing at the time of the investment and also to any particular assurances given to him at the time of the investment upon which he relied on to invest.[140] Any treatment meted on the investor will be assessed by reference to such legal framework and specific assurances. This required that the legal and business framework should be made clear by the Host State at the time of investment. The Investment tribunal gave an elucidatory exposition of the principle in the case of *Tecmed v. Mexico*[141] and the

projects on ground of environmental concerns and protection of Native American religious practices. In the claimant's taking claims before the ICSID tribunal, the tribunal rejected its argument that the FET standard has been violated. The tribunal relied on the customary international law standard laid down in the Neer's case and ruled that the international standard for FET is 'for all intent and purposes frozen at the 1925 Neer standard'. Referring to the previous NAFTA decisions such as *International Thunderbird, SD Meyers and Mondev* cases which had used particular adjective modifier like 'gross' denial of justice and 'manifest arbitrariness', 'shock or surprise' in their award respectively to show strict FET standard, the tribunal concluded that 'the fundamentals of the Neer standard still apply today: to violate the customary international law minimum standard of treatment codified in Article 1105 of the NAFTA, an act must be sufficiently egregious and shocking-a gross denial of justice, manifest arbitrariness, blatant unfairness, a complete of lack of due process, evident discrimination, or a manifest lack of reasons-so as to fall below accepted international standards and constitute a breach of Article 1105 (1).'

Also the BIT case between *Toto Construzioni General S.P.A. v. Republic of Lebanon* (*supra*) appeared to have followed the test laid down in the Neer's case. The tribunal in the Toto's case stated that 'the threshold for finding a violation of the FET is high as confirmed by *Biwater Gauff Tanzania Ltd. case.* In *EDF Services Ltd. v. Romania*, it was held that the idea that legitimate expectations, and therefore, FET imply the stability of the legal and business framework, may not be correct if stated in an overtly-broad and unqualified formulation. The FET might then mean the virtual freezing of the legal regulation of the economic activities, in contrast with the State's normal regulatory power and the evolutionary character of economic life'.

139. Mclachlan QC et al., 'International Investment Arbitration: Substantive Principles', at 226.

140. See *Toto Construzioni General S.P.A v. Republic of Lebanon* (*supra*), paras 331-333.

141. *Tenicas Medioambientales Tecmed SA v. United Mexican States*, (Award) (2004) 43 ILM 133, 173 ICSID (AF), 2003. The tribunal declared that 'this provision of the Agreement, in light of the good faith principle established by international law, requires the contracting Parties to provide to international investments treatment that does not affect the basic expectations that were taken into account by the foreign investor to make the investment. The foreign investor expects the Host State to act in a consistent manner, free from ambiguity and totally transparently in its relation with the foreign investor so that it may know beforehand any and all rules and regulations that will govern its investments as well as the goals of the relevant policies and administrative practices or directives, to be able to plan its investments and comply with such regulations. The foreign investor also expects the Host State to act consistently, i.e. without arbitrarily revoking any pre-existing decisions or permits issued by the State that were relied upon by the investor to assume its commitments as well as to plan and launch its commercial and business activities. The investor also expects the State to use the legal instruments that govern the actions of the investor or the investment in conformity with the function usually

standards of conduct espoused in the case have been followed by subsequent cases. In *Occidental v. Ecuador*,[142] the applicant, a US company entered into a participation agreement with a State owned corporation, Petroecuador, to undertake exploration for and production of oil in Ecuador.

Under the contract, the applicant was entitled to Value Added Tax (VAT) reimbursement on purchases required for its exploration and production activities and ultimate the exportation of the oil produced. The applicant had been applying for reimbursement of VAT from the State's tax authority on regular basis and has always been refunded. However, beginning from year 2001, the tax authority denied further reimbursement of VAT to the applicant and other companies in the oil sector and compelled the applicant to return the amounts already reimbursed. The applicant, in reliance on the BIT between Ecuador-US which guaranteed FET, challenged the inconsistency in the practice of the State's tax authority concerning VAT refund at the London Court of International Arbitration (LCIA). The tribunal declared that the germane issue is whether the legal and business framework meets the requirements of stability and predictability under international law and not whether there is an obligation to refund VAT. Furthermore, even though there is no obligation to refund VAT under international law, there is an obligation not to alter the legal and business environment in which the investment has been made. The tribunal held that the treatment accorded the investor in this regard has not been fair and equitable in that the tax law was changed significantly 'without providing any clarity about its meaning and extent and the practice and regulations were also inconsistent with such practice.'

In *CMS Transmission Company v. Republic of Argentina*,[143] under an emergency law, the respondent revoked the earlier guarantees given to the investor in legislation, regulations and under a licence for price adjustments for the transportation of natural gas. The claimant alleged that the legal and regulatory framework existing at the time the investment was made entitled it to calculate the tariff in US Dollars, conversion into Peso at the time of billing and periodic adjustment of tariffs in accordance with the US Producer Price Index. The claimant further alleged that the new emergency laws had changed this arrangement by imposing the devalued Peso on the tariff arrangement. The tribunal referred to the preamble to the Argentina-US BIT which provides that it is desirable 'to maintain a stable framework for investment and maximum effective use of economic resources' and concluded that '... In addition to the specific terms of the treaty, the significant number of treaties, both bilateral and multilateral, that have dealt with this standard also unequivocally shows that fair and equitable treatment is inseparable from stability and predictability.' Accordingly, it was held that the new

assigned to such instruments, and not to deprive the investor of its investment without the required compensation. In fact failure by the Host State to comply with such pattern of conduct with respect to the foreign investor or its investments affects the investor's ability to measure the treatment and protection awarded by the Host State and to determine whether the actions of the Host State conform to the fair and equitable principle'.

142. Final Award, 1 July 2004, 12 ICSID Reports 59.
143. Award 12 May 2005, ILM 1205, 1235 ICSID (2005).

arrangement imposed by the State by emergency laws violates the FET standard. Several other cases followed the standard set out in the cases above.[144]

The principle above however, has some limitations. The tribunals have held that it is the duty of the Host State to decide for itself the legal framework which it will apply to foreign investment in her territory and that the investor must take the law as he finds it.[145] The investor is therefore, bound by the Host State law at the date of the investment. If the law is faithfully applied to his investment, he cannot complain of unfair treatment in the absence of any specific representation to the contrary.

In GAMI v. Mexico,[146] the tribunal opined that 'International law does not appraise the content of a regulatory programme extant before an investor decides to commit. The inquiry is whether the State abided by or implemented that programme. It is in this sense that government's failure to implement or abide by its own law in a manner adversely affecting a foreign investor may but will not necessarily lead to a violation of Article 1105'. The tribunal has also recognised the need of the State to maintain a reasonable degree of regulatory flexibility in order to be able to respond to changing circumstances in the interest of the public. Therefore, the Host State's legitimate right to subsequently regulate domestic affairs in the public interest must be taken into consideration also in order to determine whether the breach of the investor's expectation was justified and reasonable. This is because a foreign investor should reasonably expect that the circumstances prevailing at the time of investment may change.[147]

4.1.4 *Due Process Principle*

The principle of due process concerned with the treatment of the investor in the administrative decision making process.[148] It is a fundamental tenet of the rule of law enshrined in the municipal legal order and also an important element of the FET principle. The tribunals have held that the regulatory authorities of the Host States have a duty to accord due process to the foreign investors. The duty is breached where the regulator accord preferential treatment to the local investor to the detriment of the foreign investor[149] or where the measure taken is arbitrary or discriminatory against

144. *LG&E v. Argentina, Decision on Liability,* 3 October 2006; *Eureko v. Poland, Partial,* (Award, 19 August 2005, 12 ICSID Reports 335; *Bayindir v. Pakistan,* Decision on Jurisdiction, 14 November 2005; *Saluka v. Czech Republic,* (Partial Award, 17 March 2006); *PSEG v. Turkey,* (Award, 19 January 2007), at paras 240-256 and *Enron v. Argentina,* (Award, 22 May 2007), paras 260-262.
145. Campbell Mclachlan QC et al., 'International Investment Arbitration: Substantive Principles', at 236. This principle has been recognised by the PCIJ in the Oscar Chin Case (1934) PCIJ Report Series A/B No. 63. The court opined that the investor must take the State's laws as he finds it and that he cannot complain subsequently if his business fails merely because of laws, policies and practices in place at the time of investment and which he ought to have known very well before he decides to invest.
146. *GAMI Investment Inc v. United Mexican States,* (Award) (2005) 44 ILM 545, 560 (NAFTA/UNCITRAL, 2004).
147. *Saluka v. Czech Republic* (*supra*).
148. Campbell Mclachlan QC et al., *supra* n. 959 at 239.
149. *S D Myers Inc v. Government of Canada* 8 ICSID Rep. 3 (NAFTA/UNCITRAL).

the foreign investor.[150] Also, where the regulator reaches a decision that adversely affects the investment (e.g., revocation of a licence) without giving the investor opportunity to be heard, the tribunals have held that the duty has been violated.[151] However, the standard of due process and procedural fairness applicable in administrative proceedings are lower than a judicial process.[152] Therefore, where the investor has been given a full opportunity to be heard and present evidence by the administrative body, coupled with the fact that the administrative proceedings were made subject to judicial review by the court, the tribunal had found that the standard has not been breached.[153] There are cases to show that the due process standard is not absolute. In *Genin et al v. Republic of Estonia*,[154] the tribunal held that the standard has not been breached in spite of its finding that the claimant's banking licence was revoked by the Regulators without formal notice to or hearing of the investor which the tribunal considered were contrary to generally accepted banking and regulatory practice.

4.1.5 *Good Faith Principle*

The principle of good faith is also inherent in FET which is also one of the fundamental principles in international law. Several treaty tribunals have recognised the principle. In *Waste Management v. Mexico (supra)*, the tribunal observed that the principle is a basic obligation under the FET standard as contained in Article 1105 of the NAFTA. The tribunal declared that:

> The Tribunal has no doubt that a deliberate conspiracy – that is to say, a conscious combination of various agencies of government without justification to defeat the purposes of an investment agreement – would constitute a breach of Article 1105 (1). A basic obligation of the State under Article 1105 (1) is to act in good faith and form, and not deliberately to set out to destroy or frustrate the investment by improper means.

Also in *Saluka v. Czech Republic (supra)*, the tribunal emphasised the role of good faith principle when it declared that:

> A foreign investor protected by the treaty may in any case properly expect that the Czech Republic implements its policies bonafide by conduct that is, as far as it affects the investor's investment, reasonably justifiable by public policies and that such conduct does not manifestly violate the requirements of consistency, transparency, even- handedness and non-discrimination.

The tribunal would find action of bad faith on the part of the Host State as prove of violation of the principle of FET but it is however, not a requirement.[155] However, good

150. *Saluka Investments BV Netherlands v. Czech Republic (supra)*.
151. *Tecmed v. Mexico (supra)* and *Middle East Cement v. Egypt*, (Award, 12 April 2002), 18 ICSID Review-FILJ (2003) 602; *Metalclad Corp. v. Mexico*, (Award, 30 August 2000), 5 ICSID Reports 209.
152. *Thunderbird v. Mexico*, (Award, 26 January 2006).
153. *Ibid.*, paras 197-201.
154. (Award) 6 ICSID Rep.
155. *Glamis Gold Ltd. v.United States of America*, (Award) (*supra*).

faith cannot be a defence for the State where its action causes harm to the foreign investor. Several investment tribunals have ruled on this. In *Mondev v. USA*,[156] the tribunal declared that:

> [T]o the modern eye, what is unfair or inequitable need not equate with the outrageous or the egregious. In particular, a State may treat foreign investment unfairly and inequitably without necessarily acting in bad faith.

4.1.6 *Applying the above Investment Treaties Principles to Unilateral Capture*

Intangible rights such as contractual right to 'search for, bore and get petroleum' granted by the Host State to an investor are protected property under international investment law. The question to be asked is what happens if after exercising the right to 'search for, bore and get petroleum'; an investor could not extract the resources he discovered as a result of the action or inaction of the State or by State-sanctioned action of another investor? Would treaty protect the investor if another investor interferes with or converts all or part of the underground petroleum resources that the investor discovered and the Host State or its agency fails to prevent such interference or 'taking' as provided by the Host State's law and regulations?[157] It could be argued that failure by the Host State to protect the investor from such 'taking' or 'interference' could be as result of the fact that the Host State only recognises the investor's 'right to search for, bore and get petroleum' as proprietary but denies recognition of the rights of the investor to the underlying un-extracted resources as proprietary. If this is the case, such position of the Host State will make the proprietary rights to search for, bore and get petroleum' granted to the investor meaningless. Could this position of the Host State create dual investments - one in which the treaty will protect because the State recognises it and another which it will not protect because it lacks recognition by the State? The jurisprudence of the investment treaties tribunals as well as U.S.-Iran claims tribunal have shown that the State's position in this regard will not create dual investments.

It is regarded as one investment in which the grant of proprietary rights to search for, bore and get petroleum by the Host State to the investor encompasses his rights to the underlying resources or assets discovered, but yet untapped.[158] Analogy could also be drawn from a situation in which the Host State denied the investor's rights to export his products or repatriate profits after granting him administrative permits to carry out approved activities or where the Host State changes its law to impose punitive tax on

156. Award of 11 October 2002, 42 ILM (2003) 85. See also *Tecmed v. Mexico* (*supra*); *Occidental v. Ecuardor* (*supra*) and *CMS v. Argentina* (*supra*) at para. 280.
157. This question is considered further below.
158. See *Starret Housing v. Iran* (*supra*); *Philips Petroleum v. Iran* (*supra*); *Amco v. Indonesia* (*supra*) and *CMS V. Argentina* (*Supra*). See Chapter 4 for a discussion of these cases in relation to the valuation method for expropriated contractual rights.

the income of the investor.[159] By such action, the investor's licence to carry out the approved activities will be rendered useless.

As a result, State's responsibility may arise where the Regulatory agency of the Host State fails to enforce compulsory unitisation regulations of the State to prevent unilateral capture of petroleum by one licensee from straddling reservoirs especially where the foreign investor has suffered substantial diminution of his investment.[160] If a foreign investor whose country has a BIT with the Host country suffers substantial loss of petroleum as a result of drainage by either local licensee or another foreign licensee or State oil company, it can bring a claim against the Host State at the treaty tribunal, for failure of the Host State to provide full protection and security as provided in the applicable BIT.[161] The State's obligation to take active measures to protect the investment from adverse effects covers situation in which the State officials failed to exercise due diligence and also cases of omission to provide protection to alien's property. It also goes beyond physical protection to legal protection of the investment of the investor. Where the State organ had knowledge of the straddling reservoirs either *suo moto* or on the information supplied by the licensee and yet failed to order compulsory unitisation as provided by law, the State cannot be held to have exercised due diligence especially if the unilateral drainage continues for considerable length of time before stoppage.[162]

Moreover, obligation to protect will arise from the guarantees in the compulsory unitisation laws that the Minister will compel unitisation whenever there are straddling fields. This is a form of guarantees against violation of investor's right by operation of laws and regulations. Compulsory unitisation provisions constitute an assurance and legitimate expectation that investor's underlie assets will be protected from violation by any individual including Host State entity and that the State could compel unitisation and halt unilateral drainage. The State's obligation in this regard goes beyond physical security; it includes stability afforded by secure investment environment which should include secure legal environment as well so that investor can

159. See Thomas Walde & Abba Kolo, 'Environmental Regulation, Investment Protection and "Regulatory Taking" in International Law'. (2001) 50 International and Comparative Law Quarterly at 835.
160. A clear case of an investment suffering substantial diminution as a result of unilateral drainage of petroleum from straddling fields has been shown in Chapter 6. As at September 2008 the cumulative oil production by NAOC from the common reservoir with SPDC was 123,162,453 MMstb out of total recoverable oil of 137.19 MMstb. The remaining oil reserve was 13.99 MMstb as at September 2008. The total recoverable gas in the common reservoir was 329.56 BSCF as at January 2008. NAOC has produced 203.49 BSCF leaving a balance of 126.07 BSCF as at September 2008. This shows that SPDC's investment has been severely diminished having regards to the volume of oil and gas withdrawn from the common reservoir by NAOC.

    In another straddling reservoirs operated by SPDC and NAOC (Afuo field / Ogbainbiri field), in which the reservoir was unitised in 1991, there had been unilateral production by NAOC from the straddling reservoirs. The tract participation was split into 75% and 25% between NAOC and SPDC respectively, when the fields were unitised. NAOC was recorded to have drained about 37 MMstb of oil from SPDC side.
161. See *CME v. Czech Republic, (supra)*; *Azurix Corp v. The Argentine Republic (supra)*; *Siemens v. Argentina (supra)* and *Saluka v. Czech Republic (supra)*.
162. See the examples given between SPDC and NAOC in Nigeria and the Supreme Court of Netherland's case of *Unocal v. Conoco* discussed in Chapter 6.

reasonably expect that all laws and regulations that will enhance security of the investment will be enforced. One commentator has rightly pointed out that:

> once the investor has taken cognizance of the legal framework applicable to his investment, he should be reasonably entitled to expect a just and even-handed application of the law to his investments.[163]

Because the State has failed, either wilfully or negligently to enjoin unitisation or halt unilateral capture and a foreign investor has thereby suffered substantial depreciation in the value of his investment, State responsibility or obligation may be breached under the full protection and security clause.

Applying the principle of FET in the context of unilateral capture, entails an assessment of whether the legitimate expectation of the licensee has been impaired by failure to order retroactive unitisation. A licensee has legitimate expectation in having the field developed so as to reap the benefits of the underlying assets. Where one licensee refrained from development because he is by law prohibited to develop a straddling reservoir until an arrangement for unitised development is agreed with the other party, his legitimate expectation may be impaired if the other party proceeds with unilateral development and production of oil from the common reservoir and the Regulator failed to stop such production until an arrangement for unitisation had been made. This also requires a determination of the legal and business framework existing at the time the investment was made. The legal and business framework existing then was the compulsory unitisation regulation which offers protection to the underlie assets of the investor in a straddling field,[164] which the minister was meant to enforce whenever there is straddling reservoirs. An investor could be said to have a legitimate expectation that this provision will remain stable and enforced by the minister throughout the duration of the investment. This principle entails that the enforcement of this legal and business environment should meet the standard of stability and predictability under international law. Once this standard is not met, the tribunal will probably find that the investor has not been fairly treated.[165] The State could argue that it has the right to decide the legal frame work which it will enforce or apply in her territory. However, even if investment tribunal cannot appraise the content of a law existing before the investment is made; it can inquire into whether the State abided by or implemented the law or programme faithfully. That was why the tribunal has held that government's failure in this regard may lead to a violation of Article 1105 of NAFTA.[166] Therefore, where the regime does not encapsulate the rule of capture, failure by the regulator to make unitisation order effective retroactively may raise the issues of whether the investor suffering drainage has been fairly and equitably treated and also whether the measure taken by the State's Regulatory agency amounts to indirect taking of property (i.e., the State sanctioning the taking of the property of an investor by another investor). The practice of the treaty tribunals is to define FET in a

163. August Reinisch & Christina Knahr, 'International Investment Law in Context' (Eleven International Publishing, 2008), at 190.
164. *Tecmed v. Mexico* (*supra*).
165. *Occidental v. Ecuador* (*supra*).
166. *GAMI v. Mexico* (*supra*).

broad and flexible manner so that it can be adapted to specific cases. Its meaning will therefore, depend on the circumstances of each case. The FET standard keeps evolving or developing. This is seen from the position taken by the treaty tribunals when they embraced the less stringent standard laid down in the case of *United State v. Italy* (*supra*) and have departed from the high threshold laid down in the 1926 Neer's case (*supra*). The FET has been employed by the treaty tribunals as standard against which an administrative decision that has adverse effects on the investor can be reviewed. The decision of the Regulatory Authority to make unitisation order effective from the date the order was made would obviously have adverse effect on the investment of the investor who suffered drainage. This may result in an unfair and inequitable treatment of the party who suffered drainage.[167] This is more pronounced in States where petroleum laws and regulations do not encapsulate the rule of capture and where unitisation clause mandated the minister to order unitisation whenever it is in the interests of the licensees to do so and the minister failed to exercise such power whenever the condition is present.[168] Moreover, the Administrative Agency could also be held to be in violation of due process where the drainage is by a local investor from the fields operated by the foreign investor and the Regulator fails to order retroactive unitisation. The duty is breached where the Regulator accords preferential treatment to the local investor to the detriment of the foreign investor[169] or where the measure taken is arbitrary or discriminatory against the foreign investor.[170] Moreover, where the State oil company drains oil from field operated by foreign investor and the State Regulatory Agency fails to order unitisation retroactively or compels one before drainage occurs, a case of deliberate conspiracy of the two Government Agencies to destroy or frustrate the investment of the foreign investor might be established.[171] This might violate good faith principle enshrined in the FET principle. In this circumstance, failure by the Regulator to compel unitisation or to make unitisation order effective retroactively could result into a finding of breach of this duty by the Host sate.

Also from the above, we have seen that certain acts and /or omissions have been held to constitute indirect expropriation. These include excessive or arbitrary taxation, interference with contractual rights especially where accompanied by discrimination,

167. This may also raise the issue of national treatment and most favoured nation (MFN) Principle. Investment treaty usually obligates States to treat an investor no less favourably than its own national investors or investors from third countries. See Article 3 of the United Kingdom-Venezuela BIT and Articles 3 (2) and 4 of the Kingdom of Netherlands – Federal Republic of Nigeria BIT. The import of these provisions is that it imports beneficial provisions from other investment agreements to the agreement at hand thereby giving investors an added protection. Accordingly, where the party draining petroleum from a common reservoir is the National oil company (NOC) or a local investor, and unitisation is not ordered retroactively, the affected foreign investor may have regard to other decisions made by the State on unilateral capture to determine whether it has been subject to discriminatory treatment. Also, if an NOC or local investor is given undue advantage in the context of unilateral capture there could be a breach of national standard treatment.
168. See section 48 (1) (b) of the Petroleum (Drilling and Production Regulation), 1969 (Nigeria) – the minister will order unitisation if it is in the interests of Nigeria, the grantee and the licensees or lessees.
169. *S D Myers Inc v. Government of Canada* 8 ICSID Rep. 3 (NAFTA/UNCITRAL).
170. *Saluka Investments BV Netherlands v. Czech Republic* (*supra*).
171. *Waste management case* (*supra*) and *Saluka case* (*supra*).

interference with management of an investment, appointment of managers by Host State, and revocation or denial of government permits or licences. It has also been seen that even though the investment arbitral tribunals have tried to formulate important principles for identifying indirect expropriation, there are no hard and fast rules for determining acts and / or omission that may constitute an indirect expropriation. Determination of what may constitute indirect expropriation depends on the facts and circumstances of each case. Therefore, the list of acts and / or omission that may constitute indirect expropriation is not closed.

In relation to the acts and/ or omission of the Regulatory Authority with regards to oil and gas straddling fields as discussed in the preceding chapters, we have seen that in defiance of the legislative provisions, the Regulatory Authority had failed to enforce compulsory unitisation laws and regulations at the appropriate time. We have also seen that it has failed to enforce unitisation retroactively to the date of first production or to the date when the affected investor established straddling in spite of the fact that petroleum laws do not encapsulate the common law rule of capture. As a result, one investor has suffered substantial loss of oil and diminution in the value of his contractual licence.

These sequential acts and/or omissions probably present a case of 'creeping' or 'acts tantamount to expropriation.' It does not matter whether the State benefited from the taking or not. It is also immaterial whether the intention of the State measures is for public welfare or legitimate purpose. What matters is whether 'it is a measure, being legitimate and serving a public purpose, should give rise to compensation.' Chapter 4 of this book has shown that company's reserves base has impacts on its credit rating as well as the value of its shares in the capital market. A substantial diminution of this reserves base through unilateral extraction and subsequent approval of same by the State may amount to an indirect taking of property.

4.2 International Human Rights Law

On a theoretical level, the concept of 'possessions' and the nature of the responsibility of the State in the protection of 'possessions' under the ECHR, have been considered in our analytical framework in Chapter 2. The chapter also examined whether an individual can vindicate his property rights through the mechanisms provided by the ECHR especially where there is interference or violation of his property rights by another individual.

This section therefore, considers the jurisprudence of the ECHR on the above issues and also on when interference by State or by its Organ constitutes taking of property. In addition, it considers whether failure by the Regulator to enjoin unitisation at the appropriate time or to order unitisation retroactively to the date of first production can amount to a breach of the State's obligation under AIPI of the ECHR.

4.2.1 *The Rights Guaranteed by A1P1 and Responsibility of State*

The rights guaranteed by Article 1 Protocol 1 to the ECHR (A1P1) are not absolute. It gives to State a wide power to interfere with property. This is confirmed by the practice of the Court. There is also no express provision on right to compensation in the event of interference with property except if reference is made to general principles of international law. Both natural and artificial persons have rights under the A1P1. It is instructive to note also that rights to property is a liberty right and not a claim right. Therefore, the State's obligation is limited to protection of existing property right and not to ensure that an individual acquires property. The State only has responsibility to preserve a system of private ownership. This is done by providing a legal system or avenue through which property rights can be enforced. For example, the Convention Organs have held that there is a breach of the applicant's right to property where the State fails to provide police assistance to the applicant in order for him to evict a tenant against whom he had secured court eviction order.[172] Similarly, in the case of *Cyprus v. Turkey*,[173] though the case was dismissed for lack of evidence to prove that there was an administrative practice of denying individual's access to court for redress, it can be inferred from the judgment of the court that there is a positive obligation on the part of the State to protect property against wrongful interference by private individuals. Moreover, in the case of *Plattform Arzte fur das Leben v. Austria*,[174] the court held that there is an obligation of the State to take reasonable and appropriate measures to protect demonstrators against interference of other private individuals who intended to disrupt their demonstration in breach of Article 11 of the Convention.

It is to be noted that the Convention has a horizontal effect meaning that the rights provided in the Convention is applicable in the legal relations between private parties and not only in legal relations between an individual and the public bodies.[175] Consequently, a State may be responsible for interferences with property rights arising from legal relations between individuals.[176] However, there is no State interference if the acts complained of emanated from purely contractual relationship between individuals and not resulting from exercise of governmental authority.[177]

Instances in which the European Court of Human Rights (ECtHR) has readily found the responsibility of the State is where the State exercises its legislative or executives powers in connection with the civil law relations between private persons.[178] Also, where the deprivation does not transfer property to the State but resulted from the plans adopted by the Forestry Board, the court found that the deprivation incurred State responsibility.[179]

172. See the cases of *Immobiliare Saffi v. Italy* Judgment of 28 July 1999; *A.O. v. Italy* Judgment of 30 May 2000 and *Ghidotti v. Italy*, Judgment of 21 February 2002, (App. No. 28272/95).
173. Judgment of 10 May 2001.
174. Judgment of 1988, Series A, No. 139.
175. Dijik and Hoof, 'The Theory and Practice of the European Convention on Human Rights', at 23.
176. *MN v. Bulgaria*, (App. No. 29785/96) Decision 4 September 1996.
177. *Gustafsson v. Sweden*, Judgment of 25 April 1996 at 60.
178. *James & others v. UK*, Judgment of 21 February 1986, Seriea A, No. 98.
179. *Hiipakka & others v. Finland*, App. No. 29069/95, 15 May 1996.

On the other hand, exercise of judicial power has been held not to amount to interference by State in property right. This is because the court is merely providing an avenue through which resolution of private disputes can be carried out.[180] Positive obligation of the State to protect property rights of an individual does not arise in the context of ensuring that all argument concerning the dispute between individuals will be fully considered by the courts.[181] The exception to this rule is that State's responsibility will be incurred where the decision of the court in a dispute between private persons contravenes the right to fair trial provisions in section 6 of the Convention.[182] The Commission has also held that public authorities and judicial bodies should not force some individuals to bear a loss in favour of other individuals. Where this is lacking, then State responsibility would be incurred. In *Bramelid and Malmstrom v. Sweden*[183] the Commission held that State organs - public authorities and judicial bodies - must ensure that in the determination of the legal relations between individuals, the 'law does not create such an inequality that one person could be arbitrarily and unjustly deprived of property in favour of another.'[184]

4.2.2 *Interferences with Property*

Even though A1P1 guarantees right to property, it also provides that an individual can be deprived of its possession under certain conditions and that States can control the use of property in accordance with the general interest. This basic principle is acknowledged in a number of decisions of the Convention Organs. However, the Convention Organs have acknowledged that the powers of the State to deprive an individual of its property and to control the use of property must be construed in light of the provisions of A1P1 which guarantee peaceful enjoyment of property.[185]

The A1P1 provides that:

> Every natural or legal person is entitled to the peaceful enjoyment of his possessions. No one shall be deprived of his possessions except in the public interest and subject to the conditions provided for by law and by the general principles of international law.
>
> The preceding provisions shall not, however, in any way impair the right of a State to enforce such laws as it deems necessary to control the use of property in accordance with the general interests or to secure the payment of taxes or other contributions or penalties.

180. Coban, 'Protecting Property Rights within the European Convention on Human Rights', at 168 n. 138.
181. *Ibid.*
182. *Ibid.*, at 169. See also the Cases of *Estima Jorge v. Portugal*, Judgment of 21 April 1998 (Reports 1998-II, P.762 contrast, *O.N. v. Bulgaria* (App. No. 35221/97) Decision 6 April 2000.
183. App. No. 8588/79, 29 DR 64; App. No. 12462/86, 13 July 1987, 53 DR 234.
184. Coban, 'Protecting Property Rights within the European Convention on Human Rights', at 169.
185. *James and others v. The U.K.* (*supra*); *Holy Monastries v. Greece*, Judgment of 9 December 1994, Series A, No. 301-A at 56; *Beyeler v. Italy*, Judgment of 5 January 2000 (APP. No. 33202/96) at 98; *Papamchalopoulos and others v. Greece*, Judgment of 15 February 2011(App. No. 37095/97).

From the above, there are three rules regarding regulation of interferences with property under A1P1. The first rule which is contained in the first sentence of the first paragraph provides for the peaceful enjoyment of possessions. The second rule which is contained in the second sentence of the first paragraph covers deprivation of possessions and subjects it to certain conditions. The third rule is provided in the second paragraph to the effect that the State can control the use of property in accordance with the general interest or to secure payment of taxes or other contributions or penalties.

The connection between the three rules was explained by the ECtHR in the cases of *Sporong and Lonnroth v. Sweden* (*supra*) and *James v. UK* (*supra*). The court explained that interference with enjoyment of possessions that do not qualify as a deprivation of a person's possession or a control of use of property could fall under the first rule, i.e. as an interference with peaceful enjoyment of possession. However, the court in analysing the nature of interference, will only consider whether the interference falls under the first rule after it is satisfied that the second and third rules do not apply.

4.2.2.1 Deprivation of Property (The Second Rule Contained in the Second Sentence of the First Paragraph)

Deprivation of property is allowed on the ground of public interests and subject to the conditions provided by law and by the general principles of international law. What constitutes deprivation may not be difficult to determine since deprivation involves a transfer of property or destruction of it. A subject is said to have been deprived of its property if all his rights to it are extinguished either by the operation of the law or by exercise of legal authority. The applicant therefore, must show that he has title to the property.[186] However, difficulty arises when deprivation is considered in light of the definition of property. Chapter 2 has shown that under the common law, property is defined as bundle of rights while under the ECHR, it is not so defined. Different rights arising from property is not regarded as different property rights but as use of property.[187] Therefore, where the applicant has been deprived of one right, the court may hold that he has not been deprived of ownership but that it is a control of use of property. In the case of *Tre Traktorer Aktiebolag v. Sweden,* (*supra*) the court held that a withdrawal of the licence to sell alcoholic beverages did not amount to deprivation of property but control of the use of property because the applicant could still enjoy other economic interests embedded in the premises like leasing the premises and the property assets contained in it. Also, in *Fredin's v. Sweden* (*supra*), a revocation of a licence to exploit gravel in one plot of the applicant's property does not amount to deprivation of property as the court took into consideration applicants' other surrounding parcels when evaluating the effect of the interference. In *Mellacher v. Austria,*[188]

186. *Lithgow v. UK* A 102 (1986); EHRR 329 PC.
187. David Harris et al., 'Law of the European Convention on Human Rights' 2nd edn (Oxford University Press), at 677.
188. Judgment of 19 December 1989, Series A no. 159.

where the State placed restrictions on rent contracts that has the effect of reducing the rent that landlord could charge, the court held that the measures did not amount to either formal or de facto expropriation because there was no transfer of the applicant's property and neither was he deprived of the right to use, let or sell it.

The cases above may be distinguished from cases involving oil and gas exploitation licence. In a domanial regime, licence for the exploitation of oil and gas resources is usually granted by the State and the resources are owned by the State. The land from which the resources are to be exploited is not owned by the licensee but by the State or the community. Once the license is withdrawn, the licensee loses any right to exploit the resources even where considerable amounts of money has been spent. Since the licence constitutes possession under ECHR, a deprivation may occur because the licensee's right to the premises as well as to the underground resources has been taken away. This is unlike the above decided cases where the premises in respect of which the licence activities took place belong to the applicants so that even if their licences were withdrawn, the premises could still be used for other economic activities.

Therefore, where interference took away all meaningful use of the property, deprivation will occur but where title to the property has not been lost either formally or de facto, deprivation may not occur. Accordingly, interference with one or some of the use rights does not amount to deprivation of property.[189] Where public authorities adopted measure that leads to loss of title to the property, the court will make a finding of deprivation even if there is no formal taking of property. The court inquiries into the realities of the situation rather than the appearances of the matter so that where the situation constitutes de facto expropriation, the court will find deprivation. Therefore, in cases where there is even no transfer of property to a public authority but the action of a public authority forces the owner to transfer his property to other private owners, there is deprivation of property.[190] In the case of *Papamichalopoulos and others v. Greece (supra)*, the court held that the transfer of the applicant's land to the Navy by the Government and the fact that the Navy exercised full de facto control over the land for a period of twenty-eight years constituted de facto expropriation because the applicants were precluded from exercising ownership controls over their land and neither were

189. Ali Coban, 'Protecting Property Rights within the European Convention on Human Rights', at 176.

190. See also the case of *Hakansson and Sturesson v. Sweden*, Judgement of 21 February 1990, Series A, No. 171-A. Here the applicant bought a farm land at an auction but because the authorities refused to grant him permit needed to retain the land, he had no option than to resell it. Thus, the action of the authority had forced him to sell the farm land. In *Vasilescu v. Romania*, Judgment of 22 May 1998, Reports 1998-lll at 55 the court held that there was de facto confiscation of property where valuables were unlawfully seized from the applicant and as result of which he lost ability to dispose of them. All attempts made to seek redress from the national authorities and courts also failed. Also in *Hentrich v. France*, Judgment of 22 September 1994, Series A, No. 296-A, the court found deprivation where there is transfer of property to the tax authority due to its exercise of a right of preemption over the applicant's property. However, in *Bramelid and Malmstrom v. Sweden* (1982) 5 EHRR 249, the Commission held that regulations that allow a majority shareholder to buy out a minority shareholder in certain circumstances concerns the relations of shareholders inter se and has nothing to do with the notion of 'public interest' as commonly understood in the realm of expropriations. Consequently, the commission ruled that deprivation rule applies only to seizures by the State or to whom the State gave right to seize property for public interest.

they provided any form of redress. It is to be noted that the applicant's land were never formally expropriated by the authority and they still remained owner of the land. The court however took into consideration the length of the period in which the Navy was in occupation and the fact that they could not exercise any of the incidents of ownership in arriving at a finding of expropriation.

However, the mere fact that deprivation of property was founded is not conclusive that interference has violated A1P1. The court will usually find out whether the deprivation is legitimate (i.e., lawful) and whether it is for legitimate aim, (i.e., whether it is in public interests).

4.2.2.2 Lawfulness of Deprivation

For the interference to be legitimate, it must possess certain qualities. It must be based on an accessible, precise, and foreseeable national law. The law should also provide enough safeguards against arbitrary interference with the respective substantive rights.[191] The requirement of lawfulness may be breached where the law concerned is fashioned in such a manner that provide avenue for the national authorities to apply it in an inconsistent manner, thereby resulting into unforeseeable or arbitrary outcomes or depriving a person effective protection of his right.[192] This requirement is expressed in the second sentence of the first paragraph of A1P1 as 'the conditions provided for by law and the general principles of international law'. It is also expressed in the second paragraph of A1P1 as 'such laws as it deems necessary'. In applying these requirements, the court has held in several cases that any interference by public authority in the peaceful enjoyment of possessions must be lawful.[193] Thus, where the requirement of lawfulness is not satisfied, the Court will not bother to examine whether other requirements have been satisfied before ruling that A1P1 has been breached.[194] The requirement of rule of law has been regarded by the court as inherent features of the Convention articles including A1P1. However, the Convention Organs will not concern themselves with the issue of whether the national law has been correctly applied by the domestic court unless it has been applied 'manifestly erroneously or so as to reach arbitrary conclusions'.[195] It does have limited power to look into whether the measures complained of comply with the domestic law.

191. *Hovig v. France*, Judgement of 24 April 1990, Series A, No. 176-B para. 27.
192. *Hentrich case (supra)*; *Carborana and Vetura v. Italy (supra)*. See also *Latridis v. Greece* 1999-II; 30 EHRR 97 where the court ruled that the interference was clearly in breach of the national law and therefore, incompatible with A1P1.
193. *Latridis v. Greece* 1999-II; 30 EHRR 97 para. 58 GC; *Hentrich v. France* A 296-A (1994); 18 EHRR 440; *Carbonara and Ventura v. Italy* 2000-V; *The Former King of Greece v. Greece (supra)*; *Belvedere Alberghiera v. Italy*, Judgment of 30 May 2000 (App. No. 31524/96).
194. *Beyeler v. Italy (supra)*.
195. *Sporrong and Lonnroth v. Sweden (supra)*; *O.N v. Bulgaria*, Judgment of 6 April 2000 (9 App. No. 35221/97) where the court opined that it will not deal with error of law or fact committed by the domestic court unless they had violated the rights and freedoms protected by the Convention.

However, the court has in certain cases conducted proportionality test[196] or the fair balance test[197] in addition to the lawfulness requirement.[198] This is done also in cases bothering on the conduct of administrative authorities in the application of the national law.[199]

The reference to 'principles of international law' in the second rule, has been interpreted by the court as applicable only to cases where there is a taking of alien property by the State and not to cases of taking of national's property. Therefore, cases where the expropriation of alien's property is unlawful, full compensation is payable but where it is lawful it is not clear whether full or appropriate compensation should be paid.[200] Where the property of State's own national is expropriated in the public interests, there is no obligation on the State to pay compensation unless it is provided for in the national law.[201]

However, this distinction has been eroded by the decision of the court in the case of *Lithgow and others v. UK* (*supra*) where the court opined that the taking of property without compensation is normally incompatible with A1P1.

4.2.2.3 Public Interest / General Interest of Deprivation

The court has placed the role of determining what constitutes public interests on the democratic Government or Legislature. The court has held therefore, that it has a limited role in the review of what the democratic Government or Legislature considers as public interests.[202] Accordingly, the State has a wide margin of appreciation in determining what is in the public interests. The limited role that court performs in this regard is to determine whether the aim pursued by the interference is a legitimate one and also whether the measure taken to achieve the legitimate aim is proportional.

The requirement of legitimate aim spanned through the entire three rules. It is referred to as public interests in the second rule and as 'general interests' or to secure the payment of taxes and other contributions or penalties' in the third rule.[203] The court has ruled that there is no distinction between the requirement of the 'public interests' and the 'general interests.'[204] The only difference could be that compensation is payable only in cases of deprivation of property and not in cases of control of use.[205] The burden is on the applicant to prove that the State's judgment is 'manifestly without reasonable foundation'. As a result of the low standard of proof placed upon the State

196. *Sporrong and Lonnroth case* (*supra*).
197. *Beyeler case* (*supra*).
198. See a discussion on the proportionality test or fair balance test in p. 351.
199. *Broniowski v. Poland* 2004-V; 43 EHRR1 para. 154 GC.
200. Coban, 'Protecting Property Rights within the European Convention on Human Rights', at 198, citing P.M. Norton, 'A Law of the Future or a Law of the Past? Modern Tribunals and the National Law of Expropriation', (1991) 85 American Journal of International Law 474.
201. *Gudmundsson v. Iceland*, (App. No. 511/59) Yearbook III (1960) p. 394.
202. *Beyeler v. Italy*, Judgement of 5 January 2000 (App. No. 33202/96) para. 112; *The Former king of Greece v. Greece*, Judgement of 23 November 2000 (App. No. 25701/94) para. 87.
203. Harris, 'Law of the European Convention on Human Rights', at 668.
204. *James v. UK* (*supra*).
205. Coban, 'Protecting property rights within the European Convention on Human Rights', at 175.

as to what constitutes public interests vis-à-vis the high standard required of an applicant to prove otherwise, it has been contended that the circumstances in which the court would dispute the purpose alleged by the State or contest the assertion that the measure has a legitimate aim cannot be foreseen.[206] This view is reinforced by the decision of the court in *James v. UK* (*supra*) where it was held that compulsory transfer of property from one individual to another may in some circumstances constitute a legitimate aim to promote public interests. Consequently, the court held that the taking of property in pursuance of a policy calculated to enhance social justice within the community can properly be described as being 'in the public interests.'[207] In this case, the Applicants were the trustees of the Westminster family. The Westminster and its trustees owned the Belgravia estate comprising 2000 houses in central London. These properties were held on two types of leases (1) a building lease for ninety-nine years subject to payment of ground rents and building of a house on the land which would be delivered to the landlord on the expiration of the lease, (2) premium lease subject to the payment of a capital sum and rent to the landlord. However, the Labour Government of that time introduced legislation which grants long lease holders the right to buy compulsorily the freehold at approximately the value of the land and house. The legislation further provides that where the tenants and the landlord could not agree on the price, an independent tribunal would determine the prices to be paid. Consequently, several tenants exercised their rights under the legislation and some of them resold the houses within one year of acquiring the properties and realised 'windfall profits'. The Applicants complained to the Commission that the compulsory transfer of their freehold rights under the legislation violated A1P1.[208]

Therefore, it has been suggested by one commentator that for an applicant to successfully challenge expropriation, the attack should be on the conditions that attach to it rather than on the reasons for which it was done.[209] This is because the court had hardly ruled that the aim of the interference was not in the public interests in spite of its expressed scepticisms on the reasons adduced by the government in some cases.[210] However, the approach adopted by the Convention Organs was to examine through the principle of proportionality, how the rights of the individual in question is affected by the governmental action rather than whether the decisions are in principle right.[211]

206. *Ibid.*, at 669. See also *Hentrich v. France* A 296 (1994); 18 EHRR 440 para. 99; *Lithgow v. UK* A 102 (1986) EHRR 329 PC; *The Former King of Greece v. Greece* 2000-XII; 33 EHRR 516 GC and *Chassagnou v. France* 1999-III; 29 EHRR 615 GC.
207. *James v. UK* (*supra*) (1986); 8 EHRR 123 para. 49.
208. See also the case of *Latridis v. Greece*, Judgment of 25 March 1999, Reports 1999-ll at 55.
209. Harris et al., 'Law of the European Convention on Human Rights', at 669.
210. See *The Former King of Greece v. Greece* (*supra*) where the court even though expressed doubt as to the reasons given by the expropriating government, it nevertheless held that the doubt could not suffice to deprive the overall objective of the expropriation of its legitimacy as being in the public interests.
211. Coban, 'Protecting Property Rights within the European Convention on Human Rights' at 204 citing Alexy, R. 'Individual Rights and Collective Goods', in C. Nino (ed.) Rights (Aldershot: Dartmouth, 1992).

4.2.2.4 *Control of the Use of Property (The Third Rule Contained in the Second Paragraph of A1P1)*

This is the power used by the State to restrict or regulate the use or disposal of property to serve the general interests or to secure payment of taxes or other contribution or penalties. The conditions for deprivation of property and that for the control of use of property are identical in substance.[212]

The State has a wide margin of appreciation in this aspect as its power is very wide. This power is exercised by the State or its agency by either imposing an obligation on individual or by imposition of restrictions on the activities of the individual. The Convention Organs have held that the decision of the State agency to require an individual to plant trees in the interest of environmental protection,[213] or to take some security measures in order to open a building into a business, and regulate shop opening hours[214] amounted to control of the use of property. Where the State has imposed restrictions arising from town planning,[215] environmental protection, housing policy, rent control,[216] inheritance laws, economic regulations of professions,[217] the seizure of property for legal proceedings, or demolition of a dilapidated house to prevent danger to the public,[218] the court has held that the State's action constitutes control of use of the property. Moreover, cases in which there was a transfer of hunting rights over the applicant's land by a law to members of an Association,[219] and the abolition of exclusive fishing rights of the owners of water areas[220] were regarded by court as control of the use of property.

From the above cases, where the measures taken by the State did not deprive the applicant title to his property, it may be regarded as control of the use of property. The cases also showed that measures taken by the State to regulate use or disposal of property that fall short of deprivation rule, could amount to control of the use of property.[221] In some instances however, interferences that is short of deprivation rule may be considered as interference with the substance of property and not control of the use of property.[222]

212. See p. 345 above for their differences.
213. *Denev v. Sweden, Decision of the Commission* (App. No. 12570/86) DR no. 101.
214. *Admissibility Decision of the Commission* CD 9, P.53.
215. *Fredin v. Sweden*, Judgment of 18 February 1991, Series A, No. 192; *Pine Valley Developments Ltd. and others v. Ireland*, Judgment of 29 November 1991, Series A, No. 222; *Chapman v. UK*, Judgment of 18 January 2001 (9 App. No. 27238/95) para. 120.
216. *Mellacher & others v. Austria*, Judgment of 19 December 1989, Series A, No. 169 where the court held that reduction in the amount of rent by laws amounts to control of the use of property.
217. *Van Marle and others v. Netherlands*, Judgment of 3 June 1986, Series A, No. 101.
218. *Admissibility Decision of the Commission*, App. No. 7965/77.
219. *Chassagnou & others v. France* Judgment of 29 April 1999, Reports 1999-III.
220. *Aschan & others v. Finland*, Judgment of 12 February 2001 (App. No. 37858/97).
221. Coban, 'Protecting Property Rights within the European Convention on Human Rights' at 182.
222. *Sporrong and Lonnroth v. Sweden*, A 52 (1982) 5 EHRR 35 PC; Also in the case of *Katte Klitsche de la Grange v. Italy* A 293-B (1994); 19 EHRR, the court characterised a prohibition imposed on construction imposed by the land use plan as an interference with peaceful enjoyment of property.

Also, cases involving confiscation or temporary seizure of property to prevent obscenity,[223] smuggling,[224] importation of drugs,[225] and contravention of town planning regulations[226] have been considered as control of use of property.

4.2.2.5 Fair Balance / Proportionality Test

In deciding whether a State complied with the two rules above, the court has devised a 'fair balance' test. That is, whether a fair balance was struck between the demands of the general interest of the community and the requirement of the protection of the individual's fundamental rights'.[227] This test may be used by the court solely when deciding the nature of interference in cases falling under rules 2 or 3. However, the court could decide the case by reference to rule 2 and 3 separately and focus on the particular languages of this rule when this is done.

In applying the 'fair balance' test, the court concedes to the State a wide margin of appreciation in that the court hardly review State's decision as to what it identified as community interest. Where the State decides that the community interest outweighs the individual interest, the court will hardly review it despite the fact that rules 2 and 3 stipulates the conditions that the State needs to take into account The jurisprudence of the convention organ have shown that because it is difficult to determine the particular rule that a case falls, the court sometimes makes its decision without indicating under which particular rule the case was decided.[228] As a result of this it has been argued that the process of applying the 'fair balance' test is more important to the outcome of the court's decision than identification of the type of interference.[229]

From the above analysis, an applicant may face serious difficulty in challenging the claim of the State that the interference is to secure 'general interest.' However, with the 'fair balance test' introduced by the court to control of use rule, the challenge might be successful since the court will be able to investigate the lawfulness and the proportionality of the impugned measure.[230] In other words, the State must not only show that the control measure is lawful but that in the light of the public good underlying the control, the burden which fell on the individual is not excessive and the measures are not disproportionate. In the case of *Hutten-Czapska v. Poland,* a rent control scheme was put in place with the aim of reforming the Polish housing sector.

223. *Handyside v. UK,* Judgement of 7 December 1976, Series A, No. 24, para. 63.
224. *Agosi v. UK,* Judgement of 24 October 1986, Series A, No. 108.
225. *Air Canada v. UK,* Judgement of 5 May 1995, Series A, No. 316-A.
226. *Vendittelli v. Italy,* Judgement of 18 July 1994, Series A, No. 293-A.
227. See *Sporonng* case.
228. See *Papamichalopoulos v. Greece* at p. 668 note 98 where the applicants land had been subjected to occupation by the Greek Army without any compensation. Although the Greeks courts had upheld their title to them, they were not returned to them and neither were they compensated. The applicants were precluded from having any dealings with the land even though they remained formally the owner. The court was of the view that the de facto interference was serious enough to amount to expropriation of the property. This technically may mean that the case was decided under rule 2 of A1P1 but court refrained from saying so but merely ruled that there had been a breach of A1P1.
229. Harris et al., 'Law of the European Convention on Human Rights', at 667.
230. *Ibid.,* at 687.

The rent control had been declared by the Polish Constitutional court on several occasions as incompatible with the constitutional principles of the right to property, the rule of law and social justice. Before the ECtHR, the scheme was analysed in terms of its suitability for achieving the public good pursued. The Court held that because of the severity of the impacts on the landlords' entitlements: the right to derive income from their property, the right to use and to possess it, there is a violation of AIPI. The court was of the view that striking fair balance required securing the protection of the landlords' property rights and respecting the social rights of tenants. The court found that there was harsh impact of the scheme on the landlords alone and that there was no procedure that would reduce the economic impact of the scheme on landlords so as to achieve a fair distribution of the cost of reform of housing throughout the community.

The court can also examine the lawfulness of the purpose of the measures taken by the State. For example, in *Handyside v. UK*[231] the court opined that 'this paragraph sets the Contracting States up as sole judges of the 'necessity' for interference. Consequently, the Court must restrict itself to supervising the lawfulness and the purposes of the restriction in question.'[232] However, subsequent cases have shown that the court's power of review has been extended to include the proportionality between the measures adopted by the State Organs and the purpose of the law on which they are based.[233]

The court adopted the fair balance test to assess the proportionality of interference, both with regards to the enforcement measures and the underlying legislation. As have been pointed out above, because of the wide margin of appreciation enjoyed by the State in this regards, circumstances in which the court would conclude that a fair balance has not been achieved cannot be easily discerned.[234] Therefore, for an applicant to succeed, he must show that he did not only bear an excessive burden, but also that the control of the use of his property suffered from procedural irregularities such as non-implementation of domestic court judgments, or (otherwise) from lack of application of domestic law.'[235]

Furthermore, in cases bothering on preventive measures such as seizure or enforcement measures such as forfeiture,[236] the court has examined the basis of the

231. A 24 (1976); 1 EHRR 737 PC.
232. *Ibid.*, at 29.
233. *Sporrong and Lonnroth Case* (*supra*); *AGOSI v. UK* A 108 (1986); 9 EHRR 1.
234. See the case of *Allan Jacobsson*, Judgment of 25 October 1989, A 163 at p. 9.
235. Disk & Hoof, 'The Theory and Practice of the European Convention on Human Rights' at 639 referring to the cases of *Raimondo v. Italy* A 281-A (1994); 18 EHRR 237 at p. 18; *Venditelli*, A.293-A, P. 13 Judgment of 18 July 1994; *Scollo*, A. 315-C, at p. 54 Judgment of 29 September 1994.
236. See *Handyside case* (*supra*) where the court held that destruction of books for obscenity was justified under AIPI; *Agosi v. UK* (*supra*) where confiscation of a gold coin belonging to the applicant was held to be justified as the gold coin was being unlawfully imported into the UK; *Vildirum v. Italy*, (*supra*) where the seizure and subsequent destruction of the applicant's bus was held to be justified because the bus was being used for transporting clandestine immigrants. The contention of the owner of the bus before the ECHR that he cannot be held responsible for the offence for which the driver of the vehicle has been convicted was rejected. The court held that the confiscation served the legitimate aim of crime prevention and that the State enjoys wide margin of appreciation in this regard. Consequently, the court held that given the nature of the general interests and the State's wide margin of appreciation, the confiscation

requirements of 'fair balance' and of a 'reasonable relationship of proportionality'. In carrying out an assessment of the proportionality of these preventive measures, the court usually considers the rationale for the measure, the serious nature of the offence and the threat it posed to the rule of law in the State.[237] Cases have shown that greater margin of appreciation is accorded the State when taking such preventive measures.[238]

Interference with property may also be allowed on ground of taxation. State enjoys a wide margin of appreciation in this regard because there is no limitation on the power of the State to impose tax except the non-discrimination provision of Article 14 of the convention.[239] By virtue of A1P1 the State's power covers both adoptions of measures to enforce payment of taxation as well as imposition of taxation.[240] However, the wide margin of appreciation enjoyed by the State has not precluded the Convention Organs from investigating whether the measures adopted are lawful, or arbitrary, abusive, discriminatory or disproportionate going by their newer decisions on the taxing powers of the contracting States. The 'fair balance' test demands that there are procedural guarantees to establish the applicant's liability to make payments. In the case of *WASA Omsesidigi and others v. Sweden*, the Commission opined that 'the financial liability arising out of the raising of tax or contributions may adversely affect the guarantee secured under this provision if it places an excessive burden on the person or the entity concerned or fundamentally interferes with his or its financial position.'[241] The court adopted proportionality test as a balancing tool to resolve this issue. However, in doing so the distinction between deprivation and control of use of property has been made blurred. This has resulted to a situation in which though tax measures had deprived the persons involved of their property, they were considered as control of the use of property.[242]

is not a disproportionate interference with peaceful enjoyment of the applicant's possession. In *Raimondo case* (*supra*), where the land and vehicles belonging to the applicant were confiscated (at the same time as criminal proceedings being brought against him for belonging to a mafia-type group), on the ground that the property formed proceeds of unlawful activities, the court held that the confiscation order was in the general interests and that it is to ensure that the property acquired by unlawful activities did not procure 'advantages to the detriment of the community' for the applicant or the criminal organisation.

237. See *Arcuri v. Italy* No. 52024/99, 2001-VIIDA.
238. *Butler v. UK* No. 41661/98, 2002-VIDA. In this case the sum of £250,000 which the applicant has asked his friend to take to abroad, was seized by the Customs and Excise Officials and subsequently confiscated by the order of the UK Courts under the Drug Trafficking Act 1994. In spite of the fact that there was no evidence that the applicant or anyone else would use the money for drug trafficking and that the applicant had no criminal history, the human rights court held that the problems faced by States in combating the problem of drug trafficking justified the wide margin of appreciation accorded the State in this regard.
239. The control of use power of the State may not be used discriminatorily. See *Pine Valley Developments Ltd v. Ireland* A 222 (1991); 14 EHRR 319.
240. *Darby v. Sweden*, Judgment of 23 October 1990, Series A, No. 187.
241. (App. No. 13013/87), 14 December 1988, DR 58 (1988).
242. See the cases of *Hentrich v. France*, Judgment of 22 September 19994, Series A, No. 296-A contrast *Gasus Dosier-und Fodertechnik Gmbh v. Netherlands*, Judgement of 23 February 1995, Series A nos. 306-B at 59 and *The National Building Society, Leeds Permanent Building Society and Yorkshire Building Society v. UK*, Judgment of 23 October 1997, Reports 1997-VII, at 79.

Therefore, the attitude of the court is to first consider whether the measures is taken by the State to secure payment of taxes, penalties or other contributions before considering whether the conditions attached to deprivation rule are satisfied.

In the case of *Gasus Dosier-und Fordertechnik v. Netherlands*,[243] where the tax authority had seized the property in possession of a tax debtor in spite of the fact that title to the property was still retained by a third party vendor, the court held that it was not a deprivation of possession but a measure for securing payment of taxes falling under the second sentence of A1P1. It was contended that the applicant ought to have appreciated the risk of seizure of the property by the tax authority under the Dutch law and to have taken measures to protect itself against this eventuality. The Court held that the Dutch law which allows such seizure in this circumstance is not without reasonable foundation and therefore, the legislature's assessment of measures adopted to secure payment of taxes in this regard ought to be respected. The court concluded that the measure taken by the government to secure the payment of tax obligation of the debtor is proportional.

4.2.2.6 *Interference with Peaceful Enjoyment of Possession (The First Rule Contained in the First Sentence of the First Paragraph)*

The AIPI specifically protects the right to 'peaceful enjoyment of possessions'. In substance, AIPI guarantees the right of property.[244] It therefore, provides a separate and additional ground for regulating interferences with a person's peaceful enjoyment of his possessions. It covers instances in which a person is not given an opportunity to use his property because the necessary permit is denied or because such restrictions arose from legislation or from government measures to the extent that peaceful enjoyment is eroded.[245] In *Sporrong and Lonnroth v. Sweden* (*supra*), the applicant's property was affected by expropriation permits issued by the government for the purposes of redevelopment of a City Centre. The actual expropriation was not carried out but was left hanging over the property for a period of twenty-three years in one instance and for twenty-five years in another instance. However, the implication of this is that the applicants recognised that any expropriation would be lawful as it authorises the City of Stockholm to expropriate whenever it chooses to do so. As a result, they were prohibited from carrying out construction on the property. The court held that the prohibitions on constructions were measures of control of use and that neither the expropriation permits nor the prohibitions amount to deprivation of property because they were initial steps towards deprivation. Nevertheless, the court held that they effectively constitute interference with the applicant's enjoyment of their possession under rule 1 of the first sentence of A1P1.

From the above case, it is clear that what the court looked at was the effects of the expropriation permits and the prohibitions and not their purpose. This appears to be a

243. Judgment of 23 February 1995, Series A no. 306-B, at 59.
244. See *Marckx case* A 31 (1979); 2 EHRR 330 para. 63.
245. Disk & Hoof, 'The Theory and Practice of the European Convention On Human Rights' at 625-626.

better approach because if the court had placed more reliance on the purpose, given the facts of this case, it will likely result into an unjust outcome. One commentator has suggested that this rule 1 is 'concerned with the expropriation of resources for public use, where such appropriation is not in the form of a taking of full ownership.'[246] The court had applied this criteria in some other cases, for example in *X v. Netherlands*,[247] the court held that imposition of financial liability that is not concerned with the securing of payment of taxes amounts to interference with peaceful enjoyment of possessions. Similarly, where economic value of possession is affected adversely by interference, the State has been held responsible.[248] In *Chassagnou v. France*,[249] the court held that there was an interference with property because of the law enacted by the French Government to permit public entry onto the applicants' lands for hunting activity to which they objected on strong ethical grounds. Also the court had relied on the effects of the measures taken by the Government in the case of *Matos e Silva, Lda and others v. Portugal*[250] to rule that there was no formal or de facto deprivation of possessions as the effects of the measures were not irreversible unlike in the *Papamichalopoulos case.* Several cases have followed the Sporrong and Lonrroth cases especially cases bothering on denial of access to property. In *Loizidou v. Turkey*,[251] the applicant could not gain access to her property for a period of 16 years because the area had been occupied by Turkish Cypriot forces following the civil war in Cyprus. The Commission held that her case fell under the freedom of movement and as such the denial did not constitute interference with peaceful enjoyment of possessions. The Court reversed the Commission's decision and held that the continuous denial of access over a period of sixteen years had gradually affected her right as a property owner, particularly her right to peaceful enjoyment of her possessions. Consequently, the court held that she has 'effectively lost all control over, as well as all possibilities to use and enjoy her property.' The Jurisprudence of the court has further shown that where there is a violation of this rule especially in cases concerning denial of access, payment of compensation were ordered for the period the applicants were denied access. In addition, the government was ordered to facilitate their return to their property.[252]

However, in the ***Handyside*** case the court used the purpose of the measures taken by the State to arrive at its decision that the forfeiture and destruction of the books, although deprived the applicant ownership of the book permanently, it falls under control of use rules because items whose use has been lawfully adjudged illicit and dangerous to the general interests are forfeited with a view to a destruction. This

246. Harris et al., 'The Theory and Practice of the European Convention On Human Rights' at 672 at n. 135.
247. 14 YB 224 (1971) (social security contributions).
248. See *Arshworth v. U. K.* NO. 39561/98 hudoc. (2004) DA where an interference with a possession held by the company led to the reduction in the value of the shareholders' shares. See also *S v. France* No. 13728/18, 65 DR 250 (1990).
249. 1999-III; 29 EHRR 615 GC.
250. Judgment of 16 September 1996, Reports 1996-IV, Vol. 14, p. 114.
251. Judgment of 18 December 1996, Reports. 1996-VI.
252. *Dogan and others v. Turkey* 2004 VI;41 EHRR 231.

however, can be regarded as an exception to the effect criterion used in the above cases.[253]

5. AN ASSESSMENT OF THE APPLICABILITY OF AIPI TO UNILATERAL CAPTURE

From our analytical framework in Chapter 2, the concept of 'property' or 'possession' under the ECHR covers both tangible property and a wider range of rights and interests and it has autonomous meaning.[254]

Drawing together the analysis of the concept of property in Chapter 2, the examination of the proprietary character of petroleum production licence in Chapter 3 and the analysis of the proprietary character of the Licensee's right to Discovered Petroleum Reservoir in Chapter 4, it is our submission that reservoir oil constitutes possession under the ECHR. Chapter 6 has shown that the licence granting clauses of the selected countries - United Kingdom, Nigeria, Canada, Australia and Netherlands - do not encapsulate the common law rule of capture. Their unitisation laws also provides for compulsory unitisation with conditions that can easily be misconstrued by the Regulators as given them wide discretion as to when and whether or not to order unitisation. This can result into abuse as the Regulators may fail to order unitisation when there is straddling reservoir. This is also prone to error of inconsistent decisions being made especially where the Regulator is called upon to determine the appropriate date that unitisation should commence in instances where unilateral capture has already occurred.

On the other hand, if the various 'conditions' that must be present before the minister exercises his power, can properly be regarded as 'conditions' in the strict sense of the word, it would then mean that the power given to the minister under the law to compel unitisation is limited and therefore, insufficient to deal with all instances where unitisation will be suitable or necessary. The interest of the licensee is generally not taken into consideration in the exercise of power to compel unitisation as it is not usually stated in a unitisation clause. In Nigeria and Netherlands, we have seen cases in which the Regulator either failed to exercise this discretionary power to order unitisation at the appropriate time or failed to make unitisation order retroactive to the date of first production. The effects of these failures are that property is taken by the licensee who gets to the straddling reservoirs first and he keeps what he takes permanently to the total loss of the adjoining licence holder. In the jurisdictions mentioned above, unitisation laws provide neither procedural guide for redress nor compensatory provisions. We have seen also in Chapter 6 that part of the reason behind the Regulator's policy of non-application of the unitisation law retroactively, is

253. Peter Van Den Broek, in DJ Gijlstra et al. (ed.) 'Legal Issues of European Integration', 1986/1 Law Review of the EUROPA Instituut, University of Amsterdam at p. 74.

254. The protected interests are described as possessions in the English version of the convention while that of the French version described them as "biens". This suggests that wider range of proprietary interests were meant to be protected. See Harris et al., 'The Theory and Practice of the European Convention On Human Rights' at p. 656.

the objective of protecting government share from the petroleum taken, having been comingled with other sources of revenues and expended. Calling upon the State to pay past production in cash where there is nothing left in the straddling pool may not be in the public or general interests. Since part of the Government's policy goals is also to promote petroleum development for revenue generation and discourage indolence, it would tacitly encourage the aggressive party to continue production unilaterally. Consequently, the Regulators have by implication, allowed the common law rule of capture to prevail. In Netherlands, the Regulators had refused to order unitisation retroactively by arguing that there is no unitisation of historical (past) revenues. The rule of capture by necessary implication defeated the proprietary character of the Licensee's right to discovered reservoir oil contrary to the conception of property under the ECHR. However, it must be noted that the concept of 'property' or 'possessions' has autonomous meaning under ECHR. It is independent of the conception of property at the domestic level.

The question that arises from the above assessment is whether failure to enjoin unitisation at the appropriate time or to order unitisation retroactively to t he appropriate date can amount to a breach of the State's obligations under the A1P1 of ECHR. The first segment of this question concerns the obligation of the State to protect property right while the second segment concerns circumstances under which State measures amount to an interference with property.

The first segment has been dealt with in Chapter 2 and as such our analysis in this section will focus on the second segment. It must however be noted that, as shown by our analysis above, if part of the oil in straddling reservoirs is taken by one licensee and is subsequently approved by the Regulatory Agency, it would amount to case of government indirectly taking the property of one individual and giving it to another individual. This means that there is the presence of governmental action in the process of taking of property of one individual by another individual. As our findings in Chapter 4 reveals that there is proprietary right in unexploited petroleum resources, State responsibility may be engaged under the ECHR for failure to protect this right against interferences by other private persons.

With regards to the second segment of the question, the circumstances under which interference with property can take place are in three ways as provided by AIPI. Whether State measures constitute deprivation or not must be assessed against the provisions of the three rules on interference. Therefore, the order of the Regulator to the effect that petroleum taken by one licensee through unilateral extraction from straddling fields should not be shared with the adjoining licensee must be assessed in line with the three rules. However, it must be determined whether it falls within the second and third rule before it can be considered under the first rule. In accordance with rule 2 on interference, the order of the Regulator must be assessed to determine whether it is in the public interest/or general interest and whether it is legitimate and for legitimate aim. While rule 3 will be applied to determine whether the Regulator's order is necessary for control of use of property, or to secure payment of taxes or other contributions or penalties.

Having regards to the policy behind the refusal of the Regulator to make unitisation order retroactive to date of first production, it can be argued that the property taken was in the public interest and therefore, no deprivation. Furthermore, as a result of the State's wide margin of appreciation in this regard, the court usually concedes to the State its definition of what constitutes public interests. However, this will not preclude the ECtHR from inquiring into whether the means employed to achieve the aim is not disproportionate. A measure must be both appropriate for achieving its aim and not disproportionate thereto.[255] The requisite balance will be upset if the licensee involved suffers excessive burden or one that is disproportionate.[256] The circumstances of each case are taken into consideration by the Court. The court will consider the degree of protection from arbitrariness that is afforded by the proceedings brought, the possibility for the State to have recourse to other means for achieving the aim, and the consequences of the measures on the licensee affected. It is submitted that the Regulator could still have achieved optimal revenues through unitised development if unitisation is ordered at the appropriate time rather than allowing unilateral development which though, may increase production and government revenue in the short run but may result in price decrease and wastes at the long run. The measure adopted to increase government revenue at the detriment of the licensee cannot be said to be proportionate in this circumstance as the licensee suffering drainage has been made to bear an excessive burden. This inquiry is done through the principle of 'proportionality'. In applying this principle, the court employs 'fair balance' test. That is, whether a fair balance was struck between the demands of the general interest of the community and the requirement of the protection of the individual's fundamental rights. In Chapter 6 and 7, we have seen that once reservoirs straddle, both parties are refrained from carrying out unilateral development. The licensee who suffered drainage because he chose to obey the law by notifying the Regulator of his intention to unitise under sections 4.2 (d) and 4.4 (b) of the 2008 Nigeria Unitisation Guidelines,[257] and who refrained from production while waiting for the field to be unitised by virtue of section 4.2 (a) of the Guidelines, will be made to bear excessive burden if unitisation order fails to take effect retroactively to the date of first production. In spite of the fact that the Convention does not embrace the principle of compensation, the court will ascertain whether the licensee received adequate compensation as the court has been of the opinion that 'the taking of property without payment of compensation that is reasonably related to its value would normally constitute a disproportionate interference'. However, legitimate objectives of public interests may demand for less than market value reimbursement and that the State has discretion in assessing the amount of compensation.[258] The court will not interfere in

255. See *James v. UK* (*supra*).
256. See *Sporrong and Lonnroth case* (*supra*).
257. Section 4.2 (d) provides that the 'Reference date shall be the date that DPR states in writing to be the time at which the non-producing party established straddling through seismic data, drilling and Discovery … .'

    Section 4.4 (b) provides that the Reference date shall serve the purpose of determining the date when unitisation is deemed to have commenced, and to establish when the re-adjustment of past costs and production shall take effect.
258. *James v.UK* (*supra*) at 54.

the judgment of the national authority in this regard unless that judgment is manifestly without reasonable foundation.[259]

In addition, the lawfulness of the measure taken by the Regulator, that is, ordering a non-retroactive unitisation must be considered. The measures taken must be based on accessible, precise and foreseeable national laws. Where the Petroleum law is silent on whether the rule of capture applies and the licence granting clause does not encapsulates the Rule, non-application of retroactive unitisation by the Regulator cannot be said to be based on foreseeable national law. The unitisation laws of the selected countries above were fashioned in such manner that gives the minister discretionary powers to decide when to order unitisation. Their compulsory unitisation laws are also silent on whether unitisation can be ordered retroactively or not. This has provided avenue for the law to be applied in an inconsistent manner thereby resulting into unforeseeable or arbitrary outcomes or depriving a licensee effective protection of his right.[260] Although the Human rights court has limited power to look into whether the measures complained of comply with the domestic law, the requirement is fundamental because where it is not satisfied; the court will uphold deprivation and breach of A1P1. It is to be noted too that the unitisation laws contained no procedural guides for redress and also no compensatory provisions. If the affected licensee is a foreigner, international law applies and it requires payment of full compensation as the reference to the principles of international law' in the second rule has been interpreted as applicable only to cases where alien property is taken by the State. It is also necessary to look at the effect of the measure on the affected licensee rather than its purpose.

In assessing whether the measure taken by the Regulator in this instance amounts to control of use of property, the court usually looks at the purpose of the measure rather than the effects which is the criterion under deprivation rule in rule 2. In all the control of use cases, the applicants were not deprived of the title to their property. Where the measure falls short of deprivation in rule 2, it will amount to control of use. However, there were few instances where it may amount to interference with the substance of property under Rule 1. In the case of unilateral capture, it is clear that the purpose of the order of the Regulatory Agency is neither to enforce payment of taxes nor to enforce payment of other contributions or penalties, but rather to allow the wrongful licensee and the government to keep petroleum drained from the straddling assets. The courts have ruled that the word 'public interests' mentioned in rule 2 and the 'general interests' mentioned in rule 3 means the same thing in substance.

259. *Lithgow & others v. UK* (*supra*) 102 at 122.

260. See Olufemi A. Ajayi et al., 'Current Challenges in Unitisation – The Nigerian Experience' A paper presented at the 34th Annual SPE International Conference and Exhibition held in Tinapa-Calabar, Nigeria, 31 July-7 August 2010, published in SPE International (SPE 140614) at p. 4. The author commented that the main challenge in Nigeria is the consistency with which unitisation rules are applied and the uncertainties it might create for the affected parties. He said further that though, the 2008 unitisation Guidelines does not encourage the rule of capture, the application of this principle has not been consistent.

Applying the 'fair balance' test, it must be shown that the control measure is not only lawful in the light of the public good underlying the control, but also that the burden which fell on the licensee suffering drainage is not excessive and the measure is not disproportionate. Having regard to the severity of the impacts of the measure on the innocent licensee's entitlements – the right to derive income from the oil taken, the right to use and to possess it – there is likelihood of a violation of A1P1. The economic impact on the licensee (especially where the volume of the petroleum drained from his licence is substantial) is harsh and since there is no compensatory procedure to reduce the severe impacts to achieve a fair distribution of the straddling reservoir oil between the licensees inter se and the Government, the measure is not proportionate. In addition, the licensee has also suffered from procedural irregularity arisen from non-application of the compulsory unitisation laws at the appropriate time.

An assessment of the measure under Rule 1 of AIP1 (Interference with peaceful enjoyment of possession) would show that there had been an interference with the reservoir oil of the innocent licensee. In this case, the effect of the measure and not the purpose is examined by the court. Even though the State has not taken full ownership in that the licensee still maintains control over his licence and acreage/ field, there had been interference with the quantity of the reservoir oil taken. The court has held that where economic value of possession is affected by interference, the State will be held responsible.[261]

It is submitted that the relevant factor that should be considered in the application of the principles embedded in A1P1 to cases of unilateral capture, is the severity of the impacts rather than the purpose of the Regulator's non-application of the unitisation law or non-ordering of retroactive unitisation. The severity of the impacts on the licensee should be the norm while the purpose should be an exception.[262] The licensee suffering drainage has not only borne an excessive burden, he has also suffered from procedural irregularities as a result of non-application of the unitisation laws.

6. CONCLUSION

In summary, to the extent that licensee's entitlements to the reservoir oil has been substantially or severely impacted by the unilateral action of an adjoining licensee and which is subsequently sanctioned by the State's Regulatory Agency, avenue for protection of the licensee's property right entitlements or possession is available under the International Investments treaty laws and the ECHR. Also where the State fails to compel unitisation at the appropriate time or to order retroactive unitisation to the date of first production would in certain circumstances lead to a breach by the State of its international obligations regarding the FET, National treatment, and full protection and security standards under the relevant BITs/MITs. It may also lead to expropriation claims (i.e., indirect taking of property). This means that an alternative avenue for redress is available to a licensee who though suffered drainage but could not obtain

261. See *Astworth v. U.K* (*supra*) and *Chassagnou v. France* (*supra*).
262. See *Hutten-Czapska v. Poland* (*supra*).

remedy under the domestic private law. Therefore, where the rule of capture is applied, it could expose the Host State to law suits at the international tribunals as the Rule appears to have run contrary to the principles embedded in both Investment treaties and the Human rights laws considered above.

CHAPTER 8
Conclusions

1. ANSWERS TO THE MAIN QUESTIONS

We have stated our conclusions at the end of each chapter of this book and therefore, need not restate them here. This chapter is aimed at answering the main question of the book which is significant to the security of Licensee's title to un-exploited petroleum resources. It also explained the steps taken to answer the question having regard to the analytical framework established in Chapter 2 and the comparative study carried out on the six selected countries - United States, United Kingdom, Australia, Canada, Nigeria and Netherlands. The findings from the different countries and the analytical framework are also explained. The new property right concept - 'Property right in Discovered Petroleum Reservoir' is also tested in order to determine its capacity to tame the rule of capture.

The main question asked in Chapter 1 of this book is: *How can unilateral capture of petroleum from straddling reservoirs be averted so that parties can mutually develop the reservoirs as a single unit?* Two lines of enquiries were also raised in order to be able to address the main question. These are: (1) *what is the legal nature of the rights (if any) held by the licensee in an un-exploited petroleum reservoir? (2) Can failure to enjoin unitisation at the appropriate time or retroactively amount to a breach of the State's international obligations (i.e., in particular under BITs/MITs and/or Human rights instruments?*

One of the consequences of failure to unitise is unilateral development and extraction of petroleum from straddling reservoirs which in turn results into physical and economic wastes of scarce natural resources. The findings in Chapters 5 and 6 of this book have shown that while unitisation may be one option of ensuring development of straddling reservoirs as a unit, it is not enduring as it has not prevented all times unilateral capture owing to the reasons stated therein. Moreover, in spite of the fact that there is no statutory codification of the rule of capture in our selected countries, the potential for parties failing to unitise or government failing to enforce unitisation provision has not been completely removed. As a result of these findings, a solution was developed which as has been said is the recognition of a protectable property right in discovered petroleum reservoir. In other words, the argument in this book is that because unitisation laws and/ or the Regulators are failing to secure unit development of straddling reservoirs, it is expedient to expressly give recognition and protection for the licensee's property right to discovered petroleum reservoir.

Therefore, the book argues that this solution can be derived from the understanding of the modern conception of property right and that recognition and protection of *'property rights in discovered petroleum reservoir'* is the superior approach to ensuring that unitisation principles prevent unilateral capture, eliminate wastes and guarantee consistent and predictable court's decision. The book then went on to examine whether protectable property right in petroleum reservoir is plausible. The combined findings from Chapters 2 and 3 have shown that petroleum production licence is a form of property and that it encompasses or is a constructive possession of unexploited petroleum reservoir. In arriving at this conclusion, the book developed analytical framework in Chapter 2 that focuses on the conception of property right from the olden times to the modern day, in order to show that property is no longer tangible things but consists of 'every valuable right' even if it does not involve 'things'. Chapter 2 also shows that there is commonality between investment law and human rights law to the effect that every legal claim that has economic value is regarded as property and that other economic interests will be protected. In both laws therefore, the notion of property as a material thing is out of fashion. It has been replaced by the modern conception which includes managerial control over components of a process that is wealth producing. This view of property is also in accord with the Realist's conception of property.[1] In Chapter 3, an analysis was carried out on the legal nature of oil and gas lease in both Accession and Domanial petroleum mining regimes. United States and Canada were used as examples of Accession regimes while Nigeria, UK, Netherlands, Canada and Australia served as examples of Domanial regimes. Within the Accession regimes, our finding is that the legal nature of oil and gas lease is contractual as well as a conveyance (Ownership in place States) while in Non-ownership States, it is regarded as only contractual with exclusive right to take underlying oil and gas because a conveyance of oil and gas in place, according to the Non-ownership theory, is not possible. However, one factor that has eroded this important distinction is the application of the rule of capture to both Ownership regimes. In spite of this important factor, our finding is that the practical difference between the various ownership regimes is inconsequential with regards to the nature of lessee's interest created by the oil and gas lease because whether the nature of the lessee's interest in oil and gas is classified as corporeal or incorporeal, real or personal, the lessee's interests is in real property object within the meaning of common law classification of property interests. Their difference lies only in the duration of the lease and not on any ownership theory. As a result, the reasonable conclusion that can be reached is that the nature of the lessee's interest created by oil and gas lease in Accession system of mining law is an

1. See Honore and Hohfeld in sections 3.2.1, 3.2.2 and 3.2.3 of Chapter 2 of this book.

interest in real property and therefore, qualified to be regarded as a 'property' within our theoretical analysis in Chapter 2.

In the Domanial regimes, our findings showed that there is commonality among our selected jurisdictions as regards the legal character of production rights whether coined as a licence or a permit or a lease except in Australia. It may generally be regarded as a contract with statutory flavour but the statutory nature has not displaced the contractual element. The legal nature of the interest conferred on the licensee can be generally regarded as an interest in land (i.e., proprietary interest). We arrived at this conclusion from the following step and the findings therefrom:

(1) The nature of the interest of the licensee in a production licence is reminiscent of the legal character of that licence and the interests of the State grantor in the underlie petroleum. It appears that it has no much bearing with the terrain of the applicability of the licence that is, whether based on the onshore or offshore. This is reinforced by the findings from our theoretical analysis of the nature of rights granted by international law to coastal States in the oil and gas resources of the CS. From the analysis, it was found that the 'sovereign rights' purportedly granted by international law could be construed as ownership rights to the oil and gas resources of the seabed and subsoil of the CS.

(2) In all the States examined in this book, full ownership of petroleum in situ is claimed onshore and it is logical to infer that the State can transfer by licence such interests to the licensee except otherwise stated in the licence granting clause. For example, in the UK, the licence granting clause in both onshore and offshore are the same and yet full ownership is claimed in the onshore whereas sovereign rights is claimed in the offshore. The licence granting clause has been interpreted as conveying a proprietary interest in the nature of a *profit a prendre* under English law or *mineral lease* under Scots law. In Nigeria however, the OML granting clause, when interpreted with analogy to similar private lease granting clause in the US, in which the courts have held amounted to a grant of oil and gas in place to the lessee, we concluded that an OML in Nigeria in both onshore and offshore could be said to have conveyed mineral in place to the lessee (corporeal interest) because this granting clause applies to OML granted in both terrains. This assertion is reinforced by the fact that the operating oil mining lease is for unlimited duration or for so long as oil shall be produced in paying quantities and the lessee pays rents and royalties and performs all its obligations under the lease. In Netherlands, the nature of the interests of the holder of a production licence granted under the 1810 and 2003 Mining Acts with regards to onshore minerals is full ownership (concession) while in the offshore the production licence can be regarded as conveying a proprietary interest in land. Even if not full ownership, it is proprietary in the nature of *profit a prendre*. This is because in the offshore, property in the petroleum vests in the State. In the offshore of Canada, certain features of the licences (Significant discovery and production licences) such as indefinite duration, exclusivity and the facts that their terms are to be agreed between the minister and the licensee showed that they are not bare

> licences. They are irrevocable licences coupled with interests or *profit a prendre* within the common law classification of property interests and as such, convey such interests to the holder of the licence. In Australia, though there is no judicial decision on the issue with respect to production licence, there is a judicial authority to the effect that an exploration licence is sui generis and that it is only statutory in nature.[2] Here the court held that an exploration licence conveys no proprietary interests in the licensee. This decision as has been shown in Chapter 3, is very controversial even among the judges as there was no unanimity as to the reasons given for their judgment and therefore, may not represent good authority.

Based on our findings in Chapters 2 and 3 as stated above, in Chapter 4, a conceptual framework was developed from the Analytical framework in Chapter 2 and when contextualised, it shows that since reservoir oil possesses economic value to the licensee, it is a property right under the common law, Investment treaty laws and International human rights norms. The findings in Chapter 4, therefore, have shown that Licensee's right to the discovered unexploited petroleum resources is 'proprietary'. To test whether this concept of property right is plausible, the quality of this property right was thereafter assessed against the traditional incidents of property. We found that it possesses all the characteristics of property. Chapter 4 further reveals that oil and gas in the reservoir is relatively stable having been confined by traps and will only migrate due to human activity or escape naturally where there is no trap to lock the resource in the reservoir. We found this as having satisfied the important excludability criteria of property discussed in Chapter 2. We argued in Chapter 4 pages 152-153 of the book that even if because of the ambulatory nature of oil and gas, physical exclusion is not possible, legal excludability has been used to secure exclusion through the issuance of the production licence. As a result of this understanding, the book argued that migration of petroleum from one portion of a straddling reservoir to another which did not occur on its own but caused by human interference or activity can amount to an invasion of property rights in petroleum reservoir. This is because what the court should concern itself with is whether the right regarder has a duty to exclude himself from the property of the right claimer and not whether the right claimer has a right or ability to exclude the right regarder from the property.[3]

Within the context of unilateral capture, the question therefore, should be whether the licensee that captured petroleum has a duty to exclude himself from taking the oil lying under his neighbour's fields from a well bore on his own land. We therefore concluded that by virtue of the legal character of his licence, the granting clause and the compulsory unitisation clause, he has a duty to exclude himself.

A theoretical comparison between the property rule of capture and the property right in petroleum reservoir concept was further made against the backdrop of

2. *Commonwealth of Australia v. Western Mining Corporation Ltd* (*supra*).
3. Penner, 'The Bundle of Rights Picture of Property' at 743. See the cases of *International News Service v. Associated press*, 248 U.S. 215 (1918) and *Victoria Park Racing & Rec. Grounds Co. v. Taylor* (1937) 58 C.L.R. 479.

philosophical justificatory arguments on property. This reveals that there are legal, economic and moral reasons justifying the existence of property right in discovered petroleum reservoir in our jurisprudence and therefore, should be protected. This shows that theoretically and practically, property right in discovered petroleum reservoir is plausible or exists in Common law jurisprudence. It is only that it has neither been expressly stated in the statutes nor judicially recognised (or protected) in all our selected countries except Netherlands. Netherlands was therefore, recognised by this book as representing good and modern approach to issue of unilateral capture. The apparent silence on property rights in petroleum reservoir in statutes even though existing impliedly, could be as a result of the reasons stated in our policy analysis in chapters 1 and 6.

In spite of this finding or conclusion, Chapter 6 further explored to find out if the Minister is under an obligation to compel unitisation whenever there is straddling reservoir. As a collateral question, we considered also whether a licensee is under a duty to exercise restraint in draining petroleum from straddling fields. It was found that all our selected domanial countries have compulsory unitisation clauses. However, the unitisation clauses were couched in such manner that the duty to initiate or compel unitisation is placed on the Minister rather than the licensee. This may presuppose that if the minister fails to compel unitisation where he has information that there exists straddling reservoirs; licensee may not exercise restraint in carrying out unilateral extraction. But an analysis of the various licence granting clauses would show that production licence does not encapsulate the rule of capture hence our finding that there is no statutory rule of capture in the domanial countries. Therefore, in spite of this, we have argued that the supposed 'discretion' given to the Minister would crystallise to 'compulsion' the moment there is a straddling reservoir. This is because the conditions that must happen before the Minister can compel unitisation have self-enforcement capacity as they become real the moment there is a straddling reservoir. For example, unitisation will promote ultimate recovery; it will also eliminate competitive drilling and will promote national interests and the interests of both licensees. There is, therefore, no room for the exercise of ministerial discretion once there is straddling reservoir. In addition, the fact that the licence granting clause does not encapsulate the rule of capture means that the minister is expected to order unitisation at all times. This also translates to the duty of the licensee such that where the Minister failed to order unitisation, a licensee will still be under an obligation to unitise. Therefore, where the Minister neglected or failed to enjoin unitisation in reliance on the discretion in the unitisation clause and drainage occurs, the Minister may be in violation of the laws. The only exception is where the interest of one licensee (i.e., licensee with small extension) will not be served by unitisation because the volume of petroleum on his side is so negligible that the cost of participating in unitisation discussions, development and operation of the fields will be more than the benefits. In this regard, the solution lies in 'buy-out' and where there is stale mate in negotiation for the buy-out; a third party like court or expert can objectively determine the price.

An analysis of unilateral capture regime in both Accession and Domanial systems of mining law was carried out in Chapters 5 and 6. It was found that in practice, Administrative and Judicial policies were unfavourable to this specie of property right.

Drawing together our findings and observations in Chapters 5 and 6 we concluded that the property rights of a holder of production licence in the oil and gas while still in the reservoir may be lost through drainage by an adjoining licensee. The necessary implication of this is that there is no protection for the property right of the licensee in the oil and gas while still in the reservoir. The property right, though impliedly recognised by the municipal legislations, is not protected by the court due to the Judges' adherent to precedent arising from the application of the common law rule of capture and their failure to understand or keep at pace with the technological advances in oil and gas extraction and reservoir mechanics.

As a result of the above conflicts between the law and the administrative and judicial policies, this book further investigates whether failure to enjoin unitisation at the appropriate time or retroactively amounts to a breach of State's international obligations. It also considered ancillary issue of whether there could be protection for this specie of property rights under the investment treaties and international human rights norms since disputes concerning ownership of oil in situ as between the licensees have only been confined to national courts. In Chapter 7, an assessment of the applicability of investment treaty and human rights principles to unilateral capture was therefore, undertaken. Our Analytical frame-work regarding concept of property or possession in Chapter 2 was also brought to fore in analysing the investment treaty and international human rights principles. The book applied investment treaty arbitration principles like full protection and security, FET – (legitimate expectation, due process and good faith) and indirect expropriation to unilateral capture and found that the measures taken by the Host State – failure to order unitisation at the appropriate time or to order one retroactively where unilateral extraction has occurred – may amount to breach of its international obligations under relevant investment treaty where a foreign investor suffers substantial withdrawal of petroleum from his acreage and also that it may amount to 'indirect taking' of property.[4] Similar approach or assessment was undertaken under the ECHR laws and jurisprudence. The book found that there is a positive obligation on the State to protect property of both its nationals and foreign nationals within her territory against interferences not only by government agencies but also by other private persons. Consequently, failure by the State to order unitisation at the appropriate time may amount to a violation of this obligation where the affected private party suffers loss or substantial diminution of his property. In addition, State measures in failing to order unitisation retroactively was also assessed against the three rules on interference. Fair balance test as a facet of proportionality principles was employed to determine whether the licensee who suffers drainage has borne an excessive burden given the policy behind the failure of the State to order unitisation at the appropriate time or to order a retroactive one where capture had already taken place. The book found that the measure adopted to increase government revenue at the detriment of the licensee cannot be said to be proportionate in this circumstance as the licensee suffering drainage has been made to bear an excessive burden. The book therefore suggests that the relevant factor that should be considered in the application

4. See Chapter 7.

of the principles embodied in A1P1 to cases of unilateral capture is the severity of the impacts rather than the purpose of the Regulator's measures. The severity of the impacts on the licensee should be the norm while the purpose should be an exception.[5] The book concludes that to the extent that licensee's entitlements to the reservoir oil has been substantially or severely diminished by the unilateral action of an adjoining licensee and which is subsequently sanctioned by the State's regulatory Agency, State's international obligations may be breached and that avenue for protection of the licensee's property right entitlements or possession is available under the Investment treaty principles and the ECHR considered above. At the National level, protection of this species of property is also possible under the Human Right Act of 1998 (UK). Section 3 of the Act provides that courts should interpret statutes as far as possible in the light of the Convention rights while section 6 provides that it is unlawful for public authorities to act in contravention of the Convention. This means that section 3 of the HRA enjoined the court to read and give effect to primary and subordinate legislation 'in a way which is compatible with ... Convention rights'. This suggests that courts are required by HRA to apply convention rights through statutory interpretation to not only vertical cases but also to horizontal cases. Moreover, in a horizontal dispute that involves purely common law issues, the court can under this section apply convention rights by way of analogy. Any common law rule that is incompatible with the Convention rights will be declared invalid by the court. The book therefore concludes that the common law rule of capture is incompatible with AIPI. Therefore, to effectively avert unilateral capture, secure optimum unitisation of straddling reservoirs and also avert the consequences that capture may have on the State's international obligations under investment treaties and Human rights instruments, recognition and protection of property rights in discovered petroleum reservoir is the solution.

2. PROTECTABLE PROPERTY RIGHT IN PETROLEUM RESERVOIR AS SOLUTION

If both adjoining landowners or lessees have property rights to the oil and gas underlying their respective land, rational development of the common pool will take place as neither of them can undertake unilateral development without accounting to the other, either in form of compensation or damages for drainage. This assertion could find support from Lord Macnaghten's pronouncement in the case of *Trinidad Asphalt Co. v. Ambard & Another*[6] where he declared that:

> [I]f the inhabitants of La Brea cannot dig their own pitch without invading their neighbours' rights, it is quite possible that the hope of reciprocal advantage and the apprehension of mutual liability may lead to some arrangement for their common benefit, or the difficulties of the case may induce the Legislature to step in and regulate the digging of pitch and the management of the pitch lands.

5. *Ibid.*
6. (1899) A.C 594 (P.C) at 603.

The arrangement contemplated here could be unitisation. This means that with protectable property right in petroleum reservoir, parties will be forced to enter into unitisation or some other arrangements to jointly develop the resources. This will obviously eliminate incentives to unilaterally capture petroleum from straddling fields. Chapters 3 and 5 have shown that the conflicting and irreconcilable decisions of the courts were as a result of not the differing ownership concepts but the application of the rule of capture by all the three ownership concepts in the resolution of ownership problems. The Judges also concentrated more on ownership concepts at the expense of property rights. From Chapter 2, we have seen that at common law the concept of ownership has insignificant meaning as regards land as there are other fragmented bundles of rights called interests, for example, fee simple, leasehold, *profit a prendre,* easement and rent which the court appeared to have ignored while deciding drainage (ownership) disputes between two competing users. This is what this book advocates should be protected so that the consequences of unilateral capture and conflicting decisions of the court can be avoided. It is in the light of the above analysis that the proposition stated in Chapter 1 of this book which is that *'Protectable Property Right in Discovered Petroleum Reservoir' will enhance cooperative development of straddling petroleum reservoirs, facilitate consistent courts decisions and protect the interests of the licensees and the State.'* is justified.

3. TRIGGERS FOR PROPERTY RIGHTS IN DISCOVERED PETROLEUM RESERVOIR

We have in reliance on Labour theory, argued that a licensee who has expended heavy capital investments (both human, technical and financial) to acquire acreage, worked on same and discovered petroleum reservoir has a legitimate expectation in the results of his labour and that property rights ought to be ascribed to the result of his labour.

In a PSC regime, we found that the trigger points that permit entry into Property rights to discovered petroleum reservoir are: Petroleum discovery, Appraisal of the discovery, Evaluation of the discovery, Declaration of commerciality, Submission of FDP and grants Production Licence, Lease or Authorisation. On the other hand, in the Licensing regime, some countries provide for new separate licence for each of the petroleum development phases. This means that new right is granted for each of the phases of development. In such regime, however, a Production licence is usually granted at the end of the exploration phase when licensee has made discovery of petroleum that is commercial, submits an FDP and relinquishes the portion of the acreage that is outside the FDP. This may serve as an equivalent position in the PSC regime where Production licence is granted after the contractor or IOC makes declaration of commerciality.

Moreover, other country such as UK grants Standard Production Licence (Seaward licence) and divided it into three terms to cover the various phases of the Petroleum development.

In this regime, where production licence is granted based on work programme commitments at the time of the application for award of acreage, the determination of the 'producing part', relinquishment of 'non-producing part' and obtaining an approved FDP by the Operator could be regarded as the equivalent position of 'commerciality declaration' by the Contractor under the PSC regime.

4. LIMITATION OF 'PROTECTABLE PROPERTY RIGHTS IN DISCOVERED PETROLEUM RESERVOIR AS A SOLUTION

If a State, by its licensing conditions allows unilateral capture to thrive, it may give incentive for licensees to race among themselves to quickly develop straddling reservoirs. Unilateral capture can therefore, be used by the State to achieve its goal of speedy development of its oil and gas resources. But this will in effect give positional advantage to the lessee that first reach development stage in a straddling reservoir.[7] However, where unilateral capture is excluded, this incentive will be eliminated as a licensee who is not ready to develop may be able to stymied production from straddling reservoirs until he is ready to develop.[8]

Professor Daintith, however, admitted that in domanial regimes where exploitation of oil and gas resources is secured by means of Production Sharing Contracts and other Service Agreements, a continued retention of capture will lead to wasteful production of oil and gas if the Regulators are 'lax in exercising their powers to compel unitisation or otherwise control production.'[9] The very goal of compulsory unitisation is to force parties to reach agreement to jointly develop a straddling reservoir and not only to control development. Giving property right to licensee in respect of the oil and gas in place will serve this goal. However, to ensure that it is not used as a weapon to sterilise production or used as a licence to cause 'hold out' in bargaining, certain measures may be taken by the State in their petroleum laws. These include an option of buy-out, risk penalty, etc. Where one licensee is ready to develop and the other is not ready for economic reasons, legislation may empower the licensee that is ready to 'buy-out' the interests of the party that is not ready in the common reservoir. Second, the party that is not ready should be given an option to be 'carried' for his pro-rata expenses of drilling wells coupled with penalty payment to compensate the drilling party for the risk of drilling a dry hole. These expenses will be paid immediately the drilling is completed. Alternatively, the law should be made compelling the unready party to relinquish his interests in the common reservoir to the party that is ready subject to a future interest retained by the unready party. These interests will vest in the unready party after payment of his share of cost of drilling plus the risk penalty from the oil and gas produced from the common reservoir.

The above suggested provisions would practically be helpful where the State regulator is slack in compelling compulsory unitisation or in exercising its power of imposing field development plan on the parties where they failed to reach agreement. These suggested solutions should be in addition to the express legislative provisions for

7. Daintith, 'Finders Keepers? ...', at p. 434.
8. *Ibid.*
9. *Ibid.*, at 435.

property right in petroleum reservoir and compensatory provisions in unitisation clause.

Apart from the above, technological advances such as the new ways of separation of commingle reservoirs substances, better information on reservoir mechanics and quality of seismic data to determine parties share, would assist this new property right concept to internalise some of the externalities produced by bargaining difficulty.

Also, with the recognition of Licensee's property right to petroleum reservoir, the fear that unilateral production will give rise to civil action for trespass and conversion may mitigate hold-out and thereby reduces transaction or bargaining costs.[10] This is because strategic bargaining and hold-out could also emanate from the party with larger extension and because of that may not cooperate with the owner of small extension to unitise since he can unilaterally produce from the straddling reservoir. This new property right will therefore, give rise to efficiency of private negotiations and thus, strengthen unitisation as the parties already knew that neither of them can produce from common-pool without unitisation agreement. One of the policies behind the application of the rule of capture by the courts was that because the quantity of the oil drained is difficult to ascertain, the party who suffered drainage has no remedy. The new technological advances on method of calculating recoverable oil and gas in place using computer simulation will enable ascertainment of the quantity drained, thus accounting for a claim of property right by the licensee on the ascertained portion of the oil drained by his neighbour. Even if the exact quantity of oil drained cannot be ascertained, such issue should not prevent liability, at best it should only affect assessment of damages.

5. FURTHER RESEARCH

The book is narrow in the sense that it focused on one of the problems that may arise from the failure of the parties to unitise straddling reservoirs and the solution available. However, further research could be undertaken into the legal principles that can be used to address past costs and production re-balance among the parties where there had been capture of petroleum for many years without unitisation (i.e., whether re-determination principle or equalisation principle). What will be the effects of these principles on the State as well as on the Operators with regards to production and costs pay back? Other research that could be stimulated includes:

(i) Whether there is an International rule of capture and the lessons that could be leant at the national level.
(ii) Protection of the property rights to petroleum reservoir under the national constitutions (e.g., American Bill of rights as enshrined in the Fourteenth Amendments and HRA, 1998) and other regional human rights instruments such as Inter-American human rights and the African charter on human rights.

10. The impact of these technological development on the rule of capture and how new property right could emerge in response to them is discussed in detail in Chapter 4 of this book.

Bibliography

1. Books

Adam Smith, 'Lectures on Jurisprudence' (Meek Raphael and Stein ed., 1978)

Anthony Scott, 'The Evolution of Resource Property Rights' (Oxford University Press, 2008)

Alan Watson, 'The Law of the Ancient Romans' (Dallas Southern Methodist U.P., 1970)

Ali Coban, 'Protecting Property Rights within the European Convention on Human Rights' (Ashgate, 2004)

A.G. Lang & Michael Crommelin, 'Australian Mining and Petroleum Laws' (Butterworths Pty Ltd, 1979)

A. Carter, Philosophical Foundations of Property Rights (Harvester Wheatsheaf, 1989)

B. Taverne, 'Petroleum, Industry and Governments' (Kluwer Law International, 1999)

J. Bentham, 'The Limits of Jurisprudence Defined', (Charles warren Everett ed. 1945) at p. 85

Campbell Mclachlan QC et al., 'International Investment Arbitration: Substantive Principles' (Oxford University Press, 2007)

Candian et al., 'Property-Propriete-Eigentum: Corso di Diritto Privato Comparato', (CEDAM, 1992), at 164

A. Clapham, 'Human Rights in Private Sphere' (Claredon Press, 1993)

Claude Duval et al., 'International Petroleum Exploration and Exploitation Agreements: Legal, Economic & Policy Aspects', 2nd ed. (Barrows Company, 2009)

Campbell McLachlan QC, et al., 'International Investment Arbitration: Substantive Principles' (Oxford University Press, 2007)

Civil Code of Netherlands', Hans Warendorf et al. (edn) (Wolters Kluwer Law & Business, 2009), Book 3, Section 1, Article 1

T. Daintith et al., 'U.K. Oil and Gas Law', 3rd edn (Sweet & Maxwell, 2000)

David Harris et al., 'Law of the European Convention on Human Rights', 2nd edn (Oxford University Press, 2009)

D. Rook, 'Property Law and Human Rights (Blackstone, 2001), at 60-61

D.E. Lewis, 'The Canadian Petroleum and Natural Gas Lease'(1952) 30 Can. Bar. Rev.

Eugne Kuntz, 'A Treatise on the Law of Oil and Gas', 1st ed. (West Group, 1987)

Eugene Kuntz et al., 'Cases and Materials on Oil and Gas Law' 2nd edn (West Publishing Company, 1993, at p.138

Jeremy Bentham, 'Theory of Legislation' (Richard Hildreth edn, 1975)

Harris, J.W. (ed.), 'Property Problems: From Genes to Pension Funds' (Kluwer Law International, 1998)

Harris et al., 'Law of the European Convention on Human Rights (Butterworths, 1995)

'Halsbury Laws of England', vol. 11 (1910), p. 336, at 656

Ian Brownlie, 'Principles of Public International Law', 6th edn (Oxford University Press, 2003)

J.L. Weaver, 'Unitisation of Oil and Gas Fields in Texas, A Study of Legislative, Administrative, and Judicial Policies' (RFF Press, 1986), at 27

Joseph E. Pogue, 'Economics of Petroleum' (John Wiley and Sons, 1921) 343-344

Lawrence C. Becker, 'Property Rights: Philosophic Foundations' (Routledge & Kegan Paul, 1977)

J.E. Penner, 'The Idea of Property in Law' (Oxford University Press, 1997)

Jeremy Waldron, 'The Right to Private Property' (Claredon Press, 1988)

John Christman, 'The Myth of Property – Towards an Egalitarian Theory of Ownership' (Oxford University Press, 1994)

J.E. Penner, 'The Bundle of Rights Picture of Property', (1995-1996) UCLA L. Rev. 43: 711

Jeremy Bentham, 'The Limits of Jurisprudence Defined' (Charles Warren Everett ed., 1945)

Jeremy Bentham, 'The Theory of Legislation' (Richard Hildreth ed., N.M. Tipathi, 1975);

J. Bentham, 'An Introduction to the Principles of Morals and Legislation' (Oxford Claredon Press, 1996) By J. H. Burns and H. L. A. Hart

J. Bentham, 'Theory of Legislation', (London Trubner, 1864)

John Bishop Ballem, 'The Oil and Gas Lease in Canada', 2nd edn (University of Toronto Press, 1985)

Jean-Jacques Rousseau, 'Discourse on the Origin of Inequality', (Hackett Pub Co., 1992)

John S. Lowe, 'Oil and Gas Law in a Nutshell', 5th ed. (West, a Thomson Reuters, 2009)

John Locke, 'Second Treatises on Government', edited with introduction by C.B. Macpherson (Hackett Pub Co., 1980)

John Locke, 'Two Treatises of Government', Mark Goldie ed. (EVERYMAN, 1993)

John Austin, 'Lectures on Jurisprudence or the Philosophy of Positive Law' (Robert Campbell Margaret Davies, 'PROPERTY: Meanings, histories, theories' (Routledge. Cavendish, 2007)

Lorenzo Cotula, 'Human Rights, Natural Resource and Investment Law in a Globalised World' (Routledge, 2012)

M. Sornaraja, 'The International Law on Foreign Investment', 3rd edn (Cambridge University Press, 2010)

Malcom Evans et al., 'The African Charter on Human and Peoples' Rights: The System of Practice (Cambridge University Press, 1986-2000)

Martha Roggenkamp, 'Oil and Gas: Netherlands Law and Practice' (Chancery Law Publishing, 1991)
Megarry & Wade, 'The Law of Real Property', 7th edn (Sweet & Maxwell, 2008)
S.R. Munzer, 'A Theory of Property' (Cambridge University Press, 1990)
O'Connell, 'The international Law of The Sea' (Clarendon Press, 1982), at 479
R.A. Posner 'Economic Analysis of Law', 4th edn (Little, Brown, 1992)
R. Posner, 'Economic Analysis of Law', 5th edn (Aspen, 1998)
P. Van Dijk et al., 'The Theory and Practice of the European Convention on Human Rights', 3rd edn (Kluwer Law International, 1998)
P.C. Jessup, 'The Law of Territorial Waters and Maritime Jurisdiction' (G. A. Jennings Co., 1927)
Pierri Joseph Proudhorn, 'What Is Property? An Inquiry into the Principle of Right and of Government', B. Tuker, Trans.
Richard W. Hemingway, 'The Law of Oil and Gas', 3rd edn (West Publishing Co. 1991) at 175
Richard Barnes, 'Property Rights and Natural Resources' (Hart Publishing, 2009)
Richard A. Posner, 'Economic Analysis of Law', 5th edn (1998)
Richard Clayton QC et al., 'The law of Human Rights' (Oxford University Press, 2009)
R. Dolzer et al., 'Bilateral Investment Treaties' (Martins Nijhoff Publishers, 1995)
Robert Stoneley, 'Introduction to Petroleum Exploration for Non-Geologists' (Oxford University Press, 1995)
Samuel Pufendorf, De Jure Naturae et Gentium, translation of 1688 edition by C.H. and W. A. Oldfather (Claredon Press, 1934), book IV, iv, 2-6
Stephen L McDonald, 'Petroleum Conservation in the United States: An Economic Analysis' (Resources for the Future, Inc. by The John Hopkins Press, 1971)
Stephen R. Munzer, 'A Theory of Property' (Cambridge University Press, 1990)
J.W. Singer, 'Entitlement: The paradoxes of Property' (Yale University Press, 2000)
Sir Williams Blackstone, 'Commentaries on the Laws of England', vol. 2 (Garland, 1978)
C. Schreuer, 'The ICSID Convention: A Commentary', 2nd edn (Cambridge University Press, 2009)
G. Samuel, 'Are property Rights So Simple in Europe?', in P. Jackson & D.C. Wilde (ed.), 'Property Law: Current Issues and Debates' (Ashgate, 1999).
Samuel Pufendorf, 'De jure Naturae et Gentium Libri Octo,' bk 4, c 4 (Oldfather trans, 1934)
Terrence Daintith, 'Finders Keepers? How the Law of Capture Shaped the World Oil Industry', RFF Press, The Digest of Justinian 396, vol. 3 (Theodor Mommsen, 2010)
Van Dijk et al., 'The Theory and Practice of the European Convention on Human Rights', 3rd edn (Kluwer Law International, 1998)
Whiteman, Digest of International Law, vol. 4 (Washington, D.C. 1968), 75, 756
Williams & Meyers, 'Oil and Gas Laws', vol. 1 (2004), Chapter 2, pp. 17-18
Yoram Barzel, 'Economic Analysis of Property Rights', 2nd edn (Cambridge University Press, 1997)
Zachary Douglas, 'The International law of Investment Claims' (Cambridge University Press, 2009)

2. Journal Articles

Abba Kolo, 'Legal Issues Arising from the Termination of Oil Prospecting Licences by the Nigerian Government', (2001) JENRL 19(2): 164

Alberto M. Aronovitz, 'Individual Patrimonial Rights under the European Human Rights System: Some Reflections on the Concept of Possession and Dispossession of Property', (1997) Int'l L. J. Legal Info 25: 89-90

Allan Ingelson et al., 'NAFTA Takings Update the Glamis Decision', (March, 2012) JWEL&B 5(1): p. 27.

Andrzej Rapaczynski, 'The Roles of the State and the Market in Establishing Property Rights', (1996) Journal of Economic Perspectives 10(2): pp. 87-90

Anderson, 'Compulsory Pooling In North Dakota: Should Production Income and Expenses Be Divided from Date of Pooling, Spacing, or First Run'?

Alisa Newman Hood, 'We Shale Overcome? A U.S Court Issue an Unsettling Decision on Marcellus Property Rights', (March, 2012) Journal of World Energy Law & Business 5(1): 78 at 80.

A.L. Corbin, 'Comment, Taxation of Seats on the Stock Exchange', (1922) Yale L.J. 31: 429

American Law institute, ReStatement of property s.1-4 (1936)

Billie Ann Maxwell, 'Texas Tug of War: A Survey of Urban Drilling and the Issues an Operator Will Face' (2008-2009) Tex. J. Oil, Gas & Energy L. 4: 337 at 340

Brian W. Semkow, 'Energy and the New Constitution', (1985) Alta. L. Rev. 23: 134, at pp. 118-119

Bruce, '"Maximum Efficient Rate" - Its Use and Misuse in Production Regulation', (1976) Nat. Resources L. 9: 441

Cecilia A. Low, 'The Rule of Capture: Its Current Status and Some Issues to Consider', (2008-2009) Alta. L. Rev. 46: 799

C.M. Rose, 'Cannons of Property Talk, or, Blackstone's Anxiety', (1998) Yale LJ 108: 601 at 604

Carol M. Rose, 'Possession as the Origin of Property', (1985) U. Chi. L. Rev 52: 73

Carol M. Rose, 'Property as Story Telling: Perspectives from Game Theory, Narrative Theory and Feminist Theory' (1990) Yale J. L. & Human 2: 57

D. Edward Greer, 'The Ownership of Petroleum Oil and Natural Gas in Place', (1922-1923) Tex. L. Rev. 1: 162 at p. 162

D.E. Pierce, 'Coordinated Reservoir Development - An Alternative to the Rule of Capture for the Ownership and Development of Oil and Gas,' (1983) Journal of Energy Law and Policy 4

Dylan O. Drummond et al, 'The Rule of Capture in Texas - Still So Misunderstood After All These Years', (2004-2005) Tex. L. Rev. 37: 1, at p. 16

D. Schorr, 'How Blackstone Became a Blackstonian', (2008) Theoretical Inquiries in Law 10: 103

Dean G. Acheson, 'Book Review', (1919) Harv. L. Rev. 33: 329, 330

David Lopina, 'The International Centre for settlement of investment Disputes: Investment Arbitration for the 1990s', (1988) Ohio State Journal on Dispute Resolution 107: 114-115

Eugene Kuntz, 'Recent Natural Resources Cases', (1965) Nat. Resources J. 5: 213

Marshall & Meyers, 'Legal Planning of petroleum Production', (1931) Yale L.J. 41: 33, 49-51 at 58

N. Ely, 'The Conservation of Oil' (1938) Harvard Law Review 51: 1209, 1218, 1219

Francis J. Swanyze, 'The Growing Law', (1915) Yale L.J. 25: 1, 10

Farnham, 'Waters and Water rights', 938; 53 L. R. A. (N. S.) 369

F.V.W. (Van) Penick, 'Offshore Financing: The Nature of Security Interests in Oil and Gas Projects on the Continental Shelf', (1985) Alta L. Rev. 23: 33, at p. 33

Guido Calabresi & Douglas Melamed, 'Property Rules, Liability Rules, and Inalienability Rules: One View of the Cathedral', (1972) Harv. L. Rev. 85: 1089

Grey T. 'The Disintegration of Property (Nomos, 1980), 22 at 69-85

Kevin Gray, 'Property in Thin Air', Cambridge Law Journal, Vol. 50, Iss. 2 (July, 1991), 252-307

Geoffrey Compton, 'The Proprietary Nature of Overriding Royalties in Petroleum Agreements in Australia' (2002) AMPLJ 21: 158

G. Hardin, 'Tragedy of the Common', (1968) Science 162: 1243 at 1244-1245

Harold Demsetz, 'Towards a Theory of Property Right', (1967) Am Econ Rev. 57: 347

John P. Keen, 'Commonwealth Draft Guidelines for Trans-boundary Unitisations and the Rule of Capture', (1998) AMPLA Yearbook: 440

John S. Sawyer, 'Interests Created by Oil and Gas Leases in Pennsylvania', (1937-1938) U. Pitt. L. Rev. 4: 274

John D. McKinnis, 'Directional Drilling, Subsurface Trespass, and Conversion', (1988-1989) J. Min. L. & Policy 4: 235 at 238

J.M MacIntyre, 'The Development of Oil and Gas Ownership Theory in Canada', (1969) U. Brit. Colum. L. Rev. 4: 251, at 251

J.E. Penner (Bundle of Rights Picture)

Jongwook Kim et al., 'Resource-Based and Property Rights Perspectives on Value Creation: The Case of Oil Field Unitisation', (2002) Manage. Decis. Econ 23: 225-245

Kuntz, The Law of Capture, (1957) Okla. L. Rev. 10: 406, at 406-407

M.H. Kramer, 'Book Review of Harris', P&J (1997) Cambridge Law Journal 56: 642

Kenneth J. Vandevelde, 'The New Property of the Nineteenth Century: The Development of the Modern Concept of Property' (1980) Buff. L. Rev. 29: 325 at 362

Franc I. Michelman, 'Property, Utility, and Fairness: Comments on the Ethical Foundations of "Just Compensation Law"' (1967) Harvard Law Review 80: 116-1258

Martha Roggenkamp, 'A New Mining Act for the Netherlands – The End of a 200 – Year Debate' [2003] I.E.L.T.R. at pp. 185-186.

Murray Hunt, 'The 'Horizontal effect' of the Human Rights Act', (1998) Public Law 423, available at https//login.westlaw.co.uk

P.M. Norton, 'A Law of the Future or A Law of the Past? Modern Tribunals and the National Law of Expropriation', (1991) 85 American Journal of International Law 474

Owen L. Anderson, 'Compulsory Pooling in North Dakota: Should Production Income and Expenses Be Divided from Date of Pooling, Spacing, or "first runs"?', (1982) N.D. L. Rev. 58: 537 at 539

Oliver Hart & John Moore, 'Property Rights and the Nature of the Firm', (1990) J. Pol. Econ. 98: 1119, 1121

R.I. Milliner, 'Comment on the U.S. Rule of Capture: Its place in Australia', (1986) AMPLA Year Book 299

R.E. Pelzer et al., 'Horizontal Drilling: Regulatory and Contractual Implications', (1991) Alta. L. Rev. 30

R.F.V. Heuston, 'Salmond on the Law of Torts', 16th edn (Sweet & Maxwell, 1973), at 92

Bryan Clark, 'Migratory Things on Land: Property Rights and a Law of Capture' [2002] EJCL Vol.

Robert J. Blake, 'The Oil and Gas Lease', (1939-1940) S. Cal. L. Rev. 13: 304, at 308

R. H. Coase, 'Problem of Social Cost' (1960) JL & Econ. 3: 1

Robert Cooter, 'Unity in Tort, Contract and Property: The Model of Precaution', (1985) Cal. L. Rev. 73: 1

Richard A. Epstein, '[T]he Allocation of the Commons: Parking on Public Roads', (2002) J. Legal Stud. 31: 516.

Robert J. Blake, 'The Oil and Gas Lease', (1939-1940) S. Cal L. Rev. 13: 305, at p. 306

Stuart Banner, 'Transitions between Property Regimes' (2002) 31 J. Legal Stud.

Stephen Schilde Williams, 'Can a Louisiana Unit Order Be Effective Retroactively?', (1988-1989) La. L. Rev. 49: 1119

S. Gerlach, 'Comment on the U.S. Rule of Capture: Its Place in Australia', (1996) AMPLA Yearbook, 283

Sir William Wade QC, 'Horizons of Horizontality', (2000) L.Q.R. 116: 217

Sir Richard Buxton, 'The Human Rights Act and Private Law' (2000) L.Q.R. 116: 48

Terrence Daintith, 'A Critical Evaluation of the Petroleum (Submerged Lands) Act as a Regulatory Regime', APMLA YEARBOOK (2000), 91

Thomas Walde & Abba Kolo, 'Environmental Regulation, Investment Protection and "Regulatory Taking" in International Law', (2001) International and Comparative Law Quarterly 50: 835.

Thomas D.C. Bennett, 'Horizontality's New Horizons - Re-examining Horizontal Effect: Privacy, Defamation and the Human Rights Act, Part 1', (2010) Entertainment Law Review

Thomas D.C Bennett, 'Horizontality's New Horizons – Re-examining Horizontal Effect: Privacy, Defamation and the Human Rights Act, Part 2', (2010) Entertainment Law Review 21(3): 96-104

Nicholas Bamforth, 'The True "Horizontal Effect" of the Human Rights Act 1998', (2001) 117

T. Grey, 'The Malthusian Constitution', (1986) U Miami L. Rev. 41: 21 at 30

Thomas Merrill et al., 'What Happened to Property in Law and Economics?' (2001-2002) Yale L.J. 111: 357 at 360

Thomas W. Merrill, 'Introduction: The Demsetz Book and the Evolution of Property Rights', (2002) J. Legal Stud. 31: 332

U. Mattei, 'Basic Principles of Property Law: A Comparative Legal and Economic' (2000)

Martha Roggenkamp, 'A New Mining Act for the Netherlands – The End of a 200 – Year Debate' [2003] I.E.L.T.R. at 185-186.

Martha Roggenkamp, 'The Award of Concessions for Onshore Petroleum Operations in the Netherlands' [1987/88] OGLTR 7: 199 at 200

Michael Crommelin, 'The U.S. Rule of Capture: Its Place in Australia' (1986) AMPLA Yearbook at 272

Michael Crommelin, 'The Legal Character of Resource Titles', (1998) AMPLJ 17: 57 at 68

Murray Hunt, 'The "Horizontal Effect" of the Human Rights Act', (1998) P.L, Aut, at 423-443

Nicholas Bamforth, 'The True "Horizontal Effect" of the Human Rights Act 1998', (2001) (Jan) Law Quarterly Review 17: 117

P. Marriage, 'North Sea Continental Sea Petroleum Financing in the United Kingdom', (1977) Int Bus Lawyer 5: 207

Van Penick, 'Legal Framework in the Canadian Offshore', (2001) Dalhousie L.J. 24: 5, at p. 5

F. Von Benda-Beckmann, 'Anthropological Approaches to Property Law and Economics' (1995) European Journal of Law and Economics 2: 309-336

A.W. Walker Jr, 'The Nature of the Property Interests Created by an Oil and Gas Lease in Texas', (1928) Texas Law Review 7: 1, at p. 2

Watson & El Fadl, 'Fox Hunting, Peasant Shooting, and Comparative Law,' (2000) Am. J. Comp. L. 48: I, 21

Wesley Newcomb Hohfeld, 'Some Fundamental Legal Conceptions as Applied in Judicial Reasoning', (1913) Yale L.J. 23: 16

Wesley Newcomb Hohfeld, 'Some Fundamental Legal Conceptions as Applied in Judicial Reasoning', (1917) Yale L.J. 26: 710

W. L. Summers, 'Property in Oil and Gas', (1919-1920) Yale L.J. 175 at p. 174

Walker, 'The Nature of the Property Interest Created by an Oil and Gas Lease in Texas' (1928) Texas L. Rev. 7: 1

Zachary Douglas, 'The Hybrid Foundations of Investment Treaty Arbitration', (2003) BYIL 74: 151

3. Articles in Books

Abba Kolo, 'Fat Cats and "Windfall Taxes in the Natural Resources Industry": Legal and Policy Analysis in the light of Modern Investment Treaties', in 'A Liber Amicorum: Thomas Walde', at 103

August Reinisch, 'Expropriation', in Peter Muchlinski et al. 'The Oxford Handbook of International Investment Law' (2008) at 410

Aristotle, 'The Politics', Book II, Chapter 5 Stephen Everson ed. (Cambridge University Press, 1988)

A.M. Honore, 'Ownership', in 'Oxford Essays in Jurisprudence' 107, (A.G. Guest ed. 1961)

T. Daintith, 'The Petroleum Production Licence in the United Kingdom', in T. Daintith (ed.) 'The Legal Character of Petroleum Licences: A Comparative Study' (1981) 200 at 217

David Hume, 'Treatise of Human Nature', vol. 2 (J.M. Dent & Sons Ltd, 1956) at 207

Engela C. Schlemmer, 'Investment, Investor, Nationality, and Shareholders', in Peter Muchlinski et al. (ed.) 'International Investment Law' (Oxford University Press, 2008) at 52

Garvin Philipson, 'Clarity Postponed: Horizontal Effect after Campbell and Re. S', in Fenwick, Masterman & Pililipson (eds), 'Judicial Reasoning under the UK Human Rights Act' (Cambridge University Press, 2007).

Greg Gordon, 'Petroleum Licensing', in Gregg Gordon et al., 'Oil and Gas Law: Current Practice and Emerging Trends' (Dundee University Press, 2007), at 30

J.W. Harris, P & J; J.W. Harris, 'Is Property a Human Right?', in Janet Mclean (ed.) 'Property and Constitution' (Hart Pub., 1999), at 197

Jonnette Watson Hamilton et al., 'Different Views of the Cathedral: The Literature on Property Law Theory', in Aileen Mcharg et al. eds, 'Property and the Law in Energy and Natural Resources' (Oxford University Press, 2010), at 35

L.G. Loucaides, Nijhoff Law Specials, vol. 70 'European Convention on Human Rights: Collected Essays' (2007) at p. 121

Michael Crommelin, 'Legal Character of Petroleum Production Licences in Australia', in T. Daintith (ed.) 'The Legal Character of Petroleum Licences: A Comparative Study' (1981), at p. 60

Peter van Den Broek, in DJ Gijlstra et al. eds, 'Legal Issues of European Integration' (1986/1) Law Review of the EUROPA Instituut, University of Amsterdam

Roderick Paisley, 'Aspects of Land Law Relative to the Transportation of Oil and Gas in Scotland', in Greg Gordon et al., 'Oil and Gas Law: Current Practice and Emerging Trends' (Dundee University Press, 2007), at 412

Rowland J. Harrison, 'The Legal Character of Petroleum Production Licences in Canada', in T. Daintith (ed.) 'The Legal Character of Petroleum Licensing: A Comparative Study' (1981) at 129

Terrence Daintith, 'The Rule of Capture: The Least Worst Property Rule for Oil and Gas' in Aileen McHarg et al. eds, in 'Property and the Law in Energy and Natural Resources' (2010)

Thomas W. Walde et al., 'Compensation, Damages, and Valuation', in Peter Muchlinski et al. (eds), 'International Investment Law' (Oxford University Press, 2008), 1049

4. Reports and Other Documents

American Institute of Mining and Metallurgical Engineers, Petroleum Conservation, 71 (1951) at 151

C. Donville, 'Making Hole Sideways Gives Oil Patch New Lease', [T]he Globe and Mail Report on Business, 29 March 1991

C.M. Carol Rose, 'Servitude', Arizona Legal Studies Discussion Paper No. 09-13, available at http://ssrn.com/absract=1371251

David Asmus & Jacqueling Wearver, 'Unitizing oil and Gas Fields around the World: A Comparative Analysis of National Laws and Private Contracts', available at http://www.ssrn.com

InterState oil compact commission, oil and gas production 15-16, (1951)

Weaver, Asmus, Walde, Marmud, Ifesi, Bastida, Ross in 'AIPN International Unitisation of oil and gas fields: the legal framework for analysis of international law, national laws and private contracts'

5. Conference Papers

Gary D. Libecap & James L. Smith, 'The Economic Evolution of Petroleum Property Rights in the United States', paper prepared for the conference on the Evolution of Property rights, Northwestern University School of Law, 20-22 April 2001

Garry D. Libecap & James L. Smith, 'The Self-Enforcing Provisions of Oil and Gas Unit Operating Agreements: Theory and Evidence', (3 December 1998)

Guilherme Fowler de Avilla Monteiro, 'Property rights strategy: Market Structure and Competition in Brazilian Soybean Seed Industry', at p. 5

R. Higgins, 'Ten Years of State Involvement in the Petroleum Industry: The U.K. Experience', in International Bar Association, Energy Law Seminar (1979), Vol. 2. Paper R-1.1, at p. 6

Jacqueline Lang Weaver, 'Unitisation Revisited', in Carol J. Holgren the 'Proceedings of 45th Annual Institute on oil and gas law and Taxation' (Southwestern Legal Foundation, 1994)

J. Burtner, 'Horizontal Well Completion Technology', presented at the 1990 Calgary Horizontal Drilling Conference, August 1990

Olufemi A. Ajayi et al., 'Current Challenges in Unitisation – The Nigerian Experience', A Paper Presented at the 34th Annual SPE International Conference and Exhibition held in Tinapa-Calabar, Nigeria, 31 July-7 August, 2010, published in SPE International (SPE 140614)

P.C. Crouse, 'A Review of the Reservoir Considerations for Horizontal Wells in the Bakken Formation', presented at the 1990 Calgary Horizontal Drilling Conference, August 1990

R. Arnarson, 'Property Rights as a means of Economic Organisation', in Shotton (ed.), 'Use of Property Rights in Fisheries Management. Proceedings of the Fish Rights 99 Conference', Fremantle, Western Australia, 11-19 November 1999

T. Daintith, 'Correlative Rights in Oil Reservoirs on the "United Kingdom Continental Shelf" in European Offshore Petroleum Conference and Exhibition' (1978) at p. 74

6. Magazines, Newspapers and Other Internet Sources

Last minutes Oil deals that cost Nigeria dear, http://234next.com/csp/cms/sites/Next/Home/5713375-146/last_minute_oil_deals_that_cost.csp

Shell hopes worst is out of way, Petroleum Economist, May 2004, 13

Table of Cases

Nagel v. Czech Republic (SCC 49/2002 (2004), 1 Stockholm Arb. Rep. 145 at 158, available at: http://ita.law.univ.ca, 38
Novokeletski v. Ukraine (2006) 43 EHRR 53, paragraph 100, 48
Neryildiz v. Turkey (2005) 41 EHRR 20 paragraphs 133-138, 47
New South Wales v. Commonwealth, [1973] 135 CLR 337, 73
Occidental v. Ecuador, Final Award, 1 July 2004, 12 ICSID Reports 59, 253, 266, 269, 271
Oscar Chin case (*UK v. Belgium*), Judgment, 12 December 1934, PCIJ Series A/B, No. 63 (1934), 255
Ohmart v. Dennis, 188 Neb. 260, 196 N.W.2d 181 (1972), 239
O.N. v. Bulgaria (App. No. 35221/97) Decision 6 April 2000, 50, 275, 278
Ohio Oil Co. v. Indiana (1899) 177 U.S. 190, 209, 62, 63, 149, 151
Oil and Gas Ltd v. Ministry of Petroleum Resources (Unreported) suit no. FHC/L/CS/ 481/2000, 80
Papamichalopoulos v. Greece, Judgment of 24 June 1993, Series A no. 260-B, 44
Pavey and Mathews Pty Ltd v. Paul (1987) 162 CLR 221, 213
Pierce v. Goldking, 396 So. 2d 528 (La. App. 3d Cir.), 236
People v. Warden, 145 A.D. 861, 863, 130 N.Y.S. 698, 700(1st Dep't 1911), 25
Philips Petroleum Company Iran v. The Islamic Republic of Iran, 21 Iran-US CTR 79, 38, 256
Pope & Talbot Inc v. Canada, Interim Award, Ad hoc - UNCITRAL Arbitration Rules, IIC 192 of 26 June 2000 (Available at www.naftaclaims.com), 38
Plattform Arzte fur das Leben v. Austria, Judgment of 1988, Series A, No. 139, 274
Papamchalopoulos and others v. Greece, Judgment of 15 February 2011(App. No. 37095/97), 275
Pine Valley Developments Ltd v. Ireland, A 222 (1991); 14 EHRR 319, 284
PSEG v. Turkey, Award, 19 January 2007, at paragraphs 240-256, 267
Pudas v. Sweden (1984) 20 DR 234, 45
Parsons v. Kavanagh [1990] I.L.R.M. 560, 54
Prism Petroleum v. Omega Hydrocarbons (1994) 4 W.W.R. 585 9 Alta. C.A.) at 94, 63
Parkins-Compagniet AS v. Lithuania, [443] and [445], 119
People's gas Co. v. Tyner, 152, 158
R v. Riley (1853)22 L.J.M.C. 48, 178
Richmond National Gas Co. v. Davenport (1905) 37 Ind. App. 25, 76 N.E. 525, 64, 153, 173
Rich v. Doneghey, 71 Okla. 207, 177 Pac. 86, 90, 3 A.L.R. 352, 357 (1918), 65, 151
Reference Re: The seabed and subsoil of the Continental Shelf Offshore Newfoundland (Hibernia Reference), 207
Raimondo v. Italy, A 281-A (1994); 18 EHRR 237 at p. 18, 283
Revere Copper & Brass Inc v. Overseas Private Investment Corp (1980) 56 ILR 258, 257
Railroad Commission v. Rowan & Nichols Oil Co, 311 U.S 573 at 579-80 (1940), 168
Railroad Commission v. Rowan & Nichols Oil Co, 311 U.S 570 (1941), 168
Railroad Comm'n v. Humble Oil & Ref Co, 193 S.W. 2d 824 (1946), 168
Ryan Consol. Petroleum Corp v. Pickens, 175 Tex. 221, 285 S.W.2d 201 (1955), 168

Table of Legislations, Agreements, Treaties and Guidelines

Index

O

P

Q

R

S

T

U

V

ENERGY AND ENVIRONMENTAL LAW & POLICY SERIES

1. Stephen J. Turner, *A Substantive Environmental Right: An Examination of the Legal Obligations of Decision-makers towards the Environment*, 2009 (ISBN 978-90-411-2815-7).
2. Helle Tegner Anker, Birgitte Egelund Olsen & Anita Rønne (eds), *Legal Systems and Wind Energy: A Comparative Perspective*, 2009 (ISBN 978-90-411-2831-7).
3. David Langlet, *Prior Informed Consent and Hazardous Trade: Regulating Trade in Hazardous Goods at the Intersection of Sovereignty, Free Trade and Environmental Protection*, 2009 (ISBN 978-90-411-2821-8).
4. Louis J. Kotzé and Alexander R. Paterson (eds), *The Role of the Judiciary in Environmental Governance: Comparative Perspectives*, 2009 (ISBN 978-90-411-2708-2).
5. Tuula Honkonen, *The Common but Differentiated Responsibility Principle in Multilateral Environmental Agreement's: Regulatory and Policy Aspects*, 2009 (ISBN 978-90-411-3153-9).
6. Barbara Pozzo (ed.), *The Implementation of the Seveso Directives in an Enlarged Europe: A Look into the Past and a challenge for the Future*, 2009 (ISBN 978-90-411-2854-6).
7. Henrik M. Inadomi, *Independent Power Projects in Developing Countries: Legal Investment Protection and Consequences for Development*, 2010 (ISBN 978-90-411-3178-2).
8. Nahid Islam, *The Law of Non-Navigational Uses of International Water-courses: Options for Regional Regime-Building in Asia*, 2010 (ISBN 978-90-411-3196-6).
9. Yasuhiro Shigeta, *International Judicial Control of Environmental Protection: Standard Setting, Compliance Control and the Development of International Environmental Law by the International Judiciary*, 2010 (ISBN 978-90-411-3151-5).
10. Katleen Janssen, *The Availability of Spatial and Environmental Data in the European Union: At the Crossroads between Public and Economic Interests*, 2010 (ISBN 978-90-411-3287-1).
11. Henrik Bjørnebye, *Investing in EU Energy Security: Exploring the Regulatory Approach to Tomorrow's Electricity Production*, 2010 (ISBN 978-90-411-3118-8).
12. Véronique Bruggeman, *Compensating catastrophe victims: A Comparative Law and Economics Approach*, 2010 (ISBN 978-90-411-3263-5).
13. Michael G. Faure, Han Lixin & Shan Hongjun, *Maritime Pollution Liability and Policy: China, Europe and the US*, 2010 (ISBN 978-90-411-2869-0).

14. Anton Ming-Zhi Gao, *Regulating Gas Liberalization: A Comparative Study on Unbundling and Open Access Regimes in the US, Europe, Japan, South Korea and Taiwan*, 2010 (ISBN 978-90-411-3347-2).
15. Mustafa Erkan, *International Energy Investment Law: Stability through Contractual Clauses*, 2011 (ISBN 978-90-411-3411-0).
16. Levente Borzsa´k, *The Impact of Environmental Concerns on the Public Enforcement Mechanism under EU law: Environmental protection in the 25th hour*, 2011 (ISBN 978-90-411-3408-0).
17. Tarcísio Hardman Reis, *Compensation for Environmental Damages under International Law: The Role of the International Judge*, 2011 (ISBN 978-90-411-3437-0).
18. Kim Talus, *Vertical Natural Gas Transportation Capacity, Upstream Commodity Contracts and EU Competition Law*, 2011 (ISBN 978-90-411-3407-3).
19. WangHui, *Civil Liability for Marine Oil Pollution Damage: A Comparative and Economic Study of the International, US and Chinese Compensation Regime*, 2011 (ISBN 978-90-411-3672-5).
20. Chowdhury Ishrak Ahmed Siddiky, *Cross-Border Pipeline Arrangements: What Would a Single Regulatory Framework Look Like?*, 2012 (ISBN 978-90-411-3844-6).
21. Rozeta Karova, *Liberalization of Electricity Markets and Public Service Obligations in the Energy Community*, 2012 (ISBN 978-90-411-3849-1).
22. Sandra Cassotta, *Environmental Damage and Liability Problems in a Multilevel Context: The Case of the Environmental Liability Directive*, 2012 (ISBN 978-90-411-3830-9).
23. Mark Wilde, *Civil Liability for Environmental Damage: Comparative Analysis of Law and Policy in Europe and US*, 2013 (ISBN 978-90-411-3233-8).
24. Bernard Taverne, *Petroleum, Industry and Governments: A Study of the Involvement of Industry and Governments in Exploring for and Producing Petroleum*, 2013 (ISBN 978-90-411-4563-5).
25. Anton Ming-Zhi Gao & Chien Te Fan (eds), *Legal Issues of Renewable Energy in the Asia Region: Recent Developments in a Post-Fukushima and Post-Kyoto Protocol Era*, 2014 (ISBN 978-90-411-4856-8).
26. Sabina Manea, *The Instrumentalization of Property: Legal Interests in the EU Emissions Trading System*, 2014 (ISBN 978-90-411-5420-0).
27. Joseph A. Tolorunse, *Protection of Property Rights in Discovered Petroleum Reservoirs*, 2014 (ISBN 978-90-411-5604-4).